VOICES OF THE

MATRIARCHS

VOICES OF THE MATRIARCHS

CHAVA WEISSLER

LISTENING

TO THE

PRAYERS

OF EARLY

MODERN

JEWISH

WOMEN

BEACON PRESS

BOSTON

BEACON PRESS
Boston, Massachusetts
www.beacon.org

Beacon Press books
are published under the auspices of
the Unitarian Universalist Association of Congregations.

23 22 21 20   8 7 6 5 4 3 2

This book is printed on recycled acid-free paper that contains at
least 20 percent postconsumer waste and meets the uncoated paper
ANSI/NISO specifications for permanence as revised in 1992.

Text design by Margaret M. Wagner
Composition by Wilsted & Taylor Publishing Services

Library of Congress Cataloging-in-Publication Data
Weissler, Chava.
    Voices of the matriarchs : listening to the prayers of early
modern Jewish women / Chava Weissler.
        p.   cm.
    Includes bibliographical references and index.
    ISBN 0-8070-3616-1 (cloth)
    ISBN 0-8070-3617-x (paper)
    1. Tehinnot.   2. Jewish women—Prayer-books and devotions—
History and criticism.   3. Jewish women—Religious life.
4. Women in Judaism.   I. Title.
BM675.T4Z745   1998
296.4'5'082—dc21   98-19905

In Memory of My Father
ALFRED WEISSLER
1917–1997

In Honor of My Mother
PEARL G. WEISSLER

And Most of All
To NANCY
With Love

CONTENTS

Contents

PREFACE

This [the woman] says when she puts the loaf of *berkhes*[1] into the oven:

Lord of all the world, in your hand is all blessing. I come now to revere your holiness, and I pray you to bestow your blessing on the baked goods. Send an angel to guard the baking, so that all will be well baked, will rise nicely, and will not burn, to honor the holy Sabbath (which you have chosen so that Israel your children may rest thereon) and over which one recites the holy blessing—as you blessed the dough of Sarah and Rebecca our mothers. My Lord God, listen to my voice; you are the God who hears the voices of those who call upon you wholeheartedly. May you be praised to eternity.[2]

This lovely prayer is a *tkhine*,[3] one of the supplicatory prayers in Yiddish recited by Central and Eastern European Jewish women. As a historical document, it gives a bit of evidence about the lives of Jewish women, about what they might have been thinking as they performed their religious duties and household tasks.

Tkhines—Yiddish prayers for private devotion—are the subject of this book. Like other genres of popular religious literature in Yiddish, these prayers began to appear in print in the sixteenth century and flourished during the seventeenth and eighteenth centuries. Because *tkhines*, as well as ethical works, collections of pious tales, and Bible paraphrases, were in Yiddish, the vernacular of Ashkenazic Jews, they were available to women, who rarely mastered Hebrew, the sacred tongue and the language of scholarly works. An analysis of women's religious lives forms a necessary corrective to the overwhelming majority of studies of the history of Judaism that rely primarily on sources produced by and for learned men, always a small minority of the Jewish people. Taking the religion of women—and other nonlearned Jews—into account significantly revises our understanding of Ashkenazic Judaism.

Tkhines and similar materials were not always considered of value. How does something come to be regarded as an important historical resource? All we need to remind us that all scholarship is historically situated is to look at the entry for *tehinnot* [*tkhines*] in Benjacob's *Otsar hasefarim*, one of the standard works of Hebraica bibliography, published in 1880. The entry reads: "Tehinnot le-nashim bi-leshon ashkenaz rabu mineihem ad ein mispar ve-ein le-fortam ba-sefer. (*Tkhines* for women in the Judaeo-German language; their varieties are so numerous as to be uncountable, and one cannot list them in the book.)"[4]

While this is a matter of interpreting Benjacob's tone, the implication seems to me to be that there is really no point in *trying* to list the many editions of *tkhines*, as opposed to, say, the many editions of the Pentateuch, which he carefully recorded. In any case, in the second half of the nineteenth century, prayers for women in Yiddish were not considered worthy of a detailed bibliographical entry.[5] They seemed ephemeral compared to the enduring classics of Jewish tradition, such as the Hebrew Bible, the Talmud, and the Midrash, and insignificant compared to works emerging from the major innovations in Jewish thought and responses to changing conditions, such as responsa, legal codes, and works of medieval philosophy, mysticism, and Hasidism. When and why did *tkhines* and other genres of devotional literature in Yiddish for women (and for nonlearned men) also come to be considered an important area of study?

In the first few decades of the twentieth century, the tide began to turn—or to use a more accurate metaphor, there was at least a brief trickle of interest in this material, on the part of two kinds of scholars. The first of these were the historians of Yiddish literature, such as Eleazar Shulman, Shmuel Niger, Israel Zinberg, and Max Weinreich.[6] In the wake of the rise of a modern Yiddish literature in the nineteenth century, there developed an interest in discovering a literary tradition, literary roots. Indeed, these scholars went back to the medieval period to discover and analyze biblical epic poems and courtly romances in Yiddish. Among other things, they also wrote about *tkhines*, ethical guides for women, and the *Tsenerene*, the "women's Bible."

Yet these scholars—and the writers who searched their works for literary models—were, for the most part, secularists, the creators of a new Yiddish culture detached from religious roots. They were not primarily interested in *religious* literature, nor, it must be said, in women's literature, despite Niger's pioneering essay, "Yiddish Literature and the Female Reader."[7] They preferred to cast early Yiddish literature as worldly and secular, and as a forerunner of their own "anticlerical" struggle. They loved the Arthurian romances, Elijah Bahur's elegant poetry in *ottava rima*, and the idea (now shown to be without historical basis) that there were Jewish *shpilmener*, or roving bards.[8] Somehow, women's prayers and guides to the upright life did not have quite the romantic appeal of medieval troubadours.[9] Nonetheless, authors such as Niger and Zinberg did write about them; Zinberg, in particular, cast popular religious literature in Yiddish in the role of protagonist in the struggle of the common folk against rabbinical authorities.[10]

Another passing flurry of interest came from the Reform movement. Here the impetus for an investigation of *tkhines* came from another direction; Reform leaders wanted to find precedent in Jewish tradition for praying in the languages Jews spoke, rather than in Hebrew.[11] Thus, Solomon Freehof, in his pioneering article, "Devotional Literature in the Vernacular," surveys the rise of the *tkhine* literature, its contents, and its connection to the spread and popularization of Hebrew books of mystically influenced devotions.[12] Perhaps because he wished to use this literature to show that "[the] use of the language of life for the language of prayer is not a new phenomenon in Judaism,"[13] Freehof seems a little discomfited by the fact that these prayers were written primarily for the use of *women*. He devotes a long footnote to showing that men also made use of the literature, concluding that, "although originally the *Tehinnoth* may have been written chiefly for women, the use of them soon spread among all who could not read Hebrew fluently."[14] He does not even entertain the possibility that some of the *tkhines* may have been *written* by women; in 1923, perhaps something really counted as a precedent for Jewish prayer only if it was by and for men.[15]

If I smile a little at my predecessors, it is only because I am keenly aware that my own work, too, is historically situated, influenced by the currents of the times. My interest in Yiddish devotional literature as a source for the study of women's religious lives rides the rising tide of scholarly interest in both women's history and social history. Some of the most exciting developments in recent historical research over the last two decades have broadened the scope of the historian to include those whose stories previously had not been told, the "ordinary folk" of a variety of nations. Further, both in American culture in general, and within the Jewish community in particular, it was the reexamination of the roles of women that stimulated research into their history.

For me, then, it was "obvious" that the "true" importance of Yiddish *tkhines* and other popular religious material was that they enable us to reconstruct the religious lives of "ordinary" Jews—those who were not part of the educated elite—and especially of women. This assumption was only a starting point, however, and my interests and the way I framed my questions evolved over the fifteen-odd years I have been working on these texts. The essays published below reflect the evolution of those interests.

At the beginning, I was simply excited to find women's voices, which had seemed so absent from the history of Judaism. Early on, I was most interested in discerning what was most distinctive, most womanly, about the *tkhines*. I wanted to fill in the blanks, recover women's religious experience and contrast it to men's. Further, since very little research had been done on the *tkhines* and related genres of popular piety in both Hebrew and Yiddish, I faced formidable methodological and theoretical questions in grappling with the material. How *does* one study women's Judaism? How can the study of *tkhines* help us understand the construction of gender in Ashkenazic Judaism? The essays in Part I of the book, except for Chapter 1, were the product of this period of my research. Chapter 2 directly addresses the methodological issues in the use of early Yiddish materials for the study of women's religion, while Chapters 3, 4, and 5 each explore particular topics by juxtaposing *tkhines* to other genres of popular religious literature. A central issue in all of them is the construction of gender. My revisions of these chapters for the present volume have not fundamentally reshaped the interests and perspectives they express.

Later, my interests shifted towards understanding the *tkhines* within the matrix of Ashkenazic Judaism during this period. The seventeenth and eighteenth centuries were times of turmoil and creativity; they saw the influence of mystical pietism, the spread of kabbalistic ideas, the rise and partial fall of the heretical Sabbatian messianic movement, and the genesis of the astounding religious revival of Hasidism. In standard accounts of most of these movements—Sabbatianism was a partial exception—women were almost totally absent. This is puzzling, since women have played such an important part in Christian mysticism and pietism. I wanted to discover the extent to which women were influenced by these movements, whether they participated in them, and if they shaped their own versions of mystical spirituality. The essays in Part II address these questions; Chapter 7, a study of Sarah Rebecca Rachel Leah Horowitz (1715?–1790?), a rabbinic and kabbalistic scholar, appears for the first time in this volume.

Most recently, as new research has appeared on the piety of "ordinary

Jews" in Ashkenaz, I have endeavored to set the *tkhines* into the context of the new pietistic creativity of the day. The invention of printing made it possible, for the first time, to disseminate religious practices, interpretations, and scholarship widely and cheaply, and thus extended their reach beyond scholarly elites. *Tkhines* in Yiddish were only one of a number of genres that arose in the seventeenth and eighteenth centuries. There were mystical private devotions in Hebrew, new liturgies and new rituals formulated under the influence of Kabbalah, abridgments and popularizations of ethical works, and guides to pious practices. Like the *tkhines*, these other works were not intended for scholars, but for an "intellectual middle class" that included women, artisans, traders, and children. Chapter 1, newly written for this volume, reflects this new perspective on the *tkhines*.

Finally, in publishing research on the *tkhines* over the last decade, I have helped to stimulate interest in these prayers and make them available to feminist liturgists and activists, as well as to scholars. Several anthologies of translations of *tkhines* into English have been published;[16] and new feminist "*tkhines*" have been written. In Part III, I investigate, in previously unpublished research, the development and impact of the *tkhines* in twentieth-century America. I conclude the book with reflections on what this research has meant to me, as a feminist scholar, a woman, and a Jew.

A NOTE ON TRANSLATION AND ROMANIZATION

Early Yiddish materials such as the *tkhines* present special problems of translation and romanization. Many *tkhines* quote biblical verses, prayers, and other material in Hebrew, followed by a Yiddish translation or paraphrase. The interplay between the Hebrew and the Yiddish is an essential feature of the text. To signal the presence of Hebrew, and to clarify what would otherwise seem to be unexplained repetition, I have used boldface type for Hebrew embedded within the Yiddish text.

In romanizing Yiddish, I have followed the guidelines Uriel Weinreich set out in *Modern English-Yiddish, Yiddish-English Dictionary* (New York: YIVO Institute for Jewish Research and MacGraw-Hill, 1968), although I have slightly simplified them. In romanizing Hebrew, I have eschewed technical scholarly romanization schemes in favor of a simplified system, omitting most diacritical marks, that aims at ease of pronunciation. Once again, the Hebrew-Yiddish linguistic polysystem of Ashkenazic Jewry presents special problems. Some works that are entirely in Yiddish have Hebrew titles. In such cases, I have romanized the titles according to the Ashkenazic pronunciation, e.g. *Nakhalas Tsevi*, while using the standard Sefardic pronunciation for other works, whatever their provenance, that are entirely or primarily in Hebrew, e.g. *Shenei luhot ha-brit*.

Finally, I have used translated titles for some *tkhines*, especially those that have distinctive titles and that I discuss at length: *The Three Gates*, but *Seder tkhines u-vakoshes* (Order of Supplications and Petitions).

With rare exceptions, quotations from the Hebrew Bible are rendered according to *Tanakh: A New Translation of the Holy Scriptures* (Philadelphia: Jewish Publication Society, 1985). All other translations of Yiddish and Hebrew texts are my own, unless otherwise noted.

INTRODUCTION: JEWISH SPIRITUALITY IN THE SEVENTEENTH AND EIGHTEENTH CENTURIES

This introduction will assist the reader unfamiliar with the history of Judaism in early modern Europe in placing the *tkhines* within their historical context. In Chapter 1, I introduce the innovations in everyday piety, a piety invigorated by an influx of mystical thinking. Here, I provide more background on Jewish mysticism and the three great spiritual movements of the seventeenth and eighteenth centuries, Lurianic Kabbalah, Sabbatian messianism, and Hasidism, pointing out the ways in which they did or did not influence the *tkhine* literature.

THEOSOPHICAL, THEURGIC, AND ECSTATIC MYSTICISM

The word "Kabbalah" means "received tradition," and for many centuries esoteric mystical teachings were passed along in small circles of (male) mystical adepts, who received the teachings from their spiritual masters. This was particularly the case during the early and high Middle Ages, when Kabbalah first flourished. Kabbalistic writings were purposely allusive and obscure. The teachings of Jewish mysticism were controversial, and their study was often carefully restricted to those considered worthy. However, in the fifteenth and sixteenth centuries—partly because of the rise of printing—some kabbalistic teachings became more widely available: indeed, Gershom Scholem, the greatest modern historian of Jewish mysticism, has argued that Kabbalah became the theology of Judaism.[1] The Zohar (c. 1300) is the most important work of classical Jewish mysticism.

Scholars have distinguished three phenomenological strands within

Kabbalah: the theosophical, the theurgic, and the ecstatic.[2] Of these, theosophical and theurgic Kabbalah are closely bound up with each other and are the only strands to have exerted some influence on the *tkhine* literature. Theosophical Kabbalah, about which the majority of scholarship has been written, is primarily concerned with knowledge of the secret inner life of the Godhead. Such knowledge was believed to be embedded within the Torah, revealed by God; the Torah itself, in its totality, is the secret Name of God.

Briefly, classical Kabbalah, the creation of mystics in Spain and Provence in the Middle Ages, distinguished between an utterly infinite, unknowable aspect of God, called Ein Sof (Infinity), and revealed aspects of God, the ten *sefirot* (singular: *sefirah*), or emanations. In an essentially Neoplatonic picture, the Infinite expresses Itself through these emanations, which grow like a tree from its roots, or like a man unfurling from his head down to his toes, and this process eventually descends to the creation of our material world. Indeed, the Cosmic Tree and the Primordial Man are among the most important symbols for the realm of the Revealed Divinity, the pleroma of the *sefirot*. Each *sefirah* of the ten *sefirot* is named after such abstract attributes of God as Wisdom and Understanding, Gracious Love and Stern Judgment, Beauty and Majesty. Yet each of the *sefirot* also has multiple epithets and multiple symbols, and some of them develop what could be called personalities.

Consider the image of the primordial man for the realm of the *sefirot*. The first three, and most hidden, of the ten *sefirot*, Keter (Crown), Hokhmah (Wisdom), and Binah (Understanding), form the head. The right arm is Hesed (Lovingkindness), while the left arm is known as Gevurah (Power) or Din (Stern Judgment). The trunk of the body is the *sefirah* known as Tiferet (Beauty) or Rahamim (Compassion). The right and left legs are Netsah (Eternity) and Hod (Splendor). The ninth *sefirah*, Yesod (Foundation) is the divine phallus, while the tenth *sefirah*, Malkhut (Majesty), also known as Shekhinah (Presence), is the feminine of the divine androgyne. (Recently, however, Elliot Wolfson has argued that the Shekhinah can be understood as crypto-male; see the discussion at the ends of Chapters 6 and 7.)

This imagery is developed in significant ways. The right side of the primordial man connotes lovingkindness and maleness, while the left side is associated with stern judgment, femaleness, and, ultimately, the origin of the forces of evil. The central line of the *sefirot* expresses the balance of these opposing forces. Further, Tiferet, the trunk of the divine anthropos, becomes known as the Holy Blessed One, the King. He resembles most closely the God of rabbinic Judaism. To a certain extent, he includes within himself six of the seven lower *sefirot*. The tenth and last, the Shekhinah, the Divine Presence, is his spouse. By means of Yesod, Tiferet transmits the divine blessings to Shekhinah, who transmits them to the lower worlds. She is the Presence of God within the material world. Of all the *sefirot*, Shekhinah and Tiferet are the only ones mentioned with any frequency in the *tkhine* literature, although Hesed and Din are sometimes alluded to.

Theurgic Kabbalah, the second phenomenological strand, presupposes the theosophical teachings about the structure of the Godhead and teaches the adept how to use this knowlege to affect the inner life of God. If all is well in the cosmos, divine abundance flows from the wellsprings of the Infinite through the channels connecting the *sefirot* and thence to the lower worlds, ensuring peace, health, and plenty. However, our cosmos is flawed, according to classical Kabbalah, because of Adam's sin, and, according to later Kabbalah, because of certain primordial intradivine processes. Thus, the flow of abundance can become blocked, resulting in famine, war, and disease. Israel's exile, a punishment for sin, is the most palpable expression of the loss of divine harmony. One of the most powerful teachings of Jewish mysticism is that humans, properly schooled in Kabbalah, can exercise control over these divine processes. By performing the *mitsvot* in purity and holiness, and with the proper mystical intentions and techniques, the mystic can help to keep the *sefirot* in harmony and the channels of divine abundance flowing freely. By contrast, evil-doing and sin separate the *sefirot* and block the channels.

One myth that expresses this in the Zohar and other works of the classical period is that of the exile of the Shekhinah. Building on the talmudic teaching that God's presence (Shekhinah) goes into exile with Israel, the Zohar develops the motif of the divine marriage between Tiferet, the sixth *sefirah*, the Holy Blessed One, or the King, and the tenth *sefirah*, the Shekhinah, called the Queen. Ideally, the King and Queen should be joined in eternal embrace; however, Adam separated Shekhinah (symbolized by the Tree of Knowledge) from Tiferet and the other *sefirot*, sending her into exile, and causing his own expulsion from the Garden of Eden. Later, the people of Israel exacerbated this situation by worshiping the Golden Calf and committing the later sins for which they were ultimately exiled from the Land of Israel. According to the Zohar, the goal of all Jewish religious practice is to further the divine embrace. In the short term, this will ensure abundance and well-being. However, the long-term goal is to restore the King and Queen to each other for eternity, thus bringing about the end of Israel's exile, the messianic era, and the redemption of the cosmos. Reference to the exiled Shekhinah often appears in the *tkhine* literature, especially in Eastern European *tkhines*.

While both theosophical and theurgical Kabbalah became relatively well known among scholarly Ashkenazic men, ecstatic Kabbalah, the third strand, was most influential among Sefardic and especially Middle Eastern Jews. Its major early exponent, the thirteenth-century mystic Abraham Abulafia, was less interested in theosophical details about the *sefirot,* and more interested in techniques for attaining mystical ecstasy, an unmediated experience of the divine.[3] I have found no trace of influence of the ecstatic Kabbalah on the *tkhine* literature.

LURIANIC KABBALAH

In sixteenth-century Safed, a town in the Galilee, there lived a remarkable group of Jewish mystics, poets, legal scholars, and pietists. Although many thinkers contributed to a new set of mystical teachings, the form Kabbalah took as it emerged from Safed is most closely associated with the name of Isaac Luria (1534–1572), a charismatic ecstatic who left almost no writings of his own. Thus, we know his teachings as transmitted through his disciples, Hayyim Vital and others. Lurianic Kabbalah introduced important innovations into the picture of the Godhead developed in classical Kabbalah. Not all of these changes concern us here; however, the Lurianic myth of the shattered vessels and the divine sparks was most influential in later popularizations of mystical teaching. Cosmic redemption, in Lurianic Kabbalah, is described as "raising the sparks": As a result of the original cosmic cataclysm of "the breaking of the vessels" that, according to these teachings, preceded the successful emanation of the *sefirot,* shattered fragments of divinity were trapped within base matter. By prayer, Torah study, and mystical contemplation, and especially by performing the divine commandments with the correct mystical intentions, the adept liberates the sparks from the *kelippot,* the husks or shells that surround them with base matter or even demonic powers, and restores them to the divine realm. When all the sparks have been liberated, the forces of evil will be destroyed, the messianic redemption will be achieved, and Israel's suffering and exile will end. Thus, Lurianic Kabbalah contained within itself a powerful eschatological impulse.[4] (The terms *kelippot* and *hit-sonim*, both referring to the powers of evil, do occur in some *tkhines*, although the full-fledged myth of the raising of sparks does not, as far as I have seen.)

In 1665, Sabbatai Zevi, a Jew from Izmir in the Ottoman Empire, became convinced that he was the Messiah. His claims were widely believed, especially, but not exclusively, among Sefardic Jews. His understanding of his role was based on Lurianic Kabbalah: both to redeem those sparks trapped in the demonic realm and to show that a new era had begun. In moments of religious exaltation he transgressed certain commandments, for example, eating on the fast day of Tisha B'Av. Interestingly enough, Sabbatai Zevi seems to have envisioned a transformation in the status of women to be a necessary corollary to the overall messianic transformation. As Scholem points out, he called women to the Torah, and even promised to free them from the "curse of Eve," including both painful childbirth *and* subordination to their husbands.

Sabbatai Zevi's following grew so great that in 1666, the Sultan, alarmed at the possibility of political unrest, had him arrested and gave him a choice between execution and conversion to Islam. Sabbatai Zevi chose to convert and died in captivity in 1676. While his conversion and, later, his death disillusioned many of his followers, others could not renounce their belief and attempted to justify his action. Some, indeed, believed that Sabbatai Zevi had converted in order to redeem the divine sparks caught in the realm of evil and false religion; some even converted to Islam themselves. Gradually, however, these believers were forced underground. Nonetheless, they continued to propagate their faith for many decades.[5]

For the last several decades of the seventeenth century, a time of widespread Sabbatian activity, Podolia, a region now in the Ukraine, was part of the Ottoman Empire. Thus it was readily open to influences from the vigorous Ottoman crypto-Sabbatian community. The Sabbatians of Salonika established strong ties with Podolian Sabbatians, who sent out emissaries to other areas of Eastern Europe. Many Sabbatians, convinced that mystical teachings showed the truth of Sabbatai Zevi's mission, were in the forefront of the movement to popularize the Kabbalah in simplified Hebrew and Yiddish works. Further, Sabbatian emissaries openly proselytized among women, for example, taking the Torah scroll and preaching in the women's section of the synagogue.

In the eighteenth century, a new messianic movement arose in Podolia, founded by Jacob Frank (1726–1791), who regarded himself as a new incarnation of the messiah. Frank managed to attract many crypto-Sabbatians in Podolia, Galicia, and Hungary to his sect; after his death the movement was led by his daughter Eva. Frankism was somewhat more antinomian than Sabbatianism. Frank himself promoted transgressive behavior among his followers, and eventually, for a combination of reasons, led a group of them to convert to Christianity.[6]

Scholars are just beginning to investigate the role of women among the followers of Sabbatai Zevi, in later underground Sabbatianism, and in Frankism. Here let me simply note that material from a widely read mystical guide to the Jewish festival cycle, which originated in Sabbatian circles, *Hemdat yamim,* made its way into a few *tkhines.* Further, most Eastern European *tkhines* were written by women living in precisely those regions of Eastern Europe, now Eastern Poland and Western Ukraine, in which Sabbatians and Frankists were most active.

HASIDISM

The region of Podolia, Galicia, and Volhynia was a place of great spiritual ferment from the mid-seventeenth century through the end of the eighteenth century. One contributing factor may have been the military strife that swept through the region, from the Cossack uprising led by Bogdan Chmielnicki in 1648–49, through the wars that partitioned Poland among Russia, Prussia, and Austria in the eighteenth century. Scholars continue to debate the extent of mortality, property damage, and social disorganization during this period; nonetheless, there was certainly widespread, if localized, hardship. Some historians have also argued that both religious and secular Jewish communal authorities had become corrupt and ineffective, thus leading to the rise of Hasidism as a new form of religious organization. Recent studies, made possible by the opening of Eastern European archives, call that view into question.[7]

Whatever the contributing factors, there is no doubt that Hasidism produced an amazing religious revival—for men. Hasidism traces its ancestry to Israel ben Eliezer (1700–1760), known as the Baal Shem Tov (Master of the Good Name, abbreviated as "Besht"), a charismatic figure who was a faith healer, storyteller, and mystic. In 1740, the Besht settled in Miedzyboz, a prosperous town in Podolia, where he remained a respected member of the community until his death.

In common with other charismatic figures seen as the founder of religious movements, the Besht left virtually no writings of his own, and his teachings must be pieced together from the writings of his disciples and descendents. It is not clear whether the Besht regarded himself as the founder of a movement, or simply as someone who called others to a deeper spiritual life. Contemporary archival sources suggest that he was simply seen as an outstanding exemplar of an already existing social role: the baal shem, or faith healer. Certainly, the teachings of the Besht and of other early Hasidic leaders drew upon and developed concepts already widespread among small circles of pre-Hasidic mystics.

Nonetheless, his message was clearly inspiring, and after his death his colleague/disciple, Dov Ber (d. 1772), the Maggid (preacher) of Mezhirech, a town in neighboring Volhynia, aggressively organized his disciples to spread the movement throughout Jewish Eastern Europe. Thus, it was not until the 1770s that Hasidism began to provoke opposition from the rabbinical authorities, and in fact to suffer bans and persecution by the party that came to be known as the *mitnagdim* (opponents). These conflicts took several generations to settle; by that time, Hasidism had gained the adherence of a major portion of the Jewish people in the Ukraine and Poland, with only Lithuania and White Russia as anti-Hasidic holdouts. In the nineteenth century, Hasidim and *mitnagdim* perceived a common enemy in the forces of the *haskalah*, the European enlightenment now encroaching on traditional Jewish life in Eastern Europe.

Although there was some variation among the teachings of different Hasidic leaders, we can draw the broad outlines of the message of the movement in its early years. The central goal of religious life is *devekut*, or mystical communion with God.[8] Reaching this goal involved the annihilation of the self (*bittul ha-yesh*) and the realization that God is immanent everywhere and in everything. Hasidism took a new approach to the age-old problem of distraction during prayer, known as "strange thoughts" (*mahashavot zarot*). Although earlier teachers had urged the worshipper simply to suppresss such thoughts, Hasidic leaders suggested that even thoughts of sin could, by proper concentration, be brought back to their source in holiness and thus redeemed. Further, Hasidism rejected the ascetic idea that one must turn one's back on the world in order to commune with God; Hasidim were to worship God precisely by means of their corporeal lives, eating, conversing, even smoking their pipes while in a state of *devekut*.

Certain features of the social organization of Hasidism make it unique in the history of Jewish mysticism. It was the first form of mysticism to be truly widespread among the masses of ordinary Jewish men. Further, in Hasidism the figure of the *tsaddik*, the charismatic mystical master, emerged as the center of each Hasidic community. Especially in the early days of Hasidism, young men would roam from town to town, in search of the master who could speak to the root of their souls, guide them on their spiritual quest, and help them in manifold ways. Hasidic communities thus consisted of the master and his disciples. These young men often left home and family for long periods of time to be with the *tsaddik*, who became a new, nonlocal form of Jewish authority. Further, as it became apparent that not all the followers of Hasidism were capable of the spiritual discipline required to transform "strange thoughts" and to reach *devekut*, it increasingly became the task of the *tsaddik* to accomplish these vicariously for his Hasidim. Eventually, the position of *tsaddik*—and the allegiance to a particular *tsaddik*—became hereditary, but this did not occur until around the turn of the nineteenth century.[9]

Hasidic "courts," as the residence of a *tsaddik* and the seat of his community was known, were intense social worlds. Strong emotional ties bound the *tsaddik* to his followers, and the Hasidim to each other. It was in the context of this intimate relationship that the *tsaddik* transmitted his teachings, orally, to his disciples. Further, the *tsaddik*, identified with the *sefirah* Yesod, was credited with the ability to bring down and channel the divine abundance (*shefa*)—including financial well-being, spiritual advancement, and offspring—to his followers, who, in return, were responsible for contributing financially to his support. Joyous, even ecstatic, worship was a feature of the new Hasidic communities. Song, dance, and the recounting of the *tsaddik*'s teachings and miracles were all important in the religious life of the communities; so, on occasion, was the stimulus to ecstasy provided by alcohol and tobacco.[10]

Except for the daughters, sisters, and sometimes wives of *tsaddikim*, who on occasion were credited with great spirituality and charismatic powers of their own, Hasidic courts were exclusively male communities. There were no women among the *tsaddikim* nor among the disciples (although women certainly came as petitioners for miraculous help); and even the charismatic women among the relatives of the *tsaddikim* left no writings and had no disciples of their own. Further, despite the mass character of Hasidism, none of its leaders took any thought for the spiritual needs of women, nor did they write any literature addressed to women.[11] And this is despite the fact that, cross-culturally, such ecstatic religious movements often counted women among their ranks.

Nonetheless, the spiritual explosion of Hasidism was located in those regions of Eastern Europe where women wrote *tkhines*. Did the new movement have any impact on the *tkhine* literature? The answer is no; even *tkhine* authors whose husbands had close ties to Hasidism appear not to have absorbed the basic concepts of the movement and to have rooted their writings in earlier understandings of piety. A good example is Leah Dreyzl, discussed in Chapter 1. At least according to legend, her husband was a close associate of the Baal Shem Tov. Yet her *tkhines* for the Days of Awe make no reference to either the role of the *tsaddik*, or the necessity for worship through corporeal life, even though these concepts are appropriate to her material. Further, although Shifrah bas Joseph, the subject of Chapter 6, uses such terms as "strange thoughts" and "supernal abundance," an analysis of her text shows she uses these terms in pre-Hasidic ways.[12]

WOMEN AND JEWISH MYSTICISM

While there remain many unanswered questions about the effects of all these movements within Jewish spirituality on women, the material reviewed here is suggestive. Briefly, social organization seems crucial. Those who were interested in spreading the Safed revival—and some of them were Sabbatians—propagated practices and concepts through a popular literature in Hebrew and Yiddish. Through these materials, mystical concepts, often in diluted form, made their way to women, some of whom incorporated them into *tkhines*. But Hasidism, which barely produced any books at all for several decades and concentrated on spreading its message orally in exclusively male communities, did not attempt to convey its message to women. The sole exception to this is the Yiddish translation of the Hebrew work *Shivhei ha-Besht* (In Praise of the Baal Shem Tov), a collection of hagiographic legends about the founder of Hasidism. The title pages of early editions of the Yiddish translation, published in 1816 and 1817, do address themselves to "pious women" as well as to unlearned men. (Interestingly, this was not the case for the Yiddish edition of *Shivhei ha-Besht* published in Ostraha, 1816, which was an independent version of the work, rather than a translation of the Hebrew.)

For many decades, *Shivhei ha-Besht* stood alone as the sole collection of Hasidic legends to be printed. In the meantime, a number of Hasidic masters published works, primarily consisting of homilies on the biblical portion of the week, in which they conveyed the teachings of Hasidism in a more direct fashion. In the latter part of the nineteenth century, but not before, legends about the *tsaddikim* were widely published in both Hebrew and Yiddish, and women undoubtedly read the Yiddish collections. However, almost none of the theoretical works of Hasidism were made available in Yiddish. Scholars have debated the relative merits of the legendary versus the theoretical literature of Hasidism in understanding its message; women had access only to the legendary literature. And despite the fact that women were often among those who came to ask the *tsaddik* for advice or supernatural aid, they were never admitted to the community of men to whom the *tsaddik* addressed his teachings.

VOICES OF THE

MATRIARCHS

PART I

THE *TKHINES*,
RELIGIOUS
LITERATURE IN
YIDDISH, AND THE
CONSTRUCTION OF
GENDER IN
ASHKENAZIC
JUDAISM

THE *TKHINES*: AN INTRODUCTION

Shloymele's mother Sarah was frail and slight, with small, white hands crisscrossed with tiny purple veins, and the pale face and thin lips of a pious woman. She seemed to be pure spirit, to float rather than walk. She was a learned woman, who knew all kinds of prayers [*tkhines*], prayers of the Land of Israel and prayers of Sarah Bas Tovim; she was well-versed in the laws of *khala*, menstruation, and candle lighting, which are the particular province of women, and she read such books as *Tsena Urena, The Shining Candelabrum,* and the like. It was she who showed the women how to pray: what hymns to say, when to rise, when to stand on tip-toe in the *kedusha* prayer. In the women's gallery of the synagogue, she kept a lemon and other pungent remedies to revive herself or the other women whenever they felt faint. And in fact it was hardly possible to keep from fainting when Sarah read. She would read with great emotion, her melody melting the soul and pulling at the heart strings. When she wept, everyone wept with her; her tears would have melted a stone.[1]

Here we meet a Jewish woman of some learning, a spiritual soul and a leader of other women. Yet the history of Jewish spirituality as it has been written is chiefly the history of the religious life of the educated, male elite, and indeed, the most important sources for this history are the written works produced by learned men. More generally, our understanding of the history of Judaism in any particular period has been based primarily on the writings of these small numbers of men. The result has been the relative neglect of the religion of ordinary people, those who produced no works of religious philosophy, legal rulings, or mystical speculation. But did not ordinary Jews, too, rejoice on the Sabbath and holidays, repent of their sins, hope for redemption, and express their devotion to God in prayer? To understand the religious history of the Jewish people more fully, then, we must also understand these ordinary Jews—including women.[2]

Because so few women received more than the rudiments of Jewish education throughout the ages, they left only a scant literary legacy of their own, with the result that the spiritual life of women as a group has been perhaps the most neglected area of the history of Jewish spirituality. Few women learned Hebrew, the holy language of scholarly communication, and fewer still left any written works, even in the vernacular.[3] Further, women were excluded from the major arenas of Jewish public life: the government of the *kehillah* (the organized community), the Talmudic academy, the house of study, the rabbinical court, the kabbalistic conventicle, the Hasidic gathering. And in the synagogue women did not count as one of the *minyan*, the ten adults required to make a quorum for public prayer; they were not permitted to lead the service or to read from the Torah (the scroll of the biblical text read in the synagogue); and they sat screened from men's eyes behind a partition, on a balcony, or in a completely separate room.

Some modern critics of the role of women in Jewish life have concluded from these exclusions that women had no religious lives to speak of or that their religion was only a pale shadow of the religious lives of men, who had the more direct access to the great classics of Jewish tradition and to the important spheres of Jewish religious life. Others have suggested that women did have a religious culture of their own, influenced by the scholarly and male formulations of Judaism but also in part independent of them, or that women adapted the religious language created by men for their own purposes. Because of the paucity of sources, it is nearly impossible to assess for many periods of Jewish history which of these views might be correct.[4]

A NEW SOURCE: DEVOTIONAL LITERATURE IN YIDDISH

There does exist, however, a rich array of sources for writing the religious history of women of at least one period—the Ashkenazic world of the Netherlands, the Germanic lands, Poland, and Russia from the sixteenth through the nineteenth century. In common with Jews all over the globe, Ashkenazic Jews used Hebrew, an ancient Semitic tongue and the language of the Bible, and its linguistic cousin Aramaic, the language of the lion's share of the Talmud, much as medieval Christians used Latin: as the language of worship, study, and scholarship. Together, Hebrew and Aramaic were known by Ashkenazic Jews as *loshn-koydesh* (the holy tongue). During this period, the vernacular of Ashkenazic Jews was Yiddish, a language with a Germanic grammatical base, and Germanic, Romance, Semitic, and, especially in Eastern Europe, Slavic vocabulary. Despite its predominantly European roots, Yiddish was written in Hebrew characters.

Formal education consisted almost entirely of mastering classical works written in Hebrew and Aramaic. Further, formal education was primarily for boys, almost all of whom received at least a few years of schooling. Thus, its goal was to enable males to recite the prayers, read the holy books, and, if they had the intellectual gifts, to become scholars of the classical rabbinic literature in the holy tongue. Some girls received no formal education at all, while others simply learned the mechanics of reading with little stress on actual comprehension of the Hebrew words. However, knowledge of the Hebrew alphabet enabled them to read the vernacular Yiddish. And a small number of girls, especially those from wealthy or scholarly families, received far more elaborate education.

The early modern Yiddish-speaking culture of Ashkenazic Jews stretched across a vast expanse in space and time. In the search for women's religious lives within this culture, popular religious literature in Yiddish is a precious historical resource. In the sixteenth century, not long after the invention of printing, there began to appear a voluminous literature in Yiddish, including homiletical, ethical, and devotional material and biblical paraphrases. Much of this literature consisted of adaptations of similar popular religious works in Hebrew, intended for a male readership, that were being published at about the same time. It is clear, however, from information on the title pages of the Yiddish works and from contemporary accounts that the chief audience for most of these collections was found among women, who, since they rarely mastered Hebrew, usually did not have access to literature in the sacred tongue.[5]

Literate women could read (and unlettered women could have read to them) these pious and edifying tales, which told them of the role models and heroes (though rarely of the heroines) of Jewish tradition—whether rabbis from the time of the Mishnah (second century), medieval saints and martyrs, or, later, the wonder-working hasidic leaders of the eighteenth century. The ethical literature instructed them in conducting their relations with family, servants, and neighbors in godly fashion, as well as providing a guide for proper Sabbath and holiday observance and ethical business dealings. The *Tsenerene*, the collection of Yiddish homilies on the weekly Bible reading for the synagogue that was first published around 1600, was an extremely popular work that appeared in well over three hundred editions. Women read it for inspiration and catharsis, often weeping over the text, as a regular part of their Sabbath afternoon activity.[6]

THE RISE OF THE *TKHINES*

Alongside these various genres, collections of Yiddish prayers or *tkhines*, also began to be published. The genre takes its name from the Hebrew root *le-hithanen*, to supplicate; *tkhines* (in Hebrew, *tehinnot*) are supplications. Written for a wide variety of occasions, these prayers structured women's devotional lives by defining a range of topics considered suitable for women and by establishing a realm of discourse for addressing these topics. Women chanted these prayers from small books or little booklets, often at home, sometimes with other women in the synagogue or cemetery. (The Yiddish word *"tkhine"* can refer either to an individual prayer or to a booklet of such prayers.) Each individual *tkhine* begins with a heading directing when and sometimes how it should be recited: "A pretty *tkhine* to say on the Sabbath with great devotion"; "A *tkhine* that the woman should pray for herself and her husband and children"; "What one says when one comes into the synagogue"; "A confession to say with devotion, not too quickly; it is good for the soul"; "When she comes out of the ritual bath"; "The Seven Praises *tkhine* to say with great devotion, corresponding to the Seven Heavens"; "What one says on the Eve of Yom Kippur in the cemetery"; or "A *tkhine* for Sabbaths and festivals after candle-lighting."[7] That at least some *tkhines* were written *by* women stands in contrast to other Yiddish religious genres, which were almost exclusively written by men.

The *tkhines* are a rich source of data for interpreting the meanings that various religious acts held for women. I have written "meanings" in the plural intentionally: we will see that different texts could portray the same act in different ways—whether it was lighting Sabbath candles, undergoing ritual immersion after menstruation, preparing for the Days of Awe, or greeting the new moon. Indeed, to generalize about the tone of the *tkhines* would be to imply that the spirituality of traditional Ashkenazic women was monolithic. It was not, any more than it was for men.[8]

Rather, this literature reveals an intensely lived religious life and a richly imagined spiritual world. We see from the many occasions on which women recited *tkhines* what the important religious events in their lives were and how they understood these events. Consider a *tkhine* for lighting the Sabbath candles (a ritual performed primarily by women), for example: it may contain prayers for protecting the woman's husband and children from evil spirits, or it may contain images of the candelabrum in the ancient Temple. There are *tkhines* for folk customs, as well, practices not mandated by Jewish law—such as making memorial candles for the dead. Finally, unlike Hebrew prayers, *tkhines* contain many references to the matriarchs—Sarah, Rebecca, Rachel, and Leah—and other women of the Bible; these women are figures with whom the female reader can identify.

Despite the paucity of important women in Jewish, especially post-biblical, literature and despite their total absence from the liturgy, the women's devotional literature singles out both well-known and obscure biblical women. It draws upon their portrayal in midrashic literature, the body of legend and theological reflection created by rabbis and sages over a period of almost a thousand years, and connects them to the lives of Ashkenazic women, whose lives centered around the family and the home. Hence, in one eighteenth-century *tkhine*, for blowing the ram's horn on Rosh Hashanah, Rebecca is depicted as a daughter, knowing what it is to be torn away from one's parents at an early age. Thus, the worshiper feels she can call upon her for protection for her own aging parents. Another eighteenth-century text depicts Rachel as a powerful advocate for the people of Israel, pleading with God to end the exile. The *tkhines* presented images of important women—role models—living religious lives.

There are two main groups of *tkhines*: first, those that appeared in Western Europe in the seventeenth and eighteenth centuries and that were probably written or compiled by men for women; and second, those that originated in Eastern Europe in the seventeenth, eighteenth, and early nineteenth centuries, some of which were written or reworked by women. Western European *tkhines* were published in collections addressing many topics, either in small books or as appendices to Hebrew prayerbooks, often prayerbooks with Yiddish translation. By contrast, Eastern European *tkhines* were typically much shorter, published in little booklets addressing one or two topics, usually on inexpensive paper with small, difficult-to-read type. Despite the differences, the Western and Eastern materials constitute a single genre. They use a special variety of Yiddish, sometimes called *tkhine-loshn* ("*tkhine* language"), and do not, as a rule, reflect local dialectical differences. Further, they use a common stock of terms of address for God and draw upon a broad range of shared images and concerns.[9] Finally, the term *tkhines* appears on the title pages and tables of contents of both Western and Eastern European imprints, and some of the same texts were published and republished in various parts of the Ashkenazic world over more than two centuries. Thus, the two groups of *tkhines* are most fruitfully considered in relation to one another. We shall examine each group in detail below and compare them at the conclusion of the chapter.

THE YIDDISH *TKHINES* AND THE HEBREW LITURGY

Although one can say that prayers illuminate something of how Jews, both men and women, organized their religious lives, the distinctiveness of *tkhines* as prayers specifically for women can be thrown into greater relief by comparing them with the prayers of the standard Hebrew liturgy of the siddur, the prayerbook. The differences are striking.[10]

Most obviously, the prayers of the Hebrew liturgy are composed in the sacred, scholarly language. They are fixed and obligatory, regulated by clock and calendar: men prayed three times a day, reciting a set liturgy that was expanded on Sabbaths and holidays. This liturgy marks the daily transitions at dusk and dawn, sanctifies the separation of the day of rest from the workday week, and celebrates the turning of the seasons and the formative events of Jewish history. The preferred setting for worship is with a congregation, defined primarily as a community of men. Indeed, the prayers of the siddur are typically phrased in the plural.

Tkhines, by contrast, were in the vernacular Yiddish and were voluntary and flexible,[11] recited when the woman wished, most typically at home. They were almost always phrased in the singular, and often had space for the petitioner to insert her own name, thus making them a very personal address to God. It should be noted that, according to some authorities, women were exempt from the duty of recitation of all or part of the liturgy—and by all accounts from communal prayer. Nevertheless, some women recited the Hebrew liturgy daily at home and attended synagogue on Sabbaths and holidays; some women even attended synagogue daily. In fact, there was a special prayer leader, a learned woman known as the *firzogerin* or *zogerke*, who led the women's section of the synagogue in reciting the liturgy and the *tkhines*.[12] But whether in the synagogue or not, women, too, participated in the overarching rhythm of Jewish life, in the feasts and fasts of the liturgical calendar and in the passages of the life cycle.[13] Yet to the extent that women also recited *tkhines*, they resonated to an alternative rhythm and participated in another religious world, with its own set of concerns. It is a world structured not only by the communal events of the Jewish calendar but also by the private events of a woman's domestic life. Consider the following example. Both men and women "remember[ed] the Sabbath day to keep it holy" (Exod. 20:8). But men welcomed the Sabbath in the synagogue at the Friday evening service, while women greeted it by lighting candles at home. As the burden of Sabbath preparations fell on women, so it is for the women's observances that there are *tkhines*—for baking the Sabbath loaf, lighting the candles, even making kugel, the Sabbath pudding.[14]

On the one hand, then, the *tkhine* literature reflects the general themes of Jewish life; on the other hand, it reflects the interests more particular to women. The fact that women were situated in certain social roles influenced the entirety of their religious life, even those observances shared with men.[15] In the *tkhines* the two worlds were forged into one, rooted in women's social reality. Yet what was the role of women authors in shaping this reality?

TKHINES AND THEIR AUTHORS

Some earlier scholars claimed that all *tkhines* were written by men, even if they were attributed to women. As we shall see, this is erroneous. Nonetheless, the issues surrounding the authorship of the *tkhines* are not simple. The majority of *tkhines* were published without attribution to a named author. Certainly, much of this literature was written by men for women, and the question of whether or not any of the texts attributed to female authors were actually written by women has been a vexed one. We know that beginning in the mid-nineteenth century,

Jewish intellectuals influenced by the Enlightenment (*maskilim*)—
men who had no real interest in devotional literature—fabricated
tkhines to which they attached, for commercial motives, fictitious
women's names.[16] And although these works were enormously popular
among women, certainly those written by men represent *men's* conceptions of women's religious lives. But some of the earlier, eighteenth-
century texts were indeed written by women. Leah Horowitz, who lived
in Bolechow, Poland, in the early eighteenth century, is mentioned in
contemporary sources as the author of "The *Tkhine* of the Matriarchs."
Other eighteenth-century authors as well, such as Leah Dreyzl, great-
granddaughter of Hakham Tsevi Ashkenazi, and Serl, daughter of the
Maggid (preacher) of Dubno, Jacob ben Wolf Krantz, can be readily
documented.[17]

All of these women came from noted rabbinical families. This is
hardly surprising; few *men* outside of such families wrote for publication. Further, for the first time, noted rabbis and scholars were themselves writing for a broader public, whether in Hebrew or Yiddish. The
women who wrote *tkhines* can be seen as part of this phenomenon. In
addition, we know that the male relatives of all the women mentioned
above were involved in the vigorous controversies and vibrant religious
movements of their day. How were the *tkhines* connected to the larger
religious climate?

THE *TKHINES* AND EARLY MODERN
ASHKENAZIC PIETY

The seventeenth and eighteenth centuries, the period during which the
tkhines and other Yiddish devotional genres flourished, were a time of
dynamic change within European Jewish life. The heretical Sabbatian
messianic movement arose in 1665, subsequently went underground,
and was partially succeeded in the eighteenth century by Frankism. A
vibrant religious revival movement, Hasidism, made its appearance in
the mid-eighteenth century. These large movements are discussed in
the introduction. But other changes in piety more directly influenced
the rise of the *tkhines* by creating an atmosphere in which many forms
of expression of religious devotion became available to ordinary Jews,
and not only to scholars and mystics. This epoch saw the rise of religious contrafraternities (groups devoted to pious works); the creation of
new liturgies for midnight and dawn devotions, for visiting the ceme-

tery, for preparing corpses for burial, for observing the eve of the new moon as a penitential fast, and for other events; the beginnings of "study" of mystical texts as ritual rather than intellectual exercise; the publication of guides to pious practices for groups and individuals; and even the incorporation of mystical doctrines into synagogue architecture and interior decoration.[18]

What were the factors motivating these changes, and how can we understand the place of Jewish women within them? First, this was a time of technological change and religious and intellectual ferment in Christian Europe as well: the invention of printing, which made possible the inexpensive dissemination of ideas through books and broadsides, helped to bring about both the Renaissance and the Reformation.[19] The rise of the printed book had a decisive influence on Judaism as well. For the first time, book production was cheap enough that broad masses of people could have access to published materials. This led to two results. First, halakhic, mystical, and philosophical teachings that had been the province of small elites were much more widely disseminated, if not without controversy.[20] Second, a new kind of literature emerged, one whose audience was the intellectual middle class. They were the primary consumers of guides to the ethical life, books of pious practices, and new liturgies and rituals, often in abridged and simplified form. Toward the bottom, one could say, of this middle class, were the consumers of such works in Yiddish paraphrase or translation, women along with artisans and traders.[21]

There were also internal Jewish factors leading to these religious changes. The sixteenth century saw the creation of a brilliant center of Jewish mystical and pietistic activity in the small Galilean town of Safed, in Palestine. Among its major figures were the great legist and mystic Joseph Karo, the prolific mystical systematizer Moses Cordovero, and the charismatic ecstatic Isaac Luria, who died young and left almost no writings of his own, but a legacy of myth and symbol that was transmitted and transformed by his disciples. The mystical community in Safed, which also included scores of other eminent mystics and scholars, gave rise to a mystical pietism that spread rapidly throughout the Jewish world. Because of Luria's central role in the community, this pietism is sometimes referred to as the Lurianic revival, and the mystical system that emerged from Safed is called Lurianic kabbalah. Scholars have debated the extent to which Luria's esoteric teachings were in fact known. However, at the popular level, the complexities of Luria's thought were often lost, and Cordovero's system of thought was equally influential.[22] (Thus, scholars have more recently come to prefer the term "Safed revival.") Moreover, Zeev Gries has persuasively argued that Ashkenazic pietism during this period transformed the Lurianic "mythos" to a lived and ritualized "ethos."[23] That is, the Lurianic myth, however imperfectly understood, of an exile within God that parallels the exile of Israel on earth, and of the imperative for human beings to mend both the world and the Godhead through their prayer and performance of *mitsvot*, gave rise to the pervasive ritualization of Jewish life which we have discussed above.

Women, too, were influenced by the pietistic currents of the times. They, too, wished to participate in extra ritual activities. In addition to composing *tkhines*, learned women were among those who helped to make other literature originating in the Safed revival available in Yiddish. At the beginning of the eighteenth century, Ellus bas Mordecai of Slutsk published her translations of an abridged version of *Maavar Yabbok*, a guide to dealing with the dying and the dead, and *Shomrim la-boker*, a liturgy for dawn devotions. As she says in her introduction to *Shomrim la-boker*, "many men and women chirp like birds," reciting the Hebrew prayers without understanding them; she has therefore provided a translation.[24] And a Yiddish version of an important collection of mystical Hebrew devotions (known as *tehinnot*), Nathan Nata Hannover's *Shaarei Tsiyyon* was published in Prague at about the same time.[25] The title page describes the translator as follows: "Because of her modesty, she would not let her name be published, but her learning and expert knowledge are renowned far and wide." This "important woman" provided the translation "for the pious women who only understand Yiddish," so that they too would be able to say these prayers. It was also during this period that women began treating the Sabbath before the new moon as a time of special piety, perhaps taking their inspiration from men's observances of the eve of the new moon as a day of penitence.[26]

It is indubitable that the rise of *tkhines* as a genre was also born of women's desire to shape their own form of participation in the pietistic practices of the day. As we shall see below, the introduction to an early collection of *tkhines*, published in Amsterdam in 1648, says explicitly that women wanted to recite the Hebrew *tehinnot* but could not understand them, and that therefore the (unnamed) editor acceded to the requests of these pious women and provided *tkhines* in Yiddish. The *tkhines* takes their origins, in particular, from the rise of the mystical Hebrew *tehinnot*.

YIDDISH *TKHINES* AND HEBREW *TEHINNOT*

Private devotions in Hebrew, known as *tehinnot*, formed part of the mystical literature that flowered in the wake of the Safed revival. These devotions, along with guides to the spiritual life, afforded an important channel for the popularization of hitherto esoteric kabbalistic ideas. Two significant works of this genre are the devotional manuals *Shaar ha-shamayim* (Gate of Heaven) and *Shaarei tsiyyon* (Gates of Zion). The former, composed by the eminent halakhist and kabbalist Isaiah Horowitz (1565?–1630), is an extensive kabbalistic commentary on the prayer book and includes prayers of Horowitz's own composition. (It was first published in 1717 by the author's great-grandson.)[27] *Shaarei tsiyyon*, compiled by Nathan Nata Hannover (d. 1683), was published in 1662 and reprinted numerous times. Its seven chapters contain prayers for a variety of liturgical and nonliturgical occasions.[28]

Intended for men, this mystical devotional literature, like the *tkhines*, provides for prayer outside the framework of the fixed liturgy. As we have noted, such devotions were only one genre of the wave of publications rooted in Safed pietism. Along with ethical guides, booklets of new rituals, and books of pious customs, both Hebrew *tehinnot* and Yiddish *tkhines* flourished in the seventeenth and eighteenth centuries. Moreover, there are actual points of contact between the two: Solomon Freehof has demonstrated that both *Shaarei tsiyyon* and *Shaar ha-shamayim* deeply influenced the mid-eighteenth-century Western European *tkhines* collection *Seder tkhines u-vakoshes* (discussed at length later in this chapter). The prayers for the days of the week found in this *tkhine* collection (and in the earlier *Tkhines* published in 1648 in Amsterdam) reflect the themes of the prayers for those days found in *Shaarei tsiyyon*, and some fifteen *tkhines* in all are translated or paraphrased from one or the other of these works.[29]

Nonetheless, despite certain commonalities and the fact that some *tkhines* originated in kabbalistic works, and despite Freehof's insistence that the *tkhines* contain what he calls "the usual Cabalistic ideas, the angels, the mysteries of God's name and the *Kavvanoth*," the spiritual world of the *tkhines* differs sharply from that of *Shaarei tsiyyon*, for example.[30] While *Shaarei Tsiyyon* was indeed intended for "middle class" intellectual consumers, it nonetheless retains many of the esoteric teachings of Lurianic kabbalah, if in somewhat simplified form. Central to the Lurianic myth was the idea that a primordial flaw occurred in the process of divine self-expression that led to the creation of the cosmos, and that therefore a part of the Godhead, as it were, is in exile from the rest. The people of Israel, however, have the power to aid in repairing that flaw by engaging in certain mystical techniques in prayer and in religious activity. This belief was at the heart of much of the new ritual and liturgy created in the seventeenth and eighteenth centuries. Thus, many of the prayers in *Shaarei Tsiyyon* seek to affect the inner world of the Godhead by means of mystical concentration on permutations of divine names. These *kavvanot* (intentions), which are at the heart of the Lurianic conception of prayer, disregard the literal meaning of the liturgy and seek to transform and ultimately to redeem the cosmos by rearranging, as it were, relations among the *sefirot*, the ten emanations, or aspects, of the Godhead. The prayers of *Shaarei tsiyyon* are thus suffused with a consciousness of this mystical system and often a sense of their own theurgic efficacy in bringing about the desired transformations.

These explicit mystical techniques are entirely absent from the Western European *tkhine* literature. They do, of course, make reference to demons, angels, and the evil eye, the existence of which was assumed in this era. However, they convey no clear sense of the nature of the hidden Godhead, an esoteric reality sharply at odds with the apparent reality of this world and the literal meaning of the words of prayer and sacred texts. A case in point is the *tkhine* for the blessing of the new moon, no. 66 in *Seder tkhines u-vakoshes*, which is based on the prayer for Tuesday among the prayers for the days of the week in *Shaarei Tsiyyon*. While the Hebrew source is replete with permutations of divine names, the Yiddish adaptation avoids even the mention of the technical term "Name" and contents itself with obscure references to the "power" of, for example, biblical verses. In one passage, the Hebrew refers to "the power of the great light that spreads out from the Supernal Chariot,[31] whose Name is [the permutation is given]." The Yiddish substitutes "the power of the holy [the syntax demands a following noun, but none occurs] that shines strongly and spreads out from the *Supernal Chariot.*"

What kind of sense does the Yiddish make without the Name? With no exact knowledge of kabbalistic beliefs about the mystical significance of verses, letters, and divine Names, the passages in Yiddish would be very difficult to understand. What is assumed is a passive and nonspecific knowledge that such doctrines exist, even if the reciter of *tkhines* cannot herself engage in full-fledged mystical prayer.

Further, although, as Freehof points out, the *tkhines* do stress the importance of *kavvanah* (in the sense of the desirable state of devotion during prayer), they contain virtually no *kavvanot* (in the Lurianic sense described above). Even the very prayers for the days of the week, which Freehof cites as indicative of kabbalistic influence, are missing the Lurianic *kavvanot*. Further, the Western European *tkhines* contain no obvious references to the *sefirot*.[32] I have found only one *tkhine*, in *Seder tkhines u-vakoshes*, that speaks of permutations of divine names, but it specifically denies the ability of the reciter to engage in them:

> Lord of the whole world, you are an almighty and merciful God. You know well that we are only flesh and blood, and we have no power to be able to engage in mystical intentions, or to permute your holy names, or [concentrate on] all the intentions in all the prayers and all the blessings. . . .

Yet the *tkhine* does not intend to assert that no one is able to pray mystically, for it concludes:

> May my prayer ascend before you, to make a crown for your head, with the other prayers of Jews who do know how to engage in mystical intentions, and to permute all the intentions and combinations of the holy names which are appropriate for each prayer and each blessing, which will bring together unity and holiness even unto the seventh heaven, Amen.[33]

Thus, it is the reciter of *tkhines* in particular who is unable to engage in mystical contemplation: the kabbalistic mysteries of prayer, it seems, were not deemed appropriate for women.[34] Nonetheless, as we see here, some *tkhines* presuppose the existence of mystics and their worldview, while excluding their reciters from full participation in mystical prayer. These *tkhines* do not present themselves as theurgically efficacious, even though they may on occasion refer, whether clearly, or more usually, obscurely, to mystical techniques of prayer. That obscurity of reference is important: *tkhines* that gloss over, simplify, or omit technical kabbalistic material can be very difficult to understand, even with the passive knowledge that a mystical approach to prayer exists. Perhaps this implies that the recitation of such *tkhines*, even though they are in Yiddish, could be seen as a ritual in which performance is more important than comprehension. Or perhaps they serve to reinforce a sense of mystery in the reciters.

The kabbalistic and *tkhine* prayer literatures also differ in the settings and occasions they presume for prayer. First, although *Sha'arei tsiyyon* contains some prayers that could, on occasion, be recited privately, such as *tikkun hatsot*, the midnight service bewailing the destruction of the Temple and the exile of the Shekhinah (God's presence, the tenth *sefirah*), much of its contents are to be recited in a public setting, such as the synagogue or house of study. Thus, for example, the confession of sins and declaration of faith on the part of one awaiting death but still of sound mind is addressed by the man to a *bet din*, a rabbinical court.[35] The same material reworked in Yiddish for the woman is addressed privately to Almighty God (*Seder tkhines u-vakoshes*, no. 38).

In addition, and despite some similarities, the prayers in *Sha'arei tsiyyon* cluster around occasions that are different from those that figure in the *tkhine* collection.[36] *Sha'arei tsiyyon* reflects, naturally enough, the religious life of a man and a kabbalist. The majority of the work is essentially taken up by the Lurianic *kavvanot* of prayer, along with poems and songs based on the permutations of divine names. The collection also includes prayers to be said before study and to retain what one has learned, before giving a sermon, before putting on phylacteries and the prayer shawl, before setting out on a journey, and before sexual intercourse. Since women did not study, give sermons, or wear phylacteries or prayer shawls, there are no *tkhines* for these activities. Despite the fact that women must sometimes have taken journeys, *Seder tkhines u-vakoshes* contains *tkhines* to be said only while one's husband is on a journey. Although both women and men engaged in intercourse, the *tkhines* are in general less concerned with sexuality and more with the reproductive life.[37] Thus, even though material from *Sha'arey tsiyyon* and other kabbalistic works reworked in Yiddish is found in the *Seder tkhines u-vakoshes* (and some other *tkhine* collections as well), the two literatures betray significant differences in their concerns.

We turn next to a detailed examination of the development of the *tkhine* literature, first in the West, and then in the East.

WESTERN EUROPEAN *TKHINES*

Books of *tkhines*, usually nicely printed on good paper (although poorly proofread), began to appear in print in Western Europe in the mid-seventeenth century. Beginning in 1648 and up through the first few decades of the eighteenth century, various collections, entitled *Taytshe tkhines* (Yiddish *tkhines*), *Naye tkhines* (new *tkhines*), or simply *Tkhi-*

nes, each containing about thirty *tkhines*, were published in Amsterdam, Prague, and various German towns. Around the middle of the eighteenth century, several of these collections were combined into one longer standard edition, usually entitled *Seder tkhines u-vakoshes* (Order of Supplications and Petitions), containing about 120 *tkhines*. Such shorter and longer encyclopedic collections of *tkhines* on many topics were the main form in which these devotions were published in Western Europe. These works rarely offer any statements about their authors or compilers, and many of the texts they contain are reworkings or paraphrases of Hebrew literary models, whether of mystical devotional literature, or earlier texts such as psalms.

Seder tkhines u-vakoshes was widely reprinted with only minor variations well into the nineteenth century, first in Western Europe and then in Eastern Europe. Excluding nineteenth-century Western European editions, which became "germanized," this work therefore constituted a consistent literary corpus for more than two centuries and became a standard collection; the prayers it contains can therefore be considered to define a typical range of concerns for women's piety.[38] We'll unpack this work by investigating the three major sources that became its component parts. Each has a different tale to tell about the possibilities for women's piety in seventeenth and eighteenth century Western Europe.

The Amsterdam *Tkhines* of 1648

The earliest of the Western European collections is the collection entitled *Tkhines*.[39] As its title page proclaims (in Yiddish rhymed prose), the book is intended for a female audience: "These *tkhines* are beautifully clear for pious women and girls, who all have good, pure thoughts, to praise and thank God for all the great gifts he gives to human beings all the days of their lives."

Unlike later editions of this work and also unlike most other *tkhine* collections, the 1648 Amsterdam edition contains an introduction that discusses both the intended audience and the reason for publishing the book. The unnamed author, translator, or compiler (it is not clear which)—or perhaps the printer, Joseph ben Naftali of Konskowola—states that he undertook to put this work together at the earnest entreaty of "several honorable women and pious God-fearers."[40] All human beings—and this is understood to include women—are obligated to praise God and acknowledge God's gracious gifts. While prayers exist for these purposes, they present a problem for women:

Now our sages have composed many praises and thanksgivings and prayers to the Almighty God, and to honor his Holy Name. They have composed [such prayers] in the holy tongue [i.e., Hebrew], which women usually do not understand and cannot know what they are saying. It is like a blind person standing at a window and looking out at the street to see wondrous things—this is the same as women saying the *tehinnot* in the holy tongue and not knowing what they are saying.

Thus, it is clear that women wanted to recite *tehinnot* such as those found in Hannover's *Shaarei Tsiyyon* and that some probably were reciting these prayers in Hebrew. After discussing the unavailability of adequate translations and mentioning once again the requests put to him, translator or printer states further:

Thus I could not excuse myself from acceding to all their desire, for our sages write in *Sefer hasidim* (The Book of the Pietists) that when a woman who cannot understand the prayers comes and desires to be taught, so that she will be able to understand the prayers, one is obligated to teach her so that she understands well. For prayer comes from the heart, and when the heart does not know what the mouth speaks, the prayer helps but little.[41]

Further, the compiler urges others as well to compose prayers in Yiddish for women, "so that therewith the prayers of women may be acceptable before God. . . . For the sake of their [i.e., women's] merit may we be redeemed, as our forebears were [redeemed] from Egypt because of the merit of pious women.[42] Amen."

This introduction suggests that at the time this collection was composed, there were women who wanted to be able to pray in Yiddish[43] and there were men who agreed that it was important for women to pray and to understand their prayers. Further, there was a sentiment that men were *obliged* to help women who wanted to understand the prayers they recited. It is interesting that here at least, although not in *Sefer hasidim* (a work composed in the early thirteenth century), the discussion is *not* about women reciting the required liturgy, either in Hebrew or Yiddish, but about their reciting these extra and voluntary prayers.[44]

And, in fact, the prayers in this collection are almost entirely unrelated to the prayers of the liturgy. This work contains thirty-six prayers in the following order: one *tkhine* to be recited every day; a separate *tkhine* for each of the seven days of the week; a *tkhine for* "taking *hallah"* (separating out and burning a small piece of dough in memory of the priestly tithe) and one for baking bread; *tkhines* for before and after kindling the Sabbath lights; prayers for various stages of purification from menstruation and for childbirth; *tkhines* for the four fast days of the Jewish calendar and one for "whatever day one fasts"; a total of ten *tkhines* to be recited when visiting the cemetery, including one for the eve of the New Year and the eve of the Day of Atonement; and mixed in with the cemetery prayers, two more *tkhines* for candle lighting on Sabbaths and holidays.

This collection appeared in a number of editions over the next century or so,[45] with the same basic core of concerns—adding some material here and deleting some there—but overall not showing any consistent development. Thus, in various other editions, one can find prayers for pregnancy as well as for childbirth, more material on the Days of Awe (the New Year and the Day of Atonement), one or two prayers for the eve of the new moon, and more prayers for "every day," including confessions of sins and prayers for sustenance and livelihood. Some later editions also contain a smaller number of prayers for cemetery visits than were in the 1648 edition. (Separate books of prayers in Hebrew and Yiddish for cemetery visits were also being published at this time.)[46]

This collection of prayers is firmly rooted in domestic and family life. The prayers for the days of the week are indeed related to those found in *Shaarei Tsiyyon*; however, many of the other *tkhines* deal specifically with women's lives: the three "women's commandments" (to be discussed at greater length later in the chapter), baking bread, childbirth.[47] Even the prayers in the cemetery are partly intended as "family visits," prayers at the graves of departed relative. Thus, *Tkhines* tells a tale of domestic religion, of sanctifying hearth and home.

Naye tkhines u-vakoshes (New Supplications and Petitions) (Homburg vor der Hohe: 1729)

Another collection of *tkhines*, *Naye tkhines u-vakoshes*, had an entirely different focus. The domestic domain is not missing here; there are prayers for kindling Sabbath lights and for the Friday night home ritual, and the longest prayer in the book is entitled "a powerful prayer in the holy tongue and Yiddish to pray for children." Nonetheless, fully half of the twenty-four prayers in this collection are connected with the Hebrew liturgy, to be recited before or after particular prayers in the daily, Sabbath, or festival liturgies, or at particular points in the service. It seems clear that the compiler of this collection (perhaps "Moses the typesetter, of Amsterdam," who is named as printer on the title page) assumed that those who used this book would be in synagogue.[48] Several of the prayers are in Hebrew rather than Yiddish, and virtually all the Yiddish prayers are translations from various Hebrew paraliturgical sources, such as *Shaarei Tsiyyon* and the newly popular additional Sabbath devotions, *Tikkunei Shabbat*.

Naye tkhines u-vakoshes does not state on the title page or elsewhere that it is intended for women; it presents a rather gender-neutral face to the public. An analysis of its contents, however, shows that women were its primary, although not its exclusive, audience. Some of the prayers intended for the synagogue include such phrases as "my husband and children." Another insists that the Yiddish translation of "Peace unto you, angels of peace," be recited by "every pious woman with great devotion every Friday night" when her husband comes home from synagogue, "in order to greet the angels who accompany the men from the synagogue to home." Other prayers are ambiguous about the gender of the reciter; and one is entitled "a lovely prayer for a good livelihood to be said every day by a businessman."

This collection connects women to the Hebrew liturgy, then, adding the synagogue to the other loci of women's piety—the home, the cemetery, and the ritual bathhouse—referred to in the *Tkhines* collection and its successors. These *tkhines* for the synagogue provide a kind of punctuation for or commentary on ritual high points of the service: before the *kedushah* prayer in the daily service; before the blowing of the shofar (ram's horn) on Rosh Hashanah; at the opening of the Ark to remove the Torah scrolls on the festivals. These are the same points in the service for which Hebrew meditations were also composed, and the *tkhines* are adaptations of these Hebrew prayers. Indeed, these same Hebrew devotions are still printed in traditional Hebrew prayerbooks today. Yiddish *tkhines* for significant moments in synagogue retained their importance in Western European texts and became even more important in Eastern European *tkhines*.

Seder tkhines (Order of Tkhines) by Mattithias Sobotki (Prague, 1718)

Prague is in between Western and Eastern Europe, and *Seder tkhines* by Mattithias Sobotki has some of the characteristics of the Eastern European as well as of the Western European *tkhines*.[49] Like *Tkhines* and *Naye tkhines u-vakoshes*, this work was later incorporated into *Seder tkhines u-vakoshes*. Unlike those two collections, however, it was not published anonymously, and in this resembles the many other Eastern European *tkhines* with named authors.[50] Mattithias ben Meir, formerly a rabbi in Sobota, Slovakia, like his father before him, proudly explains why he composed this work in the introduction:[51]

> My dear women, I want to explain why I have made this *tkhine* for you in Yiddish: in order to honor God, and second, to honor all the pious women. For there are many women who would gladly awaken their hearts by saying many *tkhines*. Therefore I have composed them so that they may be recited with weeping. May the tears the reciters let flow from their eyes save them from all evil!
>
> My dear pious women, I have not, God forbid, composed them for the sake of my own glory, but rather for the glory of God. . . . I have, thanks be to God, made them up out of my head, and you yourselves will say that they have never before been printed, and you will marvel over them. . . .
>
> My dear people, there are women who say their prayers in the holy tongue. It would be better if they were to say them in Yiddish, in which case they would understand better. Therefore, dear women, whoever wishes to become pious ought not, God forbid, worry about the money. For I have also not economized, and I have let [the printer] take beautiful type and good paper for it. . . . I think they will please you well.

Of the thirty-five *tkhines* in this collection, many retain the by-now familiar settings for prayer, synagogue (four), cemetery (three), and home. But among the many *tkhines* to be recited privately, Sobotki expands two areas of concern and adds a third. The most popular topic for Eastern European *tkhines* is the penitential season, from the beginning of the month of Elul in August through Rosh Hashanah (the New Year) and Yom Kippur (the Day of Atonement) in late September or early October. Sobotki includes eight *tkhines* with this theme (including one to be said in the cemetery and one or two to be said in the synagogue), for example, "the *tkhine* to say during the entire month of Elul and Rosh Hashanah at the cemetery," or "the *tkhine* to say on the eve of Yom Kippur at nightfall, before Kol Nidrei [the Yom Kippur eve service]." Sobotki also includes more material connected with the reproductive life: *Seder tkhines* contains six prayers connected with pregnancy, including two for infertility, two for safe pregnancy, and two for safe childbirth.

But perhaps most interesting, and overlapping to a certain extent with *tkhines* already mentioned, Sobotki introduces a personal subjectivity into many of the *tkhines*. That is, they are written as the prayers of women struggling with misfortune (infertility, widowhood) or danger (the illness of a child, a husband on a business trip). (Travel was hazardous in the eighteenth century, and a Jew carrying cash to purchase wares at a regional fair took his life in his hands.) One of the *tkhines* for infertility (and the death of young children) begins thus: "Lord of the whole world, I, poor woman, come before you to bemoan my suffering and the sorrow I carry in my heart, because I, unfortunately, have a difficult star for children" (Sobotki, *Seder tkhines*, no. 3). This is a prayer for emotional relief, as much as it is a plea for God's more tangible help. Note that this is Sobotki speaking, imaginatively taking on a woman's persona. This, too, has a later history in Eastern European *tkhines*, although it did not develop until the mid-nineteenth century, when men began to write *tkhines* under female pseudonyms, often in very emotional style. Is it the case that men imagined women as more lachrymose than they actually were? (Or was it a chance for them to be more emotional vicariously?) It is difficult to say; nevertheless, the frequency with which these prayers were republished shows that they had some appeal.

Seder tkhines u-vakoshes (Order of Supplications and Petitions) (Fürth, 1762)

Seder tkhines u-vakoshes, which first appeared about the middle of the eighteenth century, incorporates material from all three of these collections, and from other Yiddish reworkings of Hebrew prayers and petitions as well.[52] It contains a total of one hundred and twenty-three *tkhines*. The anonymous compiler of *Seder tkhines u-vakoshes* probably drew on a variety of sources and combined the material as he saw fit. As the title page states: in response to the requests of "many pious women," the publisher or editor gathered "all available *tkhines*."

Seder tkhines u-vakoshes was one of the most comprehensive—and most popular—collections of *tkhines* published. It thus defines a world of women's piety. What are the boundaries and regions of this world? Some of the settings for the *tkhines* are ones that touch on the religious life of both men and women: Depending on the edition, this collection contains some thirty or forty prayers connected with the liturgy of the synagogue service.[53] In addition, there is a prayer for each day of the week and four for the Sabbath. About fifteen prayers are to be said "every day" or on no particular occasion. Fourteen *tkhines* concern the penitential season, from the beginning of the month of Elul through the

Day of Atonement. Three others are confessions of sins to be said throughout the year. There are only four prayers for the festivals: one for taking the Torah scroll out of the Ark on the festivals, two for the lulav and etrog (the palm and citron) used on the holiday of Sukkot, and one for the holiday of Hashana Rabba.[54] There are *tkhines* for each of the fast days and several prayers for days on which one undertakes a private fast.

There are, moreover, *tkhines* not connected with liturgy or the liturgical calendar at all. We find eleven concerned with pregnancy and childbirth, four related to children and family (including two to be said while one's husband is away on a business trip), and one that "a widow should say with great devotion so that the dear God may once again give her what she asks of him [that is, a husband]" (no. 71; from Sobotki). Several *tkhines* petition for recovery from illness, for rain during a drought, and for sustenance and livelihood. There are eleven *tkhines* for visiting the cemetery. This collection contains four prayers connected with *Rosh Hodesh*, the new moon, a day of special significance to women on which they avoided heavy work.[55] This list of *tkhine* topics shows how the religious lives of women were constructed by Ashkenazic culture; the settings and occasions—and understandings—of religious life that the *tkhines* made available to women were part of the definition of gender in that culture.

EASTERN EUROPEAN *TKHINES*

We have seen from the Western European *tkhines* a range of occasions that constituted the framework of women's religious lives. A consideration of the Eastern European materials, originating primarily in the eighteenth century, will show that these texts, while overlapping with the Western European *tkhines*, emphasize a somewhat different different ent range of concerns. Although the *tkhines* published in Eastern Europe treat a more limited repertoire of topics than do the Western European collections, they also present a much more diverse world of individual authors. And because some of these authors were women, these texts allow us, for the first time, to hear women's voices directly.

Early Eastern European *Tkhines*

There are scattered instances of *tkhines* published in the sixteenth century, and there was a short, atypical collection entitled *Tkhine zu* (This

Tkhine) published in 1590 in Prague.[56] While until recently it was believed that other very early Eastern European *tkhines* published had been almost entirely lost, a previously unknown work, entitled *Eyn gor sheyne tkhine* (A Very Beautiful *Tkhine*) has recently been discovered.[57] Careful examination of the typeface and other details of printing of this eight-page booklet has determined that the book was published in Prague about the year 1600.[58] There is no title page, but on the first page under the title we find the following note: "[This *tkhine*] was for a long time kept secret among a group of pious women; they let it remain among themselves, and let no one copy it. Now they have rethought the matter, and have brought it for publication."

Most of the text consists of one long prayer, although a rhymed Yiddish translation of Psalm 27 is printed at the end of the booklet. (Other portions of the *tkhine* also incorporate translations of biblical verses and Hebrew prayers.) Most of the *tkhine* is taken up simply with asking God to accept the worshiper's prayer:

> Praised are you, Lord our God, and King over the whole world; you are full of mercy and compassion and are near to all who call upon you in truth. . . . Do not stop your ears to my prayer, but [accept it as you accepted] the prayer of our ancient mother Eve, . . . who prayed that you put into Adam's mind that he turn back to her, for he had separated himself from her after Cain killed his brother Abel. You increased his desire for her. . . . And accept my prayer as you accepted the prayer of our matriarch Sarah, who begged your holy Name that you protect her from Pharaoh and Abimelekh.

The *tkhine* continues by invoking the prayers of Rebekah, Rachel, Leah, Miriam, Hannah, Deborah, Bath-Sheba, Esther, and Judith, often, as in the case of Eve and Sarah, using midrashic as well as biblical material for the substance of the prayers.

Even this very early Eastern European *tkhine* exhibits characteristics that persist: this is a small booklet, devoted to just a few interrelated topics; it makes extensive use of female biblical figures; and, most interestingly, it claims some sort of female authorship, although, again typically, slightly ambiguously. Two slightly later texts, each eight pages long and printed in Prague, follow the same pattern. The first, a booklet of *tkhines* to be recited from the beginning of Elul through Yom Kippur, published around 1705, is signed on the title page: "I, the writer, Beila, the daughter of the great, holy, and brilliant scholar, the martyr Rabbi Ber R. Hezekiah's of the Horowitz family, the wife of R. Yossi Hazan [cantor], one of those expelled from Vienna."[59] The second, published at the end of the seventeenth or the beginning of the eighteenth century, is a *tkhine* "to be recited with devotion every day." Once again, the author statement is somewhat ambiguous: "And now a pious woman has brought it to publication, Mistress Rachel daughter of Rabbi Mordecai Sofer [scribe] of Pinczow."[60]

The Eighteenth Century

Although these early texts are a precious piece of the historical record, it is only towards the middle of the eighteenth century that *tkhines* really began to flourish in Eastern Europe. It is difficult to pin down dates because, unlike the Western European *tkhines*, until well into the nineteenth century most of those from Eastern Europe were published in little booklets with no place of publication or date noted.[61] Those early Eastern European collections that can be dated on the basis of typography to the late eighteenth or early nineteenth century usually appeared in short collections of eight to twelve pages, with some as short as four pages. (Sometimes, however, several short texts were collected into larger booklets.) As we have seen with the earlier texts, these *tkhines* mark a distinct shift in the range of subjects addressed, away from the broad array of occasions covered by the Western European *Seder tkhines u-vakoshes* (which, it should be remembered, was also being reprinted in Eastern Europe).

The Eastern European texts usually confined themselves to a single theme or to a few related topics, and these tended to be closely tied to the synagogue and the liturgical calendar. By far the most popular topic was the penitential season, including *tkhines* for the month of Elul and for Rosh Hashanah and Yom Kippur. The overall emphasis on liturgical events suggests that, in contrast to their counterparts in Western Europe, Eastern European *tkhine* authors and/or readers were more interested in women's relationship to the communal domain of men and somewhat less interested in the religious meanings of other aspects of their lives.

In addition, we have noted that the Eastern European texts, unlike most Western European *tkhine* collections, often name a women as the author or translator, or in some other connection with the work. These author statements can be straightforward attributions to historically documentable or ordinary-sounding women: "This *tkhine* was made by the virtuous woman, Mistress Sarah, may she live long, daughter of our teacher Rabbi Mordecai, of blessed memory." Or they can be as complex as, "We found this *tkhine* in the possession of the righteous, renowned rabbi's wife, Mistress Hena . . . who received it from her mother-in-law, the pious, renowned, righteous rabbi's wife, Mistress Leah [D]reyzel"; or, "The righteous woman who thought this up, because of her great piety, did not mention her name"; or, "This was found in the *tkhine* pouch [*be-amtahat ha-tehinnot*] left by the righteous rabbi's wife, Mistress Rachel Hinda." This language may indicate some sort of women's tradition of writing and collecting *tkhines*, as we have seen beginning with *Eyn gor sheyne tkhine*.[62] Some of the Eastern European *tkhines* were also attributed to male authors, named or unnamed, and many were also anonymous.[63]

The *Tkhines* of Leah Dreyzl

Three of these eighteenth-century *tkhines* and their authors will be discussed at length in Chapters 6, 7 and 8. Here we shall briefly consider the *tkhines* by one additional author, a woman whose husband and son were intimately connected with early hasidic circles. Two *tkhines*, one entitled *Tkhine es rotsn* (*Tkhine* of a Time of [Divine] Favor), and the other entitled *Tkhine shaarei tshuve* (*Tkhine* of the Gates of Repentance), begin with the following statement, quoted above:

> We found this new *tkhine* in the possession of the renowned, righteous rabbi's wife, Mistress Hena, may she live, widow of the departed rabbi, the great light, the righteous, pious, renowned Rabbi David Tsevi, may the memory of the righteous be for a blessing, who was the rabbi of the holy congregations of Kremenets and Mogilev, may God protect them. She had the *tkhine* from her mother-in-law, the righteous, pious, renowned rabbi's wife, Mistress Leah [D]reyzl, may her memory be for a blessing, the wife of the brilliant, pious rabbi, a leader of his generation [*mofet ha-dor*], the renowned Rabbi Aryeh Leibish, may the memory of the righteous be for a blessing, who was the rabbi of the holy community of Stanislav, may God protect it.[64]

Leah Dreyzl, named as the source of the *tkhine*, was of quite distinguished ancestry. Her great-grandfather was Hakham Tsevi Ashkenazi (1660–1718), one of the early battlers against underground Sabbatianism. Tsevi's daughter Miriam married Aryeh Leib of Amsterdam; their daughter, Nehamah Naytshe (or Naytshe Nehamah) and her husband

Moses of Zolkiew were Leah Dreyzl's parents. Leah Dreyzl's daughter-in-law Hena, who transmitted the *tkhine* in Leah Dreyzl's name, was the daughter of Aryeh Leibush of Vishnevits.

Both Aryeh Leib Auerbach of Stanislav (ca. 1710–1749) and his son David Tsevi (1743–1808) were associated with the circle of Israel ben Eliezer (1700–1760), the Baal Shem Tov, regarded as the founder of the eighteenth-century revival movement of Hasidism.[65] According to legend, the Baal Shem Tov promised a son to Aryeh Leib (who had fathered three or four daughters), on the condition that he himself be the godfather (*sandak*) at the circumcision ceremony, and that he be allowed to name the boy. Whether or not the Baal Shem Tov actually foretold David Tsevi's birth and participated in his naming, such legends, as well as those that say that the Baal Shem Tov frequently stayed with Aryeh Leib, indicate a connection with the early circles of Hasidism.[66]

Leah Dreyzl's two brief *tkhines* are to be recited during the penitential season, from the beginning of the month of Elul through Yom Kippur.[67] Even more than most other *tkhines*, they seem composed for (or transcribed from) oral performance. They contain beautifully cadenced, almost metered, rhymed prose.[68] Some passages are built on the kind of parallel construction and repetition which is particularly effective in oral delivery; indeed, passages in these *tkhines* are almost as much sermons as prayers. Texts such as these lend support to Zinberg's hypothesis that *tkhines* were the creation of the women's prayer leaders, or *zogerkes*;[69] one can easily imagine these texts being performed by the *zogerke* in the women's section of the synagogue on the Days of Awe:

> Woe is me that I have taken continuous thought for my body, and attributed no importance to my soul. Woe is me that I have sated my body with eating and drinking, and clothed it in bright colors, while taking no thought for my soul, which I have utterly corrupted. Oh, woe is me that I have blemished and deformed my 248 limbs and 365 organs.[70] Woe is me that even the three *mitsvot* of *hallah*, *niddah*, and candle-lighting have I not properly kept. Woe is me, with what sort of countenance can I approach the holy court in the next world? Woe is me for my sins, that I have not had trust in God, blessed be He, and have relied on a human being: as it is written: **"Cast your burden on the Lord, and he will sustain you"**;[71] that means in Yiddish: A person should cast his desire upon God, and He will nourish him. He abandons no one; He has mercy on Israel. Woe is me that I have cared only for what concerns the body, and have cared nothing for the punishment the soul will suffer in the next world. Woe is me, how I should weep and worry over my sins! . . . . What should I do? **I am full of sin, and you are full of**

mercy;[72] I am full of sin, and you are full of mercy. On this I may rely, that you will forgive my sins, as it is written: **"He who confesses and abandons [his sinful ways] will be treated with mercy"**; whoever confesses and abandons, so that he does no further evil, will be treated mercifully.[73]

Leah Dreyzl also emphasizes that God alone can help the sinner; neither one's own resources (except for prayer and repentance), nor friends and relations, have the power to help:

> I pray you, dear God, have mercy on me and upon my soul, as I take to heart the Day of Judgment which comes to each person before the soul separates itself from the body. All my limbs and my flesh tremble. What should I do? Who can help me on the day of my great pain and distress? Therefore, I beg my own limbs, don't stand against me, I want to go into God's house, and pour out my heart, and confess my sins with bitter tears. Perhaps he will hear my prayer. . . . My limbs answer me: You committed all those sins, and it was sweet for you. You ran quickly with your feet after the desire of your eyes, but you did not run to the dear synagogue . . . I thought [my limbs] could help me in my need, but now I see that first I must clothe myself with repentance, prayer, and charity. For if I call upon my friends and my kin, they stand far away from me; whether I call to the great or the lowly, no one answers me, no one listens to my bitter voice. I have bethought myself, why should I petition them, when they have no power to help me? Better I should pray to the living God alone, and to no one else.[74]

These two powerfully written passages express classic themes of Jewish tradition, and draw upon traditional imagery to do so. It is interesting that, while the grammatical forms used in the text show that the implied speaker is female, there is almost nothing else in the text which is specifically of concern to women. (The mention of the three women's commandments is the only exception.) Like other Eastern European women authors, Leah Dreyzl probably drew upon sources that were originally intended for a male audience. In content, these *tkhines* could refer equally well to men's consciousness of sin and desire to repent.

Indeed, this theme shows that Leah Dreyzl was well aware of the pervasive concerns of her day. Questions of sin, guilt, and penitence occupied Eastern European Jews during this period and were an important stimulus to religious literature—and to itinerant preachers.[75] Preachers trying to inspire repentance were among the founders of Hasidism, and Leah Dreyzl's *tkhine*-sermons would seem to fit right into this milieu.[76]

THE WOMEN'S COMMANDMENTS, EAST AND WEST

Finally, in order to explore the range of concerns, the similarities and differences between the Eastern and Western European *tkhines*, we shall compare texts from East and West that deal with a common topic, "taking *hallah*," one of the three so-called women's commandments.[77] This designation dates back to the first centuries of the Common Era, when the religious duties of separating a portion of dough in memory of the priestly tithes, maintaining sexual separation from one's spouse during menstruation, and lighting Sabbath candles were named in the Mishnah as particularly incumbent upon women.[78] It is perhaps the great antiquity of their association with women that gave them their special standing as "women's commandments" (*mitsvot*).[79] Indeed, Ashkenazic sources sometimes conveyed the impression that these three duties were the only ones women had been commanded to perform, as opposed to the six hundred and thirteen commandments incumbent on men. Of course, women and men were both equally obligated by the prohibitions found in Jewish law, and women were only exempted from a small number of the positive commandments as well.[80]

These three *mitsvot* were known by the Hebrew terms *hallah* (portion of dough); *niddah* (menstrual separation), and *hadlakah* or *hadlakat ha-ner* (kindling the light). The first letters of each word were combined as *h-n-h* to form an acrostic, *hanah*, which is the Hebrew for Hannah. For this reason, the biblical Hannah, the mother of the prophet Samuel, came to be associated with the women's commandments and sometimes appears in *tkhines* for these acts.[81]

Thus, when preparing bread and certain other baked goods, the woman recited a Hebrew blessing, pinched off a small portion of the dough, and burned it in the oven (see Num. 15:19–21). Jewish law prescribes (and proscribes) in detail the relations between a woman and her husband during the time of her menstruation (see Lev. 15:19–24; 18:19) and for seven days thereafter:[82] the married couple may not have any physical contact whatsoever. After the menstrual period the woman had to inspect herself twice daily for seven days to make certain the blood flow had entirely ceased. At the end of these seven "clean days," the woman immersed herself in a ritual bath, reciting a Hebrew blessing, and was then permitted to resume physical contact and sexual relations with her husband. Finally, the woman kindled at least two lights on the eve of the Sabbaths and festivals, before sunset, reciting a Hebrew blessing as she did so.[83]

Because of the long tradition that identified the three commandments with women, and because of the intimate family setting of their observance, these commandments were an obvious and popular occasion for *tkhines*.[84] The authors of the various collections approached this subject in diverse ways, however, as we shall see from an analysis of *tkhines* from *Seder tkhines u-vakoshes* and *Tkhines* from Western Europe, and *Shloyshe she'orim* (The Three Gates), by Sarah bas Tovim, from Eastern Europe.[85]

Separating *Hallah* in *Seder tkhines u-vakoshes*

As we have seen, *Seder tkhines u-vakoshes* is an anthology, rather than a unified work. The compiler did not single out the women's commandments as a unit, but rather included *tkhines* for these acts in among *tkhines* for other topics. Nonetheless, it is interesting to see in what contexts he placed them. *Tkhines* for *niddah* come, surprisingly, at the end of a set of prayers for the fall holidays and immediately precede *tkhines* for pregnancy and childbirth. Perhaps the Days of Awe were a time when women prayed most intensely for children; certainly, they were the time when God was thought to determine one's fate for the coming year. The *tkhines* for taking *hallah* and kindling Sabbath lights occur together after the *tkhines* for the days of the week, actually between the *tkhines* for Friday and Saturday. And in fact, on Friday, after her morning devotions, a woman would begin her preparations for the Sabbath; the house would be cleaned, and all food needed to be prepared in advance. Often the week's baking would be done on Friday, and certainly the special Sabbath loaves (called *berkhes* in Western Europe, and *kitke*, *koylitsh*, or *hallah* in Eastern Europe) would be mixed, set to rise, and baked. As the day waned and the house, food, and children were ready to greet the Sabbath, the housewife would wash up, change into her special Sabbath clothes, and light the candles at dusk.

Seder tkhines u-vakoshes contains the following *tkhine* to be recited before separating the dough for *hallah*.

> Praised are you, God our Lord, the God of our forebears. You have sanctified your people Israel more than all the other peoples on the earth, and have commanded them your commandments. You have commanded them: when we knead the dough for our bread, [we must] separate a portion of it for you, God Almighty. You have required us to give it to the Priest, who is

clean of all impurity. For you separated out a portion of the earth and created the human being from it, and gave him a pure soul from the place of the pure, where the pure High Priest stands; there is no impurity there. Now we have been punished because of our sins and the sins of our forebears, so that Jerusalem, the holy city, was destroyed, and the holy House in which your name was sanctified by the priests who brought sacrifices to the altar in great purity. . . .

I pray you, God, my Lord, that you grant me and my husband and my children the privilege of living to see that the holy House will be rebuilt and that Jerusalem will be once again as it was of old, and your people Israel will once more dwell in the holy Land, in which you sanctified your holy Name among them, and will give the separated portion to the priest, who is clean of all impurity, in great joy, with the ingathering of Israel. May this come true in God's name.

And recite the blessing: **Blessed are you, Lord our God and God of the Universe, who has sanctified us with his commandments and commanded us to separate *hallah*.**[86]

This prayer builds a complex of meanings around the act of removing the bit of dough. The woman doing her baking projects herself into the past, imagining herself giving the tithe to the priest during the days the Temple in Jerusalem was standing. She regrets its destruction and longs for its rebuilding during the messianic era. A striking theme is the concern for purity. Temple worship required priests and worshipers to be in a state of ritual purity, but since the Temple's destruction both the means of purification (the ashes of the red heifer; see Num. 19) and the reason for it had lapsed. Women were one of the few remaining links with the purity system through their observance of purification in the ritual bath after *niddah*; technically, in these post-Temple days, everyone is impure. Thus, this domestic act becomes a link between the glorious past and the future redemption of the Jewish people. Yet, indeed, this *tkhine* reaches even farther back. Tradition has it that God took the dust from which he created Adam from the Temple Mount; the text likens God's act in separating out a portion of dust from the earth to create Adam to the woman's act in separating out a portion of her dough for *hallah*.

Separating *Hallah* in *The Three Gates*

Unlike *Seder tkhines u-vakoshes*, *The Three Gates* is the work of a single author, who consciously shaped both an understanding of these acts and a set of *tkhines* for them. Indeed, the first "gate" (chapter) is devoted to these three women's commandments. This section of *The Three Gates* includes a paragraph explaining the background and importance of each of the women's *mitsvot*, a brief summary (in rhymed Hebrew interspersed with Yiddish translation) promising easy childbirth to the woman who observes them scrupulously, a section entitled "Laws of *Niddah*," a section entitled "Laws of *Hallah*," and the Hebrew blessing for "taking *hallah*" (separating the portion of dough) and lighting candles, each followed by a *tkhine*.[87]

Hallmarks of *The Three Gates* are its erudition and its instructional character. The introductory material concerning each commandment, including both historical background and laws of observance, prepares the woman who reads this book to understand more deeply the religious acts themselves and even the allusions contained within the *tkhines* she recites. The *tkhine* for taking *hallah* illustrates the wealth of information conveyed in *The Three Gates* and the attendant thematic richness.

The introductory material concerning the taking of *hallah* begins by quoting the biblical verse from which this *mitsvah* is derived: "As the first yield of your baking, you should set aside a loaf as a gift" (Num. 15:20).[88] The text continues by interpreting a paraphrase of Proverbs 8:21 ("By the merit of this [commandment] God will fill your storehouses to satiety") as an assurance that fulfilling the *mitsvah* of *hallah* will ensure plentiful sustenance. The author next explains the biblical system of tithes and states that since the destruction of the Temple, the *mitsvah* of taking *hallah* is the only remnant of this system. In the quick transition from the historical to the personal that is typical of *The Three Gates*, the paragraph continues:

> Therefore, Lord of the World, we pray that you accept the *mitsvah* of *hallah*, and send great blessing on us wherever we turn. May our children not be estranged [from us, or from Judaism], and may we be able to provide for our children with a livelihood, I and my husband, by ourselves, during a long life.

A later section of the work, entitled "Laws of *Hallah*," explains that the dough must be made with at least forty-three "eggs" (a rabbinic measure of volume) or at least two "quarts" of flour (another edition specifies three "quarts") for it to be required that a portion be separated as *hallah*.[89] This is followed by the Hebrew blessing for separating *hallah*, a short paragraph asking that the performance of the commandment be acceptable before God, and *yehi ratson*, a brief Hebrew prayer of kabbalistic origin asking God to rebuild the Temple. Next comes the *tkhine* for the act:

> May my *hallah* be accepted as the sacrifice on the altar was accepted. May my *mitsvah* be accepted just as if I had performed it properly. In ancient times, the High Priest came and caused the sins to be forgiven; so also may my sins be forgiven with this. May I be like a newborn child. May I be able to honor my dear Sabbaths and holidays. May God grant that I and my husband and my children be able to nourish ourselves. Thus may my *mitsvah* of *hallah* be accepted: that my children may be fed by the dear God, be blessed, with great mercy and great compassion. May this *mitsvah* of *hallah* be accounted as if I had given the tithe. As I perform my *mitsvah* of *hallah* with might and main, so may God, be blessed, guard me from anguish and pain. [The last line is in rhymed Yiddish: *Vi ikh tu mayn mitsve fun khale mit gantsn hartsn, zo zol Got borukh hu mikh hitn far payn un shmartsn.*]

The *tkhine* contains several themes: the desire to perform *mitsvot* properly, the plea for forgiveness of sins, the continued association of *hallah* with receiving adequate nourishment. As in *Seder tkhines u-va-koshes*, this text conveys the sense that by taking *hallah*, the woman is continuing the ancient system of sacrifices and tithes and identifying herself with those ancient Israelites who brought sin offerings and gave tithes to the poor and the Levites. Yet here sin and forgiveness replace purity and impurity as central concerns. Properly performed sacrifices could ensure God's forgiveness, but now the taking of *hallah* is the only substitute. Further, since taking *hallah* is an essential part of the preparation of bread, the staff of life, proper performance of the act may, it is hoped, persuade God to send plentiful food for the family.

Not all *tkhines* are this sophisticated, however, and to conclude this section we return to the Western European *tkhine* that stands at the head of the preface. *Seder tkhines* contains a prayer for baking the Sabbath loaf that contrasts starkly in style and substance with the one in *The Three Gates*.[90]

> This she says when she puts the Sabbath loaf into the oven:
> Lord of all the worlds, in your hands is all blessing. I come now to honor your holiness, and I pray you to give your blessing on what I bake. Send an angel to guard the baking, so that everything will be well baked, will rise nicely, and will not burn, to honor your holy Sabbath (which you have chosen that your people Israel may rest thereon) and over which one recites the holy blessing—as you blessed the dough of Sarah and Rebekah our mothers. My

Lord God, listen to my voice, for you are the one who hears the voices of those who call upon you with the whole heart. May you be praised to eternity! (*Tkhines*, 1648, 5a).

In its simplicity, this *tkhine* shows us how women could sanctify the most ordinary household chores. It also reminds us again that women's spirituality was far from monolithic: as one woman was moved to envision herself as a participant in the ancient Temple worship, another found holiness in her own kitchen. Whether imagining herself bringing tithes and sacrifices to the ancient Temple in purity, hoping to celebrate Sabbaths and festivals with joy, or asking God to feed her children, the woman was able to discover holiness in the act of baking bread and to connect her everyday experience with images from Jewish tradition.

The voices one hears in the *tkhines* speak to a fundamental reality of the religious life. For while the specifics of the disparity between day-to-day experience and spiritual ideals are peculiar to this women's literature, the very fact of such a disparity is not. Indeed, as perhaps any religious literature must be, *tkhines* are grounded in routine realities even as they exist in tension with them. They depict the holiness to be found in the mundane, in the activities of a wife and mother, but they also show women the angels; the patriarchs and heroes of Jewish history; and the Temple that stood in Jerusalem.

Further, *tkhines* both valorize women's traditional roles and critique them. A woman content with a religious life centered on the home and family and a peripheral relationship to the men's world of prayer and study could use *tkhines* to render that life holy. Even the domestic chore of baking bread could be understood as a sacred act, shared with the ancient matriarchs and guarded by angels. By comparing the separating of *hallah* to the bringing of tithes, a woman became, as it were, a participant in the ancient Temple worship; her baking ritual kept alive the hope for the restoration of Temple rites at the time of the future messianic redemption. Other *tkhines*, however, as we shall see in later chapters, suggested that women should make inroads into the usually male domains of liturgical prayer and Torah study. Indeed, the *tkhines* we have analyzed show that not all women were cut off from the knowledge of traditional sources. True, some *tkhines* are indeed rooted in popular religion and folk practice, but others exhibit familiarity with biblical texts, halakhah, Midrash, and various sorts of kabbalistic literature, usually transmitted through popularizations in Yiddish.

As they recited *tkhines*, generations of unknown Jewish women sanctified their daily acts and roles and at the same time transcended them. In this way Ashkenazic Jewish women—nurtured within the ritual structure of Jewish life, familiar with a limited array of Jewish sources, and hampered perhaps by the constraints of their social roles and lack of education—managed nonetheless to create a rich array of visions of the religious life.

STUDYING WOMEN'S RELIGION

What does it mean to study women's religion? How are we to define our subject matter? How are we to understand the relationship of the history of women's religious life and practice to the history of particular religious traditions? This chapter explores these questions within the specific context of the religious life of Ashkenazic Jewish women in the late seventeenth, eighteenth, and early nineteenth centuries, as seen through the popular religious literature in Yiddish. My thinking about the different approaches one could take in this endeavor was stimulated by a lecture given by Joan Scott on the study of women's history.[1] Using a framework of analysis suggested in part by Scott's work, I distinguish between three types of approaches to the study of women's religion: those that add an account of women's religious lives to an already existing history of Judaism, those that consider women's Judaism within the framework of other groups usually omitted from the history of Judaism, and those that seek to transform our understanding of Judaism by incorporating the perspective that has been gained from the study of Jewish women.

FILLING IN THE BLANKS

Women were the chief audience for the voluminous homiletical, ethical, and devotional literature in Yiddish that began to appear in the sixteenth century, judging from the title pages and introductions of these collections of pious tales, guides to the upright life, paraphrases of the Bible, and *tkhines*, as well as from contemporary accounts. Because some *tkhines* were written *by* women as well as *for* women, I regard them as an especially important source for the study of Ashkenazic women's religion.

But there are difficulties involved in using any of these sources. Foremost is the fact that most of them were written by men. They can be defined as a women's literature in terms of their audience, and indeed, there is evidence that these Yiddish works were very popular: women read and reread them. Moreover, one can argue that these works must have corresponded in some degree to women's lives and feelings; otherwise, women would not have bought and read them. Yet even with the *tkhines*, some of which were written by women, there are difficulties. First, many collections of *tkhines* were published anonymously. Were they written/compiled by men or women? Second, some of those attributed to women can be documented to have been written, pseudonymously, by men.[2] How do we distinguish the "real" female authors from the fakes? Do works written by women and men differ in definable ways?

Another sort of difficulty is more specific to particular genres. An example is the *musar* (ethical) literature. Although all the Yiddish *musar* literature was probably read by women, one work in particular, the *Brantshpigl* (Burning Mirror), written by Moses Henoch Yerushalmi Altshuler, first published in Cracow in 1596, was addressed to women in particular.[3] It includes chapter titles such as, "This chapter explains how the modest woman should conduct herself in the home," "This chapter explains who is a good wife and who is a bad wife," and even, "This chapter explains how, with much talking, women can talk their way into Eternal Life." But, we may ask, how does one extrapolate from the prescriptive to the descriptive? What is the relationship between the recommendations of Moses Henoch Altshuler and what women actually did and felt?[4] Analogous questions may be asked about the collections of pious tales, such as the *Mayse Bukh* (The Story Book), first published about 1600, in which the moral is sometimes longer than the story.[5] How does one relate the fictive to the factual?

Despite these formidable methodological difficulties, taken together, this literature reveals a rich religious life. To use the *tkhines* as an example: A survey of the many occasions on which women recited *tkhines* enables us to map out the important religious events of women's lives. Further, an analysis of the content of these prayers can reveal how women understood their religious activity. A *tkhine* for lighting the Sabbath candles might contain prayers asking protection of the woman's husband and children from evil spirits, or might describe the candelabrum in the ancient Temple, showing some of the meanings that kindling the lights might hold. Typically, as I discussed in Chapter 1, the *tkhines* expressed a *range* of meanings for any one particular act, showing that women's spirituality was far from monolithic. Finally, unlike Hebrew prayers, the *tkhines* contain many references to the matriarchs—Sarah, Rebecca, Rachel, and Leah—and other women of the Bible and Midrash. By analyzing their portrayal of these female figures, we can discern the images of women and women's religious lives described in the *tkhines*.

Now let us step back for a moment and ask what kind of answer—what kind of question—this approach represents. We might characterize it as "filling in the blanks." That is, there are certain blank spaces in the history of Judaism—blank spaces where the history of women ought to be—that need to be filled in. To use the title of Rachel Adler's well-known article, this approach tries to describe "the Jew who wasn't there."[6] This is important to do, and much of my early work on Ashkenazic women falls into this category. But it is also important to notice that this way of understanding women's religion makes it a separate domain. Women's history is additive: it adds knowledge to an already existing, albeit incomplete, history of Jewish religious life.

"WOMEN AND MEN WHO ARE LIKE WOMEN"

Perhaps, though, treating women's piety in and of itself, as an add-on to Jewish life, is too narrow an approach. Perhaps this women's Yiddish literature can best be understood as part of some broader category, a category that will give it a social location. And indeed, such a category suggests itself from the material. In the first chapter of the *Brantshpigl*, for example, the author explains why he wrote the work in Yiddish: "The book was written in Yiddish for women and for men who are like women in not having much knowledge." This is the category *nashim ve-'amei ha-arets*, "women and the ignorant." To put it into more neutral terms, this literature and the women's religious life it represents can be seen as part of folk or popular religion, of the religious life of those who are not part of the educated elite.

The attempt to set this material into a folk religious context can open the way to a number of interesting issues. First, it suggests that we investigate which men were also an audience for this literature. Second, it raises the question of the relationship between this literature and various folk religious practices, which once again requires consideration of which practices were associated with women, which with men, and which with all the "folk." Finally, it lends itself to an exploration of issues of the sociology of religious knowledge: What kinds of things could ordinary Jews know? Is there a difference between the religious knowledge of women and "men who are like women in not having much knowledge"? And who controls access to this knowledge?

Turning first to the question of audience, we must examine whether it makes sense to group together women and "ignorant" men. For Catholic devotional literature, the important distinction is between the clergy, who used Latin, and the laity, who used the vernacular.[7] One could argue that the relevant distinction in Judaism is between women and men, since there is no sacramentally and ritually set-apart clergy, and all men are potential participants in elite religious culture. But in actuality, many, perhaps most, men did not acquire enough knowledge to participate in rabbinic culture in any but the most rudimentary ways. Traditional Ashkenazic society was highly stratified, and power and knowledge were concentrated in the hands of an interlocking elite of the wealthy and/or the learned.[8]

Thus, those men who could not read the classics of Jewish tradition in the original Hebrew and Aramaic surely constituted part of the audience for the vernacular popular religious literature. We can, however, make distinctions between genres associated more with men or more with women. The *tkhines* and the *Tsenerene* (Go Forth and See) (a collection of homilies on the biblical portion of the week, a work reprinted so frequently it might be considered a genre in itself),[9] were women's genres, although there are a few *tkhines* meant to be recited by men, and many boys grew up listening to their mothers reading from the *Tsenerene*.[10] But apart from the *Brantshpigl* and some guides to the observance of women's commandments in particular,[11] the Yiddish ethical literature was addressed either to men and women equally or to men primarily. The title page of Isaac ben Elyakum's *Lev tov* (A Good Heart), first published in Prague in 1620, begins:

> All you men and women,
> And all who are fashioned by the Creator
> Who wish to build this world and the other for themselves,
> Come, all of you, and look at this splendid book.
> I believe no one will be sorry
> Who reads it through completely.

One will find in it all of Judaism
In its length and in its breadth,
Quite understandable and well explained,
Extending over twenty chapters.[12]

As Israel Zinberg notes, the author of *Lev tov* repeatedly addresses his audience as "householders and women."[13] *Kav ha-yashar* (The Just Measure), a kabbalistic morality book written by Tsvi Hirsh Koidonover, published in 1706, in Hebrew and Yiddish, addresses itself to men, but there is evidence that it was also read by women.[14] Thus, the generic distribution of this literature among men and women gives evidence that "women and ignorant men" makes a certain amount of sense as a category of audience, but also shows that one can draw distinctions between "ignorant men" and women.

The supposition that in some ways women and men participated in separate aspects of popular religion while in others they partook of a common popular religious culture is also borne out by the references in the Yiddish devotional material to acts of folk origin. These popular practices were not required by Jewish law, or halakhah, and at times were even frowned upon by the rabbinical authorities. Some of these practices were associated with women in particular. Sarah bas Tovim's book of *tkhines*, *Shloyshe sheorim* (The Three Gates), contains a long prayer for the making of memorial candles for the dead, something women usually did on the eve of Yom Kippur. The prayer refers to the making of the candles as a *mitsvah*, a divine commandment: The elite may not have considered it obligatory, but the women—or the folk—did.[15]

Consider two other such women's practices. The first seems to reflect an oral tradition. The *Tsenerene*, and also the early collection of *tkhines*, *Seder tkhines u-vakoshes*, include a prayer said by women when biting off the end of the etrog (citron) on the holiday of Hoshana Rabba, a practice that was supposed to ensure an easier childbirth. In the prayer, the woman expressly repudiates Eve's sin of eating the fruit of the Tree of Knowledge (thought by some rabbis to have been a citron) and says that therefore she ought not to suffer the consequences.[16] *Sefer ha-hayyim* (The Book of Life), a collection of prayers and practices connected with the sick, dying, and dead, and with cemetery visits, contains a prayer to be said while measuring graves in times of distress, another women's practice.[17] Women measured the grave or the entire circumference of the cemetery with candlewick, then used it to make candles that were donated to the synagogue or house of study.

While these practices seem unambiguously associated with women, others are less so. *Sefer ha-hayyim* and another collection of cemetery prayers, *Ma'aneh lashon* (The Right Response), both have versions in Hebrew and versions in Yiddish, versions for women and for men, and more and less folkloric aspects.[18] These two collections turn out to be splendidly ambiguous in relation to all these categories. The Yiddish of *Ma'aneh lashon* seems to be intended primarily for men, while the *Hebrew* version seems to reflect a more folkloric view of the relationship of the living and the dead than does the *Yiddish* of *Sefer ha-hayyim*, which is intended for women. And *Sefer ha-hayyim*, while in general taking a more elite line than *Ma'aneh lashon* (by discouraging graveside prayers to the dead, for instance), also includes instructions for keeping demons away from a corpse, stories about what to do if the dead appear in dreams, explanations about how the dead know all that goes on in the world of the living, and instructions to bury a sheet or diaper with a woman who died in childbirth, so that she can care for her dead child in the grave. This material demonstrates the great complexity of the interrelationships between folk and elite religion and between women's and men's religion.

The last issue I want to explore as part of the consideration of women's religion in the framework of popular religion is the sociology of religious knowledge. What access did women and unlearned men have to the great literature of Judaism? If they could not understand Hebrew, what could they know by reading the *Tsenerene*, the morality literature, the *tkhines*, the stories?

In fact, readers without Hebrew and Aramaic could still gain access to fairly extensive Jewish knowledge via Yiddish sources. The *Mayse bukh* billed itself as "the Yiddish Gemara"; and indeed many of the stories it contains do originate in the Talmud.[19] As the title page proclaims:

A beautiful storybook. Come here, dear men and women, and examine this lovely storybook which, since the world has existed, has never appeared in print. With three hundred and some stories, all of which are made out of the *Gemara*, and also tales out of the *Midrash Rabba* and Bahya, and none of the stories of Rabbi Judah the Pious will you miss. Also tales out of *Sefer Hasidim* and *Sefer Musar* and the *Yalkut*, as you will see in the back in my listing. Therefore, dear women, before you had the Yiddish books; now you will also have the Yiddish *Gemara*. So you will have the entire Torah.

On the verso of the title page, the compiler spells out his intentions and the merits of his work even more fully:

Glory to God alone, Blessed be His Name, who helped me realize the desire which I long ago undertook to serve pious women. I have now composed many books, but all of them are nothing in comparison with this one. From it will read rabbis and rabbis' wives and every man. Even if one knows much *Gemara*, he will bring out of it midrashim and stories and legends so that the whole world will be astonished at him and every man will say: "I believe he knows the whole Torah on one foot. As he has such great erudition in the Gemara, I believe he knows the whole Torah. Who has seen his like? To every situation he gives a law to be carried out in practice applicable to the case. . . ." Our sacred books write that it is a sin as big as a house to read [ungodly books] on the holy Sabbath day. If you wish to spend your time reading, I will write a lovely storybook. Therefore, dear women, buy it quickly before it goes away into foreign lands—to Bohemia, White Russia, and Poland. . . . Later you will say, Why did I not buy any when it was in the land?[20]

The *Tsenerene* quotes by name such popular biblical commentators as Rashi (Solomon ben Isaac, 1040–1105), Bahya ben Asher (thirteenth century), and the Hizkuni (Hezekiah ben Manoah, mid-thirteenth century). Readers of this literature could gain familiarity not only with the content of traditional sources but also with the way in which traditional Jewish exegesis uses sources and structures an argument. For example, the chapter in the *Brantshpigl* on how women can talk their way into Eternal Life quotes a number of talmudic and midrashic prooftexts demonstrating that women as well as men can receive a heavenly reward; it also quotes opposing viewpoints and attempts to reconcile them. Considering all of this evidence, it seems clear that an "ordinary Jew," male or female, who read this literature could acquire considerable knowledge of both the content and the style of the Midrash, Bible commentaries, and the aggadic portions of the Talmud, as well as a certain amount of halakhah.[21]

Nonetheless, there remains an issue of power and control. What we have here is an elite acting as gatekeeper and deciding what is appropriate for the folk to know. This comes out in interesting ways with regard to the kabbalistic material, perhaps the most problematic sort of material for broad distribution. In the earlier stages of this literature, some pains were taken to exclude or minimize kabbalistic material. For example, Bahya ben Asher's commentary on the Torah includes the four standard types of Jewish exegesis: literal, homiletical, philosophical, and mystical. The author of the *Tsenerene* quotes Bahya copiously, yet always stops short of including the kabbalistic portions of Bahya's work.[22] Similarly, *Seder Tkhines u-vakoshes*, while influenced by the mystical devotional literature in Hebrew, as Freehof has shown,[23] omits just that material which actually involves esoteric teachings—the kabbalistic *kavvanot* and permutations of divine names.

Yet some Yiddish devotional, homiletical, and ethical material contains overt kabbalistic teaching, and in some cases deliberately undertakes to popularize mystical materials. Thus, for example, *Shloyshe sheorim* (The Three Gates) contains passages from the Zohar and from *Sefer hemdat yamim* (The Book of the Days of Delight), a mystical guide to pietistic practices for festivals and other special days—although without attribution.[24] *Sefer maasei Adonai* (Book of the Tales of the Lord) and *Avir Yaakov* (Protector of Jacob), both compiled and translated by Simon Akiva Baer ben Joseph, consist of Yiddish (and Hebrew) translations of kabbalistic materials from a variety of sources, from the Zohar to *Shivhei ha-Ari* (In Praise of the Ari), a book of hagiographic legends about the charismatic mystic Isaac Luria, 1534–1572. *Nakhalas Tsevi* (Inheritance of Tsevi) is a Yiddish translation of much of the Zohar, made by Tsevi Hirsh Khotsh, and published in 1711. Further, *Kav ha-yashar* (The Just Measure), by Tsevi Hirsh Koidonover, is a morality book heavily influenced by the kabbalistic worldview. All of this literature is part of the great move to popularize Kabbalah that occurred in the wake of the Safed revival.[25] An interesting question then is the role of the Yiddish material in the popularization of the mystical tradition. Did the Yiddish material reach a wider public than the Hebrew? What differences are there between the presentation of kabbalistic material in the Yiddish sources and in the Hebrew (for example, are there more stories in Yiddish, more theoretical material in Hebrew)? How did this popularized Kabbalah affect—and how was it affected by—popular religious practice?[26]

We have seen that it can be fruitful to consider women's Yiddish devotional literature within the framework of popular religion: it has shown us the complexities of audience for religious literature in Yiddish, the ways in which this literature helped to spread both folk religious practices and knowledge of classical sources, and the role of the elite as gatekeepers of knowledge. Yet, there are also difficulties with this approach. It ignores the very real stratification among women, both in terms of wealth and in terms of knowledge. Those women authors whose existence can either be actually documented or, from the evidence of their works, plausibly assumed, were clearly far more learned than the average woman. Sarah Rebecca Rachel Leah, daughter of Jacob Yokl Horowitz, wrote her *Tkhine of the Matriarchs* in Aramaic, with an introduction in Hebrew and her own Yiddish translation of the text.[27] At the other end of the continuum were the many women who could not read. Are they represented in this literature at all? There is evidence that such women had an oral tradition of devotions in the vernacular. To what extent did that oral tradition influence the written material that we have?[28]

Or suppose, to counter the first objection, that we pinpoint a particular social stratum. If we can identify the level of "popular religion" under discussion—the religious lives of those who could read Yiddish but were by and large not learned in Hebrew and in the texts of the elite tradition in their original languages (not the bottom of the social scale by any means)—we still need to investigate the relationship between men's religion and women's religion. Is there enough common ground for us to say that there *is* a popular religion in which both men and women participate? Or, alternatively, if men's and women's nonelite religious practices, knowledges, devotions, and so forth differ substantially from one another, does it add anything to our understanding of them to include them both in the category "popular religion"?[29]

In the last analysis, then, this too is an additive approach to the study of women's religion, one that simply broadens the category of what is to be added. We fill in the blank of popular religion, but the picture of so-called normative Judaism remains unchanged. Women are subsumed under a category that is defined as being outside of what is usually studied as "Judaism." Further, placing women's religion under the rubric of popular religion does not allow the history of women's experience to challenge our received assumptions about either "elite" or "popular" Judaism.

RECONFIGURING ASHKENAZIC JUDAISM

The third approach I mentioned at the beginning of the chapter raises the question of whether what we learn about Ashkenazic women's religion can reconfigure our understanding of Ashkenazic Judaism as a whole.[30] Rewriting history to incorporate the perspective of women's history presents us with a challenge. It begins with women, but its subject is gender.[31] Making gender a category of analysis enables us to understand Ashkenazic Judaism as a *total* social system in which both men *and* women participated. Further, it reveals the cultural constructions—the structures and symbols—that defined and expressed Ashkenazic Judaism's specific visions of maleness and femaleness.

This approach sets men and women in relation to one another. Thus it leads to an investigation of the distribution of domains of the religious life between women and men and what this distribution tells us about the system as a whole. To explore this issue of domains, I want to look at the differing views in men's and women's devotional literature of how sexuality and the reproductive life relate to religious expression. A second topic I'll look at is the relationship of gender and power, and here the very existence of the category "women and ignorant men" becomes the subject of analysis. And lastly I'll examine the cultural construction of gender, both in the morality literature, with its prescriptions for proper behavior, and in the images of women and men in devotional literature, especially in the transformation of these images as they move from their original Hebrew sources to the vernacular Yiddish.

Let me discuss each of these in a little more detail. Since I have looked chiefly at the women's material, most of my examples will be drawn from the woman's perspective, but I shall try to suggest ways in which it can be juxtaposed with the "normative" view.

As we saw in Chapter 1, the *tkhine* literature can give us a good sense of the domains and occasions of women's religious lives. All in all, the *tkhines* give us the sense that women's religious lives were more private than men's: the majority of these prayers were meant to be recited when the woman wished, at home or in some other private setting. Furthermore, the prayers are phrased in the singular, and some leave space for the woman to insert her own name as petitioner. This contrasts with what we know of the man's religious life, a much greater portion of which was carried on in public settings, such as the synagogue or house of study. The Hebrew liturgy is phrased primarily in the plural and, by preference, should be recited communally. It is required and public, in contrast to the *tkhines*, which are voluntary and private.

Yet is there a way to get past this overly neat distinction between the public and private spheres? Perhaps if we examine the places where the domains cross or intersect. For example, what was the nature of the prayers women said in the synagogue (the *tkhines*, not just the regular liturgy) or the prayers husbands said during their wives' pregnancies? Why is it that cemeteries, which are, after all, public places, seem to be so important in women's religious lives? Some possible answers seem to point us back toward the private domain; many women's cemetery prayers were addressed to their dead relatives. These prayers are still, in a way, trying to keep the family together. And although the cemetery *was* public, it was only rarely—for example, during funerals—the scene of public rituals. It may be that considering cemetery devotions destabilizes the distinction between public and private domains.

A comparison of the *tkhine* literature, on the one hand, and the contemporaneous kabbalistic devotional literature in Hebrew said by men, on the other, suggests another question about the distribution of domains of the religious life: the relationship of gender, sexuality, procreation, and religious devotion. The kabbalistic devotions, which were similar to the *tkhines* in being voluntary, included many prayers concerned with sexuality. *Shaarei tsiyyon* (Gates of Zion), by Nathan Nata Hannover, contains prayers to be said before intercourse, asking God's aid in preventing impotence and in ensuring male rather than female offspring.[32] These prayers are more directly concerned with sexuality than the *tkhines*. The comparable cycle of *tkhines*, found in eighteenth-century editions of *Seder tkhines u-vakoshes*, concerns the observance of *niddah* (menstrual avoidances), conception, pregnancy, and childbirth.[33] This material contains a strong notion of menstruation as impure, stresses God's justice in causing the sufferings of childbirth, and expresses the hope for sons but finds daughters acceptable. It is far more concerned with reproduction than with sexuality. The closest the *tkhines* come to the subject of sexuality is the following, taken from a *tkhine* to be recited after ritual immersion: "Purify my heart and my thoughts that I may think no evil while my husband has intercourse with me, and may his whole deed be done in great purity, not wantonly or brazenly." The prayer then moves right to conception: "Send me the good angel to wait in the womb to bring the seed before you, Almighty God, that you may pronounce [its fate]."[34]

Women's devotional literature, though expressing chiefly private concerns, seems to exclude the erotic, which was reserved for (relegated to?) men. This distinction is also observed in a comparison of the Hebrew and Yiddish ethical literature of the period. *Shenei luhot ha-berit* (Two Tables of the Covenant) by Isaiah Horowitz (d. 1628), for example, contains a lengthy discussion of whether or not one can atone for the sins of masturbation and nocturnal emission, for which harsh penances are prescribed; and it counsels the reader on how to avoid inappropriate sexual arousal. By contrast, while *Seder mitsvas noshim* and the *Brantshpigl* both advise that intercourse be performed in a pure and modest manner, they seem to assume that women rarely have troubling sexual desires.[35] How can we account for the absence of the erotic in women's materials and its strong presence, both as a subject for prayer and petition and as part of the content of kabbalistic myth,[36] in the literature for men? This material seems to suggest that the popularization of Kabbalah during this period needs to be understood in the context of male guilt and fear, on the one hand, and of female lack of interest in, or suppression of, sexuality, on the other.[37]

The second transformative way to think about this material is to explore the relationship between gender and power. Here, as I indicated, we might start out by analyzing the category "women and men who are like women in not having much knowledge." In what contexts (halakhic, devotional, community structure, and so on) does this category appear? Examining these contexts could lead to questions concerning the relationship of gender and class and might provide a new way of looking at that problematic category, popular religion, as well. In addition, within the Jewish community, knowledge *was* power, in a very particular sense. The community was headed by an interlocking aristocracy of wealthy and learned men. The distribution of knowledge then becomes a key to the distribution of power as well. I have already discussed the question of what could be learned from the Yiddish sources, but, in regard to these sources, it might be interesting to take as a starting point ambiguities about the intended audience.[38] So many of these works have title pages or introductions that start out addressing men and women and then switch to women, or vice versa, or that address the masses in one breath and the elite in the next, as in the example of the *Mayse bukh* cited above. The cemetery prayers are equally ambiguous. For whom, exactly, was what knowledge intended?

Third, let us consider how the perspectives gained from the study of women's religion can contribute to our understanding of the cultural construction of gender in Ashkenazic Jewish society. Just taking this approach transforms some of the methodological difficulties with the literature under investigation into interesting points of departure. In the ethical literature, we pondered the relationship of the prescriptive to the descriptive. Yet now the prescriptions themselves become the object of analysis as constructors of gender roles and behaviors. In addition, it would be fruitful to compare the conceptualizations of male and female roles found in various bodies of ethical literature: Yiddish literature addressed to women with Yiddish literature addressed to men, and literature in Hebrew directed at men. Thus, the *Brantshpigl* proffers advice on how to be a good wife, while the *Lev Tov* offers counsel on how to be a good husband. How do the descriptions compare? Are they reciprocal? Symmetrical? Asymmetrical? In another genre, the cemetery prayers, prayers said by a wife or husband at the grave of a deceased spouse, there is a startling asymmetry. The husband asks his wife's pardon for his occasional outbursts of temper and expresses the hope that she will not hold a grudge against him but will intercede on his and their children's behalf before the Throne of Glory. The wife's prayer, by contrast, is full of expressions of grief and loss, none of which appear in the husband's prayer.[39]

These examples from the morality literature and the cemetery prayers, prescriptive or idealized as they might be, are about the concrete relations of real men and women. But what of the mythical images, the role models, the portraits of the patriarchs and matriarchs, for example? Unlike the Hebrew liturgy or the Hebrew kabbalistic devotional literature, which refers almost exclusively to the patriarchs, Abraham, Isaac, Jacob, and other male biblical heroes, the *tkhines* also make frequent reference to the matriarchs and other biblical women. The different ways in which these women are portrayed suggest both the hallowing of women's traditional roles and the possibilities for transcending gender categories.

Particularly interesting in this regard is the selection and transformation of motifs from midrashic and kabbalistic sources. Some *tkhines* suggest the possibility of transcending traditional roles. In one prayer, for example, the women lighting Sabbath candles identifies herself with the High Priest, an unexpected association.[40] Perhaps the best example of the transcending of categories comes from a description of the women's Paradise that originates in the Zohar (III 167a-b), the classic work of medieval Jewish mysticism, and appears in a number of Yiddish versions: within a *tkhine*, as a story, in collections of translations of kabbalistic material.[41] All of these versions change the original in significant ways. The Zohar, while honoring righteous women in general and certain heroic women of the Bible in particular (Pharaoh's daughter; Serah, daughter of Asher; Jocheved; Miriam; Deborah; and the matriarchs), makes it quite clear that even in Paradise women retain their subordinate status. Their radiant heavenly garments do not shine quite as brightly as men's robes. Further, three times a day, Pharaoh's daughter and Serah pay homage to the forms of Moses and Joseph, respectively, saying, "Happy is my lot that I brought up this light," and "Happy was the day when I brought Jacob the news that Joseph lived." Along with singing praises to God, the women in Paradise occupy themselves with studying the reasons for the commandments, particularly those they were unable (because they were women) to perform during their earthly lives.

By contrast, in almost all of the Yiddish versions, the little detail about the women's inferior garments is omitted, and many of the Yiddish versions state that women in Paradise "study Torah," pure and simple. One text, "A great tale of Rabbi Simeon bar Yohai," says explicitly that the women in Bithia's chamber study Torah "just like men."[42] The *tkhine* that contains this motif also boldly expresses women's spiritual power: "How worthy is my strength, and how knowing is my power!" proclaims Bithia, daughter of Pharaoh, recollecting the day on which she drew Moses out of the water.[43] Thus, some Yiddish versions allowed the reader to imagine herself in a radically different situation from that in which she lived: reciting these prayers or reading these stories, a woman could picture herself surrounded by other righteous women, freed from her earthly roles, devoting herself to studying Torah and praising God.

However, the "great tale" begins a shift that becomes more pronounced in later versions: it specifies the good deeds that cause these women to merit Paradise, a question with which the Zohar was unconcerned. This turns women back towards their domestic duties. As an eighteenth-century description of Paradise states:

In the first dwelling is Bithia, the daughter of Pharaoh. And many pious women are there who have raised orphans, and have shown friendly faces to the scholars who were the guests of their husbands, and who have given charity secretly. Every day they are crowned with the shining crown of the radiance of the Shekhinah. . . .

In the third dwelling is Miriam the prophet, and many pious women . . . who brought their husbands to the good way and to serve their Creator. And in each dwelling there are beautiful canopies and angels are set over each dwelling.[44]

All of this suggests that in order to delineate the images of the religious life to which women and men could aspire, we need to consider the original text—the Zohar—and its transformations. These texts were part of the popularization of the Kabbalah during the seventeenth and eighteenth centuries. It is significant that it is precisely some of the Yiddish materials—mysticism for the masses—that contained a more positive image of women.[45] Nor can one fall back on the simplistic explanation that Yiddish versions are naturally favorable to women because they were written for a female audience. Most of the changes in the portrayal of women were first introduced by a male author, Simon Akiva Ber ben Joseph, in his *Sefer maasei Adonai*, which was addressed primarily to [male] householders but also, toward the end of the introduction, and with characteristic ambiguity, to women. A careful study of the distribution and readership of the various versions (including the original) of this story, which seems to have become something of a touchstone, will enable us to delineate the varying ways in which women's spiritual potential was imagined among Ashkenazic Jews.[46]

We have seen that all three approaches to the study of women's religion —the additive, the social historical, and the transformative—can contribute significantly to the study of the religious lives of Ashkenazic women. Yet our discussion of the third approach, the transformative, suggests that viewing women's religion as an addendum to men's religion, or subsuming it under the rubric of popular religion, limits the insight to be gained from the investigation of women's religious lives. Viewing Ashkenazic Judaism as a system that incorporates both men and women allows us to move beyond a mere static delineation of "the woman's role in Judaism." Thus, for example, our discussion of the transformation of midrashic and zoharic motifs suggests a more dynamic picture, one in which women and men, folk and elite, made use of the sources and resources of Judaism to create a culture with many and complex images of men's and women's religious roles and spiritual aspirations. The analysis of these motifs and other similar materials shows us that Ashkenazic Judaism in fact offered multiple possibilities for the cultural construction of gender, possibilities that may still be explored and reclaimed.[47]

CHAPTER THREE

THE CONSTRUCTION OF GENDER IN YIDDISH DEVOTIONAL LITERATURE

Gender definitions within a culture have two aspects. First, they are *social* categories, with "men" and "women" referring to groupings of real people whose social roles prescribe the activities and the modes of interaction appropriate for each sex. But second, "male" and "female," "man" and "woman" are also *symbolic* categories. The reflexive process of the creation of identity always proceeds with reference to some other, someone who is "not me" or "not us." One's own identity and that of the other are developed in tandem. Each gender could symbolize to the other traits that it denied in itself, or that it feared, or abhorred, or coveted, or desired. And what men and women symbolize to each other is inextricably intertwined with the actual relations of power and powerlessness, hierarchy and subordination, in which they live out their interactions.[1]

Any individual culture may display variations in gender definitions, as women and men, social elites and "ordinary people" understand maleness and femaleness differently. As I have noted, the history of Judaism and Jewish culture as it has been written has been chiefly—and perhaps unavoidably—based on sources written by the learned elite. Particularly in considering the cultural construction of gender, then, attention must be paid to more popular sources, including those addressed to or stemming from women. Because writing on religious topics for women in the vernacular broke out of the frame of normal male scholarly discourse, such works prove a fruitful place to look for reflection on gender categories, and a comparison of these popular works with learned literature will convey a sense of the range of gender definitions in Ashkenazic Judaism.

This chapter will explore gender definitions among Ashkenazic Jews in the early modern period, to get at both their symbolic and their social meanings. It examines, in particular, those places where gender categories meet and cross—where men are like women, and women are like men. My goal is to gain insight into what the categories are, how much flexibility they have, and whether there is play in the boundaries between them. As it turns out, not surprisingly, that it is nonelite men who resemble women, I shall also probe the relationship between gender and other social hierarchies.

TWO VIEWS OF GENDER IN ASHKENAZIC SOCIETY

In 1596, Moses ben Henoch Yerushalmi Altshuler (c. 1546–1633) published the *Brantshpigl* (Burning Mirror), one of the earliest works of *musar*, or ethical literature, in Yiddish.[2] This comprehensive guide to the upright life went through three editions during Altshuler's lifetime (and continued to be reprinted up until 1706), yet he seems to have felt the need to explain why he wrote in the vernacular, rather than in Hebrew, the sacred tongue. Chapter 3, entitled, "This chapter explains why I write in Yiddish," begins: "The book was written in Yiddish for women and *for men who are like women.*" What can this statement possibly mean?

Among the varied definition systems for gender in Ashkenazic Jewish society, let me focus on two.[3] One is halakhah, Jewish law. Most of the provisions of halakhah apply equally to both women and men. Nonetheless, where halakhic provisions concerning men and women differ, all men (except for the mentally incompetent) are defined by one set of rules and virtually all women by another.[4] Broadly put, the halakhic system of gender definitions gives rise to rather separate spheres, roles, and responsibilities for women and men. Further, because the task of the halakhic system is to regulate real social behavior, there is very little give in the boundaries of gender definitions, very little space for men to be "like women" or for women to be "like men."

However, a second, complex system of reflection, symbolization, and definition of gender emerges from the popular religious literature in Yiddish and crosscuts the halakhic definition of gender roles. This Yiddish literature is, of course, conceived within the overall societal framework demarcated by halakhah, and draws upon a great many classic and other learned Hebrew texts. But, unlike Jewish law, the Yiddish texts (or at least those I am considering here) were not intended to determine legal practice and set precedent and thus could assume a looser and more playful stance in their definitions. Further, in addressing themselves at least in part to women, they stepped out of the normative universe of Jewish religious discourse and in some sense were forced to address questions of gender.[5] Thus, these popular religious texts in Yiddish, especially the two genres of *tkhines* and the *musar* or "ethical" literature and allied edificatory works written by men[6] for men and women, do contain reflections on the ways in which women can be "like men" and men "like women."

To return to the *Brantshpigl* and thus to the *musar* literature, when are men like women? The sentence concludes: "The book is written in Yiddish for women and for men who are like women in not being able to learn much." This category, *nashim ve-amei ha-arets* (women and the ignorant) suggests that definitions of gender in Ashkenazic culture might be approached in terms of the sociology of religious knowledge. The author of the *Brantshpigl* is talking not about general intellectual ability but about a very specific sort of learning: Torah study, the supreme religious duty of Jewish men, from which women were excused or excluded.[7] Indeed, the ideal for a man in Ashkenazic society was to devote his life to the study of the Torah, supported by his wife, the community, or wealthy patrons who could not themselves study. Although the quintessential man was a scholar, of course only a small minority of men could actually attain this ideal. Thus, definitions of social hierarchy in Ashkenazic society emphasized one's level of scholarship over one's economic status. And if access to certain sorts of knowledge is the key determinant of status for men, it is so in an even more absolute sense for women, who by definition (although not necessarily in fact) could *never* gain this access. Women did gain status—and sometimes access to knowledge of Torah—from association with rabbinical families. The wife or daughter of a rabbi had a standing in the community approaching that of the male members of her family. Further, rabbinical families sometimes educated their daughters as well as their sons.

Further, the popularization and spread during this period of Safed pietism, a mystical doctrine with a strong eschatological bent, complicates the definition of "Torah study." According to the Kabbalah, redemption could come only if all members of the People of Israel performed their religious duties, including Torah study, with the proper mystical intentions. So despite the fact that mystical texts and the mystical intentions for ritual acts were thought to be the province of a very limited elite, the internal logic of the system demanded that some form of the doctrines be disseminated among the masses. Thus, during the seventeenth and eighteenth centuries there were, in a sense, competing definitions of "Torah study": the more exoteric study of Talmud, commentaries, codes, and other legal materials, in contrast to the esoteric study of the Zohar, the great classic of medieval Jewish mysticism, and other mystical texts.[8]

MEN WHO ARE LIKE WOMEN

For the *Brantshpigl*, men who are not learned are like women, with the divide between Hebrew and Yiddish serving as the demarcation line. The norm in the Jewish literary world was that learned men wrote in Hebrew for other learned men, and any departure from that norm had to be justified. Further, publishing a work in Yiddish automatically made it accessible to a sizable number of women. It is thus no accident that the author of the *Brantshpigl* invokes gender categories in explaining his motivation for writing in the vernacular.

In Chapter 3, Altshuler offers four reasons for writing in Yiddish. Only the first two concern us here.[9] To quote him further on the first reason:

> The book was written in Yiddish for women and for men who are like women in not being able to learn much. So that when the Sabbath comes, they may read therein, and they will be able to understand what they read. For our holy books are in the sacred tongue [Hebrew], and often include complicated exegetical arguments [*pilpul*] from the Talmud, and they are not able to understand [them]. . . . The great masters of the Kabbalah teach us, and write, that not every human being possesses equal understanding. Thus I write this book for women and for men who cannot fundamentally read or understand the holy books in the sacred tongue.[10]

Thus, the author develops the category of "women and men who are like women": not all people are equally well endowed intellectually, and provision must be made for those who cannot attain the scholarly ideal.

It seems—although the author does not make this explicit—that while only some men fall into the class of those who are not well endowed, all women do. And despite his attention to nonscholarly men, Altshuler addresses his work primarily to women:

The second reason [that I write in Yiddish] is that I have learned from the Torah that the Holy One, be blessed, spoke to Moses our Teacher, "**Thus you shall say to the house of Jacob**."[11] This means in Yiddish, Thus you shall say to the household of Jacob, and announce to the children of Israel. In the Mekhilta[12] the sages interpret "the household of Jacob" to refer to the women, and "the sons of Israel," to refer to the men.[13] In the Midrash [Rabba][14] the rabbis ask why the women merited having Moses speak God's word to them before the men. This is because they accustom their [male] children to study Torah from their youth, and take them to their teacher, and watch over the children, and speak God's word to them, and awaken in their hearts the eagerness to learn and to fulfill the commandments, and [they cause them] to fear their teachers and to honor father and mother, and they teach them modesty, that they take God's name honorably, and keep the Torah and commandments honorably as well.

One notable feature of Altshuler's use of his sources is how he edits and expands them to produce a "warmer" picture of women than is found in the original. After giving the basic interpretation of "house of Jacob" as the women, and "children of Israel" as the men, the Mekhilta adds another interpretation: " 'Thus you shall say to the house of Jacob': Tell the women the main points [of the Torah] in a mild tone. 'And declare to the children of Israel': And be exacting with them."

While Altshuler implies that women cannot comprehend the details of the Torah, the Mekhilta explicitly states that only women fall into the "less well-endowed" class, and all men fall into the "better-endowed class." The view of the *Brantshpigl*, then, represents a development of the midrashic approach.

Of particular interest is Altshuler's expansion and suppression of material from Exodus Rabba:

"Thus you shall say to the house of Jacob": These are the women. He [God] said to him [Moses], Tell them the main points, which they are able to understand. "And declare to the children of Israel": These are the men. He said to him, Tell them the exact details, which *they* are able to understand. Another interpretation: Why tell the women first? Because they are quick to perform the commandments. Another interpretation: In order that they lead their children to Torah. Rabbi Tahlifa of Kesarin said, The Holy One, be blessed, said, When I created the world, I only commanded Adam, and afterward Eve was commanded [second and indirectly], and she transgressed and ruined the world. Now, if I do not speak to the women first, they will nullify the Torah; therefore it is said, "Thus you shall say to the house of Jacob."

A comparison of this midrash with the *Brantshpigl* reveals a number of interesting differences. First, of course, although the view that women are incapable of a detailed understanding of Torah seems implicit in the *Brantshpigl*, Altshuler nowhere quotes the statements that imply that all women have weaker minds than all men. In fact, by including some men in this category, he tempers the harshness of the division. Second, he omits the view that women had to be given the Torah first because of Eve's sin. Exodus Rabba, by contrast, implies that women are spiteful, perhaps, and cannot be trusted. Third, in his detailed interpretation of "leading their children to Torah," he greatly expands on and esteems the role of women as socializers and educators of children.

In this, the *Brantshpigl* differs from *Nakhalas Tsevi* (Inheritance of Tsevi), Tsevi Hirsh Khotsh's Yiddish translation and paraphrase of portions of the Zohar, published in Amsterdam in 1711.[15] This book cannot be called a *musar* work in the same sense as the *Brantshpigl*, although, as Khotsh points out, it contains the ethical portions of the Zohar and omits the "mysteries" of the Kabbalah. Rather, this work is part of the wave of seventeenth- and eighteenth-century popularizations of the Kabbalah. *Nakhalas Tsevi* raises a dilemma faced by all popularizations of mystical material: How can one make available to the masses a text such as the Zohar, the central work of Jewish mystical thought, which had for centuries been studied only by an elite coterie?[16] Khotsh explores this question in the two introductions to the work and, in the course of his discussion, transforms the meaning of the category "women and simple folk."

The first introduction is in rhymed Hebrew and is entitled *Hakdamat ha-mehaber, be-safah berurah medaber*, "The introduction of the author, speaking in clear language [i.e., Hebrew]." In it, Khotsh extends a Talmudic parable to develop a lengthy argument showing that knowledge limited to the revealed or exoteric aspects of the Torah is not sufficient to gain either eternal life for the individual soul or redemption for the people of Israel: to that end all Jews must also have some knowledge of the hidden or esoteric aspects of the Torah. But, as he concedes, not all Jews are capable of understanding the mysteries and secrets known to the kabbalists. To deal with this difficulty, Khotsh develops a fascinating theory of what might be called the "mystical unconscious." According to the Talmud, the souls of all Jews learn Torah in Paradise before they are born.[17] When the time comes for them to enter this earthly life, however, an angel flicks them on the upper lip, and they forget what they have learned. It is much easier for them to relearn it a second time, since in fact they are only recalling what they once knew. For Khotsh, of course, the Torah learned in Paradise is first and foremost the Torah understood mystically. Thus, even those who never manage to relearn the mystical lore in this life still know it, as it were, unconsciously. And when they read a translation of even the exoteric portions of the Zohar, it reminds their souls of the "secrets of Torah" they learned in Paradise, even if they are not actually aware of it.

The Hebrew introduction leaves open the question of whether or not this is also true of women. Did the souls of women also learn Torah before birth? Did women also have a repository of unconscious mystical knowledge? Was it also important for women to study the esoteric dimensions of Torah in order to gain eternal life? Neither Khotsh nor his talmudic source takes up these questions. However, the title of the Yiddish introduction, *Koh tomar le-vet Yaakov*, "Thus you shall say to the house of Jacob," would seem to imply to anyone familiar with the classic exegesis of this verse that the book must, at least in large part, be addressed to women, and that they too possess a mystical unconscious. But this turns out not to be the case, as Khotsh changes the meaning of the verse and its exegesis:

> Although many things are written [in the Torah] that appear to be stories, that is only their [outer] garb, so that not everyone will understand the great mysteries. . . . And therefore, since the Torah has both an exoteric and an esoteric aspect, and the mysteries are set forth through the revealed aspect, the Holy One, be blessed, said to Moses, "Thus you shall say to the house of Jacob." [These are] the ordinary people and the women, to whom you should teach only the plain [exoteric] meaning of the text. But "and declare to the children of Israel": to the scholars, the masters of the Kabbalah, you should reveal the mysteries. And why, in the verse, does "Thus you shall say to the house of Jacob" come before "and declare to the children of Israel"? First the ordinary people learn the plain meaning of the Torah, to show that even if they do not understand the great mysteries, but their intention is for the sake of heaven, as the Torah intends, their reward is very great.

Women then drop out of the picture entirely in the subsequent discussion. For Khotsh, the division is between the kabbalists who understand the true mysteries, on the one hand, and the ordinary folk, on the other. He is concerned, not with women, but with those men incapable of being mystics. Nonetheless, by using this verse with its exegetical tradition, he essentially collapses the category of nonlearned men into the category of women.

Thus, Khotsh's exegesis of this verse in *Nakhalas Tsevi* contrasts sharply with that in the *Brantshpigl*. First, the *Brantshpigl* is not concerned, as is *Nakhalas Tsevi*, with the distinction between esoteric and exoteric understandings of Torah. Rather, it assumes that "Torah" means either the exoteric aspects or both together and that some people, for whatever reasons, are unable to "learn Torah." Second, the author of the *Brantshpigl* is interested in real women; he acknowledges their social importance and is writing a book he considers appropriate for them. The author of *Nakhalas Tsevi*, for his part, is not really interested in women at all; for him, "women" become a symbolic category, standing for a certain kind of man. Thus, beginning with the Midrash, we can trace a complete transformation of this motif. In the Mekhilta and in Exodus Rabba, women—the "house of Jacob"—and men—the "sons of Israel"—are, as in Jewish law, discrete categories, with no overlap. In this schema, women possess inferior intellectual abilities. The *Brantshpigl* adds certain men to the category of women, and *Nakhalas Tsevi* completes the process by taking "the house of Jacob" to refer primarily to men who lack mystical understanding.

One can speculate briefly here on why these two works use the category in such different ways. One obvious factor is the geographical and chronological distance between them: the *Brantshpigl* was published in Cracow in 1596 and *Nakhalas Tsevi* in Amsterdam in 1711. Much had changed during that period, and one of the most important changes was the spread of mystical pietism and the rise and partial fall of the Sabbatian messianic movement.[18] This raises the question of the influence of kabbalistic views of women. Is the difference between the appreciation for women in *Brantshpigl* and the relegation of them to a symbolic category in *Nakhalas Tsevi* related to the greater importance of Kabbalah in the thinking of Tsevi Hirsch Khotsh than in that of Moses Altshuler? While the answer is probably yes, I would like to suggest that the Kabbalah was not a univocal influence on this literature and that different authors, as we have seen with the *tkhine* literature, could make different use of its repertoire of symbols and concepts.

Perhaps more important for the view of women in the various works of Yiddish devotional literature was the social location of their authors: I have seen much to suggest that the more "elite" the male author, the lower his view of women.[19] Khotsh was much more of a scholar than Altshuler and thus higher in the hierarchy of Ashkenazic culture. Khotsh's humbler but equally kabbalistically inclined contemporary, Simon Akiva Ber ben Joseph, author of *Avir Ya'akov* (Amsterdam, 1717), which also paraphrases material from the Zohar in Yiddish, has a much more egalitarian view of women and men *and* of their ability to comprehend mystical secrets. Touting the merits of his work in the introduction, he says:

> On the Sabbath, when they have finished their naps, wife and husband should sit down with this book. They'll find many new interpretations therein. No scholar need be ashamed to read it; it will reveal many mysteries to you, and many new interpretations of the Torah.

Thus, in his view, both men and women are capable of understanding the "mysteries."[20] The question remains, however, whether or not women were considered capable of *acting* on their mystical knowledge, of undertaking religious acts with the proper mystical and redemptive intentions.

WOMEN WHO ARE LIKE MEN

An important thing to note about the category of "men who are like women" is that a lot of real men fall into it. In Altshuler's scheme these men are not scholars, and in Khotsh's scheme they are not mystics. Next I shall examine some of the ways in which the *tkhine* literature shapes a definition of what it is to be a woman in Ashkenazic culture and the places in which "women" can be "like men." We will find that women can be "like men" only in a much more distanced and indirect way than men can be "like women." For example, as I discuss in Chapter 5, certain texts describe women in Paradise as studying Torah "like men"— but of course this is only in Paradise. There is no suggestion that real earthly women should engage in this activity. And, as we shall see, women can even be compared to as illustrious a figure as the High Priest. But of course since the destruction of the Temple in 70 CE there has been no High Priest, nor will there be one again until the Messiah comes. And even then there is really no danger that a woman could assume any priestly functions.

For the purposes of this chapter, I shall examine the *tkhines* for the three women's commandments, in particular, the *tkhines* for kindling the Sabbath lights.[21] These *tkhines* develop an image of women who can be "like men," specifically one particular man, the High Priest.

These three commandments often are described in the *tkhines* and the ethical literature as the quintessence of women's religious life.

One finds, in the case of *tkhines* for *hallah* and candle lighting, although not in the case of *niddah*, the recurring image of the High Priest performing the rituals in the Temple. How can we explain the appearance of this male figure in a prayer for a quintessentially womanly act when the *tkhines*, unlike the Hebrew prayers, more typically contain numerous references to the matriarchs—Sarah, Rebecca, Rachel, and Leah—and other women of the Bible and Midrash? How, that is, is the woman lighting candles like the High Priest?

To answer this question, let me quote portions of two different *tkhines* for kindling the Sabbath lights.[22] These two texts are found in works that originate and were published in Eastern Europe, probably in the eighteenth century.

The comparison of the woman lighting Sabbath candles to the High Priest—or rather, of her candles to the lights kindled in the Temple— appears in the *tkhine* for candle lighting found in *The Three Gates* (*Shloyshe she'orim*) attributed to Sarah bas Tovim.[23] The first section of this work contains *tkhines* for the women's *mitsvot*; the *tkhine* for kindling the Sabbath lights, found at the end of the first section, begins with the Hebrew blessing recited before lighting the candles. The text continues in Yiddish with a formula also used after the blessing for separating the dough for *hallah* and then adds a well-known Hebrew prayer for the rebuilding of the Temple, which begins, **"May it be your will, Lord our God and God of our Fathers, that the Temple be speedily rebuilt in our days, and grant us a share in your Torah."** Next comes the *tkhine* proper, in Yiddish:

> Lord of the world, may my [observance of the] commandment of kindling the lights be accepted as the act of the High Priest when he kindled the lights in the dear Temple was accepted. **"Your word is a lamp to my feet and a light to my path"** (Psalm 119:105). This means: Your speech is a light to my feet; may the feet of my children walk on God's path. May my kindling of the lights be accepted, so that my children's eyes may be enlightened in the dear Torah. I also pray over the candles that my [observance of the commandment] may be accepted by the dear God, be blessed, like the light [which] burned from olive oil in the Temple, and was not extinguished.

The comparison of the woman's Sabbath candles to the High Priest's lights in the Temple is not the only motif contained in this *tkhine*.

Nonetheless, it appears here within an overarching reference to the ancient Temple. The theme connecting the performance of the women's *mitsvot* and the Temple worship runs through Sarah's treatment of separating the dough for *hallah* as well as lighting the candles. The use in both *tkhines* of the Hebrew formula praying for the restoration of the Temple and thus, of course, for the messianic redemption highlights the central symbolic importance of Temple worship, not only in the past, but also in the future. The Temple cult, though interrupted *temporarily*, is to some extent maintained in the interim by women, in their lighting candles and also in their separating dough for *hallah*. This is in line with the rabbinic interpretation of *prayer* as a substitute for sacrifice; however, the worshiper is not usually pictured as the High Priest. And while Sarah's *tkhine* for "taking *hallah*" pictures the woman in the role of an ordinary Israelite bringing a sacrifice or giving the tithe,[24] the *tkhine* for kindling the Sabbath lights places her instead squarely in the central priestly role.

The second text, *Tkhine imrei Shifre* (The *Tkhine* of Shifrah's Words) is attributed to Shifrah, daughter of Joseph, wife of Ephraim Segal, judge in the rabbinical court of Brody.[25] Internal evidence—the statement, "we have suffered in this dark exile for more than 1700 years"—dates this text to some time after 1770.[26] An important feature of this work is its extensive use of material from the Zohar. The author of this *tkhine* used *Nakhalas Tsevi*—which was *intended*, as noted above, primarily for a male audience—as a direct source. But because she addressed the work specifically to women, it brought material from the Zohar, especially interpretations of the mystical significance of various Sabbath observances, to a wider female audience. Further, the author wove this material into an extended consideration of the mystical importance of *women's* Sabbath observance.

The passage I shall discuss employs a number of standard kabbalistic images and ideas: a conception of the Godhead as consisting of a dynamic interrelationship among ten emanations, called *sefirot*, of the utterly transcendent and unknowable God; the image of the Tabernacle of Peace for the tenth *sefirah*, the Shekhinah, God's immanent presence thought of as female and in exile from the other *sefirot*; the image of the *menorah*, the seven-branched candelabrum, as a symbol of the seven lower *sefirot*; the idea that Jews receive a special additional soul on the Sabbath; and the conviction that the human and divine worlds are interrelated as microcosm and macrocosm, and that human devotion in prayer and performing the commandments brings about love and unity among the *sefirot*, restoring, if only momentarily, the Shekhinah from her exile. In this way the people of Israel help to bring about the redemption.

Near the beginning of her "New *Tkhine* for the Sabbath," Shifrah considers the significance of candle lighting:

> The *mitsvah* of **Sabbath candles** was given to the women of the **holy people** that they might kindle lights. The sages have said that because Eve extinguished the light of the world and made the cosmos dark by her sin, [women] must kindle lights **for the Sabbath**.[27] But this is the [real] reason for it. Because the **Tabernacle of Peace** [the Shekhinah] rests on us during the Sabbath, on the [Sabbath-]souls, it is therefore proper for us to do below, in this form, as it is done above [within the Godhead], to kindle the lights.[28] Therefore, because the two souls shine on the Sabbath, they [women] must light two candles.

The complicated argument goes as follows: Making use of Numbers 8:2, a description of the candelabrum in the Tabernacle, Shifrah postulates a correspondence between an upper and a lower candelabrum, based on the fact that the verse speaks of seven lamps facing or corresponding to the candelabrum. The lower candelabrum was that in the Tabernacle, while the upper candelabrum is a symbol of the seven lower *sefirot*, or emanations, of the Godhead. Lighting the lower candelabrum—an act performed by the High Priest—brings about great arousal to love in the upper spheres, and as a consequence the male and female aspects of God unite. Now, returning to Shifrah's text:

> When the priest below lit the **seven lamps**, he therewith caused the **seven lamps above** to shine. Therefore, by kindling the lamps for the holy Sabbath, we awaken great **arousal** in the upper world. And when the woman kindles the lights, it is fitting for her to kindle [them] with joy and with **wholeheartedness**, because it is in honor of the Shekhinah and in honor of the Sabbath and in honor of the extra [Sabbath] soul.[29]

The *tkhine* then moves on to other matters.

The woman lighting candles in this text is "like a man" in two different senses. First, she is explicitly compared to the High Priest lighting the candelabrum in the Tabernacle, and in this text, the acts of the High Priest are understood to have cosmic and redemptive significance. Thus the woman, too, must light the candles with "joy and wholeheartedness." Note that Shifrah rejects the view of the sages that women were commanded to light candles to make up for Eve's sin and substitutes an interpretation that portrays women as significant religious actors.

The second way in which the woman lighting candles is "like a man" is that her ritual acts, too, can have mystical significance.[30] In Safed pietism, all Israel had to pray and fulfill the commandments with the proper mystical intentions in order to bring the redemption. Of course, it is always a question in such cases whether or not a term like "all Israel" includes women. This *tkhine*, at least, asserts that it does—that women are "like men" in their ability and responsibility to carry out *their* religious duties with full mystical intention and significance.

This *tkhine* depicts the participation of women in the mystical life in a way that goes beyond anything I have found in other texts. In other instances, women can become like men only metaphorically or indirectly, by comparison. This is what we find in Sarah bas Tovim. And yes, women in Paradise can become like men and study Torah—but *only* in Paradise, not in this earthly life. In *Tkhine imrei Shifre* alone can women performing a quintessentially womanly religious duty act as men are required to act, in full consciousness of the religious significance of what they do and with full mystical import.[31]

At the outset of this chapter, I raised questions about gender as a symbolic category and about its relationship to other social hierarchies. We have seen that in the *Brantshpigl* and especially in *Nakhalas Tsevi* gender is used *as a symbol* of social location, because both works define gender roles *and* social hierarchies with reference to the sociology of religious knowledge. Women, who by definition cannot have access to certain sorts of knowledge, come to stand for men who fall short of the cultural ideals. Thus, "women" come to symbolize men who are not, in the one case, scholars or, in the other, mystics. Further, *Nakhalas Tsevi*, the more kabbalistic of the two texts, more thoroughly transforms gender into a symbolic category, perhaps because full mystical competence is so much more difficult to attain than rabbinical scholarship, and thus many fewer men—let alone women—attained it.

Note the asymmetry here: it is easier for women to symbolize "real men" than for "real men" to symbolize women—an outgrowth of the hierarchical ordering of these categories. In Ashkenazic culture to be a man was more highly valued than to be a woman, and it was easier to lose status in the social hierarchy than to gain it. In the *tkhine* texts, unlike the ethical works, it is the significance of religious actions, rather than the sociology of religious knowledge, that defines gender. Nonetheless, one encounters this same asymmetry in the *tkhine* texts. The man—the High Priest—who symbolizes women in certain circumstances is an impossibly distant model; not even men can aspire to this role until the Messiah comes, and, even then, only one man will be High Priest. Further, it is important to distinguish between the kabbalistic and nonkabbalistic texts. In traditional nonkabbalistic Judaism, while women had fewer religious acts to perform, one could argue that the significance of the performance of a particular *mitsvah* was the same for everyone, women and men. According to the Kabbalah, by contrast, there is a world of difference between a *mitsvah* undertaken with full mystical intention and one performed without such intention. This raises the stakes for women and almost always excludes women from meaningful religious action.

Yet there is another aspect to consider, the fact that in traditional Judaism, mystical and nonmystical alike, the three women's commandments were seen as the quintessence of womanhood. Men did not routinely perform these acts. Thus, in *Shloyshe sheorim*, women are compared to the High Priest not when they perform just any *mitsvah*, let alone when they are acting in some *real* sense "like men," but rather when they perform one of the acts that most clearly defines them as women. So that while the comparison to the High Priest may enhance the value of the act, it neither transforms its meaning nor suggests that women could actually become "like men."

Imrei shifre, by contrast, opens the way for the woman to act like a real man, at least in some small degree. Indeed, symbolically speaking, the woman becomes male. In the kabbalistic understanding of the text in Numbers, the High Priest arouses the Shekhinah, the feminine aspect of the Godhead, so that she will unite with her consort Tiferet; in Shifrah's text, the woman replaces him in this role. To some extent, this just reinforces the hierarchical ordering of the categories. For a woman to become a full-fledged kabbalistic actor, she must on some level become a man. Even when lighting candles, a woman *as a woman* cannot be a kabbalist.

Nonetheless, by the late eighteenth century, several different uses of this motif were simultaneously available in the culture. Women could interpret the meaning of their religious act in kindling the Sabbath lights in a number of different ways, contributing to the variety of Ashkenazic women's spiritual expression, and the multivocal quality of Ashkenazic Jewish life.

Finally, to expand on this last point, let me reflect on the broad implications of this material for the study of Judaism. Just this cursory examination of two motifs from popular religious literature points up the limitations of relying only on halakhah and other elite sources for an understanding of Jewish life; such an approach yields too univocal a perspective on gender definitions and on the possibilities for women's religious life within Ashkenazic culture. Ashkenazic Judaism as reflected in Yiddish devotional literature is less rigid in its gender categories than the halakhah and tends to invoke them in more playful and symbolic ways.

CHAPTER FOUR

MITSVOT BUILT INTO THE BODY: TKHINES FOR NIDDAH, PREGNANCY, AND CHILDBIRTH

One of the important insights of feminist theory is the alterity, or otherness, of women: men are the rule, women the exception. Thus, in considering the significance of the body in Judaism, we are in the first instance thinking about the significance of the *male* body. The female body, like the female person, is the exception. What, then, does the *female* body signify in Judaism? Perhaps the obvious question is, to whom? While women as well as men are socialized to see men as the norm, it still may make a difference, in understanding the meaning of the body, whether one is embodied as male or female. By exploring two genres of popular religious literature in Yiddish I hope to see the connections they draw between women's bodies and the women's commandments, especially *niddah*, the observance of menstrual avoidances and purification.

This chapter draws in particular upon an important work from the Yiddish *musar* (ethical) literature, a guide to the observance of the women's commandments, *Ayn shoen froen bukhlein* (A Pretty Little Book for Women), also known as *Seder mitsvas ha-noshim* (The Order of Women's Commandments), by R. Benjamin Aaron Solnik, first published in 1577.[1] It also refers to Moses Henoch Altshuler's *Brantshpigl* of 1596.[2] Material in these works will be compared with *tkhines*. While many *tkhines* were written by women, most of the texts discussed in this chapter are anonymous, and I suspect that some of them were written by men.

Both the *tkhines* and the ethical works consider the relationship of women's bodies, the biblical story of Eve, and the three women's commandments.[3] And both kinds of texts pay special attention to menstruation as symbolic of the way in which Eve's punishment implicates later women. Nonetheless, the two genres display markedly different attitudes toward women's bodies and bodily processes. Ethical literature, written by men, treats women, especially women's reproductive processes, in mythic terms, whereas *tkhines*, some of which were written by women, treat women's bodies more concretely.

WOMEN'S BODIES AND THE WOMEN'S MITSVOT

A well-known rabbinic trope connects human anatomy and God's commandments. According to this traditional physiology, human beings have 248 limbs and 365 organs, corresponding to the numbers of positive and negative commandments, respectively, for a total of 613, the traditional number of commandments in the Torah.[4] This describes only *male* human beings, however; women, with their different anatomy, have a different number of limbs. A long *tkhine* to be recited "every day," found at the beginning of the mid-seventeenth-century work *Tkhines*, expounds the implications of this difference:

> Strengthen my bones so that I can stand before you and serve your awesome Name with my whole heart, with all my limbs that you have created within me, two hundred and fifty two. You have given and commanded your children Israel to perform two hundred and forty-eight commandments, the same number as [the number] of limbs men have. And you have promised them that if they keep and do these commandments, you will give them the light that is hidden for the righteous men and women in the next world.[5] And you have given us women four extra limbs, and you have also given us four commandments: kindling lights to honor the holy Sabbath, and to purify ourselves of our impurity, and to separate *hallah* from the dough of our baking, and that we are obligated to serve our husbands. You have also placed in my body three hundred and sixty five organs—the same number as the negative commandments that you have given to your children Israel.[6]

Thus, the three women's commandments, here bound up with subservience to the husband, are built into women's bodies. Truly, in this case, anatomy is destiny.[7]

THE SIGNIFICANCE OF THE WOMEN'S COMMANDMENTS

The three women's commandments are obviously related to women's traditional activities: separating *hallah* and kindling Sabbath lights can stand for domesticity, while the observance of menstrual avoidances structures sexuality and reproduction. Texts dating back to the rabbinic period add another level of meaning, however: they see both the three women's *mitsvot* and women's post-Edenic physiology as emblematic of and punishment for Eve's sin. In Midrash Tanhuma, we read:

> And why were women commanded these three commandments? The Holy One, be blessed, said, Adam was the beginning of my creation, and was commanded concerning the Tree of Knowledge. And it is written with regard to Eve, When the woman saw, etc. [that the tree was good for eating and a delight to the eyes, and that the tree was desirable as a source of wisdom, she took of its fruit and ate.] She also gave some to her husband, and he ate [Gen. 3:6]. Thus she caused his death and shed his blood. And it is written in the Torah, "Whoever sheds the blood of man [Adam], by man shall his blood be shed [Gen. 9:6]." So she sheds her blood, and keeps her period of separation [*niddatah*], in order to atone for the blood of Adam that she shed. Whence comes the *mitsvah* of *hallah*? She polluted the *hallah* of the world, as Rabbi Yose ben Dusmeka said: Just as the woman slaps her dough with water and afterward takes *hallah*, so did the Holy One, be blessed, with regard to Adam, as it is written, "And a mist came forth from the ground and watered [the whole surface of the earth]" [Gen. 2:6], and then afterward, "The Lord God formed Adam from the dust of the earth" [Gen. 2:7]. Whence comes the kindling of the lights? She extinguished Adam's light, as it is written, "The light of the Lord is the soul of man [Adam]" [Prov. 20:27], therefore she must observe the kindling of the light.[8]

Thus, the women's commandments are seen as punishment and atonement for Eve's sin, which is understood here as causing Adam's death. Menstruation, in this text and others, is seen as part of God's punishment of Eve.[9]

In *Seder mitsvas ha-noshim*, R. Benjamin Aaron Solnik picks up this midrashic motif and lovingly develops it. He begins by retelling the tale of Eve's sin in the Garden of Eden.

> After Eve ate of the apple and realized she must die, she wanted her husband to eat of it as well. She said, If I have to die, you have to die with me.

And she gave it to him so that he would also have to eat of the apple. Adam, poor thing, at first did not want to eat of the apple. So she took a tree branch in her hand and beat him until he also ate of the apple. As the verse says, **She gave me of the tree, and I ate** [Gen. 3:12: *Hi natnah li min ha-etz va-okhel*]. She gave [it] to me with the tree, and I ate. And because that foolish Adam let his wife beat him, God, blessed be his name, cursed him, for he should not have let a woman beat him, but he should have beaten her . . . for God made the man to rule over the woman.[10]

Thus, Eve's sin includes insubordination to Adam—even though the biblical text declares that Adam will rule over Eve only *after* they have eaten the fruit, as part of Eve's punishment (Gen. 3:16). But according to *Seder mitsvas ha-noshim*, Eve's sin is even worse than that:

Therefore the woman must also . . . suffer torment and misfortune. And therefore she must have her period every month, and must fast once or twice [a month], so that she will always remember her sin and remain in a constant state of repentance. Just as a murderer continuously does, who must all his days fast once or twice a month so that he will think about repentance, and regret his sin, so must the woman do as well. Every month she immerses herself in the ritual bath, so that she will remember her sins and be pious. . . . Therefore, it is fitting for her to recite the prayers for a repentant sinner.[11]

Thus, every month a woman's very body offers evidence against her as a murderer; the implication also seems to be that, because of Eve's sin, all women are "naturally" more sinful than men and therefore need the monthly reminder of their sins that the observance of *niddah* provides. This periodic penitence will ensure the woman's piety, says the author, even after she reaches the age of forty and, presumably, menopause. "Therefore, dear daughter," this chapter concludes, "God has commanded you these three commandments. If you keep them and do them properly, he will forgive you your sins in this world and the next."[12]

What should give us pause here is the picture of woman as murderer.[13] Solnik uses the midrashic sources to develop it even further, with reference to the other two commandments as well:

Women were commanded to kindle the lights, and they are obligated to observe this commandment, because they extinguished the light of the world [no longer just Adam's light], and darkened it. . . . And because of her sin, because she ate from the apple, all of us must die. Since she has extinguished the light of our life, she must kindle the lights.[14]

After giving a variety of interpretations for the requirement that two candles be lit, the author returns to this theme:

> Therefore women must kindle the lights, for they have extinguished our light. And for that reason they must also suffer the pain of menstruation, because they shed our blood. Therefore they have the suffering of menstruation and must immerse themselves. For the immersion is like the repentance of a penitent sinner who was a murderer. And so it is with *hallah*, too. For she has spoiled things for us, we who are called "**Israel was holy to the Lord, the first fruits of his harvest**" [Jer. 2:3]; this means in Yiddish: Hallow, Israel, to God, the firstling of his fruit. Therefore she must "take *hallah*." For she is commanded, "**As the first yield of your baking, you shall set aside a loaf** [*hallah*] **as a gift**" [Num. 15:20]; this means in Yiddish, the first part of your dough shall you separate as *hallah*. Therefore the woman must keep the three commandments.[15]

What is fascinating here, even beyond the punitive theory of the women's commandments is the author's complete collapse of all women into Eve. They are all the same, and thus the sixteenth-century women he addresses must repent continuously for Eve's "murder" of Adam. Of course, the text of Genesis does indicate that the punishments of both Adam and Eve will apply to future generations, and the midrashic sources also conflate Eve and later women. Solnik goes beyond his sources in two ways, however. First, he repeatedly uses the term "murderer," which does not appear in the rabbinic sources. Second, he implicitly describes all women as the murderers of all men, not just of Adam: "They have extinguished *our* light. . . . They have shed *our* blood" (emphasis added). Near the end of the final chapter of the section on *niddah*, which makes up the lion's share of the book, Solnik remarks, "Women, with their apple eating, brought death to the world, and with their piety, which means behaving as set out above, they can bring about the end of death. . . . Thus has the Lord God spoken; may it come to pass speedily and in our days, . . . amen."[16]

THE VIEW OF THE *TKHINES*

While Solnik builds on well-known themes in rabbinic literature, and while these themes are also echoed, if less elaborately, in the discussion of the women's commandments in the *Brantshpigl*,[17] I have yet to discover a *tkhine* that links the three women's *mitsvot* to Eve's sin. The biblical figure more likely to appear in *tkhines* for these *mitsvot* is Hannah (the mother of the biblical prophet Samuel), whose name is an acronym of *hallah, niddah,* and *hadlakah*.[18] According to talmudic exegesis (B. Berakhot 31b), Hannah repeated the phrase "your handmaid" three times in her prayer for a son in order to remind God that she had never transgressed any of the three women's commandments. As God answered her prayer, Hannah's observance was rewarded with a son, a theme explicitly played out in some *tkhine* texts. Thus, in the *tkhines* the observance of the women's *mitsvot* is connected to fertility, rather than to penance.

In general, *tkhines* for the women's commandments stress the rewards for observance and the positive religious significance of the acts. (Some of the specific motifs are also found in the *musar* literature.) The reward most frequently mentioned is pious, scholarly offspring. The light of the Sabbath candles symbolizes the light of Torah and Sabbath peace and joy, while the taking of *hallah* is likened to God's creation of humanity, *without* mention of how Eve spoiled that first human loaf.[19] Both taking *hallah* and kindling Sabbath lights recall Temple rituals: the *hallah* is in memory of the system of priestly tithes, while the kindling of the lights is compared to the High Priest kindling the candelabrum in the sanctuary:

> We must kindle lights for the holy day, to brighten it and to rejoice on it; therewith may we be worthy of the light and the joy of eternal life. . . . Lord of the world, I have done all my work in the six days, and will now rest, as you have commanded, and will kindle two lights, according to the requirement of our holy Torah, as interpreted by our sages, to honor you and the holy Sabbath. . . . And may the lights be, in your eyes, like the lights that the priest kindled in the Temple. And let our light not be extinguished, and let your light shine upon us. Deliver our souls into the light of paradise together with other righteous men and women.[20]

Only a small number of *tkhines* for *niddah*, pregnancy, and childbirth raise the topic of Eve's sin. Rather, most *tkhines* for *niddah* are concerned primarily with the themes of purity and impurity, and most *tkhines* for childbirth plead that mother and child may come through the birth alive and unharmed. And rather than assuming with *Seder mitsvas ha-noshim* that all women are complicit in Eve's sin and must suffer for it, those few *tkhines* that mention Eve are troubled by the relationship between Eve's sin and later women's suffering. Further, Eve's sin is never described as murder; it is, rather, disobedience to God.

Three *tkhines* that mention this motif are found in *Seder tkhines u-vakoshes*, first published about 1750, although at least one of them is considerably earlier. All of these texts raise the question of the relationship between women's present suffering and Eve's sin, even if they also accept the punishment with resignation. Thus, for example, a *tkhine* to be said during childbirth begins:

> Almighty God, righteous judge, with truth and with justice have you punished us women from the creation of human beings, that we women must bear our children with pain. It is within your power; whomever you punish is punished, and whomever you show mercy is shown mercy, and no one can contradict you. Who would say to you, What are you doing?[21]

There *is* a question here, even if the *tkhine* asserts that it is improper to ask it. Further, God's "justice," the text implies, is partly a matter of brute power.

A *tkhine* to be said when the woman inspects herself to make certain the flow of blood has ceased, which she must do for seven days before purifying herself by ritual immersion, again articulates and then stifles a question:

> God and my King, you are merciful. Who can tell or know your justice or your judgment? They are as deep as brooks of water and the depths of springs. You punished Eve, our ancient Mother, because she persuaded her husband to trespass against your commandment, and he ate from the tree that was forbidden them. You spoke with anger that in sadness she would give birth. So we women must suffer each time, and have our regular periods, with heavy hearts. Thus, I have had my period with a heavy heart, and with sadness, and I thank your holy Name and your judgment, and I have received it with great love . . . as a punishment.[22]

This prayer seems designed chiefly to reconcile the women who recited it both to the discomfort of their menstrual cycles and to an interpretation of this discomfort as a just punishment. By portraying God's justice as inscrutable, the *tkhine* does recognize, at least indirectly, that women's situation might seem unjust, but it then squelches this thought by having the reciter thank God for her periodic punishment.

Only one text—significantly, the one that seems to be the oldest and the one that gives some indication of having emerged from women's oral tradition—actually dissociates the woman from Eve's sin. This is the prayer for biting off the end of the etrog on Hoshana Rabba, a practice thought to ensure an easy childbirth.[23] Although it was later incorporated into *Seder tkhines u-vakoshes* and several other *tkhine* collections, it appears first in the *Tsenerene*, known as the "women's Bible," the enormously popular homiletical work. Since the *Tsenerene* was first published about 1600, this *tkhine* is contemporaneous with the *musar* literature quoted earlier.

The way the *Tsenerene* introduces this prayer makes it sound like a record of women's practice. The context is a discussion of the Tree of Knowledge in the Garden of Eden:

> Some sages say that it was a citron tree. Therefore, the custom is that women take the etrog and bite off the end on Hoshana Rabba (the seventh day of Sukkot), and give money to charity, since charity saves from death (Prov. 6:2), and they pray to God to be protected from the sufferings of bearing the children they are carrying, that they may give birth easily. Had Eve not eaten from the Tree of Knowledge, each woman would give birth as easily as a hen lays an egg, without pain. The woman should pray and should say:
>
> Lord of the world, because Eve ate of the apple, all of us women must suffer such great pangs as to die. Had I been there, I would not have had any enjoyment from [the fruit]. Just so, now I have not wanted to render the etrog unfit during the whole seven days when it was used for a *mitsvah*. But now, on Hoshana Rabba, the *mitsvah* is no longer applicable, but I am [still] not in a hurry to eat it. And just as little enjoyment as I get from the stem of the etrog would I have gotten from the apple that you forbade.[24]

By implication, then, since the woman would not have committed Eve's sin, she should not suffer Eve's punishment.[25]

To a greater or lesser degree, all of these *tkhines* distance the woman reciting them from Eve and her sin, whether directly or by implication. Further, while one finds reference to Eve's sin in these texts, it is not offered as justification for the observance of *niddah* (let alone the other women's *mitsvot*). Eve's sin explains why women menstruate and why childbirth is painful. But the observance of *niddah* itself is not described as eternal penance for Eve's murder of Adam or even for Eve's disobedience of God's command. Rather, the *tkhine* before ritual immersion, for example, uses a vocabulary of purity and cleansing and articulates the connection of the woman reciting it to other pious Jewish women: "God, my Lord, may it be your will that my cleanness and washing and immersion be accounted before you like all the purity of all the pious women of Israel who purify themselves and immerse themselves at the proper time."[26]

The *tkhine* to be said after immersion is concerned primarily with hopes for pious offspring, whether male or female.[27] In both cases the meaning of the observance of *niddah* for the woman is pictured quite differently than it is in *Seder mitsvas ha-noshim*. Further, the very language describing women's physiological states differs between the two genres. The *tkhines* consistently use a vocabulary of purity, or cleanliness, and impurity. Both *Seder mitsvas ha-noshim* and the *Brantshpigl*, by contrast, prefer a terminology borrowed from the language of cuisine: they describe the woman as either *kosher* or *treyf*.[28]

TKHINES, MUSAR, AND WOMEN'S ALTERITY

In comparing the *musar* literature and the *tkhines* on the subject of the women's *mitsvot* and women's bodies we begin with one point in common. Both genres inquire as to the meaning of women's bodies and bodily processes, and both genres take men as the norm and women's bodies as in need of explanation.

But here the similarities end. In the *musar* works, women are less individualized: they constitute a kind of cosmic class. And they are more anomalous. The disobedient and sinful Eve is paradigmatic for all women, whose post-Edenic bodies testify monthly to their sinful natures. Indeed, the *Brantshpigl* sees the connection as direct and physical, asserting that the blood of menstruation and childbirth originate in the impure venom that the serpent deposited in Eve.[29] Further, according to this text, men find the sight of menstrual blood revolting, and women should therefore keep bloodstained chemises and sheets hidden from their husbands.[30]

The *tkhines*, by contrast, view women's bodies in less mythical terms and more as rooted in physical realities. The question most urgently addressed by the *tkhines* is that of suffering: the physical discomfort, pain, and danger women experience in menstruation and childbirth. The authors of the *tkhines* want to know why women suffer, not why they bleed, and the blood itself does not inspire them with disgust. Further, these texts are troubled by the idea that all women suffer because of Eve's sin.

Can we account for the differences between these two genres by the different genders of the authors? The issue is complex, especially since, to be precise about these anonymous *tkhines*, we need to speak of the gender only of the authorial voice. Yet it does seem that men speaking as men and women (or men) speaking as women express different attitudes toward women's bodies and have different questions about them. Let me be clear here that this is not a matter of individual male malice or prejudice toward women. As other parts of the *Brantshpigl* make abundantly clear, Altshuler rather liked women and keenly appreciated their social importance.[31] Solnik, as a *posek*, an adjudicator of Jewish law, was quite concerned to extend as much opportunity for religious expression to women as he thought could be justified halakhically.[32] And both men took the quite unusual step of troubling to write books for women in Yiddish. Rather, the differences between the two genres are evidence of the multivocality of gender constructions in Ashkenazic culture. And these differences might be phrased as two contrasting questions. The authors of the *tkhines* want to understand how God's justice can require women's suffering. But the authors of the two *musar* works want to know why women are the way they are, whence springs the archetypal nature of the irreducibly Other.

CHAPTER FIVE

WOMEN IN PARADISE

How can we imagine spiritual fulfillment? What in a religious system can give us a sense of the possibilities inherent in the religious life? Ashkenazic Judaism offered various answers to these questions, answers embedded in Jewish law, ethical literature, and mystical literature, as well as in custom, folk religious practice, and social structure. The legal and ethical materials address such issues primarily in the context of our mundane realities: Given the circumscribed and limited nature of earthly life, how should a Jew live? To what standards of behavior should a Jew aspire? How can one live a holy life? Yet if we remember that religion exists in tension with mundane reality, that it strives both to sanctify the everyday and to transcend it, we realize that there are other ways of posing the question, other kinds of ideals to which a Jew may aspire. Thus, one may ask, can we imagine ourselves untrammeled by earthly limitations? How high can our liberated souls reach? Such transcendent visions are more prevalent in the esoteric mystical literature and for many centuries were available only to a restricted intellectual elite.

To look at the question of spiritual aspiration from a different angle: It is clear that Ashkenazic Judaism implicitly differentiated between the religious goals of the learned elite and those of the *amei ha-arets*, the ignorant or the common people, who might be called the "folk," and it explicitly distinguished between the religious duties, responsibilities, privileges, and aspirations of men and those of women. As we have seen, women's mundane reality was circumscribed indeed. There is, of course, much in Yiddish devotional literature, especially in the *tkhines*, that hallows the everyday: prayers for a sick child, or for baking bread, or for the three women's commandments. There are prescriptions for how to be a good wife and strictures against idle chatter in the synagogue. Yet did anything in this literature suggest that women could transcend the limitations of their earthly roles? How could women—and men—imagine the spiritual aspirations of Jewish women? How high could *women's* souls reach?

One place to look for the answer to these questions is in material that quite literally transcends the life of this world: descriptions of Paradise. Paradise can, of course, be imagined in ways that *reinforce* earthly roles and limitations—witness the well-known motif of women in Paradise serving as their husbands' footstools.[1] There is even a chapter in the *Brantshpigl* entitled, "This chapter explains how women, with much talking, can talk their way into eternal life." The *Brantshpigl* does not waste much time describing Paradise, except to state that husbands and wives will be there together, and moreover that the joy of a righteous *man* in Paradise is only complete when he is together with his wife. But the work does discuss the question of whether and how women can earn a heavenly reward. In general it follows the talmudic view that women gain eternal life by bringing their children to school or to the house of study, by awaiting their husbands with a nice hot meal when they come home from the house of study or (the *Brantshpigl* adds) from business, and in general by caring for their husbands' needs.[2]

Another description of Paradise gives a very different picture of the religious possibilities for women's souls, however. In this, a description of a separate Paradise for women, they are unencumbered by their earthly roles and occupy themselves with prayer, study, and contemplation. I first came across this description in *The Three Gates*. The striking contrast it presented to other depictions of women in early Yiddish literature intrigued me and set me searching for its source and for parallel versions. I discovered that this motif derives from the Zohar (the Book of Splendor), the great classic of medieval Jewish mysticism, and that it was widespread in seventeenth- and eighteenth-century Yiddish literature (and through reprinted editions, also in the nineteenth century) in a number of different versions. The early part of this period in particular saw the popularization of Jewish mysticism, a phenomenon that made new visions of the religious life available to those outside the learned elite—women and unlearned men. But this is only half the story, for the visions were also transformed in the process of popularization and translation.

In addition to the text in *The Three Gates*, I found Yiddish descriptions of the women's Paradise in two sorts of literary settings: as a portion of running translations or adaptations of large sections of the Zo-har;[3] and as a separate "story" or "tale" (*mayse*), variously entitled "A Grand Story of Rabbi Simeon bar Yohai" and "A Wondrously Beautiful Tale from the Zohar," appended to other texts.[4] These versions differ from each other and from the original text of the Zohar in a number of significant ways, even when the differences are only small details, and all of these versions, including the original, were circulating during roughly the same period. These texts were aimed at and/or accessible to particular audiences, whether male or female, learned or unlearned. For us to understand how women's spirituality was imagined among Ashkenazic Jews, by women and by men, we must investigate the distri-bution of versions to audiences. There is no simple or single picture to be drawn of the spiritual aspirations appropriate to women.

Three of these versions—the Zohar, one of the running translations, and the *tkhine*—form a direct literary chain and are an illuminating ex-ample of changes in content depending on the audience being ad-dressed.

Let me begin, then, with the original (Zohar III 167b). In this ac-count, Rabbi Simeon bar Yohai, the hero and putative author of the Zo-har, is receiving a report of various heavenly secrets from one of his dis-ciples:

> O my teacher, they showed me six palaces that contained enjoyments and delights, in the place where the curtain is spread in the Garden, for from that curtain onwards, males do not enter at all.
>
> In one of the palaces is Bithia daughter of Pharaoh,[5] and several myriads and thousands of righteous women are with her. Each one of them has places of light and delight without any crowding. Three times a day, criers announce, Behold, the image of Moses the faithful prophet is coming! Then Bithia goes out to the place where she has a curtain, and sees the image of Moses, and bows before it, and says: Happy is my lot that I brought up this light. And this is her special pleasure, more than all the other women.
>
> She returns to the other women, and they devote intensive study to the commandments of the Torah. All of them are in the forms they had in this world, and they are clothed in garments of light like the garments of males, except that [the women's garments] do not shine as brightly. In that world, they devote intensive study to the commandments that they were unable to fulfill in this world, and the reasons for them. And all the women who dwell with Bithia daughter of Pharaoh are called "tranquil women,"[6] because they have not suffered the pains of Hell at all.
>
> In the next palace is Serah daughter of Asher,[7] and several myriads and

thousands of women with her. Three times a day it is announced before her: Behold, the image of Joseph comes! She rejoices, and goes out to a curtain she has, and sees the light of the image of Joseph, and rejoices, and bows down before him and says: Happy was the day on which I gave the good news about you to my grandfather. Afterward, she returns to the other women, and they busy themselves with the praises of the Lord of the World, giving thanks to his Name. And each of them has several places and joys. Afterward, they turn once again to the commandments of the Torah and the reasons for them.

At this point, the text describes the palaces presided over by Jocheved, the mother of Moses, and Deborah the prophet, and then continues:

> O my teacher, O my teacher! Who has seen the rejoicing of the saintly men and righteous women who serve the Holy One, be blessed! Way inside all of these palaces are the four hidden palaces of the holy matriarchs, which it is not permitted to reveal, and no one has seen them.
>
> And all day long, [the women] are by themselves, as I told you, and so are the men. But every night, they all come together, since the hour of copulation is at midnight, both in this world and in that world. The copulation of that world [consists of] the cleaving of soul to soul, light to light.

The text concludes by explaining that the fruit of these heavenly midnight trysts are the souls of those who become converts to Judaism.

The author of the Zohar, it is clear, honors the saintly women of Paradise. Nonetheless, though they are depicted as freed from the cares of their earthly roles as wives and mothers and devoted to such spiritual pursuits as singing the praises of God, these women retain their inferior status, even in heaven. Even their heavenly garments do not shine as brightly as men's. Further, both Bithia and Serah bow humbly to Moses and Joseph, respectively, and acknowledge their good fortune in acquiring merit through their association with these male figures. And finally, the women's study of "the reasons for the commandments" is focused on those commandments that they were unable to fulfill on earth—by implication, because they were women. *Taamei ha-mitsvot*, speculation concerning the reasons for the commandments of the Torah, has a long history in rabbinic, philosophical, and mystical Jewish thought. Compiling comprehensive lists of the commandments justified in mystical terms was a popular activity of Jewish mystics. Women, however, were forbidden to engage in such speculation, even when they were permitted to study such practical matters as the religious laws they themselves were required to observe.[8] It seems, then, that here the author of the Zohar allows women in Paradise to repair or make up for their female disabilities.

Neither does the author of the Zohar single this narrative out. Although he was sufficiently interested in the fate of women in Paradise to include a discussion of it, he sets this passage into a narrative that describes many other features of Paradise. This contrasts most sharply with those "wondrously beautiful tales" in which the entire narrative is devoted to this one motif. Finally, there is the audience for this text in the period under discussion. Despite the fact that the study of mystical materials was spreading in the seventeenth and eighteenth centuries, the original text of the Zohar was in Aramaic and thus accessible only to a rather limited segment of the population, and one that may safely be presumed to have been almost exclusively male.

Striking as the Zohar's depiction of the women's Paradise is, the version contained within *The Three Gates* changes it in significant ways. The description of the women's Paradise is contained within the section of the *tkhine* that deals with the blessing of the new moon. After an impassioned plea for the messianic redemption and a paraphrase of a version of the prayer recited in synagogues for the blessing of the new moon, the text makes an abrupt shift, as follows:

> Lord of the World, I pray to you, God, as Esther the Queen prayed. Lord of the whole world, with your right hand and your left hand, you have created the whole world with both your hands. May you spread your mercies over me.
>
> There are also there in Paradise six chambers in which there are several thousand righteous women who have never suffered the pains of Hell. Queen Bithia, daughter of Pharaoh, is there. There is a place in Paradise where a curtain is prepared to be opened, which allows her to see the image of Moses our teacher. Then she bows and says, *How worthy is my strength and how knowing is my power!* I drew such a light out of the water, I brought up this dear light! This happens three times a day.
>
> In the next chamber, there are also thousands upon thousands upon myriads of women, and Serah daughter of Asher is a queen. And every day it is announced three times, Here comes the image of Joseph the Righteous! Then she bows to him and says, *Praised is my strength, and how worthy is my power*, that I was privileged to tell my lord Jacob that my uncle was alive. And in the upper chamber, he studies Torah, and in the other chamber, they sing hymns and praises, *and study Torah* (emphasis added).

After describing the chambers of Jocheved and Deborah, the passage concludes:

And the chambers of the matriarchs cannot be described; no one can come into their chambers. Now, dear women, when the souls are together in Paradise, how much joy there is! Therefore, I pray you to praise God with great devotion, and to say your prayers, that you may be worthy to be there with our mothers.

This remarkable passage bespeaks a different view of women's spiritual status from what one finds in the original. Three changes are particularly noteworthy. First, there is no mention of women's inferior garments; indeed, the whole discussion of garments is omitted. Second, women are no longer studying the reasons for the commandments they could not perform on earth; they are no longer repairing or compensating for the disabilities they had suffered as earthly women. Rather, they are simply, in the Yiddish phrase, *lernen Toyre*—studying Torah—the primary religious duty of Jewish men, from which women were excused or excluded. But in the paradise of *The Three Gates*, at least, women engage in this most holy of activities.[9] (The Yiddish tales [*mayses*] about the women's Paradise, incidentally, make this even more explicit. They state that women study Torah "just like men.")[10] The assertion that women could study Torah, even if only in Paradise, must have seemed quite radical, so much so that it was omitted from some later editions of the text, which say only that Joseph studied Torah in an upper chamber, while the women sang God's praises below. Third, and perhaps the most striking feature of this text, Bithia and Serah boldly proclaim their strength and their spiritual power. They express a sense of their own worth in this passage, not just their good fortune at having been the agents of events concerning important men. A fourth change, the expunging of the erotic element from the conclusion of the description, seems characteristic of the popularization of kabbalistic texts.[11]

All of these changes occur in a Yiddish text explicitly addressed to women. Yet do these changes suggest that a woman was the *author* of this text? Certainly, the fact that the changes in the text expanded women's spiritual horizons makes a female author seem plausible. But could a woman have actually read the original text of the Zohar, from which this description derives? Only a few women acquired fluency in Hebrew, let alone Aramaic, and an esoteric text like the Zohar was not a likely one for a woman to study.[12] This problem set me searching for an intermediate source in Yiddish and led to my discovery of all the versions of the description mentioned at the outset.

And I found in the process that my hypothesis—that these textual changes must have been introduced by a woman—was wrong. This became apparent when I found the intermediate source. Yes, the author of *The Three Gates* was almost certainly a woman, Sarah bas Tovim. But she based her text on *Sefer maasei Adonai* (Book of the Tales of the Lord), in which the description of the women's Paradise appears in a Yiddish paraphrase of a long section of the Zohar.

The author of this work, Simon Akiva Ber ben Joseph, lived in Germany and Bohemia in the seventeenth century and spent much of his life wandering, teaching Talmud, and preaching. In addition to two works in Hebrew (a mystical commentary on the daily prayers, and an encyclopedia of Midrash Rabba), he composed two very popular works in Yiddish. These were *Avir Yaakov* (Protector of Jacob), a collection of legends from medieval mystical sources about the biblical patriarchs, and *Sefer maasei Adonai*, which contains stories collected, translated and adapted from various mystical works. Part 1 first appeared in 1691, part 2 in 1694, and a revised combination of the two in 1708.[13] This was an author actively engaged in the popularization of mystical literature. His works, while in Yiddish, were primarily directed, not to a female audience, but to nonscholarly men.

Many details prove that this work is in fact the source used by the author of *The Three Gates*.[14] It is, indeed, even possible to show that it was the revised, combined version of 1708, rather than the versions based on the 1694 edition, that was used. The clincher is that strange detail about the "upper chamber" in which, according to the *tkhine*, Joseph studies Torah. This "upper chamber" first appears in the 1708 edition. In any case, let me quote the passages comparable to those cited for the other two texts:

Dear Rabbi, there are six chambers in which there are women. And there is a curtain spread out in Paradise, past which no man can go. And in the first chamber sit several thousands and myriads of women none of whom have suffered the pains of Hell, and Bithia daughter of Pharaoh is their queen. And every day there comes a cry that says that the image of Moses is coming. Now there is a place in that chamber where Bithia can open a curtain and see the image of Moses. As soon as she sees him, she bows down to him and says, *How worthy is my power* that I brought up such a light! This happens three times a day.

Now in the next chamber there are thousands of myriads of women, and Serah daughter of Asher is their queen. And every day it is called out three times, Here comes the image of Joseph the Righteous! She bows down to him, and says also, *Praised is my power, and how beautiful is my strength*, that I was worthy to tell the good news to my lord Jacob that my uncle Joseph was still alive. *And in the upper chamber* [in the 1694 version: in the first chamber] *they study Torah, and in this next chamber they sing praises and hymns and also study Torah* (emphasis added).

After describing the chambers of Jocheved and Deborah, the description concludes:

> And in the chambers where our matriarchs are, it is not to be described what joy and purity there are, and no one is privileged to see their purity. Now, dear Rabbi, when the souls in Paradise come together, they have great delights, and they rejoice fully in Paradise. And a great light is created from their joy, and from this light are created the souls from which come the converts to Judaism.

To run briefly through the comparison: *Sefer maasei Adonai* omits mention of the inferior garments. Second, women study Torah, and we can see that the introduction into the *tkhine* of Joseph studying Torah in the "upper chamber" is both a watering down of the original force of the statement and an attempt to explain a typographical error or misreading. The earlier edition, referring to the fact that Torah study went on in Bithia's chamber as well as Serah's, referred to the *first* (*ershtn*) chamber; the later edition erroneously substitutes the word *eybershtn* (upper) for *ershtn*. A later reader could have reasoned, What upper chamber could have been meant? It must have been a segregated spot in which a man could study. Which man appears in the text? Joseph. Third, Bithia and Serah once again proclaim their power. Fourth, the conclusion seems just about halfway between the original text and the *tkhine*'s complete exclusion of erotic elements. Further, the wording of the final address to Simeon bar Yohai is clearly the literary model for the appeal by the author of the *tkhine* to women to be good girls and to say their prayers.

Despite my exhilaration at having discovered the intermediate source between the *tkhine* and the Zohar, I was also at first somewhat disappointed to realize that Akiva Ber, a man, was the source of all the key changes. But how intriguing that *Sefer ma'asei Adonai* was not only written *by* a man but was also addressed primarily *to* men, as the introduction makes clear. Indeed, this positive portrayal of women for a male audience becomes one of the most interesting features of this array of materials concerning the fate of women in Paradise. Nonlearned men could read about women who said things like, "Praised is my power, and how beautiful is my strength."

In the analysis of all these texts, we may seem to have descended from spiritual heights to a morass of detail. So let us now ask again, how high could women's souls reach? How were women's religious aspirations imagined by Ashkenazic Jews? This study of a single motif, however widespread, may be only a modest foundation on which to base an answer to this question, but it can at least point us in some interesting directions.

The evidence of the texts examined here suggests that the answer to these questions depends on whom you ask. The most restricted view of women's spiritual prospects was that available to the intellectual elite, to those who could read the Zohar in the original and who did not need to resort to—and perhaps would not stoop to—Akiva Ber's popularizations in Yiddish. For this audience, women, even in Paradise, remained distinctly subordinate. Nonlearned men and women, by contrast, encountered versions of this motif which asserted that, at least in Paradise, women could become like men, having intrinsic spiritual worth and attaining unambiguously to the paramount male religious activity, Torah study. How striking it is that there seems to have been more sympathy for or appreciation of women among (or conveyed to) the uneducated than among the learned.

In addition, these texts suggest that the answers to these questions about women's spirituality also depend on *when* historically you ask. This can be seen most clearly in the changes that take place in this passage in successive editions of *The Three Gates*. During the first half of the nineteenth century, the text developed in one of two ways: either it omitted the reference to Joseph studying Torah in the upper chamber, or it omitted the mention of women studying Torah. And thus it eliminated the ambiguity and came out either for or against the full-fledged and self-sufficient study of Torah by women. By the late nineteenth century, however, the reference to women's study was often omitted, whether or not Joseph's study was retained. In addition, one late (1894) version of this description (which was, incidentally, pirated from *The Three Gates* and incorporated into a completely different *tkhine*) also removed Bithia's and Serah's exclamations of power, perhaps revising the text to bring it back into line with the original. Thus, the affirmation of women's spiritual power and worth and the assertion, found in early editions of this text, that women can aspire, at least in Paradise, to something like equality with men has faded somewhat by the end of the nineteenth century.[15]

At this point, it is difficult to be certain of the reasons for this change.

One factor may have been the desire of certain modernizing Jewish intellectuals, or *maskilim*, to transform the traditional Jewish household into a model middle-class family along nineteenth-century Western European lines. This involved restricting women to the role of housewife and removing them from their traditional economic and other activities outside the home, while encouraging men to abandon Torah study for more economically productive vocations that could support their families. It has been shown that some of these *maskilim* used the vehicle of popular Yiddish literature, including the *tkhines*, to convey their views to a female audience, an audience they did not hold in high regard.[16] Thus, these later versions of the fate of women in Paradise could reflect both the decline of Torah study as an ideal and a lowered estimation of the intellectual and spiritual aspirations suitable for women.

It is worth remembering, however, that all of the texts examined, from the Zohar to the *tkhines*, were, in varying degrees, liberating: they enabled women and men to imagine a Paradise filled with "thousands of myriads" of righteous women, unencumbered by their roles as wives and mothers, freed from at least some of their earthly limitations, devoting themselves to studying Torah and praising God.

PART II

THE *TKHINES* AND MYSTICAL SPIRITUALITY

KABBALISTIC CANDLE LIGHTING

WOMEN AND KABBALAH

The absence of women from Jewish mystical movements presents an enduring puzzle for the historian of religions. How is it that women have been present in Islamic mysticism, and were among the crucial shapers of Christian mysticism, and yet have played so negligible a role in Jewish mysticism?[1] While this is ultimately an unanswerable question, reflection on it can lead us to a deeper understanding of early modern Jewish spirituality. In this chapter, we will explore the problematic of women and Kabbalah chiefly through the lens of *Tkhine imrei Shifre* (The *tkhine* of Shifrah's Words), attributed to Shifrah bas Joseph, a late eighteenth-century Eastern European text that makes use of kabbalistic motifs and sources. First, however, we need to lay out the basic issues.

The problem of the absence of women from Jewish mysticism is both social and theological. In sociological terms, women and members of other relatively powerless groups are often participants in ecstatic and mystical movements, leading sociologists of religion to speculate that temporal powerlessness has led women to seek spiritual power.[2] But not in Judaism—the social organization of Jewish mystical circles seems to have made no room for women. Kabbalah is a mysticism of the learned that requires a knowledge of languages and texts that was simply not available to most women or, for that matter, to most men.[3] The kabbalists, that is, were an esoteric elite. However, Safed pietism, Sabbatian messianism, and Hasidism all possessed more of a mass character, meeting, in eighteenth-century Eastern Europe, in a struggle for the hearts and minds of Jewish men. But did they also appeal to women, providing opportunities for women to participate or to assume leadership roles?[4]

Hasidism is a particularly interesting case. Some earlier scholars have argued that Hasidism was decisively different from earlier mystical movements and gave women greater scope as participants, even leaders. However, as Ada Rapoport-Albert has shown, Hasidic teachings had no special concern for women.[5] Hasidic teachers produced no works for a female audience, nor did they concern themselves with the education or spiritual development of women. Indeed, their attitude to women was essentially a continuation of pre-Hasidic rabbinic and kabbalistic views. What is more, women were never a part of the institutionalized leadership of Hasidism. The women who are depicted in oral tradition as charismatic figures, usually mothers, sisters, or wives of *tsaddikim*, produced no body of hasidic writings, nor did they have an enduring following. Even Hannah Rachel Verbermakher (born c. 1815), known as the Maid of Ludmir, who tried to act as a hasidic master, in the end must be seen as a failed *tsaddik*, a deviant who could not play her chosen part.

But several decades before Hannah Rachel's birth, during the formative years of Hasidism, women from Volhynia and Galicia were credited with the authorship of texts in Yiddish, some of which incorporated kabbalistic symbols and other material derived from kabbalistic sources.[6] The question is whether these texts contradict the generally accepted view that women played no role in the world of Kabbalah. Are they evidence that Hasidism did in fact provide women with greater spiritual outlets than before? Or do they support the view that Hasidism, as compared with the earlier Safed pietism, was of little consequence to women? An even more basic question concerns the sources these women used: where did they get their kabbalistic material?

Because very few women knew Hebrew, and even fewer mastered Aramaic, the classic works of Kabbalah were closed to all but the most exceptional among them. However, kabbalistic material was available in Yiddish, which many women learned to read. While a detailed study of kabbalistic literature in Yiddish has yet to be made, a cursory review shows that by the mid-seventeenth century kabbalistic material began to be incorporated into various genres of popular religious literature in Yiddish.[7] Compendia of material from the Zohar and other kabbalistic sources were also published in the late seventeenth and early eighteenth centuries. Examples are the anthology of material from a number of kabbalistic sources, *Sefer maasei Adonai*, collected and paraphrased by Simon Akiva Baer ben Joseph; the same author's tales of the patriarchs from the Zohar, *Avir Yaakov*; and the Yiddish paraphrase of the Zohar, *Nakhalas Tsevi*, by Tsevi Hirsh Khotsh).[8] These are all books that were available to Ashkenazic women who could read Yiddish. My examination of the sociological aspects of the negligible role of women in Jewish mysticism, therefore, asks to what degree these Yiddish versions expunged or transformed technical theosophical and theurgic concepts, and to what extent women utilized these adaptations as sources for their own writings.[9]

Theologically, too, Kabbalah presented obstacles to the full participation of women. Within the kabbalistic system, "male" generally signifies and symbolizes the spiritual and the holy, whereas "female" descends into the material and the demonic. If women are indeed so intimately connected with physicality (*gashmiut*), it would seem inconceivable for them to engage in asceticism and strive for spiritual elevation. Furthermore, while kabbalistic theosophical teaching paid great attention to the female aspects of the Godhead, especially the Shekhinah, they were depicted in their relationship to the male mystic, for it was his task to arouse the Shekhinah to unite with her consort, Tiferet. Could there be a place for women in this symbolic universe? It is difficult to separate cause and effect here; it seems that the symbolic system and the absence of women mystics fed off of and reinforced each other. Nevertheless, even if scholarly mystics dismissed—for both mystical and practical reasons—the possibility that women *could* strive for spiritual perfection, we must ask whether other segments of the Jewish population—for example, women and nonlearned men—viewed the matter differently. In other words, the problem should be considered from the bottom up as well as from the top down.

It is instructive to compare the kabbalistic system of gendering with Christianity's. Medieval Christianity also identified women with physicality and men with spirituality. But, as Caroline Walker Bynum has shown, there was a solution to the difficulty this posed for medieval Christian female mystics: in Christianity, the human aspect of Jesus Christ's dual nature was just as important as the divine. In identifying with the humanity of Jesus, women could therefore give spiritual meaning to their association with physicality.[10] The theological ramifications of the kabbalistic system, then, lead me to question whether the symbolic system of the *sefirot* presented Jewish women with similar possibilities. Could women identify with the feminine *sefirot*, Malkhut (Shekhinah) and Binah, as contemporary Jewish feminists sometimes argue?[11] Conversely, could they have a special devotion to the masculine *sefirot*, Tiferet or Yesod, parallel to the male kabbalists' devotion to Malkhut? Either possibility would require reinterpreting the symbol system of the *sefirot*, but the evidence suggests that, insofar as women made use of kabbalistic symbolism, they did not significantly transform its gender representations.

THE *TKHINES* AND KABBALAH

Many of the *tkhines* in the standard, often reprinted collection, *Seder tkhines u-vakoshes*,[12] derive from voluntary or supplemental devotions in Hebrew that are rooted in Lurianic Kabbalah—in particular, *Shaarei Tsiyyon* (Gates of Zion) by Nathan Nata Hannover and *Shaar ha-shamayim* (Gate of Heaven) by Isaiah Horowitz.[13] Yet these *tkhines* contain little overtly kabbalistic material. On some level, however, they cannot be understood if one does not know that there is such a thing as mystical intention in prayer and *mitsvot*; they imply a model of women as distanced participants in the mystical system. One *tkhine* from *Seder tkhines u-vakoshes* acknowledges that "we do not have the power to engage in the mystical intentions and combinations of the holy names . . . in all of the prayers" but nonetheless petitions God: "May my prayers rise before you to make a crown on your holy head together with the prayers of those Jews who do know how to engage in mystical contemplation and to combine all the intentions and combinations of the names."[14]

Some of the Eastern European *tkhines*, such as *The Three Gates* (*Shloyshe sheorim*), attributed to the legendary Sarah bas Tovim, use kabbalistic sources in much the same way as the Western European texts.[15] In its paraphrases of material from *Sefer hemdat yamim* (Book of Days of Delight),[16] *The Three Gates* summarizes or glosses over technical kabbalistic matters, sometimes to the point of making the text extremely difficult to follow. Others, however, such as *The Tkhine of the Matriarchs* by Sarah Rebecca Rachel Leah daughter of Jacob Yokl Horowitz (b. c. 1720),[17] contain much more explicitly kabbalistic material. This *tkhine* consists of three sections: a Hebrew introduction, an Aramaic liturgical poem, and a Yiddish paraphrase of the poem. The Hebrew introduction includes a kabbalistic interpretation showing the importance of women's prayer; the poem refers to *imana shekhinta* (our Mother the Shekhinah), and other *sefirot*; and the Yiddish paraphrase contains not a trace of kabbalistic material. Although Leah, as the author was known, read kabbalistic literature and was able to make use of kabbalistic symbols and concepts, she knew that her audience was not familiar with kabbalistic terminology and concepts. In the Yiddish portion of the text, she therefore transformed the kabbalistic concept of prayer for the sake of the Shekhinah into something women who were not mystics could grasp—tearful prayer for redemption.

TKHINE IMREI SHIFRE

In contrast to the two *tkhines* mentioned above, *Tkhine imrei Shifre*[18] contains a great deal of explicitly kabbalistic material *in Yiddish*, most or all of which is ultimately derived from the Zohar, via an intermediate source in Yiddish.[19] *Imrei Shifre* consists of four sections: a long *tkhine* on the themes of exile, repentance, and redemption; a *tkhine* to be recited every day; a *tkhine* for the Sabbath, which contains the material to be considered here; and a *tokhakhas musar le-shabes* (moral reproof for the Sabbath), which consists almost entirely of translations of portions of the Zohar into Yiddish.

The author attribution found in this text may be substantially correct. Whether real or fictitious, it is an interesting portrait of a *tkhine* author. The title page reads:

TKHINE IMREI SHIFRE

This *tkhine* was made by the prominent, learned, wealthy woman Mistress Shifrah daughter of the late marvelous [*ha-mufla'*] and learned rabbi, our teacher Rabbi Joseph, of blessed memory; the wife of the learned and pious rabbi, the acute Rabbi Ephraim Segal, *dayyan* (rabbinical judge) in the holy community of Poznan.

Unlike other *tkhines*, *Imrei Shifre* contains something resembling a rabbinic approbation (*haskamah*). On the verso of the title is the following:

INTRODUCTION [HAKDAMAH]

Inasmuch as the important, learned woman, wife of the Torah scholar and rabbi, the great luminary in Torah and piety, outstanding *dayyan* of the holy community of Brody, our teacher Rabbi Ephraim Segal, as I say that I knew her and was acquainted with her in the past, and now, even more, that all of her deeds are for the sake of heaven; and now, her excellent plan is to travel to the holy land with her husband;[20] therefore, several rabbis and sages agree [*maskimim*] that she should publish this *tkhine*. One ought not to cause her any financial loss. And she has approbations and bans [*haskamot ve-haramot*] from the eminent scholars of the land, except that the page is too short to hold [all the names].

This is followed by half a page of blank space. Either there were no *haskamot*, or "the eminent scholars of the land" did not wish to have their names used in a Yiddish pamphlet for women.[21] Clearly, in seeking rabbinic approbation, the author wished to have the legitimacy this would convey. *Haskamot* functioned as both imprimatur and copyright, and very few Hebrew books were published without them. And while some Yiddish books by men were published with *haskamot*, there is only one case known to me in which a woman succeeded in getting approbations for her Yiddish work.[22]

In any case, although there remains some doubt about the author's historicity, for convenience, I refer to the author, who I assume was a woman, as Shifrah. Like most Eastern European *tkhines* published before 1835, *Imrei Shifre* does not refer to a publisher or place or date of publication. Fortunately, however, it does contain an internal date. "We have tarried in this dark exile," laments Shifrah, "for more than seventeen hundred years." This places the text sometime after 1770,[23] during the formative years of Hasidism.

Like other *tkhine* authors, whether historically identifiable or not, Shifrah is described as a member of the elite—wealthy, wise, and belonging to a rabbinical family. I have not yet found any direct historical evidence about the author, and there are certain inconsistencies in the statements on the title page and introduction, particularly in reference to her husband. On the title page he is said to be from Poznan; the introduction says he is from Brody. Another edition of the *tkhine* gives his location only as Brody.[24]

Whether these statements are accurate or merely the publisher's fabrications, the association of this *tkhine* with certain localities is significant. Poznan was the residence of Shabbetai Sheftel ben Isaiah Horowitz (1590?–1660?) who was appointed rabbi of Poznan in 1643. Shabbetai Sheftel's Hebrew *tehinnot*, adapted into Yiddish and entitled *Ayn sheyne kestlikhe tkhine* (A Beautiful, Precious *Tkhine*), were frequently reprinted. On the title page, he is always referred to as Rabbi Sheftel of Poznan. Perhaps the publisher of *Imrei Shifre* wished to associate it with an earlier best-seller.

More interesting is the association of *Imrei Shifre* with Brody. This Galician city was in the heartland of eighteenth-century religious ferment among Eastern European Jews. Bans were published in Brody against the Frankists in 1752 and against the Hasidim in 1772, just about the time *Imrei Shifre* was composed. In addition, for much of the eighteenth century, members of the *kloyz*, mystical pietists of the older Lurianic school, were active in Brody. While some of these mystics were involved in early hasidic circles or were sympathetic to Hasidism, others were hostile, and the *kloyz* as a whole supported the 1772 ban.

Further, inhabitants of Brody were well represented among the three hundred or so Eastern European Jews who accompanied Rabbi Menahem Mendel of Vitebsk, Rabbi Abraham of Kalisk, and Rabbi Israel of Polotsk when they departed in 1777 to settle in Safed in the Holy Land. While the organizers of this group were prominent hasidic leaders, and its core members were their followers and disciples, they were joined by a "mixed multitude" of Jews of varying religious persuasions. Menahem Mendel and his colleagues appear to have been motivated by a desire to perfect their inner spiritual lives; others who accompanied them may have had messianic hopes, or even connections to underground Sabbatianism. In addition, many of the emigrants were indigent people, displaced by the wars associated with the partitions of Poland. Although I have not yet uncovered any direct evidence that Shifrah and her husband were among these emigrants, their participation, suggested by the introduction to the *tkhine,* is quite plausible. Shifrah's husband Ephraim was a learned man, a judge in the rabbinical court, and Shifrah herself was, like the organizers of the emigration, deeply moved by a mystical understanding of the *mitzvot.*[25] In addition, Shifrah laments the troubles that afflicted the region, remarking that rabbis and scholars "travel from city to city and walk in the streets swollen with hunger, and the poor cry out and beg for bread, while the gentiles plunder and drive us out."

In general, as noted above, the region of Galicia and Volhynia is rich in attributions of *tkhine* authors. However, it is difficult to assess the significance of the association. It is likely that numerous *tkhines* were composed and published in this region at this time because of the religious ferment in the air. Further study is needed to determine whether any of these texts were hasidic, antihasidic, or even Sabbatian. *Imrei Shifre* does not seem to contain any specifically hasidic teachings. It does make reference to the problem of "strange thoughts" during prayer, an idea developed in hasidic teachings. But this motif had a long history before the rise of Hasidism and is discussed in various popular Yiddish ethical works.[26] Indeed, it is likely that the sources for *Imrei Shifre* were these prehasidic ethical works, rather than any of the new hasidic teachings.[27] The *tkhine* breathes the spirit of these works, with their emphasis on repentance, judgment, and punishment of the soul after death. The author of *Imrei Shifre* drew on one such Yiddish work, *Nakhalas Tsevi*, and probably knew others as well. Thus, the kabbalistic material found in this *tkhine* is most likely influenced by the Safed revival—which led to the publication of mystical morality literature—and not by Hasidism and its putative opportunities for women. That Brody was a center of prehasidic Lurianic mystical piety further supports this hypothesis.

Tkhine imrei Shifre goes further than any other *tkhine* I have seen in attributing explicit kabbalistic significance to women's religious performance. Furthermore, the text argues for the importance of women's Sabbath observance and takes for granted the importance of women's prayer. The author is conversant with and has borrowed from several earlier *tkhine* texts, including *Seder tkhines u-vakoshes* and *Tkhine imohos* by Leah Horowitz.[28] This places Shifrah within the literary tradition of the *tkhines*. This is important, for she takes from *tkhines* a common nonkabbalistic motif for lighting Sabbath candles and gives it a kabbalistic interpretation.

Since the text contains a great deal of material derived from the Zohar, it assumes and makes use of a number of standard kabbalistic images and ideas: the Shelter of Peace for the tenth *sefirah*, the Shekhinah; the candelabrum (*menorah*), as a symbol of the seven lower *sefirot*; the idea that Jews receive a special additional soul on the Sabbath; the belief that the human and divine worlds are interrelated as microcosm and macrocosm, and that human devotion in prayer and in performing the commandments brings about love and unity among the *sefirot*, and restores, if only momentarily, the Shekhinah from her exile.

Shifrah begins her "New *tkhine* for the Sabbath" with a general statement about God's grandeur and power and about the significance of the Sabbath as sanctifying the memory of the creation. She then stresses the importance of women's observance of the Sabbath: "And women must be as scrupulous about the Sabbath as men." She mentions that women are obligated to recite *kiddush*, the prayer of sanctification over wine that begins the Sabbath meal. She then moves on to the significance of candle lighting:

The commandment of **Sabbath candles** was given to the women of the **holy people** that they might kindle lights. The sages said that because Eve extinguished the light of the world and made the cosmos dark by her sin, [women] must kindle lights **for the Sabbath.** But this is the reason for it: Because **the Shelter of Peace** [=the Shekhinah] rests on us during the Sabbath, on the [Sabbath-]souls, it is therefore proper for us to do below, in this form, as it is done above [within the Godhead], to kindle the lights. Therefore, because the two souls shine on the Sabbath, they [women] must light two candles. As it is written in the verse, **"When you raise** [*be-ha'alotekha*, here usually understood to mean "when you kindle"] **the lamps, let the seven lamps shine against the face of** [*el mul penei*] **the candelabrum."**[29] [It seems that the verse] should have used a term for kindling, rather than one for raising up; but by his kindling **below** the verse *means* raising up: "And the lights that are against the candelabrum, may the seven lights—the candelabrum—shine."[30] He raised the **arousal to the Upper World** [*hit'orerut le-ma'lah*]. All this was set out **below** corresponding to the **Tabernacle above** [*mishkan shel ma'lah*]. Therefore the verse says that the **heavenly candelabrum** corresponds to the **earthly candelabrum.** When the priest below lit the **seven lamps,** he therewith caused the **seven lamps above** to shine. Therefore, by kindling the lamps for the holy Sabbath, we awaken great **arousal** in the upper world. And when the woman kindles the lights, it is fitting for her to kindle [them] with joy and with **wholeheartedness**, because it is in honor of the Shekhinah and in honor of the Sabbath and in honor of the extra [Sabbath] soul. Thus she will be privileged to have holy children who will be the light of the world in the Torah[31] and in fear [of God], and who will increase **peace in the world**. And by this means she gives her husband long life; therefore, it is appropriate for women to take great care concerning this.[32]

The text then continues, at some length, with other matters.

Shifrah offers a complex argument countering the view of the sages that lighting the Sabbath candles is a religious duty that was assigned to women as atonement for Eve's sin. She explains it as an expression of women's spiritual power and significance.[33] And because the tenth *sefirah*, the Shekhinah, rests on the people of Israel on the Sabbath and bestows the additional Sabbath souls on them, women must kindle two Sabbath lights.

The earthly act of lighting candles corresponds to the kindling of lights in the realm of the divine, which is a symbol of the union and harmony of the *sefirot* that occurs on the Sabbath.[34] To develop this idea, Shifrah uses Numbers 8:2, which is a description of the candelabrum in the (earthly) Tabernacle. She postulates a correspondence between an upper and a lower candelabrum, based on the reference in Numbers to seven lamps facing or corresponding to the candelabrum. The lower candelabrum was in the earthly Tabernacle, while the upper candelabrum is a symbol of the seven lower *sefirot*, whose divine light illumines the Shekhinah, the heavenly Tabernacle. Lighting the lower candelabrum, an act performed by the High Priest, causes great arousal to love in the upper spheres. In other words, the High Priest below acts on and symbolically as the Shekhinah; as he lights the seven lower lights, She lights the upper candelabrum of the seven lower *sefirot*. In classic kabbalistic terms, the act of the High Priest contributes to the *hieros gamos* (the sacred marriage) of the male and female aspects of God, Tiferet (together with the rest of six lower *sefirot*) and Shekhinah (the seventh of the lower *sefirot*). Facilitating this union is the sacred and mystical heart of kabbalistic ritual. In her most daring move, Shifrah likens the act of the woman to that of the High Priest: by lighting their weekly Sabbath candles, women arouse the *sefirot* to love and union. This act should be undertaken with joy, because it is in honor of the Shekhinah, of the Sabbath, and of the Sabbath-souls.

The Source of the Passage

The full significance of Shifrah's *tkhine* can be assessed only in comparison with its source. Much of this passage is a relatively close paraphrase of the following text from Zohar I 48b:

> The Sabbath light was given to the women of the holy people to kindle, and the Company have said that she extinguished the light of the world, and darkened it, etc., and this is a good explanation [*ve-shafir*]. But the secret meaning of the matter is that this Shelter of Peace is the Lady of the Cosmos, and the souls which are called Supernal Candles rest in her. Thus, the woman must light the candles, for the Lady adheres to her and acts [through her]. [Or: Thus, the woman must light the candles, for she is in the place of the Lady, who adheres to her when she performs the act: *Ve-al da matronita baya le-adlaka de-ha be-dukhtaha itahadat ve-avdat uvda.*] And the woman must light the Sabbath candles with joy of the heart and good will, for it is a supernal honor for her, and of great merit for her, so that she will be worthy to have holy sons who will be the light of the world in the Torah and in fear [of God], and who will increase peace in the world. And she gives her husband long life. Therefore she must take care in [the act of kindling the lights].

Note that the motif of the High Priest lighting the candelabrum, as it appears in the *tkhine*, is interpolated into the middle of this passage.

In addition, there is no passage in the Zohar that corresponds precisely to the *tkhine*'s description of the High Priest.[35] There are two possible explanations for this lack of a source passage in the Zohar for the motif of the High Priest. Shifrah might have used an intermediate source that does contain this passage, or she might have added material of her own composition. Both in fact turn out to be the case.

Analysis of the texts shows that Shifrah made creative use of the material she found in Khotsh's *Nakhalas Tsevi*, her immediate source.[36] Although the book was written in Yiddish, it was addressed to nonscholarly men, not to women.[37] Nonetheless, Shifrah appropriated it for her own purposes. She also combined two separate passages from *Nakhalas Tsevi* and, in so doing, conveyed a new understanding of the significance of women's candle lighting.

> The first passage Shifrah used is Khotsh's paraphrase of Zohar I 48b:
> And the commandment of **the Sabbath candle** was given to the women of **the holy people**, that they might kindle the lights. The sages gave a reason [for this]: Because Eve extinguished the light of the world, and made the cosmos dark by her sin, therefore, they [women] should kindle lights **for the Sabbath**. But the secret meaning of it is this: Because the **Shelter of Peace** rests on us on the Sabbath, and [on] the [Sabbath] souls, therefore, it is proper for the women **below** to act as in the form **above**: to kindle the lights. And because the two souls of human beings shine on the Sabbath, therefore she must kindle two lights. And when the woman kindles the lights, it is fitting for her to kindle them **with joy and with wholeheartedness**, because it is in honor of the Shekhinah. And thus she will be privileged to have holy children who will be the light of the world in Torah and in fear [of God] and who will increase **peace in the world**. And by this means she also gives her husband long life; therefore, it is proper for the women to take great care concerning this.[38]

The wording in this passage is very close, although not identical, to that of Shifrah's *tkhine*. The High Priest, however, is missing.

We find him in another part of *Nakhalas Tsevi*, in a passage that begins by translating Zohar III 149a, an interpretation of Numbers 8:2, and continues on into a section interpolated and apparently written by Khotsh himself. Shifrah uses *only* this interpolation:

> Therefore the text uses the term "*beha'alotekha* [raising]" here, when it would seem it should have used the term for kindling, not for raising. But by kindling the candelabrum below, he [the High Priest] raised the **arousal to the Upper World**. Everything **below** is set out in correspondence with

the **Tabernacle above**. Therefore [the verse] says: **against the face of the candelabrum**. The candelabrum **above** corresponds to the candelabrum **below**. When the priest below has kindled [the candelabrum], then **"the seven lamps shine"**; by this means he has kindled **the seven lamps above**.[39]

Although the wording here does not correspond as precisely to Shifrah's text, this is clearly her source.

A comparison of Shifrah's text with the Zohar and *Nakhalas Tsevi* yields several interesting differences. First, Shifrah rejects the view that women are commanded to light candles to compensate for Eve's sin rather more definitively than her source. She gives the view of "the sages" (*hakhamim*) and then says, "But *this* is the reason for it" (*Ober di zakh iz der tam der fun*). *Nakhalas Tsevi* describes the second view as the "secret" explanation, thus implying that the first reason given has legitimacy as midrashic exegesis (*derash*).[40] Unlike *Nakhalas Tsevi*, Shifrah does not accept an interpretation that sees women's religious activity as punitive.[41]

The Motif of the High Priest in the *Tkhines* for Candle Lighting

Even more interesting is the interpolation of the motif of the priest lighting the candelabrum in the Tabernacle. *Nakhalas Tsevi* and the Zohar do not associate the High Priest with the Sabbath candles. Yet Shifrah does. Why? The answer lies in the literary tradition of *tkhines* for lighting Sabbath candles. Let me give two brief examples. The first is from a *tkhine* that appeared in the collection entitled *Tkhines*, published in Amsterdam in 1648; it was reprinted in *Seder tkhines u-vakoshes*, which first appeared about 1755. Other passages in *Tkhine imrei Shifre* also seem to have been influenced by this work.

> Lord of the World, I have done all my work in the six days, and will now rest, as you have commanded, and will kindle two lights, according to the requirements of our holy Torah, as interpreted by our sages, to honor You and the holy Sabbath. . . . And may the lights be, in your eyes, like the lights which the priest kindled in the Temple, and let our light not be extinguished, and let your light shine upon us.[42]

The second example is from *The Three Gates*, attributed to Sarah bas Tovim, perhaps the most popular collection of *tkhines* ever published:

Lord of the World, may my [observance of the] commandment of kindling the lights be accepted as the act of the High Priest when he kindled the lights in the dear Temple was accepted. **"Your word is a lamp to my feet and a light to my path"** (Ps. 119:105). This means: Your speech is a light to my feet; may the feet of my children walk on God's path. May my kindling of the lights be accepted, so that my children's eyes may be enlightened in the dear Torah. I also pray over the candles that my [observance of the] commandment may be accepted by the dear God, be blessed, like the light [which] burned from olive oil in the Temple and was not extinguished.[43]

Although both passages enhance the significance of the woman's act by comparing it to that of the High Priest, neither contains even a trace of a kabbalistic interpretation of either act. Whatever the origin of this comparison,[44] Shifrah endows it with a very different meaning by placing the motif of the High Priest in the passage that establishes a correspondence between the woman lighting Sabbath candles below and the Shekhinah, who rests upon the Sabbath souls, above. As far as I know, this motif does not appear in other *tkhines*. Thus, in comparison with *Nakhalas Tsevi* and the Zohar, Shifrah's innovation is to introduce the High Priest into the discussion of the Shekhinah and the Sabbath candles. Within the literary tradition of the *tkhines*, her innovation is to join material about the Shekhinah and the Sabbath souls to the motif of the High Priest.

Both Shifrah's *tkhine* and *Nakhalas Tsevi* soften the boldest assertion of the Zohar: "Thus, the woman must light the candles, for the Lady [*matronita*; the Shekhinah] adheres to her and acts [through her]. And the woman must light the Sabbath candles with joy of the heart and goodwill, for it is a supernal honor for her." While *Nakhalas Tsevi* draws a comparison between the woman and the Shekhinah,[45] it does not describe the identification as an embodiment. Thus, in the two Yiddish works, as opposed to the Zohar, the woman honors, but does not embody, the Shekhinah: "And when the woman kindles the lights, it is fitting for her to kindle [them] with joy and with wholeheartedness, because it is in honor of the Shekhinah and in honor of the Sabbath and in honor of the extra [Sabbath] soul."[46]

In diminishing the significance of the woman's act, Shifrah follows *Nakhalas Tsevi*, which, like other popularizations and adaptations of kabbalistic texts in Yiddish, often blunts the edge of the most daring material. Yet whereas *Nakhalas Tsevi*'s adaptation of the Zohar means that the woman is no longer seen as acting theurgically and mythologically, Shifrah's combination of the two passages transforms the lighting of Sabbath candles into a fully kabbalistic act.

Nakhalas Tsevi understands the acts of the High Priest as having cosmic significance. By kindling the earthly candelabrum, the High Priest raises the lights to the heavenly candelabrum and arouses the *sefirot* to love and union. Thus, when the woman in the *tkhine* acts as the High Priest, her deed, too, possesses full mystical significance and theurgic efficacy. In the words of the *tkhine*, "Therefore, by kindling the lamps for the holy Sabbath, we awaken great arousal [*hit'orerut*] in the upper world." This sentence is not found in either passage in *Nakhalas Tsevi*. It is Shifrah's own.

In its adaptation and transformation of material from *Nakhalas Tsevi*, *Tkhine imrei Shifre* is evidence for a limited sort of participation by women in kabbalistic thinking. Whether or not this was the intention of their authors, the Yiddish adaptations of kabbalistic materials that sprang from the Safed revival made some kabbalistic symbols and concepts available to women. It may be that the religious ferment surrounding the rise of the Sabbatian, Frankist, and hasidic movements stimulated women to use these materials to construct their own religious understandings. Even so, among *tkhines*, Shifrah's text is exceptional for its explicitly kabbalistic interpretation of women's religious activity.

The theological question is how women understood their place in the kabbalistic symbol system and whether they adapted the materials available to them to create a distinctive religious language. *Tkhine imrei Shifre* transforms the symbol system, but not in a fully coherent way. It rejects the association of women with sin inherent in the idea of lighting Sabbath candles as punishment. Yet the woman lighting candles does not act in concert with—or as an echo of—the Shekhinah, as the text of the Zohar suggests she should. Rather, she assumes the active role of the male High Priest. The High Priest represents the kabbalistic worshiper, who approaches the world of the Godhead through his relationship to the lowest and mediating *sefirah*, the Shekhinah. Thus, for a woman to become a full-fledged kabbalistic actor, she must become, symbolically, male.[47] This text, at least, has not achieved a transformation of the kabbalistic system that allows a woman *as woman* to be a kabbalist.

Perhaps Shifrah did not grasp the fine points of sefirotic symbolism and did not realize how ambiguous an image she was creating. She was, after all, working within a textual tradition that already contained a comparison between the woman and the High Priest. Or perhaps she was making use of the gender ambivalence built into the kabbalistic symbol system. As Elliot Wolfson has argued, in arousing the Shekhinah, the male adept—in our example symbolized by the High Priest— is actually integrated into Her, and feminized.[48] In addition, until I have verified that Shifrah bas Joseph or some other woman was the actual author of this text, I cannot be absolutely certain that the adaptation was indeed made by a woman.

Despite these unsolved problems, this text does challenge, in however small a way, the view that Kabbalah was made exclusively "for men and by men."[49] Even if this passage was authored by a man, *someone* thought that women could perform at least one *mitsvah* the way men are supposed to perform all *mitsvot*. Furthermore, this view of the significance of *likht-bentshn*—candle lighting, a quintessentially womanly act—is found in a *tkhine*, a text specifically aimed at a female audience. The women who *read* this text, who recited it as they performed the gender-specific *mitsvah* of kindling the Sabbath lights, could think of this act as having cosmic ramifications.

CHAPTER SEVEN

TEARS FOR THE SHEKHINAH

LEAH HOROWITZ

Considering the difficulty of establishing authorship of the *tkhines* with certainty, we are fortunate in possessing at least one, entitled *The Tkhine of the Matriarchs* (*Tkhine imohos*), whose author is amply documented in many sources in addition to the *tkhine* itself.[1] Thus, we can sketch a fuller portrait of her than of any other *tkhine* author. Sarah Rebecca Rachel Leah (usually known as Leah) was the daughter of Jacob Yokl ben Meir Ha-Levi Horowitz (1680–1755) and Reyzel bat Heshel. Leah Horowitz was a highly unusual woman in the traditional Ashkenazic world, both in writing for publication at all, and in the extent of her knowledge of the classical Jewish sources. Unlike other women who composed *tkhines*, she wrote not only in Yiddish but also in Hebrew and Aramaic:[2] her *Tkhine of the Matriarchs* contains a Hebrew introduction, a *piyyut* (a liturgical poem) in Aramaic, and a prose Yiddish paraphrase of the poem.[3] Leah is thus one of the most learned Jewish women of her era, and, in reading her work, we learn something of what a truly exceptional woman *could* know, as well as something of what she thought less learned women could and should know and do.[4]

Because Leah came from a distinguished and learned family, members of the aristocracy of Ashkenazic culture, much information about her immediate family is easily recoverable. Leah's father, Jacob Yokl, became rabbi of the city of Brody after serving as rabbi of Bolechow, in Polish Galicia (southern Poland), from 1711 to 1735.[5] While in Brody, Yokl seems to have been involved in the *kloyz*, a circle of scholars and mystics important in the very early stages of hasidism.[6] Because he joined other noted scholars of Brody in denouncing the adulterous behavior of a wealthy woman, her influential relatives forced him to abandon his post, probably in 1742.[7] He then settled in Gross-Glogau, where he remained as rabbi until his death.[8]

Leah was one of about seven children. Three of her brothers were rabbis: Menachem Manes (1700–1768), rabbi of Zmigrod Nowy and Lvov; Isaac (1715–1767), rabbi of Brody and the community of Hamburg, Altona, and Wandsbeck; and Mordecai, who succeeded Yokl in Bolechow. Isaac, known as Reb Itsikl Hamburger, was especially renowned. Leah's sister Pessil had a reputation as a very spiritual person: their grandnephew, the hasidic rebbe Naftali of Ropczyce, reportedly said of her that she had the soul of the matriarchs. There may have been another brother, Israel, and another sister whose name is no longer remembered, the wife of Zeev Wolf Landau, rabbi of Krzeszów.[9] As the sister of eminent brothers, Leah disproves the old canard that the only educated woman were the daughters of learned rabbis who had no sons.

When Yokl left Bolechow for Brody, his son Mordecai was appointed to fill the vacancy he left. The memoirist Ber of Bolechow, who was then a boy of twelve, used to come to R. Mordecai's house on Sabbath afternoons for a Talmud lesson. He recalls meeting R. Mordecai's learned sister:

> At that time there dwelt with him his modest sister, the learned and famous Mistress Leah, of blessed memory, who remained here after the departure of her father and mother for the holy community of Brody, and she was married to the rabbi, our teacher, Aryeh Leib son of the rabbi, the head of the rabbinical court of the holy community of Dobromil.[10] It would happen that the rabbi [Mordecai] would show me a law in the Talmud to read, and then lie down to take a nap after lunch, as he was always a sickly man. His sister, the above-mentioned woman Mistress Leah, used to sit at a distance, and she would look over and notice how I did not understand the discussion in the Talmud and Rashi's commentary. She would say to me, "What are you puzzled about over there? Tell me which words of the Talmud you are in doubt about." So I would begin to tell her some of the words of the Talmud that was before me, or the words of Rashi,[11] and she would begin to recite the words of Talmud or Rashi by heart, in clear language, explaining it well as it was written there, and I learned from her words. And when the rabbi awoke from his sleep, I knew how to explain the passage in the Talmud to him properly.[12]

From this passage we can ascertain the approximate dates of Leah's life. Ber of Bolechow, born in 1723,[13] was twelve at the time of his encounter with Leah, so it must have taken place in 1735, shortly after her father's departure for Brody. Ber also mentions that Leah was married. Because she and her husband were living with Mordecai, she had probably married within the previous few years, since it was customary for young couples to board for several years with one or the other set of parents, usually the wife's. This arrangement, called *kest*, was written into the marriage contract: its primary purpose was to allow the young husband to continue his studies (or, in less scholarly families, to establish himself in business). Considering the young ages at which children of upper-class Jewish families usually married during this period—her brother Isaac married at twelve—Leah was probably born about 1720.

From Ber's memoir, we can also estimate Leah's date of death. He adds the locution "of blessed memory" after her name, thus indicating that at the time of writing she was already dead. While the date of composition of Ber's memoir is not known with certainty, Mark Vishnitzer estimates that it was written between 1790 and 1800.[14] Thus, Leah had almost certainly died by 1800.

Ber's encounter with Leah also tells us something of her character. He refers to her as "famous," although it is not clear whether she was famous at the time or became so only later. Nonetheless, it is clear that she knew the Talmud well. Other authors also mentioned her talmudic scholarship. The great halakhic authority Joseph Saul Nathanson cites an interpretation of a point in the Talmud that he heard attributed to her. While this attribution is probably erroneous,[15] it shows that Leah was well known for her talmudic expertise.

Leah's talmudic learning is also evident from the text of the *Tkhine of the Matriarchs* itself, especially the introduction. Equally apparent from the text is her knowledge of kabbalistic sources, particularly the *Zohar*, although none of the biographical sources I examined mentions her knowledge of Kabbalah, which was probably even rarer among women than expertise in halakhic literature. That Leah possessed such knowledge, however, is shown by her citations from the *Zohar* and her free use of kabbalistic concepts and imagery.

ON BEING A LEARNED WOMAN

Leah Horowitz was passionately concerned with the religious place and role of Jewish women, and she was keenly aware of her own anomalous status as a learned woman. While she defended her right to her own learning, she seems to have thought of herself as so exceptional that she could not imagine other women like herself. Other women, she seems to agree, live up to the stereotypes: they chatter away in synagogue, more concerned with their wardrobes than with salvation. But, she would also say, they have the potential for real spiritual power. For this reason, she seeks to fashion a paradigm that even unlearned women can follow to actualize that spiritual power.

Leah addresses these issues both explicitly, in the Hebrew introduction to her *tkhine*, and by implication, in the Aramaic *piyyut* and the Yiddish paraphrase. This is the only premodern text known to me in which an Ashkenazic woman discusses such issues as the significance of women's prayer, the proper way for women to pray, and the circumstances under which women should and should not submit to their husband's authority. Thus, the two-page introduction to this *tkhine* is an extremely precious historical document. Yet it is a text we must read with pain. Writing in Hebrew for women, Leah literally had no audience: men were not interested, and women could not read Hebrew. Indeed, after the first few editions, the printers simply dropped the Hebrew introduction and usually the Aramaic *piyyut* as well.[16] Leah's efforts to speak about women's prayer and women's power, and her attempts to legitimate her own voice as authoritative, were silenced.

Leah *was* an anomaly: one can distinguish what she says about herself from what she says about women in general. She seems particularly concerned, both in the introduction to the *tkhine* and according to some of the external sources about her, to establish the legitimacy of her own involvement in "Torah study," that is, in talmudic discussion.

After all, from the mishnaic period (the first centuries of the Common Era), the study of the Torah was defined as the highest religious duty of Jewish men.[17] Throughout most of Jewish history Torah study was primarily understood to mean the study of the Oral Torah, especially the Talmud. The Talmud itself contains a discussion about whether or not one is *permitted* to teach women Torah. (The fact that women are not *obligated* to study Torah is undisputed.) While Ben Azzai does say that a man should teach his daughter Torah, or at least certain parts of it for rather particular reasons, the majority opinion follows Rabbi Eliezer that "one who teaches his daughter Torah is as if he taught her foolishness (or lewdness)."[18] In all of the Mishnah and Talmud, one finds only a single woman scholar, Beruriah.[19]

For most of Jewish history, most authorities forbade women to study Torah. In its broadest interpretation (for example, among Yemenite

Jews), this was taken to mean that women were forbidden even to learn to read and write.[20] Understood more narrowly, women were permitted to study practical *halakhah*, to learn the commandments that applied to them, and sometimes the Written Torah, but they were forbidden to study the classic halakhic works, such as the Mishnah and Talmud, as well as speculative and mystical material.[21] In the Ashkenazic world, even those exceptional women from learned families who were known for their scholarship usually were expert in the Hebrew Bible and rabbinic Midrash.[22] Moreover, because women were not obligated to study Torah, it followed according to a general principle of Jewish law that those who did were considered to merit a lesser reward than did men who studied, because for them study was a religious duty.[23]

Considering this background, it is not surprising that Leah's learning was sometimes greeted with criticism or astonishment. One source reports a sharp exchange between Leah and the chief rabbi of Berlin on the subject of women's learning. Whether it records an actual historical event, we have no way of knowing, but it is consistent with the picture we get from Leah's own writings and other sources.

Our teacher the eminent Yokl Ha-Levi Horowitz, head of the rabbinical court of Glogau, had a daughter, the rabbi's wife, Sarah Rebecca Rachel Leah, who wrote the *Tkhine of the Matriarchs*, the wife of our teacher, the eminent Shabbetai, head of the rabbinical court of Krasnik. She was a great scholar, well versed in the Talmud. Once she was invited to a wedding, along with our teacher the eminent Tsevi Hirsh, head of the rabbinical court of the holy community of Berlin,[24] and there as well was the rabbi's wife, Mistress Dinah, wife of our teacher, the eminent [Saul], head of the rabbinical court of the holy community of the Hague.[25] And together they [the women] engaged in Talmudic discussion. When our teacher the eminent Tsevi Hirsh heard this, he was very surprised, and he said to them, "It is the practice of scholars to make a jest before beginning study, and I would like to hear your skill at this." And the rabbi's wife, the daughter of our teacher the eminent Yokl, answered that the reason for this is because of the holiness of the Torah, according to the command of the sages of blessed memory, for they feared that the evil inclination and Satan might also come to seize onto this, God forbid. So therefore, when they begin with a jest, the externality[26] of the Torah would go to him [Satan], and they would then be able to study Torah for its own sake. But this is not the case with us, who are not commanded [to study Torah]. There is nothing strange within us that can come to suckle from the holiness of the study, and this is what Solomon said (Prov. 31:26), "She opens her mouth with wisdom," that the woman can begin [literally "open"] with Torah study without her having to make a jest first, and therefore it is written "and the teaching of kindness [the Torah of Hesed] is on her tongue," that is, Torah for its own sake; and see Sukkah (49b), where they interpret "the teaching of kindness" to mean "Torah study for its own sake."[27]

Leah's "jest" is a stunning retort to the challenge posed by the rabbi of Berlin. She takes the disadvantage under which women labor—of not being commanded to engage in Torah study—and turns it to their advantage. The custom of beginning the study of halakhah with a jest is mentioned in the Talmud, where it appears in a discussion of whether joy or awe is the proper state for such study.[28] Probably, this talmudic reference is all that Tsevi Hirsch had in mind, but Leah gives the matter an additional twist, by making use of the later kabbalistic view of the significance of this custom of jesting.

According to kabbalistic doctrine, Satan and his demonic forces are drawn to acts of holiness from which they try to nourish themselves. They are able to do this, however, only if there is something impure in the performance of the act. In the case of Torah study, men are in danger of feeling prideful in fulfilling their religious duty or of harboring ambitions for fame and power because of their scholarship. Yet the demonic forces can be "bought off," much as one throws a dog a bone, by some sop—in this case a jest, not true Torah study, but the "externality" of the Torah.[29] The jest provides an outlet for pride or ambition. Once that has been gotten over, the men can then get down to study Torah "for its own sake," with a pure heart. But women, Leah says, who are not commanded to study Torah, are in no such danger and may begin their study directly without such a jest or pleasantry. Indeed, women speak the "Torah of Hesed," the Torah that stems from the Right Side of God, far from the wellsprings of the powers of evil on the Left. Leah's "jest," then, turns on the fact that women need not jest, whereas male scholars, such as her challenger Tsevi Hirsh, rightfully fear the demons of pride and ambition.

In her own writing as well, Leah was quick to deflect possible challenges to her authority to address halakhic matters, and to rebut denigration of the latent spiritual power of women. The sharp tongue she turned on Tsevi Hirsh is still detectable, if more muted, in the introduction to the *Tkhine of the Matriarchs*. Already, early on in the introduction she writes, "Although you may say that a woman is not competent in reasoned argument, nonetheless, 'the crown of Torah is left [for the generations],' and in my view, I am bringing merit to the many."[30] Quoting Ecclesiastes Rabba 7:2 here, Leah is perhaps thinking of Avot de-Rabbi Nathan 41: "But the crown of Torah is not thus [restricted to certain segments of the population, as are the crowns of priesthood and kingship]. Whoever wishes to undertake to toil in the Torah may do so"—even, she implies, herself, a woman.

THE *TKHINE OF THE MATRIARCHS*

This *tkhine* also sheds light on Leah's view of the proper religious role for women, especially the nature and importance of women's prayer. Leah, as we shall see, is engaging in an explicit polemic about several aspects of women's religious activity. Her views about other women are also implicit in the Yiddish paraphrase of the Hebrew and Aramaic portions of her text: she omits technical kabbalistic and talmudic material in the Yiddish. On the surface, this approach resembles the transformations found in Western European *tkhines* based on kabbalistic models; these, as we recall from Chapter 1, simply excluded women from the kabbalistic mysteries. But while those *tkhines* could be seen as disempowering women, Leah sought to empower them. As is evident from its title, this text assigns a central role to the matriarchs. One sees from an analysis of the images of the matriarchs, and especially of the changes in the depiction of Rachel in the Aramaic and Yiddish portions of the text, how Leah sought to help women with no knowledge of Kabbalah enact their religious power.

The Hebrew Introduction:
Women's Prayer and Women's Power

Leah was a poor Hebrew stylist: the Hebrew introduction contains a series of convoluted and complex discussions and is often difficult to decipher. Her two major themes are the importance of women's prayer and the nature of proper prayer; these topics are closely interrelated. Secondary themes include critiques of behavior and practices she considered improper, as well as consideration of the proper balance of authority between husband and wife. Throughout, Leah argues that women have greater religious importance than is usually thought.

In her introduction, Leah underlines the power of women's prayer when it is undertaken with proper devotion. Her point is that women too can be a source of "prayer for the sake of heaven," a point she supports with a medieval commentary by Rabbi Jacob ben Asher on Exodus 38:8, concerning the "ministering women at the door of the tent of meeting." She then tartly remarks, "I have many other proofs. . . . This matter has certainly not escaped the discerning eye, and I will not speak in the ears of a fool."

Yes, more commandments apply to men, but, she stresses, women have the power to bring redemption: "Well-known are the words of Rav Aha which are cited in Yalkut Ruth,[31] that the generations are only redeemed by the merit of women." This is partly because of the redemptive power of tears, and "tears are common among women." Sadly, however, the full redemptive power of women's prayer is unrealized, because prayer is only heard in synagogue,[32] and in these generations, women do not attend synagogue for daily prayers. But Leah insists that women should attend synagogue every day, morning and evening. "It is proper for the women of our day, 'for the day of the Lord is near,' to go to the synagogue morning and evening to pray with 'copious tears.'" Unfortunately, as she notes, when they do come to synagogue, it is often to spend their time in idle chatter, comparing their clothes and jewelry, instead of praying with true devotion.

Because this particular criticism of women's behavior in synagogue is found in so many sources,[33] it is hard to know in this instance whether Leah's strictures against women's behavior in synagogue derive from her own experience or represent her acceptance of the stereotype. Earlier in the introduction, she supports the generalization that "women are talkative in the synagogue on the Sabbath" by citing a story derived from rabbinic literature,[34] not by describing what she herself has witnessed.

Leah devotes considerable attention to the matter of true prayer, because women can realize the spiritual power of their prayer only if they know how to pray properly. Proper prayer, in her view, is for the sake of the Shekhinah (divine presence), the tenth *sefirah*, or emanation, of the Godhead, who mediates between the human and the divine worlds. This understanding of prayer sets Leah squarely within the religious universe of early Hasidism. Dov Ber, known as the Maggid (preacher) of Mezhirech (d. 1772), the leader of the movement after the death of Israel Baal Shem Tov in 1760, denied the legitimacy of petitionary prayer: "Let not a person pray concerning matters of his needs, but let him always pray only on behalf of the Shekhinah, that it be redeemed from its exile." The Maggid's disciples transmitted, elaborated, and debated this teaching just at the same time that Leah was likely to have written *The Tkhine of the Matriarchs*, and used some of the same terms.[35]

As I have noted, according to Jewish mystical teaching, the Shekhinah, like Israel, is in exile, and it is the goal of all true prayer and religious performance to end this exile and reunite her with her divine consort, Tiferet, the sixth *sefirah*. The full and final reunification will only come in the era of messianic redemption. Jewish religious activity strives for that final redemption, but also for smaller moments of love and unity among the *sefirot*. Sexual imagery is often used to describe the reunion of Shekhinah and Tiferet. The role of human devotion in prayer, then, can also be described as providing the initial sexual arousal that brings about this union.[36]

In a kabbalistic exegesis of Isaiah 1:12, Leah contrasts the arousal —the "female waters," in the Kabbalah's graphic image[37]—which the Shekhinah (called *zot*, "this") requires from the worshipers, with the "trampling of the courts" that occurs when they instead engage in idle chatter in synagogue. And by interpreting the Talmud's comments (B. Shabbat 32b-33a) on Amos 4:1 ("Hear this word, you cows of Bashan . . .") to mean that Amos criticized these women because they prayed only for their own sustenance, Leah seeks to show that the problem with women's prayer is that they pray for their own material benefit instead of for the sake of the exiled Shekhinah.[38]

Yet another aspect of women's religious practice that Leah regards as improper actually motivated her to write the *Tkhine of the Matriarchs*. Leah explains in her introduction that she is writing this *tkhine* to combat the practice women have of reciting another *tkhine* for the blessing of the new moon, one that contains a confessionary formula and request for forgiveness of sins. She remarks that every schoolchild knows that one ought not to recite confessions on festive days such as the Sabbath and the new moon. Yet these themes made their way into prayers for the blessing of the new moon because women took over material from men's kabbalistic prayers for the Eve of the New Moon, a monthly penitential day in mystical ritual. It is likely that Leah was polemicizing against one particular and popular text, the *tkhine* for the blessing of the new moon, no. 66 in *Seder tkhines u-vakoshes*, discussed in Chapter 1. Ironically, in later years, the latter text was often printed together with the Yiddish portion of Leah's text, both in *tkhine* pamphlets of prayers for the blessing of the new moon and in prayer books, at that juncture in the service.[39]

Interestingly, the prayer preceding the blessing of the new moon, which was entering the Ashkenazic Hebrew liturgy during the eighteenth century,[40] concerns precisely these material needs:

> May it be Thy will, Lord our God, God of our fathers, to bring on the coming new month for our good and blessing. Grant us long life, a life of peace, a life of goodness, a life of blessing, a life with sustenance, a life of vigor and vitality. May it be a life with reverence for Heaven and with fear of sin, a life without shame or ignominy, a life of riches and honor, a life in which there shall be among us love of the Torah and veneration for Heaven.[41]

The *tkhine* for blessing the new moon from *Seder tkhines u-vakoshes* is thematically related to this Hebrew prayer. Its concerns, as well, are sustenance and livelihood, good luck, and protection from evil. Thus, Leah's *tkhine* may represent an implicit criticism both of the newly popular liturgy for this occasion and of *tkhine* no. 66 from *Seder tkhines u-vakoshes*. Clearly, her objections to the latter included more than the problem of reciting confessions on the Sabbath. These selfish requests for material benefit are not prayer at all, according to Leah, but merely the barking of greedy dogs: "They bark like dogs, give us life, etc. There is no one who repents for the sake of the Shekhinah, but all the good that they do, they do only for themselves."[42] Leah offers her own *tkhine* for the Sabbath before the new moon as a substitute for these greedy, self-centered prayers.[43]

Leah also takes up the question of women's obedience to their husbands and, together with this, the famous talmudic passage that inquires: "By what means do women acquire merit? By bringing their sons to read in the synagogue, and sending their husbands to study in the academy, and waiting for their husbands to return from the academy."[44] She finds it astonishing that these vicarious acts could be the only means by which women acquire merit, since all of the negative commandments and most of the positive ones that apply to men also apply to women. Surely, she reasons, this cannot be what the Talmud meant. Rather, she argues, relying on a commentary by Obadiah of Bertinoro on a passage from the Mishnah, the root that we have understood to mean "to acquire merit" (*zkh*) should be understood in its Aramaic sense, "to prevail." Thus, the Talmud is actually asking, Under what circumstances should women prevail over their husbands? Under ordinary circumstances, women should obey their husbands. As Leah puts it, "In all the matters of this world [in which] it is fitting for him to be a man, let him be a man. 'Even a weaver is a policeman in his own house!'"[45] But regarding "matters of the world to come," such as Torah study, the Talmud specifies that women should prevail over their husbands and prevent them from neglecting Torah study or from causing such neglect on the part of their children.[46]

In sum, the introduction gives a mixed picture of women and their religious role. While stressing their great potential power for bringing redemption, Leah is critical of their actual behavior. And as she argues that key religious texts about women have been misunderstood, to the detriment of women, she also states unambiguously that "a worthy woman does the will of her husband." Leah understands that women's subordination to men is, under most circumstances, a fact of life.

One edition of this text, published in Grodno in 1796, includes a Yiddish paraphrase of the introduction instead of the Hebrew original, along with the *piyyut* in Aramaic, and its paraphrase, the Yiddish *tkhine*. It is impossible to be sure whether Leah herself prepared the Yiddish paraphrase of the introduction. Considering the late date of publication, however, I think it unlikely, although the title page does not indicate that the author is deceased. Still, a comparison with the original Hebrew introduction offers us additional information about women's religious roles, regardless of who was responsible for the paraphrase.

First, the Yiddish is considerably easier to understand than the Hebrew. Clearly, much thought was devoted to getting at the meaning of the original: whoever did the translation consolidated and ordered the scattered pieces of Leah's various arguments, polemics, and exegeses and also consulted at least some of Leah's sources.[47] The omissions are also significant: for example, the entire discussion of when a woman should prevail over her husband is simply dropped. Further, although Leah is usually careful in how she cites most of her sources in rabbinic and kabbalistic literature, the Yiddish paraphrase gives the sources in a much more general and sometimes misleading form. Most interpretations or citations are simply attributed to the Talmud, the midrash, or the "Holy Zohar." Thus, where Leah cites Yalkut Shimoni, a collection of midrashim, on Ruth, the Yiddish paraphrase attributes the interpretation to the Talmud. Since it is apparent that the paraphraser has actually consulted the source whose title he or she omits, the motivation for making such a change is not obvious.

Nonetheless, the Yiddish version of the introduction retains the assertion that redemption will come because of the merit of righteous women, because redemptive tears are more common among women than men. It further asserts, although less vigorously than the original does, that women should pray in the synagogue morning and evening. (It also retains the condemnation of women's improper behavior in synagogue.) Perhaps most striking, the Yiddish version forcefully makes the point that one should weep and pray for the sake of the Shekhinah:

> And it is known that prayer is called **service**, and the key aspect of prayer [is weeping]. And one must weep for the sake of **the exile of the Shekhinah**, but not for the sake of food, because that cannot be called either prayer or **service**. . . . [48]
>
> . . . And they should pray, and weep about **the exile of the Shekhinah**, and not for the sake of **the needs of this world**. And because of our many sins, today . . . people are wont to go straight to the subject of livelihood. . . . And they exchange the world to come, which is **an enduring world**, for this world, which is a **transitory world**.

This is a more straightforward formulation than Leah's original, in which one has to puzzle through the citations, allusions, and exegeses. Here again, the Yiddish version omits technical kabbalistic material: no mention is made of the requirement of the Shekhinah for the "female waters"; proper prayer seems simply to consist in praying for the end of the exile of the Shekhinah and disregarding one's material needs.

Did anyone think that this sort of "scaled-down" prayer for the sake of the Shekhinah could actually bring redemption? Was this a sop to women, or was it a serious attempt to include them in the Safed revival? Was it a conscious rejection of the overblown complexity of the Lurianic *kavvanot* of prayer, akin to that found in Hasidism?

Several factors suggest that the paraphraser has caught Leah's true intent: this text is indeed meant to show women how to pray efficaciously for the Shekhinah, despite their having no knowledge of Kabbalah. We see, further, that Leah offers the midrashic picture of the weeping Rachel and the weeping children of Israel as a paradigm for redemptive prayer. That is, she wrote this text to *show* women how to pray "for the sake of the Shekhinah."

It is quite relevant that for the kabbalists, as Moshe Idel points out, weeping was a technique of both theosophical contemplation, that is, of envisioning the hidden nature of the Godhead,[49] and theurgical manipulation, that is, of bringing about changes in the relations among the *sefirot* so as influence earthly life.[50] Idel cites a sermon by R. Hayyim Vital, the disciple of Isaac Luria, who remarks that theurgical weeping works "automatically." One need not be a learned kabbalist or even a righteous man: "There is no need that the weeper should be a righteous and honest [man], since everyone who sheds [tears] is causing this . . . even if the weeper is [part of] the vulgus."[51] For Idel this signals "a shift from elitist theurgy, characteristic of Lurianic Kabbalah, to a popular one, characteristic afterward of Hasidic mysticism. . . . By means of this change, the spread of Kabbalah among large masses was facilitated."[52]

Leah seems to have held a similar view, whether or not she knew this text by Vital. The *Tkhine of the Matriarchs* thus transforms certain kabbalistic ideas in a way that facilitates their transmission to "the masses."[53]

The Aramaic *Piyyut* and the Yiddish *Tkhine*

In addition to the introduction, Leah's text consists of a liturgical poem (a *piyyut*) in Aramaic and a prose paraphrase of it in Yiddish, both of which contain acrostics of the author's name, a standard way of indicating authorship. The Yiddish paraphrase is the *tkhine* proper; most later editions of the *Tkhine of the Matriarchs* include only the Yiddish portion of the text. Let me briefly summarize those elements of the *piyyut* and the *tkhine* that parallel one another; divergences will be noted later.

In both, Leah begins by briefly recapitulating God's creation of the world in six days and the institution of Sabbath rest. Relying on a rabbinic tradition that God rested *from speech* (the means of creation) on the seventh day, she stresses here, as well as in her introduction, that the Sabbath is a time to avoid idle talk[54] and to speak only of heavenly matters and Torah study. "And ignorant folk and women should busy themselves in their homes in the easy language [i.e., Yiddish] concerning what they are obligated to do according to the commandments."

Next, Leah recalls that, in addition to the gift of the Sabbath, God gave Israel festivals and new moons. When Israel still dwelt in Zion, the new moon was proclaimed according to the testimony of witnesses.[55] But now, in this era of exile, all that remains is the blessing of the new moon, an appropriate occasion for supplication.

This supplication constitutes the thematic heart of the work, the plea for redemption from exile. Leah describes Israel's suffering in exile and asks God to take vengeance against Israel's oppressors. Most importantly, she asks that God redeem Israel because of the merit of the four matriarchs, Sarah, Rebecca, Rachel, and Leah, and she describes the merit of each. Returning to the occasion of the blessing of the new moon, she asks that that the "Daughter of Abraham" be redeemed from her degrading servitude "this month."

Finally, Leah adds a little coda that introduces a new theme. She briefly restates the reciprocal love between Israel and God (described as "my beloved" in Aramaic and "our dear father" in Yiddish), and then prays that teachers and authors of holy books, including authors of "prayers and supplications" (*tefillot u-tehinnot*), be granted male offspring, sons who will be scholars and serve God "with perfect hearts."[56]

I will focus on only two of the issues suggested by these parts of the text. First, in what sense—theurgic or nontheurgic—are the Aramaic and Yiddish sections prayers for the sake of the Shekhinah, which Leah in her introduction has stressed is the only true prayer? Second, what views of women's religious role and power are implied in these parts of the text? What can be learned of this from the comparison between the Aramaic and Yiddish texts? And what is to be learned from the portrayal of the matriarchs as paradigms of spiritually powerful women? Here, too, the differences in the Aramaic and Yiddish texts provide the key to unlocking the meanings of the text.

Prayer for the Sake of the Shekhinah. I have noted that "prayer for the sake of the Shekhinah" can have two interrelated goals. First, mystical prayer can strive to bring about the union of Shekhinah and Tiferet now, a fragile union that is liable to disruption as long as the cosmos remains in its unredeemed state. In her introduction, especially in her exegesis of Isaiah 1:12, Leah seems to stress this aspect of devoted prayer: to bring about the arousal of the Shekhinah, the "female waters." When Shekhinah and Tiferet are united, and all the *sefirot* are in balance and harmony with each other, the Shekhinah is the conduit to the lower spheres of divine abundance and blessing. The second and ultimate goal of mystical prayer, then, is to bring about the redemption of the cosmos, which on the heavenly plane includes the unceasing union and harmony of the *sefirot*, and on the earthly plane, the end of Israel's exile.[57]

Leah's *piyyut* and *tkhine* are prayers for the Shekhinah in this second sense: they are about exile and redemption. Further, they are intended for the time of the announcement of the new moon, the moon being a symbol of the Shekhinah. This prayer heralds the waxing of the moon and the increase of the Shekhinah's power. The Aramaic *piyyut* begins:

And thus, you have given us festivals for joy and new moons for remembrance. And when we were in Jerusalem, city of beauty, the seat of the dwelling house of our Mother the Shekhinah, of all beauty, the heads of the community would consecrate [the new moon] according to eyewitnesses. But in this era of exile, nothing is left to us except the blessing of the new moon.

And it is a time appropriate for supplication, when the appointed time has come to bless the new moon. We spread out our hands to our merciful Father in heaven: Cause us to return as in days of yore, for the endurance of the tender young kid is failing as in the noonday heat. Our joy, our festivals, and our new moons have ceased. We are like orphans without a father and like sheep without a shepherd. The enemy has stretched out his hand over all that is precious, and there is none to say, Restore! God of vengeance, shine forth from Mount Paran! He who answered our fathers, he will answer us on this new moon, and that by the merit of the ancient mountains and hills [i.e., the patriarchs and matriarchs].[58]

This is not a kabbalistic prayer for the reunification of Shekhinah and Tiferet; it contains no kabbalistic techniques of prayer, such as *kavvanot* or *yihudim*.[59] Nonetheless, it is a prayer for the redemption of the children of Israel from exile, by definition, a plea for the restoration of cosmic harmony. This identification is expressed, in kabbalistic symbolism, by equating *Keneset Yisrael* (the community of Israel) with the Shekhinah. Thus, Israel and the Shekhinah are one. The vengeance wreaked upon the earthly Israel's enemies is symbolic of the victory of Shekhinah over the forces of evil that beset her and try to keep her from Tiferet.[60]

Farther on in the text, Leah uses the symbol of the Daughter of Abraham to express these two levels of meaning:[61] "The Daughter of Abraham our father is under the law of the exile that degrades [her]; the Daughter of Abraham dwells under harsh masters; this one says, Strike! and his fellow says, Let me be like him."

In the words of a talmudic interpretation, "'How graceful are your feet in sandals, O daughter of a noble! (Song 7:2)' [This refers to] the Daughter of Abraham our father, who is called noble." Because this remark occurs within the framework of standard rabbinic exegesis of the Song of Songs as a dialogue between God and Israel, this means that the Daughter of Abraham is identified with the people of Israel.[62] However, the kabbalists, drawing on a talmudic passage which speculates that Abraham had a daughter named "Ba-kol" (with everything), identify this daughter with the Shekhinah.[63] Thus, "the Daughter of Abraham dwells under harsh masters" means the Shekhinah is in exile. Further, since the exile of the Shekhinah is the cosmic enactment of the earthly exile of Israel, the two meanings of "Daughter of Abraham" echo one another. The Yiddish version of the text, however, identifies the daughter of Abraham less ambiguously, simply as "us," that is, the people of Israel: "We will certainly be called **Daughter of Abraham**, the children of Abraham our father; but today we must be in unmerciful hands."

So this seems to be prayer *for the sake of* the Shekhinah. But it is not theurgic prayer, which, according to esoteric techniques, can actually effect some change in her status. Technically speaking, this is not prayer that *can* bring about the "female waters" which the Shekhinah demands, except insofar as all "good deeds" help to tip the balance toward the forces of light. Does this mean that Leah was not familiar with the techniques of mystical prayer? Or did she consider them unsuitable for her audience? Neither, I would argue. Rather, she thought that nontechnical prayer about redemption and the Shekhinah, and especially prayer that includes weeping, *could* be efficacious in bringing about love and union among the *sefirot*.

Aramaic Transformed into Yiddish. As the foregoing discussion has suggested, the Aramaic and Yiddish versions of this prayer differ in significant ways. First, as in so many Yiddish adaptations of Hebrew or Aramaic texts, the paraphrase is "dekabbalized." While the Aramaic does not qualify as *theurgic* prayer, at least according to the kabbalistic elite, it does contain many more kabbalistic references than does the Yiddish. The Aramaic refers to Jerusalem as "the seat of our Mother the Shekhinah," while the Yiddish omits any mention of the Shekhinah. As we have seen, in the Aramaic, "the Daughter of Abraham" seems to be a dual symbol of the Shekhinah and the people of Israel, while in the Yiddish it refers unambiguously to the people of Israel. Finally, the Aramaic version of the prayer for sons asks for "male children, from the Male World, the Right Side, wise in the Torah, and obeying the will of their Father in heaven, in most supernal fear and love, like Moses the Faithful Shepherd, the beloved son of the supernal Father and Mother."

This is a purely kabbalistic description. The right side of the Godhead, of course, contains those *sefirot* associated with loving kindness and maleness, whereas the *sefirot* on the left side are associated with stern judgment, femaleness, and, ultimately, the origin of evil. In zoharic terminology, "Male World" refers to Binah, the third *sefirah*, the "upper mother," while "Female World" refers to Shekhinah, the "lower mother." Sometimes "Male World" refers to all of the *sefirot* between Binah and Yesod, the ninth *sefirah*, while the "Female World" includes the Shekhinah together with the demonic forces attached to her from below. "The root of the soul of the male is from the *sefirot* Binah to Yesod (as is explained in Zohar II 105b), and the root of the female . . . is in Malkhut [=the Shekhinah]"; thus, if a son is desired, his soul *must* come from these upper *sefirot*.[64] Further, the desired son is to be like Moses, who was described in the Zohar as the son of Tiferet and Malkhut: "His Father is none other than the Holy Blessed One, and his Mother is none other than *Keneset Yisrael*."[65] The Yiddish, by contrast, simply asks for "**worthy, living, and healthy offspring**; may they be scholars, and may they serve God **with perfect hearts** and with love, [together] with [all] the pious ones, Amen." (Despite Leah's passionate defense of the spiritual power of women, her text makes no mention of the desirability of *female* offspring.)

Thus, at one level, it seems that in adapting her own text into Yiddish, Leah is following the (probably male) adapters of Hebrew paraliturgical devotions into the Western European *tkhines*, which we discussed in Chapters 1 and 2.[66] Leah, too, seems to feel that technical kabbalistic terminology and references are not appropriate for (most?) women. Why she thinks this is not clear. Perhaps it simply represents her acknowledgment that women do not have the requisite knowledge to understand such matters.

This is consistent with her earlier statements in the Aramaic *piyyut*, in which she argues that Sabbath rest includes rest from worldly speech:

> And you commanded the holy people that they rest from all words, except as they occupy themselves with the business of heaven and the secret mysteries [i.e., study of Kabbalah]. And ignorant folk and women should busy themselves in their homes in the easy language [i.e., Yiddish] concerning what they are obligated to do according to the commandments.

In Yiddish this reads, in part:

> You dear folk Israel . . . should also rest on the Sabbath, from all work and from words that you ought not to speak. [On the Sabbath, one] should speak only words of Torah, and one should study Torah, each according to his ability. And he who cannot study Torah, and also women, should read in Yiddish and should also understand how to serve God; they should know how to observe their commandments, which God has commanded [them].

Two features are noteworthy here. First, here, too, the reference to "secret mysteries" is omitted in the Yiddish, in which Torah study is presented *tout court* as unattainable for women; mystical study is not even mentioned. Second, in both languages, Leah lumps all women together with those ignorant men who cannot study Torah.[67] She herself was a learned woman, but it does not occur to her to mention other learned women or to include them explicitly in the reminder to devote one's speech to Torah study on the Sabbath. Perhaps the number of learned women was so small that Leah did not consider them as any sort of potential readership.

Images of the Matriarchs. There is yet a further aspect to Leah's Yiddish adaptation of the Aramaic, one bound up with the central thematic feature of this *tkhine*, indicated in its title: the appeal to the merit of the matriarchs in aid of the promised redemption. It seems at first that, except in the case of the matriarch Leah, the power of these women to bring redemption has nothing to do with weeping but rather is related to a fairly standard list of meritorious acts or qualities derived from the Midrash. However, a careful examination of the Yiddish portrayal of the matriarch Rachel (one of the most common symbols of the Shekhinah) shows that this text provides a paradigm for efficacious, redemptive prayer to be followed by women who were not kabbalists. It is a unique treatment. For the other matriarchs, the Aramaic and Yiddish texts are quite similar, except that the Aramaic assumes its readers will recognize the allusions it contains, whereas the Yiddish is more explicit. Let me quote them (except for the Yiddish on Rachel), side by side:

ARAMAIC	YIDDISH
Sarah, for whose sake you commanded, "Touch not my anointed ones (Ps. 105:15)." So may it be for her descendants; may all who touch them be destroyed.	By the merit of our mother Sarah, for whose sake you have commanded and said, "**Touch not my anointed ones**," which means in Yiddish, You nations! Do not dare to touch my righteous ones! Thus too, may no nation have any power [over] her children to touch them for evil.
Rebecca, who caused the blessing [to come] to us; may it soon be fulfilled for us.	By the merit of our mother Rebecca, who caused our father Jacob to receive the blessings from Father Isaac. May these blessings soon be fulfilled for Israel her children!

Rachel, whom you promised, "and your children will come back to their own country (Jer. 31:17)"; cause us to return quickly for her sake.	(see below)
Leah, whose eyes were weak for fear she would fall to the lot of the wicked one; for the sake of her merit, cause our eyes to shine out of the darkness of exile.	And for the sake of the merit of our mother Leah, who wept day and night that she not fall to the lot of the wicked Esau, until her eyes became dim. For the sake of her merit, may you enlighten our eyes out of this dark exile.

This listing of the merits of the matriarchs relies on common biblical and midrashic motifs. Sarah's ability to protect her descendants is linked to her preservation of her own chastity while in the houses of Pharaoh (Gen. 12:10–20) and Abimelech (Gen. 20); the connection is made in the commentary of Midrash Psalms on Psalm 105. Rebecca, as related in Genesis 27, made sure that Jacob (symbolic of the people Israel) rather than Esau (in later Jewish interpretation, symbolic of Christianity—or of the powers of evil) received God's blessing from Isaac. In Jeremiah 31:15–17 God promises the weeping Rachel (although the Aramaic text does not mention her weeping) that her children, though now being sent into exile, will return to their land. And according to the Talmud (B. Baba Batra 123a), Leah's eyes were made weak or soft (Gen. 29:17) by her incessant weeping, caused by her assumption that, as Laban's older daughter, she was destined for Isaac's firstborn son, the wicked Esau.[68] Thus, the merit of the matriarchs consists of their concerns for chastity, for endogamy, for the fate of their offspring. In other words, that they behave like good Jewish wives and mothers is precisely the source of their power to help the people of Israel.

The most powerful section of this *tkhine*, which probably accounted for its great popularity and which, in my view, is the key to its significance, is the account of Rachel in the Yiddish version:

By the merit of our faithful mother, Rachel, to whom you promised that by her merit, we, the children of Israel, would come out of exile. For when the children of Israel were led into exile, they were led not far from the grave in which our mother Rachel lay. They pleaded with the foe to permit them to go to Rachel's tomb. And when the Israelites came to our mother Rachel, and began to weep and cry, "Mother, mother, how can you look on while right in front of you we are being led into exile?" Rachel went up before God with a bitter cry, and spoke: Lord of the world, your mercy is certainly greater than the mercy of any human being. Moreover, I had compassion on my sister Leah when my father switched us and gave her to my husband. He told her to expect that my husband would think that I was the one. No matter that it caused me great pain; I told her the signs [that Jacob and I had agreed upon to prevent the switch]. Thus, even more so, it is undoubtedly fitting for you, God, who are entirely **compassionate and gracious**, to have mercy and bring us out of this exile now. So may it come to pass, for the sake of her merit.

What a dramatic depiction of the children of Israel—they on their way into an exile that punishes them for their unfaithfulness to God, pleading at Rachel's tomb for her aid; and Rachel, for her part, pleading passionately with God for mercy for her children. Rachel, the matriarch most typically identified with the Shekhinah, is moved to recall her own struggles with passion and jealousy. She calls upon God to have compassion for Israel, as she had compassion for her sister. It is a portrayal that expresses the anguish of later Jews in exile and their hope for redemption.

But this passage is more than a heartrending picture: it is the paradigm, graphically depicted, for "prayer for the sake of heaven." As the children of Israel come to Rachel's tomb and *weep*, their tears in turn stir Rachel to respond with a bitter cry of her own. And her tearful plea to the Holy One causes him to respond with redemption. Not only is tearful prayer depicted as theurgically effective, but the passage suggests a further transformation: The "female waters" are no longer sexual fluids, but tears. This is consistent with the pervasive de-eroticization of kabbalistic and midrashic motifs that one finds in Yiddish paraphrases. It can be seen more explicitly yet when this passage is compared with its source, Midrash Lamentations Rabbati.[69]

The midrash first describes how the three patriarchs, Abraham, Isaac, and Jacob, and then Moses plead unsuccessfully with God to abandon his fierce anger against the Israelites, who are being led into the Babylonian exile in punishment for their sins, especially the sin of idolatry. At that moment, Rachel springs up before God and retells the whole history of her romance with Jacob, how he served for her for seven years, and how she realized that her father intended to substitute

Leah for her on her wedding night. She and Jacob then arranged secret signs between them, so that the imposter could be exposed. But, she says:

> Afterward, I changed my mind, and I endured my desire, and I had compassion for my sister, that she not be exposed to disgrace. And in the evening, they gave my sister to my husband instead of me, and I told my sister all the signs I had given to my husband, so that he would think that she was Rachel. And not only that, but I went in under the bed on which he lay with my sister, and when he spoke to her, she would keep silent and I would answer him each and every time, so he would not recognize my sister's voice. . . . And if I, who am but flesh and blood, was not jealous of my rival, and did not expose her to shame and disgrace, you, who are the living, eternal, and merciful King, why are you jealous of an idol that has no reality, and why have you exiled my children?

God relents at once and has mercy on the children of Israel: "Immediately, the mercies of the Holy One, be blessed, prevailed, and he said, For your sake Rachel, I will bring Israel back to their place."

This midrash is even more dramatic than Leah's version of it, but both her additions and her omissions are significant. Leah leaves out the erotic elements of the original. She omits Rachel's night under, rather than in, her marriage bed and does not explicitly equate Rachel's conquering her jealousy for her sister and God's forgiveness of Israel's unfaithfulness. In contrast with the *tkhine*'s setting of this motif among the motherly merits of the matriarchs, in the midrash, even the setting of the story has an erotic tinge to it: Only the *female* advocate of Israel, Rachel, could touch the heart of the Holy One, blessed be he. Her arrival is the climax of the story, following on the unsuccesful pleas of the patriarchs and Moses.[70] Despite the sexual imagery of the Kabbalah, then, and the appearance of this imagery in her introduction, Leah deemed the erotic elements of the Midrash unsuitable for the Yiddish-reading audience of the *tkhine* and transformed the erotic into tears.[71]

Equally important, however, is what Leah has added to this passage. Rather than setting Rachel's plea as the culmination, following upon the failed pleas of the various male figures, Leah makes it a direct response to Israel's tears.[72] This is the most persuasive piece of evidence that Leah intended her depiction of Rachel to be a paradigm for tearful, redemptive prayer that is theurgically efficacious even if recited by a woman with no kabbalistic knowledge. This may also be the key to the great expansion of the treatment of Rachel in the Yiddish portion of the text. From the kabbalistic terminology in the Hebrew introduction and the Aramaic *piyyut*, it appears that these portions were directed to readers *with kabbalistic expertise* (even if such female readers, as we have seen, were so rare as to be nonexistent). Thus, they did not need to be instructed in kabbalistic techniques of prayer. Only the readers of the Yiddish portion needed to learn how to pray "for the sake of heaven," or "for the sake of the Shekhinah." And it is all the more important to teach them, because "it is in their power to bring the redemption."

Leah Horowitz, as we have seen, was a highly unusual woman, a member of the intellectual elite who took serious thought for "ordinary Jews." Convinced of the latent spiritual power of women, she sought to help women bring that power to fruition. Elaborating upon what was already a focus of women's piety, the blessing of the new moon in synagogues, she provided a framework that she believed could bring redemption, and she tried to correct the prevalent improper practices—confessions and pleas for livelihood. Her *Tkhine of the Matriarchs* brings together a powerful nexus of themes: At the time of the renewal of the moon, which symbolizes the waxing of the Shekhinah's power, weeping women provide the transformed "female waters" for the Shekhinah, the weeping Rachel, whose pleas for the redemption of her children cannot be resisted by the Blessed Holy One. Taking into account as well her images of the other matriarchs, Leah's *tkhine*, like her introduction, combines an appreciation of women's traditional roles with an assertion that women have far more theurgic power than is usually recognized.

The *Tkhine of Three Gates*, by Sarah bas Tovim, the subject of the next chapter, shares some themes with the *Tkhine of the Matriarchs*, although it also differs in significant ways. Sarah, too, seems to have believed that women could transcend their traditional roles. However, she does not discuss this explicitly. Far more rooted than Leah in folk religious practice, Sarah also more wholeheartedly affirms the power inherent in traditional female roles and activities. The messianic impulse found in Leah's text, however, is even more fully developed in the *Tkhine of Three Gates*. Perhaps both texts reflect the religious ferment—Sabbatianism, Frankism, and Hasidism—found in Galicia, Volhynia, and Podolia in the eighteenth century.

CANDLES FOR THE DEAD

This chapter examines the work of the most famous of all *tkhine* authors, Sarah bas Tovim. It begins with a discussion of what can be known about Sarah, information gleaned from her two authentic *tkhine* collections, and then considers the most beloved portion of one of her collections, her *tkhine* for *kneytlakh legn* (laying wicks)—making candles of the wicks used to measure graves in the cemetery. Like Shifrah, Sarah draws on popularizations of kabbalistic material in Yiddish, and, like Leah, Sarah presents women's actions as having the power to bring redemption. But unlike both of these women, Sarah turns to women's folk ritual, rather than to Jewish mysticism, for her paradigm of religious power. A comparison of this *tkhine* with other contemporaneous material will elucidate the meaning of the ritual and the *tkhine* that accompanies it.

THE AUTHOR AND HER WORKS

Sarah, daughter of Mordecai (or sometimes daughter of Isaac or Jacob) of Satanov, great-granddaughter of Mordecai of Brisk, known as Sarah bas Tovim, became the emblematic *tkhine* author, and one of her two works, *Shloyshe sheorim* (The Three Gates), perhaps the most beloved of all *tkhines*. As literary evidence attests, Sarah bas Tovim's *tkhines* eventually became part of the standard knowledge of pious women,[1] and her influence eventually extended well beyond her native Podolia. An elusive figure, in the course of time she took on legendary proportions. Indeed, some have insisted that she never existed at all.[2] Sarah even became the subject of a short story by I. L. Peretz, in which she appears as a sort of fairy godmother.[3] The fact that the name of her father (although not her great-grandfather) changes from edition to edition of her work, and the unusual circumstance that no edition mentions a husband,[4] make documenting her life quite difficult.[5]

The skepticism about Sarah's existence is rooted in the older scholarly view that the tkhines were not written by women, that all were maskilic fabrications. Yet so many women authors have been historically authenticated that there now seems no reason to doubt that there was a woman, probably known as Sarah bas Tovim, who composed most or all of the two texts entitled "The *Tkhine* of the Gate of Unification Concerning the Aeons" (*Tkhine shaar ha-yikhed al oylemes*) and "The *Tkhine* of Three Gates." (In Hebrew books, influenced by Arabic, the word "gate" frequently means "chapter" or "section.") The author repeatedly refers to herself as "Sarah." In *The Three Gates*, she even works her name into an acrostic, a common form of claiming authorship in Hebrew works.[6] All the information we have about her comes from her own texts, which are unusual in that they contain extensive autobiographical sections, thus enabling us to grasp something of her personality and history.

The bibliographical problems associated with Sarah's work are formidable.[7] The publishers of *tkhines* took great liberties with their texts, changing and rearranging them as they saw fit. When no edition can be given clear priority, it is very difficult to establish the correct text. And although all the extant editions of *The Three Gates* before the mid-nineteenth century contain the same three sections in the same order; this order does *not* match that described at the opening of the text. Further, some sections of the text are repetitive: two successive paragraphs, for example, may differ somewhat but also contain many nearly identical sentences. The reasons for this are not clear. Sarah could simply be repeating herself, or this could be evidence of a rootedness in oral performance, or it could simply be further evidence of the liberties taken by printers. Finally, the third section of the *tkhine* seems somewhat garbled even in what appear to be early editions. The subject under discussion can change utterly from one sentence to the next.[8] This could be poor editing on Sarah's part or on the part of the publisher.

The question of authorship has another set of complexities, however. Sarah bas Tovim herself composed only part of her two texts and compiled other portions from other works. She is quite forthright about this, and indeed this is more typical of the *tkhine* literature than is simple authorship. She says that the *tkhines* contained in *The Gate of Uni-*

fication are "taken out of holy books"; thus, in fact, she claims for them more prestige than if they were merely her own invention. Of both of her *tkhines* she says that she "put them into Yiddish," implying a source in Hebrew.[9] Yet even as she says of both works that she "arranged" them, she also lays claim to having "made" the *tkhines*, refers to them as "both my *tkhines*," and says that they "came out of" her. Thus, she takes responsibility for these texts—the portions that she compiled and perhaps reworked, as well as those she actually wrote. An additional complicating factor here is the possible role of the publishers. It may be that some of the passages from other sources have been added by a publisher and were not originally included by Sarah herself. This is made less likely by the fact that all of the early editions of *The Three Gates* contain the same sections in the same order, even though the texts vary.[10] There are fewer extant editions of *The Gate of Unification*, so it is harder to be certain about the components of the text.

The fact that Sarah uses material from other works allows us to date her *tkhines*. *The Gate of Unification* uses material from Tsevi Hirsh Khotsh's *Nakhalas Tsevi* (Inheritance of Tsevi), the Yiddish paraphrase of the Zohar, published in Amsterdam in 1711, and in Zolkiew, closer to home, in 1750. *The Three Gates* paraphrases material from Simon Akiva Ber's *Sefer Maasei Adonai* (Book of the Tales of the Lord), from the 1708 edition. Perhaps most interesting is Sarah's use of material from *Hemdat yamim* (Days of Delight),[11] the anonymous Sabbatian work first published in Eastern Europe in Zolkiew in 1740. This guide to the meaning and observance of the Sabbath and festival days was reprinted several times before its heretical character was recognized and further publication in Ashkenazic communities was therefore abandoned—although even that did not suppress all interest in the work. I have not yet identified an intermediate source in Yiddish for the material Sarah uses, but there is evidence that there was such a source. Nonetheless, this suggests that *The Three Gates* cannot date from any earlier than 1732, unless *Hemdat yamim* also drew this passage from an earlier source.[12]

Tkhine of the Gate of Unification

The earlier of Sarah's two works was entitled "*Tkhine* of the Gate of Unification concerning the Aeons" (a title with mystical overtones) or *Sheker ha-hen* ([Physical] Grace is Deceitful). This *tkhine* seems to have been far less popular than *The Three Gates*, and for good reason: its literary style is more pedestrian and less powerful, and in some ways the content is less interesting. Nonetheless, the introduction and the last *tkhine* in the book, as well as certain other passages, display Sarah's distinctive literary style. The work begins as follows:

> O dear women and maids, if you read this *tkhine*, your hearts will rejoice. They are taken out of holy books. By their merit, you will be worthy to enter the Land of Israel. Also I have put down a lovely new *tkhine* that should be said on Mondays and Thursdays and fast days and on the Days of Awe. **Grace is deceitful and beauty is vain.**[13] Beauty is nothing, only righteous deeds are good. **The wisest of women builds her house.**[14] The important thing is that the woman should run the house so that one can study Torah therein, and that she should guide her children **in the straight path** to God's service.
>
> I, poor woman, I have been **scattered and dispersed**,[15] I have had no rest, my heart has moaned within me. I recalled from whence I come and whither I shall go, and where I shall be taken.[16] A great fear came over me, and I begged the living God, blessed be he, **with copious tears**,[17] that the *tkhine* might come out of me.[18]
>
> I, the renowned woman Sarah bas Tovim, of distinguished ancestry, who has no **strange thought**, but has made this *tkhine* only for the sake of the dear God, blessed be he, so that it may be a memorial for me after my death.[19] Whoever reads this *tkhine*, her prayer [*tfile*] will certainly be accepted before God, may his Name be blessed. I, the woman Sarah bas Tovim [daughter of] the rabbinical scholar, learned in Torah, the renowned Rabbi Mordecai, son of the great luminary, Rabbi Isaac, of blessed memory, of the holy community of Satanov, may God protect it.

This introduction reveals several preoccupations that reverberate through Sarah's work: her view that women are to be taken seriously as religious actors, while still honoring their roles as wives and mothers; the significance of her own suffering in her life and in her literary activity; her sense (more clearly expressed here than anywhere else) of her own worth despite the suffering she has endured. The intensity of her prayer for self-expression is noteworthy; clearly, the composition of this *tkhine* was deeply significant and tremendously difficult for her.[20]

As this introductory material indicates, *The Gate of Unification* contains one long *tkhine* to be recited on Mondays and Thursdays (the days when the Torah is read, sometimes considered minor penitential days) and on fast days. This portion of the text includes, among other things, a Yiddish paraphrase of Ecclesiastes 12:1–7 and a confession of sins that expands and explicates the standard alphabetic formula. (As far as I have been able to discover, the *tkhine* for Mondays and Thursdays, although it contains many Hebrew phrases and verses, is not a Yiddish paraphrase of any of the usual penitential prayers and supplications (*selihot, tahanun*) for Mondays and Thursdays.) The work concludes with a *tkhine* to be said before making memorial candles for Yom Kippur, which differs from the prayer for the same occasion found in *The Three Gates*.

The Tkhine of Three Gates

Sarah's second work, *The Three Gates*, is one of the most popular *tkhines* and also one of the most unusual. By the time she wrote this work, Sarah had developed a distinctive and powerful literary voice. In addition, this one work contains *tkhines* for three of the most popular occasions for which *tkhines* were published in Eastern Europe: the three women's *mitsvot* (the first gate), the penitential season (the second gate), and the new moon (the third gate).[21]

Sarah's writing is both intimate and intense. The intimate effect of the *tkhine* is achieved in part by the inclusion of autobiographical material. The author has suffered much and longs for the redemption that will bring an end not only to her own tribulations but also to the sufferings of all Israel. Her intensity stems from her desire to impart to other women what she has learned, both from books and from life. The literary power of this work is enhanced by her use of such devices as rhyme, internal rhyme, and assonance.

Sarah opens *The Three Gates* with an invocation that expresses her purposes in writing this work and that describes her lot in life. The tribulations only hinted at in the introduction to *The Gate of Unification* are here spelled out:

> I take for my help the living God, blessed be he, who lives forever and to eternity, and I set out this second beautiful new *tkhine* in Yiddish with great love, with great awe, with trembling and terror, with broken limbs, with great petition, with great . . . [22] May God have mercy upon me and upon all Israel. May I not long be forced to be a wanderer, by the merit of our mothers Sarah, Rebecca, Rachel, and Leah; and may my own dear mother Leah pray to God, blessed be he, for me, that my being a wanderer may be an atonement for me for my sins. May God, blessed be he, forgive me for having talked in synagogue in my youth, during the reading of the dear Torah.
>
> Lord of the whole world, I lay my prayer before you. As I begin to edit my

second lovely new *tkhine*, with my complete devotion, and with the entire foundation of my heart, may you protect us from suffering and pain.[23] I pray the dear God, blessed be he, that, just as he heard the prayer of our patriarchs and matriarchs, he may soon have great mercy on all Israel, and also on the years of my old age, that I not be forced to wander. . . . And I beg heaven and earth and all the holy angels to pray for me, that both of my *tkhines* may be accepted; may they become a crown for his holy name upon his head, Amen.[24]

Sarah's intense faith and difficult life emerge from this text. She feels that she has been punished for the sins of her youth, especially talking in synagogue, with a life of wandering. Her wandering may in fact reflect the unsettled conditions in eighteenth-century Podolia.[25] Relying on God's mercy, on the merit of the matriarchs, on the intercession of her own deceased mother, Leah, and on the merit of her own act in writing two *tkhines*, Sarah asks God for forgiveness and a peaceful old age. She also asks God to have mercy on all the people of Israel, thus implicitly asking for the redemption of the messianic age.

The sin of talking in synagogue preoccupied Sarah. At the end of the second gate, she writes a long excursus on the topic, entitled "Moral Reproof for the Women." This portion of the text is particularly rich in autobiographical material and reveals something of her personality, religious concerns, and theology.

I, the woman Sarah, entreat the young women not to chat in the beloved synagogue, for it is a great sin. For I remember that the Tanna Rabbi Eliezer b. Rabbi Simeon[26] met the officials who led two donkeys carrying punishments. He asked the officials, For whose sake is this? They said, For those people who talk in synagogue between the *barukh she-amar* prayer and the end of the *shemoneh esreh*.[27] Therefore, I warn you, so that you may not, God forbid, be punished as I was punished, with wandering. Thus, you should take proof from me and confess your sins before God, blessed be he.

I also entreat you to have compassion for widows and orphans and proselytes and captives, and for all elderly people, and for all ill people. For just as when you fast, your heart is bitter, so should you believe that it is bitter for the poor man who has nothing for his wife and children to eat. Therefore, I entreat you to do this for the sake of the dear God, blessed be he, that you should see that you have great care. For I, the woman Sarah, hope in God's blessed Name for great prosperity, and I pray to the dear God, blessed be he, that he may have great providence for my old age.[28] I have also composed a second lovely *tkhine* so that I might thereby have atonement for my great sins. Through our recalling of our sins, may God, blessed be he, send us life.[29]

I remember all the things [I used to do] when I used to come into the beloved synagogue, all decked out in jewelry. I would do nothing but joke and laugh. Today I remember and recall that God, blessed be he, does not forgive, as it is written, "**He who is quick to anger, and extends his wrath**,"[30] he waits long and pays quickly. Today, I go wandering, and my heart moans within me, for I recall that God, blessed be he, will forgive no one. Therefore, I entreat you to listen to my words and take them to heart. When you enter the beloved synagogue, a great terror should overcome you: You should know before whom you have come and to whom you pray, and to whom you must answer for your life.

I also entreat you to have great compassion for widows and orphans and proselytes and captives and elderly people, and for ill people. For when you fast, your heart aches; therefore you should believe the poor people—as if he were not in enough distress, it pains him even more when he sees his wife and children and has nothing with which to refresh them. Therefore, I, the woman Sarah, entreat that you do this for the sake of the dear God, blessed be he. May you see that you take great care. For I, like all paupers, hope in God's promise. I also entreat the dear God that he have great care for my old age. May our children not be driven away from us. I have also composed this second lovely new *tkhine* that we may be cured of our sins and of the Angel of Death this year. And because of this merit, may God, blessed be he, send [us] life.

In this passage the stereotypical critique of women's behavior in synagogue becomes autobiography. Unlike many of her contemporaries,[31] Sarah does not simply criticize women's unseemly behavior in synagogue, she confesses to it and testifies to its terrible consequences.

Further, this passage allows us to locate Sarah and her intended audience in a particular socioeconomic class. In her youth, Sarah came to synagogue "all decked out in jewelry." This means that she came from a wealthy family, even if she has become impoverished in her old age. The text addresses other wealthy women: "For just as when you fast, your heart is bitter, so should you believe that it is bitter for the poor man who has nothing for his wife and children to eat." As the women who constitute her audience have no experience with hunger, she must make hunger and need concrete for them by reminding them how they feel on a fast day, when food and drink are forbidden.[32] She reminds them of the obligations of the wealthy: compassion for widows and orphans (who are poor), proselytes (who may have lost the economic resources of their families as a result of conversion), captives (who must be ransomed), and the elderly and the ill (who may also be in need of material assistance).

We also get a glimpse of Sarah's theology. God is awesome and punishes sin; one should come before him in terror and trembling. Yet God is also merciful to those who confess their sins and do good works. Other passages in this text show us that Sarah also believed that one could establish reciprocal relationships with the dead; thus the matriarchs, patriarchs, and other biblical figures could be made powerful advocates for the living. The closing words of this passage sound a leitmotif that echoes through the second and third gates of the *tkhine*, the hope to be "cured . . . of the Angel of Death this year." This is not merely hope for a healthy old age, but expresses longing for the resurrection of the dead and the eternal life of the messianic era. This theme and others will reappear in Sarah's *tkhine* for "laying the wicks."

MEASURING GRAVES AND LAYING WICKS

The Texts and the Rituals

The second of the three gates is rooted in a centuries-old women's ritual. During the High Holiday season (and also in times of illness or trouble) women went to the cemetery, where they walked around the circumference of the cemetery and measured the cemetery or individual graves with candlewick, all the while reciting *tkhines*. Between Rosh Hashanah and Yom Kippur, and often on the Eve of Yom Kippur, they made the wicks into candles "for the living" and "for the dead," again, reciting *tkhines* as they did so. On Yom Kippur, according to some customs, the candles were burned at home, while, according to others, one or both of them burned in the synagogue. There are hints of this practice in sources going back nearly a thousand years, and it is well attested in literary and ethnographic material over the last three centuries.[33]

While the text in *The Three Gates* is the best known and most powerful *tkhine* connected with these candles, there are others. Sarah herself composed one of them: the final *tkhine* in *The Gate of Unification* is to be recited before making the candles. A *tkhine* by another author, Simeon Frankfurt, published in his 1703 *Sefer ha-hayyim* (The Book of Life)[34] is for the actual measuring of the graves. In addition, several later literary and ethnographic sources paraphrase or summarize texts

very similar to the one found in *The Three Gates* itself. It is quite unusual for any one *tkhine* to be the subject of so many descriptions; this
testifies to the tremendous popularity of Sarah's text (and of the practice
of making the candles), whether it was attributed to her by later generations or had entered anonymous oral tradition.[35]

In 1906 S. Weissenberg published a description of the ritual of measuring the cemetery (*feldmesn*), complete with photographs.[36] At the
behest of any woman who wished to order candles, two or usually three
women (who specialized in performing the ritual), would measure the
cemetery: one, in the middle, would hold two skeins of candlewick
thread, while the other two would wind up the thread she let fall while
walking counterclockwise around the cemetery. All the while, the
woman who had ordered the candles would walk behind them, reciting
tkhines. (Weissenberg does not give the text.) Alternatively, a poorer
woman might choose to measure only a single grave (*keyvermesn*),
which required the services of only one professional and smaller
amounts of candlewick and wax.[37]

The measuring finished, the woman would bring the threads home.
Later, in the synagogue, on a Monday or a Thursday between Rosh Hashanah and Yom Kippur, they would be made into candles for Yom Kippur (the ritual of making the candles was called *kneytlakh leygn*, laying
the wicks). A poor woman who knew how to make the candles would
receive the wicks. First she would make the candle "for the living" or
"for the healthy." She would take up each wick in turn, while the woman
who had asked her to make the candle would say, "This wick is for my
husband, may he live long; this is for my daughter, may she have a good
match," and so forth, expressing her wishes for each family member for
the coming year. Next, all the wicks for the living family members
would be twisted together to make one thick candle.

After laying the wicks for all the relatives and close family friends,
they would proceed to the making of the candle "for the dead," also
called the "soul candle." The woman who had asked to have the candle
made would say, over each wick, "This is for Adam and Eve, Abraham
and Sarah," and so forth for all of the patriarchs; "this is for my departed
mother, may she have pleasant rest in Paradise and be a good advocate
for me and my children; this is for my [deceased] little son," and so
forth. Then these wicks would be twisted into one heavy candle. Any
leftover wicks were made into individual candles to be used for Hanukkah and a variety of other purposes. The candle for the living was lit at
home on the eve of Yom Kippur, to bring good luck for the coming year;

other sources say that it was used as an oracle to predict whether family members would all live out the year. The candle for the dead was lit in synagogue at the same time.

While Weissenberg's account dates from at least a century and a half after Sarah published *The Three Gates*, his summary of the text bears striking similarities to hers. Other nineteenth- and twentieth-century accounts differ somewhat in the details of the ceremony, but the overall picture of the ritual that emerges is clear.[38] Thus, we may cautiously accept this picture as essentially consistent with the evidence of earlier texts.

There are two other important pieces of evidence, roughly contemporaneous with Sarah, that confirm this description. The first, slightly earlier than Sarah's text, is the mention of the custom of measuring graves in a legal commentary. Zechariah Mendel ben Arieh Loeb of Cracow (fl. 1671–1707) wrote the commentary Baer Heitev on the Yoreh Deah section of the Shulhan Arukh. In a comment on one of the laws of burial, he first quotes *Sefer ha-Agudah*, a legal source written by Alexander Zuslein ha-Kohen (d. 1349) on the custom of walking the circumference of cemeteries in times of illness, and then says: "And from this the custom has spread to measure the cemetery's circumference with wicks that are afterward made into wax candles and given to the synagogue, and this is a good custom."[39] Zechariah Mendel does not explain the rationale for the custom, nor does he specify whether any prayers or supplications were recited during the measuring and candle making. And he does not report whether women or men, or both, performed the ritual. Also, the occasion for the candles is different: this text records a custom connected with healing illness, rather than with the penitential season.[40] Nonetheless, this suggests that a custom similar to that for which the *tkhine* in *The Three Gates* is the liturgy was in existence by the late seventeenth century. Since we know of the existence of other prayers for visiting graves by this time (in *Maaneh lashon* and *Maavar yabbok*, for example), it seems reasonable that there may have been prayers to be said for this ritual too.

The second piece of evidence is found in *Mateh Efrayim*, by Ephraim Zalman Margoliot (1760–1828).[41] Margoliot lived most of his life in Brody, not too far from Satanov and not much later than Sarah, so his evidence is particularly valuable. He notes that on the day before the eve of Yom Kippur women made candles for use in the synagogue on Yom Kippur. He specifies that the candles should be attractively made, from good quality wicks and wax, preferably from white wax, which burns well. He warns that women who sell wicks that they claim have been used to encircle the cemetery often sell inferior merchandise of coarse flax or hemp, which does not burn well.[42] If one wishes to use wicks that have encircled the cemetery, one should arrange in advance for high-quality thread to be used. Margoliot mentions the custom of reciting supplications while making the candles (although he gives no text), and states: "One should not abolish this custom or mock it, for the custom of Israel is Torah." Margoliot also specifies that one candle is to be made for each married man and his living family members, called "the candle of the healthy," and one for departed parents, called "the soul candle." Despite the prevalent custom of bringing only the "candle of the healthy" to synagogue, Margoliot directs that both candles should burn in the synagogue on Yom Kippur.[43]

Thus, one can recover in Margoliot's text and in the ritual suggested by Sarah's text a level of women's religious creativity—a genuine folk practice—that is rarely approached through the mainly literary genre of *tkhines*. Sarah has composed—or adapted—a liturgy in Yiddish for a religious act of folk origin, apparently created by women: as by all accounts, the making of candles for Yom Kippur was practiced only by women. Nonetheless, Sarah's text repeatedly describes the making of the candles as a *mitsvah*, that is, a divine commandment and obligation upon women—even though it is not found in any standard halakhic code.[44]

In any case, the evidence shows that the candle-making ritual existed for centuries before Sarah lived and also long after. As with other long-standing rituals, its significance undoubtedly changed and evolved over time. What did it mean in Sarah's texts? Were these meanings contested in her own time?

Since the text from *The Three Gates* is the best-known *tkhine* for this ritual, we shall consider it first. The text begins:

> Lord of the world, I pray you, most merciful God, to accept my [observance of] the *mitsvah* (commandment) of the lights that we will make for the sake of your holy Name, and for the sake of the holy souls.
>
> **May it be [God's] will** May it be God's will that today, on the eve of Yom Kippur, we be remembered before you with the *mitsvah* of the lights that we shall make in the synagogue. May we be remembered for good, and may we be worthy to give lights to the Temple, as used to be done. And may the prayers which are said by the light of these candles be with great devotion and **fear and awe**, that Satan may not hinder our prayer.[45] And may the lights that are made for the sake of the holy souls . . . [words missing?] May

they awaken and each inform the next all the way back to the holy patriarchs and matriarchs, who should further inform each other back to Adam and Eve, so that they may rectify the sin by which they brought death to the world. May they arise out of their graves and pray for us that this year may be a good year. For they caused death to enter the world, so it is fitting for them to plead for us that we may be rid of the Angel of Death.

As I lay the next wick for the sake of our Father Noah, it is fitting for him, too, to pray for us, for he was in great trouble. Of him it is written: **"For the waters have reached my neck"**;[46] the water came up all the way to his neck. May the God who saved him save us from fire and water and from all evil that we fear; may it not, God forbid, come to us.

The *tkhine* then continues with the laying of wicks for Abraham, Sarah, Isaac, Rebecca, Jacob, Rachel (Leah is omitted), Moses, Aaron, David, and Solomon, and for "all the righteous and pious people who have ever lived." Each name is accompanied by a short paragraph constructed on the model of the one for Noah, with some characteristic of the person as portrayed in the Bible or in later midrashic material mentioned as making that person an especially appropriate intercessor. The paragraph for each person then concludes with a prayer that is connected in some way with this feature. After the laying of all the wicks, the *tkhine* contains some further prayers. It asks for forgiveness of sins, sustenance, and good matches for one's children, but most especially it asks for redemption and the accompanying resurrection of the dead.

May these lights, which were made for the holy and pure souls, awaken them so that they arise and inform one another back to the holy patriarchs and matriarchs, and further back to Adam and Eve, that they rectify the sin by which they brought death to the whole world. May they arise from their graves and pray for us, that this very year, may it come for good, there may finally be the Resurrection of the Dead. May [God's] Attribute of Stern Judgment become the Attribute of Mercy; may they be unified.[47] May [the souls] pray for us that the resurrection of the dead will come to pass. And may all the holy and pure angels pray that the dry bones live again,[48] speedily and soon.

This *tkhine* concludes on a similarly eschatalogical note:

Lord of the world, I pray you, merciful God, accept the lights that we make for the holy pure souls. For each thread that we lay, may you increase life for us. May the holy souls awake out of their graves and pray for us that we may be healthy. It is fitting for us to pray for the dead, for those who died in our own generations, and for those who have died from the time of Adam and Eve on. Today we make candles for the sake of all the souls—for the sake of the souls who lie in the fields and the forests, and for all the martyrs,[49] and for all those who have no children, and for all the little children[50]—so that they may awaken the dry bones; may they come alive speedily and soon! May we be worthy to see the resurrection of the dead this year, Amen, Selah.

The ritual of making the candles for the dead and the living, together with its liturgy, embodies condensed and complex symbolic meanings, tying together the woman, her family, and the people of Israel from its beginnings until its final redemption. The text in *The Three Gates* vibrates with eschatalogical tension and messianic hopes. It also endows the women's ritual with the power to enlist the aid of the dead in helping their own families and in bringing the redemption. This relationship of mutual aid and reciprocity between the living and the dead is also found in Sarah's earlier *tkhine, The Gate of Unification*. By contrast, the prayers for the cemetery by the slightly earlier author Simeon Frankfurt portray a more one-sided relationship. We shall consider each in turn.

The Living and the Dead

Sarah first lays out the reciprocity between the living and the dead in *The Gate of Unification*:

> **May it be your will** may it be your will, God, my God, the God of my fore-bears, Abraham, Isaac, and Jacob, and of Sarah, Rebecca, Rachel, and Leah, the God of righteous men and women, of male and female martyrs, [that] for the souls who have already been forgotten, and for the souls who died before their time, in their youth, and for the souls who have no one to make lights for them in the synagogue; may it be your will, God, my God, that they may have a portion in these lights, so that our lights will not be extinguished, heaven forbid, before the [proper] time. As we have not forgotten the souls who sleep in their graves—we go to entreat them and measure them—thus may we be measured for good in the heavenly court, so that our sentence may be with great mercy, not with anger. . . . Therefore we entreat the dear God, blessed be he, that our sentence may be [pronounced] with great mercy, not, heaven forbid, with anger, so that we may not, heaven forbid, leave any little orphans. May these souls inform the souls that sleep in the Cave of Machpelah[51] that they should pray for us, that we may have a good

year, that we may be worthy to see the red thread turn white,[52] that we may be delivered, and that we may have **a year of mercy for good, Amen**.

The text expresses a touching concern for those Jews who, because they died anonymously and were never given proper burial or because they were childless, have no one to make candles in their memory. Thus, one element of the reciprocity between living and dead is that the living remember the dead, even those who have otherwise been forgotten. They give the dead a portion in the merit of donating candles for the synagogue. (Long-burning candles were especially necessary on Yom Kippur so that people would be able to read the unfamiliar, daylong liturgy for the entire holiday, from dusk to darkening dusk.) In return for their meritorious act, the women making candles hope that their own candles, the oracle for the coming year, will not be extinguished before the holiday is over. Another aspect of the ritual is that the living remember the dead by entreating them and measuring their graves. They thus hope that they will be measured with mercy before the divine Court of Justice. And finally, by coming to the cemetery, measuring the graves, and entreating the dead, the living hope to rouse the souls of those in that cemetery to communicate with other souls, all the way back to the patriarchs and matriarchs, buried in the Cave of Machpelah in Hebron, to pray for the living. Specifically, the living hope for a good year to come, to see the red thread turn white. That is, they hope to see the restoration of Temple worship in the messianic era, when the scapegoat will once again be sent to the wilderness and the scarlet thread of Israel's sins will miraculously turn white as snow. Failing that, they hope that their sins will be forgiven, and they hope to be delivered and redeemed.

What is the origin of this conception of reciprocity between the living and the dead? The Zohar recounts that when human beings in trouble weep at the graves of the righteous (later in the passage it says they should bring a Torah scroll to the cemetery), the dead become concerned and rouse "those who sleep in Hebron," that is, the patriarchs and matriarchs and Adam and Eve, to plead for mercy for them.[53] Paraphrases of this passage occur in two Yiddish sources from which Sarah quotes: *Sefer maasei Adonai* and *Sefer nakhalas Tsevi*, the latter containing more of the relevant material.[54] However, neither of these sources connects this practice to the penitential season, although there is some suggestion of an association with the new moon. Further, neither of them contains the text of an actual appeal to "those who sleep in Hebron." Nor does either of them mention prayers for the messianic redemption or the resurrection of the dead; rather, both imply a desire for relief from some temporary difficulty, such as plague or persecution.

However, this passage from the Zohar is also quoted or paraphrased in additional *Hebrew* sources,[55] among them, *Hemdat yamim*. Particularly interesting is the fact that this work quotes the Zohar passage immediately after the "Lament for the Exile" that Sarah includes in Yiddish paraphrase in the gate for the new moon. That lament pleads with Abraham, Isaac, Jacob, Moses, and the Messiah to arise and beg God to bring the redemption. Further, the author states that it was his custom to recite the lament and pray for redemption in the cemetery on the Eve of the New Moon. Thus, the actual content of the text of *The Three Gates*, the appeal to the patriarchs and matriarchs and to Adam and Eve, points us back toward the connection with *Hemdat yamim*. This suggests that Sarah could have gotten her inspiration for this *tkhine* from a Yiddish work that contained more of *Hemdat yamim* than simply the "Lament for the Exile." To the extent that Sarah was influenced by the subterranean messianic message of *Hemdat yamim*, this might account for the eschatalogical tension in her works. Alternatively, she might actually have participated in crypto-Sabbatian circles in Satanov or elsewhere in Podolia. There is as yet no way to be certain, however.

In *The Three Gates*, Sarah takes the general idea of an appeal to those who sleep in Hebron and develops it into a full-fledged plea to various biblical figures (not all of whom are said to be buried in the Cave of Machpelah), laying a wick for each figure. And she further develops the idea of reciprocity between the living and the dead. This text assumes that the dead can aid the living, in some cases simply because God remembers their merit and in other cases because of more active intercession:

> As I lay the third thread of the wicks for our father Abraham, whom you saved from the fiery furnace, may you purify us of **sins and trespasses**. May our souls become pure, just as they were given to us, without guilt, **without any fear or terror**, as they came into our bodies.
>
> By the merit of my laying the thread for our Mother Sarah, may God, blessed be he, remember for us the merit of her pain when her dear son Isaac was led away to be bound on the altar. May she[56] be a [good] advocate for us before God, may he be blessed, that this year we not, God forbid, become widows, and that our little children may not, God forbid, be taken away from the world during our lives.
>
> By the merit of our laying a thread for our Father Isaac's sake, may you

have compassion for us. You have commanded us to blow the shofar on the New Year: **The horn of a ram, in memory of the binding of Isaac.**[57] May you remember this merit for us, that we may be able to tend to our children's needs, that we may be able to keep them in school, so that they accustom themselves to God's service, to repeat **Amen, may his great name be blessed forever and ever.** . . .[58]

By the merit of my laying a thread for our mother Rachel's sake, may you cause to be fulfilled, by her merit, "**Your children shall return to their country**;"[59] that means, by Rachel's merit, God, blessed be he, will bring us back to our land, Amen. May her merit defend us, that she did not let herself be comforted until the coming of the righteous redeemer, may he come speedily and soon, in our days, Amen. . . .

And by the merit of our laying a thread for our father Aaron the priest, and by his merit, may we be worthy to give candles to the Temple. May we live to see how he performs the priestly service. May his merit defend us, and enlighten the eyes of our children and our children's children in the dear Torah, like a light. . . .

The act of laying the wick connects the woman with the ancestors of Israel, which allows her to claim their aid. As in *The Gate of Unification*, this act creates a reciprocal relationship in which the dead benefit from the meritorious act of supplying candles for the synagogue, and thereby become obligated in turn to help the living.[60] Further, it graphically expresses the connection of the woman and the members of her very own family with past generations of Jews, all the way back to the patriarchs and matriarchs, and even to Adam and Eve. While modern Jewish scholars and theologians have been chary of the idea that the dead can intercede with God for the living and have tended to collapse this into the concept of *zekhut avot*, "ancestral merit," in fact, the concept of the dead as intercessors has had rabbinical proponents from talmudic times on.[61] And both views are found in tandem in *The Three Gates*: God is asked to remember the merit of Abraham and Isaac (as well as the merit acquired by the woman making the candles), and Sarah is asked to intercede with God.[62]

East Is East and West Is West

At a somewhat earlier date at the other end of the Ashkenazic world, in Amsterdam, Simeon Frankfurt (a rabbi born in Schwerin, in the Duchy of Mecklenburg, in the first half of the seventeenth century, but active in Amsterdam after 1656) recorded (or more likely, composed) a different *tkhine* for measuring graves. Although superficially similar to Sarah's, this text in fact portrays a very different relationship between the living and the dead. In 1703 Frankfurt published *Sefer ha-hayyim* (The Book of Life), which contains prayers for the sick and the dying, for funerals, and for visiting the cemetery, and also instructions for caring for the sick and preparing the dead for burial. The work is intended as a manual for village Jews who do not have easy access to rabbinical authority, and especially for the members of the *hevra kadisha*, the burial society, those members of the community who cared for the dying and prepared the dead for burial.[63] *Sefer ha-hayyim* consists of two sections, the first, in Hebrew, for learned men, and the second, in Yiddish, for women and uneducated men. Moreover, the contents of the two sections differ; the Yiddish is not simply a translation of the Hebrew.

In composing the prayers for visiting graves in *Sefer ha-hayyim*, Frankfurt drew upon and rewrote earlier material, chiefly *Sefer maaneh lashon* (The Right Response), dating from about 1615, by Jacob ben Abraham Solomon, a Bohemian rabbi; the expanded edition, by Eliezer Liebermann Sofer ben Loeb, dates from about 1658. Frankfurt's revisions are intended to reconfigure the relationship between the living and the dead as found in these earlier prayers. Whereas the text of *Sefer maaneh lashon* situates the worshiper primarily as a family member, who may rightfully appeal to deceased kin for aid, Frankfurt situates the individual worshiper as a member of the entire people of Israel and stresses the individual's and the people's direct relationship with God. Further, Frankfurt's prayers downplay the role of the dead as intercessors and stress instead the benefit the living bring to the dead by their prayers, as well as the worshipers' primary relationship with God, not the dead.[64]

There is no prayer for this ritual in *Sefer maaneh lashon*,[65] and thus it is not clear what source(s) Frankfurt drew upon. Nonetheless, his version of the prayer for measuring graves would likely exhibit the same tendencies as his other prayers for the cemetery:

The women who measure the graves should say this prayer. . . .
I pray You, O Lord my God, I pray you, my dear God, accept my prayer which I pray before you in this holy place [i.e., the cemetery] where lie the pious ones who sleep in the earth. We are come here for the sake of Your glory, and for the sake of the pious souls who are in the light of Paradise, and whose bodies rest in the earth, to measure the cemetery and all the graves, so that all may have a part in the candles that we shall bring into the holy

synagogue, to honor You with, and that the lamp may bring atonement for the souls, who are called **"the human soul is the lamp of the Lord"** [Prov. 20:27]. And when we say our prayers in synagogue by [the light of] these [candles], may you accept and receive our plea to forgive all our sins. And may you enlighten us with the light of your presence [Shekhinah]. And may the light be an atonement for the sin of Eve, who extinguished Adam's light, and brought death to the world.[66] O dear God, may you deliver us and enlighten us with the light from your holy candelabrum in the Temple, and make all the dead live, and do away with death unto eternity, just as you have spoken. Amen, Selah.

And they should begin to measure from the right side, and should measure all the graves with it [the wick], unless [they come to the grave of] someone who did not do right during his life. And they should make wax candles from it for the synagogue. And when they have measured, they should say, **"May it be Your will, etc."** and **"You are great, etc."**[67]

As in later accounts, this text presents a full-blown ritual: the actors are women; there is the text of a prayer; there is a procedure to follow; and the occasion, although unspecified, seems to be the penitential season.[68] And as in *The Three Gates*, the text asks God to receive the prayers recited by the light of the candles favorably, and it prays for deliverance from exile and an end to death. Further, this prayer explicitly includes the souls of the dead in the merit of the candles, and it mentions Adam and Eve, although not other biblical figures.

The similarities between the two texts suggest that they cannot have arisen entirely independently. However, it is chronologically impossible for Frankfurt to have based his text on Sarah's. *Sefer ha-hayyim* was first published in 1703. Although the date of publication of *The Three Gates* is unclear, it must be later than 1731–32, the date of publication of *Hemdat yamim*, and it is probably later than 1735, the "internal date" in the Yiddish paraphrase of the "Lament for the Exile" from *Hemdat yamim* that Sarah quotes. Thus, the thematic similarities between the two texts suggest some common source.

It is my view that Sarah did not create the *tkhine* for *kneytlakh legn* de novo, but reworked a *tkhine* already current in oral tradition, or perhaps already current in an as yet undiscovered written form—a *tkhine* reworked as well by Frankfurt, in an altogether different direction.[69] Indeed, Frankfurt's text would seem to be prime evidence for the existence of such a *tkhine*, in oral or written form.

Despite their similarities, Frankfurt's text contrasts sharply with the text of *The Three Gates*. First, this is a text for a different part of the ritual, for the act of measuring the graves; Sarah's prayer, by contrast, is for the making of the candles. Second, Sarah's text is much longer, much more dramatic, and has much higher eschatalogical tension.

Most important is the startling contrast between the valence of key elements in the two texts. Many of the themes found in *The Three Gates* are also found in *Sefer ha-hayyim* but transformed by Frankfurt's reformist program. He, for example, stresses atonement as the purpose of bringing the candles into the synagogue; this never appears in Sarah's text. The relationship between the living and the dead in Frankfurt's text is simple and one-sided: the acts of the living, such as making the candles, can bring benefit to the dead. Frankfurt is very careful here, as in all of the prayers he includes, to make it clear that the living should turn for help only to God, not to the dead. Any benefit for the living must be requested directly from God.

The Three Gates portrays a more complex and reciprocal relationship between the living and the dead, created by the measuring of the graves and the making of the candles. By this ritual women are empowered to call upon the dead for aid, and the dead are empowered to act: The making of the candles awakens the souls of the dead and communicates even to the patriarchs and matriarchs and to Adam and Eve the plea that they arise from their graves and plead before God on behalf of the living. Sarah's text attributes great power to the dead, especially to Adam and Eve, to "rectify the sin by which they brought death to the world."

For Sarah, then, the sin that brought death to the world belongs to both Adam and Eve. And she attributes to them the power to put it right and bring the messianic era, the end of death—an idea that to the best of my knowledge is not found in rabbinic sources. In Frankfurt's text, by contrast, the sin is Eve's alone.[70] Further, the candles are supposed to *bring atonement* to Eve. Here, she becomes the passive recipient of forgiveness, while in Sarah's text Eve, together with Adam, can actively bring redemption. Thus, in *The Three Gates*, Eve, the matriarchs, and the women reciting the prayers and making the candles all play an active role, as do Adam and the other male figures mentioned. Perhaps the contrast could be stated as follows: in *Sefer ha-hayyim* God is the only real actor; God may choose to respond graciously to the prayers and repentance of the living. In *The Three Gates*, the dead and the living can also act to affect the fate of the individual worshiper, her family, and the people of Israel.[71]

The *tkhines* for measuring graves and making candles for Yom Kippur by Simeon Frankfurt and Sarah bas Tovim give evidence of two sharply differing ideas of the relations between the living and the dead and the efficacy of women's ritual performance. In conclusion, let me briefly consider the question of which text is closer to the general range of views on these questions found in eighteenth-century Eastern European *tkhines*. It is safe to say that Frankfurt's Western European, reformist formulations find little echo in Eastern Europe. Eastern European *tkhine* authors generally do believe that the dead can come to the aid of the living; other texts for other occasions display a variety of means of establishing reciprocity with the dead.

One interesting example is the "Tkhine of the Matriarchs for the Blowing of the Shofar," by Serl daughter of Jacob ben Wolf Kranz (the Dubno Maggid, 1741–1804). Serl makes claims upon the matriarchs because they, like herself and other worshipers who recite her *tkhine*, have experienced the hope, loss, and pain entailed in being mothers and daughters:

> First we ask our mother Sarah to plead for us in this hour of judgment. . . . Have mercy, our mother, on your children. And especially, pray for our little children that they may not be taken away from us. For you know well that it is very bitter when a child is taken away from the mother, as it happened to you. When your son Isaac was taken away from you, it caused you great anguish.[72]

Further, other contemporaneous texts stress the efficacy of women's ritual. Like Sarah, Leah Horowitz, as we have seen in Chapter 7, was concerned with bringing the messianic redemption and argued that if women pray properly (in synagogue, with weeping), they have the power to do so. Her *Tkhine of the Matriarchs*, to be recited on the Sabbath preceding the new moon, contains an appeal to God in Aramaic and in Yiddish to remember the merit of each of the matriarchs and to redeem Israel for their sake.[73]

Interestingly both Serl and Leah used descriptions of graveside appeals to the one matriarch who was not buried in the Cave of Machpelah, Rachel, as the focal point of their *tkhines*. Leah, whose *tkhine* prays for the redemption of Israel, portrays the exiled Israelites at the grave of their matriarch. In response to their plea, Rachel arises from her grave and successfully entreats God to promise an end to the exile. Serl, whose prayer appeals for the health and welfare of the family, pictures Joseph at his mother's grave:

> And we also ask our mother Rachel to plead for us, that we may be inscribed and sealed for good, and that we may have a year of life and a year of liveli-

hood. And may we never suffer any sorrow. We know well that you cannot bear to hear of any sorrow. For when your beloved son Joseph was led to Egypt, the Ishmaelites caused him great sorrow, and he fell on your grave and began to weep, "Mother, mother! have mercy on your child! How can you look on my sorrow, when you had such love for me? . . ." And you could not bear to hear the sorrow of your child, and you answered him, "My dear child, I hear your cry, and I will always have compassion when I hear your sorrow." Therefore, have compassion on our sorrow and our anguish, and our trembling before the judgment, and plead for us that we may be inscribed for a good year in which there will be no sorrow, Amen.[74]

Thus, even without the actual ritual of encircling the graves and making the candles, the motif of graveside appeals to powerful intercessors clearly lived in the imagination of Eastern European Jewish women.

Despite the similarities between these two texts, there is one area in which they differ sharply: the proper subject for prayer. While Serl's appeal is for the concrete and the mundane, health and livelihood, Leah sharply condemns this type of prayer as trivial and selfish. For her, influenced as she was by the Jewish mystical tradition, the only true prayer is that for the sake of the Shekhinah. No other prayer can bring the desired redemption.

By contrast, one of the triumphs of Sarah bas Tovim's *tkhine* for making Yom Kippur candles is the remarkable way in which it combines eschatalogical and domestic concerns. This *tkhine* pleads for purity of soul, deliverance from exile, the resurrection of the dead, and the restoration of Temple worship—in short, for the messianic redemption. But it also asks for sufficient livelihood to keep the children in school and marry them off, just in case the Messiah tarries yet awhile longer. In other words, both kinds of concerns are legitimated.

And, as we have seen, the woman reciting this *tkhine* does more than just plead for health, livelihood, redemption—her very action helps bring them about. By laying the wicks and making the candles, she enters into a reciprocal relationship with the dead. She awakens the forebears of Israel and enlists their aid. She rouses the matriarchs, patriarchs, and other biblical figures to act as advocates for herself, her family, and all of Israel. She helps to bring the redemption: the advent of the King Messiah, the return of the people of Israel to their land, and the resurrection of the dead. Alongside the clear emotional power of such a prayer, Simeon Frankfurt's rationalized *tkhine* appears dry and sterile.

PART III

BRINGING THE

TKHINES HOME

CHAPTER NINE

AMERICAN TRANSFORMATIONS
OF THE *TKHINES*

Dear G-d, as I begin this paper, grant me the wisdom to uncover the hidden sparks of Torah. Send me your angels to guide me on my way as I stumble through sentence construction and footnotes. Bless me with the fertility of ideas as you have blessed my ancestors Sara, Rebecca, Rachel and Leah. Give me patience and endurance to finish this paper on time and the ability to enjoy my work in the process. See this effort as my humble way to draw closer to You and to bring humankind closer to redemption. May the wings of Shechinah hover over me as I work, keeping me safe from doubts and exhaustion. Grant me serenity in my endeavor and let me say, amen.
— *G E E L A R A Y Z E L R A P H A E L , 1 9 9 3*

This chapter reflects on the transformations of the Yiddish *tkhines* in America and how those transformations relate to changes in Judaism, Jewish domesticity, and the type of religious expression thought appropriate to the domestic realm. It thus traces the development of these prayers as a window on the inner history of the great wave of Yiddish-speaking Jews who migrated from Eastern Europe to the United States in the late nineteenth and early twentieth centuries, and their descendents. After looking at the somewhat modernized Yiddish *tkhines* of the late nineteenth and early twentieth century, including the immigrant period, I highlight three contemporary examples of what might be considered descendents of the *tkhines*: modern editions of *tkhines* in Yiddish; a limited reappropriation of the *tkhine* form in the recent edition of the Conservative prayer book; and new feminist prayers and rituals modeled in part on the *tkhines*. These reflections lead us in turn to questions of the nature and fate of domestic religion among American Jews, its connection with religious faith, and its varied reponses to the rise of secularism. What we find is that over the course of this century there has been a transformation of domestic religion into a more individual phenomenon.

DOMESTIC RELIGION

I begin with the concept of "domestic religion," as treated by Susan Starr Sered. In an ethnographic study of the religiosity of elderly Jewish women in Jerusalem, she distinguishes between "domestic religion" and the "great tradition":

> [T]he domestic religious realm [is] the arena in which the ultimate concerns of life, suffering, and death are *personalized*–domestic religion has to do with the lives, sufferings, and deaths of *particular*, usually well-loved, individuals. . . . Rituals and symbols become transformed when they enter or leave the domestic realm. When a literate Jewish man listens to the Torah reading in synagogue, he is obeying a divine law, learning about the history of the Jewish people, and participating in the life of the community. When an illiterate Middle Eastern Jewish woman listens to the Torah reading in synagogue, she is seeking the most efficacious moment, the moment when the channel of communication between human and God is most open, to ask God a personal favor for a particular, loved person. A pervasive problem in much of the academic study of religion is the tendency to treat the first set of motivations as more noble, beautiful, important, eternal, or true than the second set. . . . There is no reason to assume that the experience of the holy is any more immediate to a rabbi in a *yeshiva* than to a woman lighting candles to protect her family.[1]

Sered is undoubtedly correct that the experience of the holy is as readily available to the practitioner of domestic religion as it is to the scholar of the great tradition. Nonetheless, her formulation is not without its difficulties. First, the religious expression of someone petitioning God for a personal favor is likely to be suited chiefly to the particular moment and the particular individual. Heartfelt though it may be, it may also be less likely to speak to other individuals facing similar spiritual or material dilemmas than would be a prayer based in a classical tradition that has addressed the human condition over centuries. Further, such personal prayers may pay little attention to literary aesthetics: They may create a profound sense of communion with God for the person who offers them, but not appeal or be meaningful to others. Second, Sered's formulation seems especially problematic when we try to think about domestic religion in a modern, increasingly secular context. What can domestic religion as Sered describes it, embedded in faith in the efficacy of prayer to bring about divine intervention on behalf of particular individuals, mean when such faith is called into question, or reformulated in different terms?

Traditional Judaism was embedded in the everyday. Thus, even though public religious life was largely the preserve of men, the *tkhines* in particular, and traditional Judaism more generally, hallowed domestic life, for both men and women. But in the United States, Judaism inexorably came to be seen as a "religion" along the Western model, a repository of teachings about ethics and truths, expressed in the liturgy, rituals, and sermons of public worship. In America, then, the public sphere was what remained as Judaism came increasingly to be seen as something that happened in synagogue rather than at home. This shift effected thoroughgoing changes in American Judaism. As a result, the classical *tkhines,* too, lost ground as a means of religious expression for women.[2]

These concrete prayers for particular benefits, the product of domestic religion, in the immigrant language, nearly disappeared. At the same time, the classics of the great tradition, the Bible, Talmud, and Midrash, for example, did not disappear, although they were studied by an ever smaller proportion of Jewish men.

As the century has worn on, however, there have been attempts to recapture the concreteness of domestic religion, albeit in new forms. As we trace the evolution of the *tkhines* and their successors, we can chart the changes in the meaning of the domestic sphere, its relationship to the great tradition and to the sacred. We will see a shift from petitions for material benefits and communal spiritual hopes, to affective ties within the family, and, finally, under the influence of the therapeutic culture of contemporary America, to individual psychological aspirations.

TKHINES OF THE LATE NINETEENTH AND EARLY TWENTIETH CENTURIES

Europe

As we have seen, in the classical form of the genre, there are *tkhines* for the Days of Awe, for the festivals, for new moons, and for every day.

They ask God for forgiveness of sins, for pious children, for protection from evil spirits, for a decent living, for redemption from exile. They appeal to the biblical matriarchs and patriarchs, as well as to angels, for aid and intercession on high. This type of prayer, embedded in the domestic aspects of traditional Judaism, allows the worshiper to make every moment holy. But such prayer is particularly difficult for the modern westernized Jew, who is uncertain about whether or not God can do the kinds of things these prayers ask for and also about whether or not it is appropriate to pray for one's own particular material needs.

By the mid-nineteenth century the genre was beginning to change. The older *tkhines* (often rewritten, toned down, or garbled) continued to be reissued in numerous new editions, but new material also appeared. These new *tkhines* were quite different from the earlier texts, especially in their portrayal of family relations. At the same time, the Eastern European Jewish family was changing. The age of marriage shifted from the early teens to the late teens, and arranged marriage slowly began to give way to marriage based on an ideal of romantic love. Roles within the family changed. In the premodern ideal family, the wife supported her husband, so that he could devote himself entirely to Torah study. By contrast, the new ideal of the nineteenth century required that the husband work and support his wife, who was to stay home and care for the children.[3] As these changes were taking place, new *tkhines* were written about family events and family relations, for example, *tkhines* to be recited by a bride on her wedding day or by the mother of a boy beginning *kheyder* (elementary school). Such prayers are evidence of the new emphasis on emotional ties within the family; the events they address are not new, but they have become a new subject for *tkhines*.

Moreover, *tkhines* themselves became vehicles for various reformist programs. Ben-Zion Alfes (1850–1940), an Orthodox author and activist, edited, revised, and wrote a book of *tkhines* entitled *Shas tkhine khadoshe* (A New *tkhine* of Six Orders).[4] This work was an integral part of his project of spreading knowledge about Judaism and love for traditional Jewish life among the Jewish masses of Eastern Europe.[5] Alfes hoped thereby to counteract the influence of secularism and secular ideologies, such as socialism; and indeed, his *tkhines* were extremely popular, as were his other writings. Alfes, however, was no throwback to the Middle Ages or even the eighteenth century. He engaged in the controversies of his day and wrote in a modern style. In response to the struggles over the role of women and the nature of the family among

Jews at this time, his *tkhines* repeatedly point to the critical role of women in maintaining a Jewish home and raising Jewish children. Further, his view of the family was influenced by the image of the ideal bourgeois family of his day.[6]

While Alfes, like the female and male authors of earlier *tkhines*, took the religious lives of his readers seriously, a new set of authors arose at about the same time, or a little earlier, who often regarded their readers with contempt. These new authors—all men—were *maskilim* (enlighteners); their program was no less than a thoroughgoing reform and modernization of Eastern European Jewish life. They regarded women who clung to traditional ways as benighted and superstitious, and an obstacle to change. An interesting example is Isaac Meyer Dik (1814–93), known primarily for his popular fiction.[7] Like Alfes, Dik used his writing to advance his ideas of reform. However, unlike Alfes, he despised the *tkhines*: "They are completely senseless, worthless, and offer no thoughts to warm the heart or elevate the spirit."[8]

Although it may seem surprising that Dik and other *maskilim* wrote *tkhines*, they did so for two reasons. First, many of them were employed by the Hebrew publishing houses at low salaries. Since they wrote *tkhines* to make money, they composed them in a style that they thought would appeal to their audience: highly emotional and lachrymose. Presumably because they thought it would sell books, they often wrote pseudonymously, attributing new *tkhines* to fictitious female authors. Second, the *maskilim* wrote *tkhines* in order to reach the "benighted" women with their reform program. Thus, for example, *maskilic tkhines* imploring God to restore the health of an ill child also stress the importance of proper domestic hygiene, a theme that never appears in earlier *tkhines* on the same topic.[9]

America

Despite the pressures to Americanize and to use English, Yiddish *tkhines* at first flourished among the immigrants to North America. As Yitskhok Shloyme Mayer pointed out in a pioneering study, many *tkhines* were composed especially for the conditions and experiences of Jewish immigrants in America and were published alongside more traditional *tkhines* in new American editions.[10] He begins his article by quoting what he describes as an example of a classic "old-country" *tkhine* republished in an American anthology. However, perhaps because he was unfamiliar with the history of the genre, the text he in-

cludes, *A naye tkhine tsu hashkomes boyker* (A New *Tkhine* Upon Arising in the Morning) was really of recent origin; it appears to be based on
a *tkhine* for the preservation of good health composed by Alfes. Mayer
notes that the *tkhine* collection he used was reworked and edited by
Aaron David Aguz, an American Yiddish journalist, for the Hebrew
Publishing Company of New York.[11] And in the edited form Aguz gave
it, this *tkhine* fits in well with the ideals of settlement house reformers
who worked with the immigrants:

> Although you, Lord of the Universe, are our protector, yet you have written
> in the Holy Torah that human beings should not depend on miracles,[12] and
> when a person looks after himself, the Lord of the Universe looks after him,
> too. And as it is well known that many infectious diseases come from lack
> of cleanliness, I therefore petition you for the strength and the wisdom to
> know how to keep my home and the members of my household properly
> clean. May you also send me the understanding to know how to preserve my
> health and strength, the health and strength of my husband, and the health
> and strength of my entire household, both with proper hygiene, and with
> healthful and tasty foods, so that each meal and each dish may be served on
> time. Thus may we have the strength to serve the Creator, as the Ethics of
> the Fathers say: "If there is no flour, there is no Torah."[13] The Rambam[14] says
> that our knowledge and reason are stronger in a healthy body and less prone
> to error than in a weak body. Especially in the present era, when, because
> of our many sins, it is so difficult to make a living, we must hold fast to
> the resolve to strengthen our powers. And the most important thing is to re-
> joice in our own portion:[15] May I not, God forbid, envy another woman for
> her good food, or for her expensive clothing, or for her jewelry, but let me
> only envy good Jewish conduct. And may I rejoice in that which the Most
> High bestows upon me, so that my home may be always full of joy. May I
> never know evil times, and may no curse fall upon my home. And while, for
> the most part, women have weak understanding,[16] which brings them to
> talk themselves into imaginary illnesses until they truly become weak, I
> pray you, Lord of the Universe, to strengthen my understanding and my
> strength, so that I can drive these weak thoughts away from me. May my
> husband and my children be gladdened whenever they come home; may I
> gladden them with good, loving, and wise words, and in this manner may
> blessing, plenty, livelihood and success come to rest upon my home, so that
> I may be able to give charity with a joyous heart and can pray with pure
> thoughts. May you fulfill our every prayer for good.[17]

This text is worlds away from the *tkhines* of the seventeenth and
eighteenth centuries. Rather than petitioning God for health and liveli-

hood, or for protection from natural or supernatural foes, or for forgiveness of sins, or for redemption from exile, it asks only for the strength and wisdom to be a model middle-class wife and mother. Its underlying theme, self-reliance, is very American: God helps those who help themselves. The woman undertakes to keep her home and family clean, her meals well balanced, tasty and served on time, her demeanor cheerful and sweet at all times, regardless of how difficult conditions are. The *tkhine* reinforces a reformation of the Jewish home around the ideals of Western bourgeois life. Indeed, it fits right in with the conceptions of health, hygiene, nutrition, and family decorum conveyed repeatedly in classes on cooking and housekeeping at the Henry Street Settlement and other such institutions.[18]

Another *tkhine* from the immigrant period reflects specifically American conditions. This text is entitled "A new *tkhine* for candle lighting, especially for America."

But today we are in exile, where the struggle to make a living is so great that the conditions under which we live often make it impossible to keep the Sabbath and festivals according to Jewish law. Kind Father in heaven, for nearly two thousand years we have wandered, driven from one land to the next, and we have had no rest. But we have always carried your holy Torah with us, and wherever we have been, the Torah has been with us. The persecutions we endured in other lands have driven us here to America, which serves as a refuge for all the persecuted and suffering. But life here is very hard, and because of our many sins, Jewish children must profane the Sabbath and festivals. I am not, God forbid, accusing anyone of doing this to anger You, or to blaspheme your holy Name; but the times and the conditions bring this about.[19]

Here the text acknowledges sin, but stops short of actually asking God for forgiveness. Nonetheless, the idea that economic conditions could excuse the profanation of the Sabbath is thoroughly modern. This *tkhine* suggests the widespread discomfort immigrant women felt as their children disregarded Jewish law and custom, and took on American ways.[20]

There were *tkhines* reflecting other aspects of immigrant life as well—*tkhines* in memory of the young women who died in the Triangle Shirt Waist fire in 1911, and in memory of the victims of the pogroms in Russia and the casualties of the First World War. Mayer quotes "A new *tkhine* for America, when one hears bad news from the Old Country." For happier occasions, there is a *tkhine* to be said by a mother when her son becomes a bar mitzvah, a celebration that received much greater emphasis in the United States than it had in Europe, and a *tkhine* for a bride getting married far from her family. Reflecting the new way of caring for the elderly in this country are several *tkhines* to be recited by women living in nursing homes.[21]

The *tkhines* for very specific occasions such as the First World War gradually disappeared from newly published anthologies. The majority of *tkhines* published in the United States were revised and recombined versions of older texts. Thus, prayers expressing religious sensibilities from very different historical periods are found side by side in the same anthology. (It is hard to know whether the immigrant women who bought these anthologies were themselves aware of this, however.) Nonetheless, the newer material contained in these anthologies does show a distinctive evolution from the classical *tkhines*: an emphasis on self-reliance and a reluctance to ask God for specific material benefits, a reckoning with secularization and assimilation, and a new vision of the family and the woman's role in the home. And while the benefits requested from God are less material and more psychological, the newer *tkhines* are still in the individual voice and continue to focus primarily on the home and family.

MODERN TRANSFORMATIONS OF THE *TKHINES* IN AMERICA

Can the *tkhines* in any form speak to Jews increasingly removed from the traditional religious life in which domestic religion made sense? What can we make of the persistence or resurgence of *tkhines* or *tkhine*-like forms of Jewish religious expression in the United States? Is it evidence for the persistence or resurgence of forms of Judaism that sanctify the domestic and the everyday? Do such prayers express changes in the meaning of home and family and increasingly also of self? Examining three types of modern *tkhines*, I will consider them in relation to changes such as these in the lives of relevant American Jewish groups.

Recent Editions of *Tkhines* in Yiddish

After the Second World War a new wave of Jewish immigrants arrived in North America. A certain number of them were Hasidim, very traditional Orthodox Jews, grouped around charismatic religious leaders called *rebbes* or *tsaddikim*. Unlike many earlier immigrants, these hasidic Jews were uninterested in assimilating to American culture and preserved their traditional way of life much more aggressively. One of their strategies for maintaining their separate culture was to continue to speak Yiddish as their mother tongue. Nonetheless, they did (and do) adapt to American life in a variety of ways, from their use of American technology to their conformity with American laws requiring that girls as well as boys receive an education.[22]

In Brooklyn neighborhoods such as Williamsburg and Borough Park, where there are large, Yiddish-speaking hasidic communities, one can readily buy new editions of the *tkhines* in Yiddish, published both in this country and in Israel. Often these are photo-offset editions of earlier material, rearranged to suit the publisher.[23] Overall, they continue a trend that began in the nineteenth century toward a greater connection with the liturgical calendar and a lesser connection with the domestic sphere. In contrast with early *tkhines* that paid little attention to the festival cycle (except for the Days of Awe), these collections contain numerous prayers for the three pilgrimage festivals (Passover, Shavuot, and Sukkot), as well as prayers for each month of the year and for every week in the annual cycle of readings from the Torah. In short, they contain more prayers to be said in synagogue and fewer to be said at home. They do, however, contain *tkhines* for the three women's commandments (separating dough for *hallah*, kindling Sabbath lights, and observing menstrual avoidances and purification), and some contain *tkhines* for life-cycle events, such as childbirth or a son's first day at school. This shift in content suggests that even in very traditional, Yiddish-speaking communities, the focus of women's religious lives has shifted toward the public sphere. This shift may be related to the fact that women in these communities are far better educated in the great tradition than were their European grandmothers or great-grandmothers. In these books of prayers the distinctiveness of a separate women's culture, rooted in domestic life, is less evident.[24] But in addition, the private sphere has been redefined. Much of the concern is now with emotional ties within the family, most often expressed at times of life transition.[25]

A particularly interesting example of current books of Yiddish *tkhines* is *Tkhine imohos* (*Tkhine* of the Matriarchs), published in Brooklyn in 1992, and "written and adapted" by Jacob Meshullam Grinfeld. Unlike most of the others, this book is newly typeset with large, clear, attractive type, and it is available in both a standard hardbound edition, and a gilt-edged, leather-bound luxury edition. While most of the material it contains comes from earlier collections of *tkhines*, it also shows clear traces of the editor's hasidic origin.[26] In addition, it contains a section of charms, incantations, and other magical formulas for curing disease and escaping misfortune.

The introduction to this work sets forth Grinfeld's purpose in issuing this edition. In fact, much of what he says is not all that different from what one found in the introductions to eighteenth-century *tkhine* collections: that it is important to pray in a language one understands (the vernacular Yiddish rather than the sacred Hebrew) and that women's prayers are more efficacious than men's, because women are more prone to weep when they pray. Indeed, Grinfeld emphasizes that women need to become aware of their spiritual power.[27] Although it is couched entirely in traditional terms, this detailed articulation of the importance of women's prayer may be seen in part as a response to the modern feminist movement.

One of Grinfeld's other expressed motives for publishing the work is nostalgia for a genre he knows is fading: "These are the prayers of our mothers and grandmothers." He is also very careful to assure the reader of the impeccable orthodoxy of the prayers. He states that in many cases he tracked down the (Hebrew) sources of the *tkhines* and corrected the "errors" in the Yiddish text to bring it into accord with what he presumed must be the proper wording. There is a well-observed trend toward ever-greater stringency among American Orthodox Jews, especially among those already at the extreme right of the religious spectrum. In sociological terms, this represents a rationalization of religious life, an effort to bring about greater internal consistency, as a response to the threat of secularism from without and to more widespread literacy in the sources of traditional religion among both men and women within.[28] Grinfeld seems to be suggesting that even the most traditional Jewish women are losing interest in *tkhines* as a genre, except as a form of nostalgia (or is this men's nostalgia?), and that through their education and their exposure to American life, these women are turning to a form of religious expression more closely related to the great tradition.

There has been a recent revival of interest in *tkhines* among modern Orthodox Jewish women, as well. Much more fully acculturated into American life than Hasidim, modern Orthodox Jews speak English, not Yiddish, and typically receive a full secular education, including university studies, alongside their extensive Jewish education. Boys and girls may be educated separately or together; girls may have a somewhat less rigorous Jewish curriculum. Nonetheless, girls usually learn Hebrew and are exposed to a wide range of classical Jewish sources. American feminism has had some impact on modern Orthodox women. One result of this is an interest in the history and means of expression of Jewish women, in search of a "usable past" to serve as a model for the present. *Techinas: A Voice from the Heart*, edited by Rivka Zakutinsky, is a bilingual work designed for Orthodox women who do not know Yiddish.[29] This publication aims to do more than satisfy historical curiosity, however. As the editor states in the preface:

> [P]reserving the text of the *techinas* would not be enough. Presenting them as the obscure relic of an era long past simply increases our loss. These *techinas* are a formula for dialogue, a form of address to God. They are an opportunity for today's woman to find her voice and reconnect her *emuna*, her faith, as if reconnecting a severed limb. By attaching ourselves to the voices of our grandmothers, we can again become whole.
>
> Thus, my intent was to present these *techinas* as a vehicle for today's English speaking woman to reach out to her Creator in prayer. As her predecessors employed the Yiddish, so she could approach God in her own language.
>
> However, we consulted with Rav Shlomo Freifeld . . . , who advised that "because Yiddish is a language that was used by Jews for over a thousand years, it is infused with holiness. It is preferable to say the *techinas* in Yiddish while glancing at the English." We have therefore included a guide for reading the Yiddish.[30]

Here there is definite *women's* nostalgia for a time when religious faith was purer and more wholehearted, as well as *men's* reverence for the Yiddish language. It is ironic that this book urges young Orthodox women, who typically have an excellent command of Hebrew and who understand the Hebrew liturgy and recite it regularly, to pray in a language they may not even know how to pronounce. There is an uncomfortable echo here of the "ignorant" Jewish woman of the past, stumbling over the Hebrew prayers.

This collection also preserves the increasing emphasis on prayers associated with the liturgy and the public sphere. Nearly half the book is devoted to prayers associated with the blessing of the new moon in synagogues (including one *tkhine* for each month), as well as other prayers for the new moon. The rest of the book consists mostly of *tkhines* for the holidays, with some for the three women's commandments and for family events, such as a baby cutting a first tooth, or for the recovery of an ill husband or child. This parallels the redefinition of the domestic sphere we have seen in the hasidic editions of the *tkhines*.

The editor's motivations for publishing this book are rooted in the domestic world. Zakutinsky writes:

> My earliest memories are of watching my mother, after she kindled the Sabbath lights, recite her *techina*. "You don't know how beautiful they are!" she would exclaim. The Yiddish words in between those tattered red covers conveyed a special and moving message. . . . Years later, as I looked through the tearstained pages, I realized how precious these supplications were, and indeed, that they could truly overturn entire worlds. She communicated with God as if by telephone. A direct line to Heaven, so powerful and intimate are they.[31]

There is an implicit valorization of a separate women's spirituality in these words, a valorization that one also finds in the new prayers of non-Orthodox feminists.

The Conservative Prayer Book:
Siddur Sim Shalom (Prayer Book "Grant Peace")

Conservative Judaism is the centrist denomination in American Judaism. For many decades the largest of the denominations, it has recently been losing ground to the Reform movement. For decades it has been torn between the traditionality of its rabbinical seminary and its clergy and the laxity of its laity. More recently, it has been subjected to an internal critique by some of its most active members, those who have been involved in the havurah movement and Jewish feminism.[32] The result has been a number of significant changes in Conservative Judaism, among them, a reemphasis on spirituality and a new concern with women's opportunities for religious participation.[33]

The daily and Sabbath prayer book edited by Rabbi Jules Harlow, and issued in 1985 by the Rabbinical Assembly and the United Synagogue of America (both institutional organs of Conservative Judaism) contains one old prayer in Yiddish and several suggested private devotions that are modeled on *tkhines*. Harlow included this material, I believe, both to give token representation to women's voices and to encourage private prayer. Indeed, this prayer book as a whole, in contrast to the earlier edition edited by Morris Silverman, reflects Conservative Judaism's effort to recognize the private sphere as an important arena of religious life and to articulate a liturgy for home and private devotion.[34] The difference between the two prayer books is indicative of the shift in Conservative Judaism, from the institution building of the 1950s to a more inward looking, spiritual focus on the part of some in the Conservative leadership in the 1980s.

At the end of the Havdalah prayer that concludes the Sabbath, Harlow includes, without comment and without a source notation, a version of *Got fun Avrohom* (God of Abraham).[35] This Yiddish prayer, recited by Eastern European Jewish women at the close of the Sabbath, has been collected from oral tradition in dozens of variants.[36] It appears that Harlow intended it to be incorporated as part of the standard Conservative Havdalah ritual. As far as I can determine, this prayer is the only Yiddish text·incorporated into the prayer book.

Harlow also includes personal prayers to be recited after kindling Sabbath or festival lights, though he never calls them "*tkhines*." Nonetheless, they resemble *tkhines* in that they are private devotions intended primarily for women, and they are written for one of the most popular occasions on which *tkhines* were recited. Further, they are clearly modeled on the literary form of the *tkhines*. Harlow begins the section on candle lighting with the following note:

It is the special obligation of a woman to light candles for Shabbat, Festivals, Rosh Hashanah, and Yom Kippur. When there are no women present, men are obliged to light the candles.

After the candles are lit, the *berakhah* [blessing] is recited. A personal reflection, meditation, or prayer is appropriate following the *berakhah*. The selections of meditations on these pages are offered as guides to be adapted in the context of your own life. Your own thoughts are equally appropriate.[37]

There follow three brief meditations for candle lighting on any occasion, two for the Sabbath (these are written by Navah Harlow, the editor's wife), and one each for the festivals, Rosh Hashanah, and Yom Kippur. In one of the general meditations, Harlow seems to be striving to echo aspects of the literary form of traditional *tkhines*:

Ribbono shel olam [Lord of the universe], when I am lonely, help me to realize that I am never alone. When I am discouraged, help me to find new ways and new hope. When I am afraid, help me to discover my hidden strengths. When I am confronted by meaninglessness, help me to see the depth and beauty of our tradition. Hear my plea through the merit of our ancestors,

Sarah, Rebecca, Rachel, and Leah, so that the spark which they kindled will never be extinguished. Favor us with Your light, so that we may be blessed with a meaningful life. Amen.[38]

This prayer begins on an intimate note by addressing God with a Hebrew phrase often used in both *tkhines* and in private devotions in Hebrew, rather than in the standard liturgy. Further, it invokes the merit of the matriarchs. This invocation, though standard in the *tkhine* literature, means something rather different there than it does here. In the earlier *tkhines*, the matriarchs were addressed as intercessors who could bring the worshiper's concerns to God's attention, as it were. Or, alternatively, by their exemplary lives the matriarchs had accumulated a "treasury of merit" upon which the worshiper could draw to supplement her own merits, thus helping to convince God to grant her plea. Here the form of that request is preserved, but the meaning seems actually to be that the worshiper will feel an obligation to continue Jewish tradition.[39] Also, as in the earlier "*tkhine* upon arising in the morning," the worshiper asks God for psychological resouces, rather than material benefits. But the underlying theme of the prayer, the quest for a meaningful life, is thoroughly modern, alien even to the early twentieth-century *tkhines* we examined above.

One of the prayers written by Navah Harlow voices the emphasis on family typical of *tkhines* for Sabbath candle lighting. But in other ways it reflects a completely modern sensibility:

> *Avinu shebashamayim* [Our Father in heaven], as I light my candles this Shabbat eve I thank you for the week that has passed. I thank you for protecting my family and helping us to better understand each other, to share our joys, to share our triumphs and disappointments and to give strength to one another. I pray that the coming week will be a week of good health and of continued mutual pride and love in our family. Please, *Adonai* [Lord], watch over our fellow Jews who are oppressed or threatened anywhere. Amen.[40]

Once again, this prayer begins with an appellation for God commonly used in Yiddish *tkhines* and Hebrew private devotions. The text expresses gratitude to God for a variety of benefits bestowed on the family, yet the author seems unable to ask God directly for those benefits, unless they are for a much bigger group of people than her own family. This is indicative of the modern doubts about what kinds of requests it is appropriate to make of God: can God actually protect us, grant us health, free us from oppression? Further, some of the benefits for which Navah Harlow is grateful are also quite modern: mutual understanding and sharing within the family.

Thus, these private devotions found in the Conservative prayer book continue the shift from the material to the psychological aspects of home and individual life that we have already seen in the early twentieth century. If the inclusion of this material is part of a general strategy in the editing of this prayer book, it shows both the attempt to take the devotional life of the individual seriously and the new understanding of that devotional life in terms of psychological struggles and dilemmas: hope and despair, love and loneliness, meaning and meaninglessness.[41] These prayers reflect both the secularization and the relative affluence of Conservative and other American Jews: hopes for the family are for understanding and appreciation, rather than for food, clothing, and protection from the ravages of war and pestilence. Thus, these prayers adapt the literary form of the *tkhines* and infuse it with modern concerns.[42]

Feminist Prayers and Rituals

The feminist prayers and rituals composed and performed over the past twenty-odd years are more numerous and diverse than either the recent editions of Yiddish *tkhines* or the *tkhine*-like prayers in the new Conservative prayer book. Nonetheless, taken as a group, they bear some similarity to aspects of the earlier *tkhine* literature and can be understood as a transformation of domestic religion. Further, some of them are specifically called "*tkhines*" by their authors, who consciously hark back to classical *tkhines* as their model. The interest in *tkhines* has stimulated the publication of several collections of *tkhine* translations, and the availability of these translations has further stimulated the composition of new "*tkhines*."[43] Editors of volumes of new feminist liturgy and ritual have included traditional *tkhines* along with more recent liturgical compositions.[44]

A striking feature of this new feminist creativity is the sheer variety of occasions for which rituals and prayers are created and performed. And in this they resemble the *tkhines*, which were also recited on a wide variety of very specific occasions. One recent collection, *A Ceremonies Sampler: New Rites, Celebrations, and Observances of Jewish Women*, contains rituals for pregnancy, the postpartum period, naming a daughter, infertility, hysterectomy, divorce, becoming a vegetarian, becoming "a woman of vision," celebrating the lifetime commitment of a lesbian couple, and the holidays of Hanukkah and Sukkot, among others. *Miriam's Well: Rituals for Jewish Women around the Year* grows out of the reappropriation of the new moon as a sacred day for women and contains thirteen rituals, for the thirteen months of the Jewish calendar. Some of the themes of the different months include remembering our foremothers, yahrzeit (anniversary of a death) and mourning, planting and nurturing, menopause and wisdom, fertility and infertility. *Four Centuries of Jewish Women's Spirituality* includes a number of new feminist rituals, along with other writings of women in the section entitled "Contemporary Voices." Among them are a "crone ritual," sitting shiva (the seven days of mourning traditionally observed after a death) for a lost love, ceremonies for the new moon, and a ritual for healing after rape.[45]

Among the great variety of ceremonies and prayers, one major theme stands out: the events of women's biological lives. The classical *tkhine* literature contained many *tkhines* for pregnancy, childbirth, infertility, and the observance of menstrual purification. Indeed, this is one reason the *tkhines* are seen as a model for women today.

> [F]or women who feel today that nothing in the traditional prayer book, seen as a "male document," relates to them, it is an advantage that these prayers speak to women's specific concerns and lives—such as childbirth, nursing, and child rearing. . . . [The *tkhine* literature] certainly provides a precedent for prayers and rituals that relate directly to events in a woman's experience. Women today want to connect Jewishly with events in their life-cycle—including dealing with infertility, pregnancy loss, weaning, baby-naming, and menopause, and there are now ceremonies and rituals that focus on these.[46]

However, feminist rituals and prayers are *more* focused on these biological events than were the traditional *tkhines*. It is, to say the least, interesting, that these rituals are so centered on the affirmation of women's biology. It would seem that the creators of such rituals have a view of women that puts motherhood and, more broadly, embodiedness, at the center—an echo of themes found in the liturgical creations of other American feminists, whether Christian, "pagan," or New Age.[47]

As we have seen, classical *tkhines* were usually recited by women privately, rather than as part of an organized group.[48] This has been seen as a drawback in the use of these prayers as models for Jewish women today, who prefer to create rituals for group performance:

Most of the [*tkhines*] were said by the woman at home or by herself, for example, on visits to the cemetery, or to the *mikvah* (ritual bath). . . . The rituals we see now have more of a ceremonial aspect and also more of a sharing with others in the nature of a public statement. They share, with the traditional prayers and devotions, the connections with the collective past as Jews, or as Jewish women, but they come from a different tradtion, not of individual petition and personal supplication, but more of a communal story-telling. This, more than the fact that they deal not only with adult *bat-mizvahs* and 60-year-old birthdays, but with recovering from a rape or abortion, marks these new rituals off from the traditional ones.[49]

The first new ritual I shall consider illustrates the concern for the biological aspects of womanhood and contains an actual *tkhine* as well. This ritual, written by Rabbi Jane Litman, is entitled "M'ugelet: A Pregnancy Ritual."[50] As is typical of modern *tkhines* and other liturgical creations, this ceremony was written by Litman for herself and later made available, through publication, to other women. In this ceremony, the members of Litman's women's group stood around her in a circle, holding a long cord that had been wrapped around Rachel's tomb in Bethlehem.[51] Litman describes the ceremony as follows:

The women stood around me in a circle, holding the cord. I recited the following prayer, which is written in the style of Ashkenazi *techinas*, Yiddish women's folk prayers of the 16th through 20th centuries. . . .

Merciful and gracious Creator, have compassion on your loving hand-maid, —— bat ——, that she may have her child safely and in good health. May the merit of our holy foremothers Sarah, Rivka, Rachel, Leah, Bilha, and Zilpah, and the merit of our great leaders Miriam, Deborah, Hannah, and Judith, sustain me through my time of danger. May you help me avoid unhealthy acts and stay far away from any drink, smoke, or food which might harm the precious life within me. May this child be born in spacious straits, with room to spare. As You opened the Red Sea so that the children of Israel could pass through it unharmed, please open my waters and birth canal so that this child is born safely and without pain. May this little one grow to be a righteous person, always living in the path of Torah and *ma'asim tovim* (good deeds), and may the Jewish people merit true redemption in this one's lifetime. Amen.

Following the recitation of the prayer, the women encircled Litman's belly with the cord, at each turn whispering blessings for an easy delivery. This was followed by the "Blessing Song," by Jewish feminist composer Faith Rogow. Later, Litman took the cord with her to the hospital and held it while in labor.

Litman based her creation on the following Yiddish *tkhine*:

> Merciful and gracious God! Mighty Creator, have compassion on the woman *ploynes bas ploynes* that she may have this child safely. May the merit of our holy matriarchs—*sore, rivke, rokhl,* and *leye*—and the merit of our prophetesses—*miryem, dvoyre, khane,* and *khulde*—and the merit of *yo'el* sustain her in this time of danger so that she may have the child easily and without suffering. For You God, can perform such a miracle, through the merits of the righteous women from among our ancestors, that the child should be born a pure soul for Your service, a righteous person who will devote himself to the study of *toyre* and perform *mitsves.* And if it is a female, may she be a modest woman, a God-fearing woman, and may she have good fortune. May both mother and child be healthy and may she come into the world to help bring salvation and comfort to all *yisro'el.* May the Jewish people merit a true redemption in her lifetime. *Omeyn.*[52]

These two texts, we see, are very similar. In fact, several references in Litman's *tkhine* that do not appear in this Yiddish text are simply taken from other *tkhines.*[53] Litman's reliance on earlier models ensures that her *tkhine* breathes an earlier spirit. Litman asks God not for generalized spiritual or psychological benefits but for the specific intervention of a safe childbirth and a healthy baby.

Nonetheless, Litman introduces changes that also bring her *tkhine* into line with contemporary feminist consciousness. First, the seemingly trivial matter of the matriarchal figures named: only a modern feminist would make a point of including Bilhah and Zilpah among the matriarchs, thus raising them from their lowly status as handmaids and concubines. And note that Litman changes the second group of women from "prophetesses" to "great leaders" and omits the obscure Huldah for the better-known Judith. And consider the setting: the Yiddish originals contain no hint of a group ritual; presumably, they are to be recited in private. As noted, this isolation in religious devotion is at odds with most modern feminist creation—an important element of modern feminist ritual is the presence of the supportive feminist community.[54] This is well illustrated in Litman's ceremony. Nonetheless, Litman easily integrates the recitation of the *tkhine* into the communal context.

The most striking feature of this ceremony for a student of ritual is its specificity: it was written by one woman for her own use, to help her through a specific life transition. And, indeed, Litman testifies to its efficacy in the birth of her first child. While the very fact that it was published has made it available to others, the overwhelming impression one receives on reading this literature is that each woman prefers to write her own ceremony rather than use one that is ready-made.[55]

This is a pervasive characteristic of recent liturgical creation. In traditional societies the making of meaning is primarily the task of the culture rather than of the individual. The rituals, prayers, and other works of both the great tradition and domestic religion teach people their roles in society, and the meaning of their life transitions and crises, and of their joys and sorrows. Yet in societies such as contemporary America, great value is placed on individualism. Each person is expected to forge his or her own way in the world and find individual meaning in life. For some, this means a turn to psychotherapy to explore their inner world.[56] (Indeed, the rise of psychotherapy as a meaning-making enterprise can be seen as a result of the breakdown of the canopy of meaning provided by religious traditions in the past.) For others, this drive for personal meaning leads to the creation of new and individual rituals and prayers, whether within the framework of established religions or outside them.[57]

Thus, it not surprising to discover that many of the new *tkhines* are concerned with the author's psychological and spiritual state, rather than the family, the people of Israel, or some other group or community. Jewish feminist rituals are one Jewish manifestation of the therapeutic culture of the late twentieth-century United States. A pertinent example can be found in a collection of contemporary *tkhines* composed by Geela Rayzel Raphael, who was then a student at the Reconstructionist Rabbinical College.[58] Her "Techinah for Easy Labor," while also based on earlier *tkhines*, contrasts in spirit with that written by Litman:

TECHINAH FOR EASY LABOR: TO BE SAID WHEN BITING OF[F] THE PITOM OF AN ETROG ON HOSHANAH RABA

Mother of the Universe and all Universal Knowledge, our tradition has taught us that Eve suffered on account of her eating of the fruit. I know however, that our eyes have been opened as a result of her courageous act. Eating of the Tree of Knowledge, although a disobedient act, gave us the ability to discern injustice and oppression. We see and are aware of your justice and mercy as well as the wounded places in the world.

Eve, the crown of Your creation, was assertive and strong as she ran wild with the wolves. She delivered her children with strength. As I eat this pitom, may I be infused with Eve's birthing powers. Let my labor be only mild pangs of discomfort, yet may I labor for the revelation of Your presence in the world.

Primal EarthMother Eve tended and cared for Your garden as I will care for my child. May this child grow to be conscious of your world and environment as Eve did. Let this child blossom as a garden blooms in the springtime. May this child grow to respect Your creation–treasuring the sweetness and the tartness just like the etrog.[59]

This *tkhine* is loosely based on and is a response to the *tkhine* for biting off the end of the etrog discussed in Chapter 4 above, but it transforms its model far more completely than Litman does. God is addressed as Mother, and Eve's rebellious act is valorized. The *tkhine* pictures Eve as a wild, powerful "Primal EarthMother." Reciting the *tkhine*, the woman imagines herself as Eve, in her bonds with nature, courage, and "birthing powers."[60] Further, this prayer expresses wishes for the reciter and her child but does not ask the Mother of the universe directly to fulfill them. The chief benefit sought is the psychological and spiritual one of placing oneself in relation to a tradition, an ancestor, and God as one faces a difficult life passage.

As I discussed in Chapter 1, even the tables of contents of *tkhine* collections have something to teach us. By noting the list of occasions for which *tkhines* were recited, we mapped out the domains and occasions of women's religious lives. Rabbi Raphael is the only modern author of *tkhines* to have written an entire collection of texts. Despite the fact that these *tkhines* are not intended to address the full round of women's religious life, it can still be instructive to compare her table of contents with those of early *tkhine* collections. Her work contains ten *tkhines*:[61]

1. Techinah of a Woman Rabbi: To be recited before leading a service
2. Techinah for Infertility
3. Techinah for Dreams: To be said upon retiring
4. Techinah for Health
5. Techinah for Children's Safety
6. Techinah for Easy Labor: To be said when biting off the pitom of an etrog on Hoshanah Raba
7. Techinah for Rosh Hodesh
8. Techinah for Feminist Awareness in a Sexist Culture
9. Techinah for "Femstruation" [Menstruation]
10. Techinah for Mikveh

Once again, there is a very broad range here. Some of these topics (such as mikvah) are found in the oldest of *tkhine* collections; others are found in or are compatible with texts in later collections. (Of course, the language used in these texts may be quite different from that found in the classical *tkhines*, for example, addressing God as "Oh Holy Rachamema, Compassionate WombMother," in the *tkhine* for infertility.) We see here once again the valorization of the biological and maternal aspects of women's lives, on the one hand (five of the ten *tkhines*), and a somewhat lesser concern with contemporary spiritual concerns on the other (four of the ten *tkhines*). The *tkhine* for Rosh Hodesh (the new moon), for example, explicitly refers to the renewal of Rosh Hodesh observance by groups of modern women:

> This Techinah was written by the woman Rabbinical student, Geela Rayzel Raphael, daughter of Mitchell and Natalie, wife of Simcha, mother of Yigdal.[62]
>
> Sacred Mother of the Moon, You have given us this time of Rosh Hodesh for enjoyment and renewal. As your daughters gather in the darkness, we attune to Your sacred energy. Your crescent sign, a reminder of the waxing cycles of the Jewish people, is for us a symbol of Your ever present ability to restore our souls. We light candles to honor your presence and welcome You with warmth as our female ancestors did in the desert.
>
> Shechinah, Feminine Divine Presence, You have remained with us through hard times. Observing Rosh Hodesh was almost a forgotten observance, yet You have again demonstrated Your steadfastness by helping us recover our sacred time. Be with us again as we enter this new month filling our life with bounty and blessing.

This *tkhine* is clearly intended for a group ritual. And what is sought is "restoration of soul," "bounty and blessing"—primarily, that is, inner psychological transformation. Yet there is also a desire to connect to Jewish tradition, even as that tradition is transformed. It is interesting to see what represents tradition in prayers such as these and, specifically, the part played by the reappropriation of the *tkhine* genre. For while the *tkhines* of Raphael and Litman, as well as of other authors not quoted here,[63] make use of Bible, Midrash, a variety of feminist rereadings of primary sources, and materials from non-Jewish feminists, they write in the form of *tkhines* in order to claim for themselves an authentically Jewish *and* an authentically female tradition. As Heather Altman writes in the introduction to her "Dream *Tkhine*":

> Jewish feminism encourages newly created women's rituals as well as women's involvement in traditional rituals. My *tkhine* is part tradition and

part innovation. The genre of *tkhines* was once the cornerstone of Jewish women's spirituality. . . . I felt the need for *tkhines* on 20th century topics, so I revived this special, personal, female type of prayer.

I believe that the *tkhines* are a rich source of nourishment for modern Jewish women because they show us that our foremothers were indeed intelligent, articulate, educated, confident, and spiritual. In this spirit, I hope to honor the memory of Sarah bas Tovim, Serel, Sarah Rebecca Rachel Leah, and other nameless women, who recorded their prayers.[64]

The three contemporary examples of *tkhines* we have examined open an interesting window onto American Judaism today. Modern editions of *tkhines* in Yiddish reveal certain changes among even the most traditional, Yiddish-speaking Hasidim. Paradoxically, in this group, in which the daily and domestic element of religious life is still very strong, *tkhines* show women's religious lives moving in the direction of the great tradition. This is consonant with other things we know about these communities. Although they still maintain strict separation between male and female religious and social spheres, the legal requirement for the education of girls in this country means that hasidic women today have received greater formal instruction in the great tradition.

Among Conservative and feminist Jews, we see a different trend. Both groups are far more acculturated to American society and share the psychological and spiritual dilemmas and approaches of the larger society. Thus, among both groups, new liturgical creation expresses the psychological quest for meaning and wholeness. While earlier in the century, Conservative Judaism focused its creative energies on institutions, especially on the synagogue and on public liturgy, its new prayer book places a new emphasis on the domestic realm and on meaningful private devotion. Among the creators of feminist *tkhines*, the emphasis on the individual quest goes even farther, and there is also a desire to create a women's spirituality within Judaism, at once drawing upon the great tradition, but also distinct from it.

Is it justifiable to consider these new forms of religious expression as "domestic religion" or as successors to the *tkhines*? When we compare them with the religious practices Sered describes or with the classical *tkhines*, we see in both the Conservative meditations and the feminist rituals a shift away from a desire for material benefits to a desire for psychological benefits, and away from asking for benefits for others, usually family and household, to seeking benefits for oneself. Thus, the term "domestic" appears less appropriate to these forms of religious expression.

The difficulty with Sered's formulation of domestic religion I raised at the outset of the chapter continues to trouble me. These very individual prayers bear the clear stamp of their authors' personal concerns and are limited by their authors' literary talents. Composed either for their authors alone or for a very limited circle, these feminist *tkhines* and rituals may not prove as durable as the classical Hebrew liturgy. Even Navah Harlow's meditation on candle lighting, intended for a large audience, may prove too rooted in late twentieth-century concerns to last for generations. Of course, similar critiques can be raised about the classical *tkhines*. All of this appears to contradict Sered's assertion that domestic religion is no less "noble, beautiful, important, eternal, or true" than the great tradition.

Further, most of the creators of the modern devotions have real difficulty in asking God (or Shekhinah) for anything very specific; the modern uncertainty that God can bestow specific benefits is clear. Nonetheless, both forms of modern religious expression express a move away from a more abstract understanding of Judaism as a repository of truths and values, of publicly performed rituals, and a move toward something more concrete, something lived in the home and the heart.

CHAPTER TEN

THE FEMINIST SCHOLAR
AND THE *TKHINES*

You see what you want to see and what you can't help seeing.
— *AMY RICHLIN*

We are in the midst of a national debate on multiculturalism: the role of tradition and traditions, majority and minority voices within our national life. Feminist scholarship—a scholarly tradition, albeit a relatively new one, within which I stand—has sought to give voice to some of those who have been voiceless and to raise to consciousness the hidden and unspoken conventions of society that have sustained that voicelessness. To the extent that such scholarship has succeeded, it has inevitably presented us with a picture of histories, cultures, traditions, and religions as more fragmented than unified, more contested than harmonious. This picture can be unsettling—witness the outrage it has provoked. And it can challenge how we relate to our past.

Let me suggest that such questions plague not only those whose views are being challenged, but also those doing the challenging. When one begins to study a group of people or an aspect of a culture that was previously excluded from consideration, the incorporation of the topic demands a fundamental revision of how one thinks about the entire field. Equally important, though less often articulated, is the change this process demands on the part of the scholar. I wish, in this chapter, to address both aspects of the question: how the study of the religious lives of Jewish women, so long excluded from considerations of the history of "Judaism," changes our picture of Judaism, and how this study changed me. I chose this field of research out of deep conviction of its importance, yet I found that it challenged some of my deepest assumptions and loyalties.[1]

The materials I studied angered me, in ways that took me by surprise. What does one do with anger in scholarship?[2] The issue is complicated by a further question: What does the scholar do with loyalty, whether loyalty to a scholarly tradition or to a religious tradition? Feminist theory—along with cultural theory and other recent reflections on the nature of scholarship—has taught us the impossibility of scholarly impartiality and the importance of engaged, passionate scholarship. A feminist scholar strives to be engaged, responsible, and honest, and aware of the importance of her own position in the shaping of her account. I write as a scholar of Jewish studies and of women's studies, trained as a folklorist; I write, as well, as a woman and a Jew. At least in part, this chapter is a meditation on the role of anger and of loyalty, on how anger and loyalty shape a scholarly account. Perhaps most fundamentally, it is a reflection on how, as I struggled for a way to stand within the traditions I hold dear, I sought a language that could encompass both anger and loyalty, a language that would help me discover whether or not they must necessarily conflict. Have I found it? I am not sure.

Most folklorists who study women's culture engage, relatively unreflexively, in advocacy of women and valorization of women's culture. Two recent collections of essays concerning women's folklore[3] tend to stress either the real power women hold (of which we may previously have been unaware) or women's resistance to male domination, to gender stereotypes, or to male definitions of female roles. Such folklorists typically do not write about the ways in which women's culture and folklore express *submission* to ideologies of male domination or *acceptance* of male gender constructions.[4] Yet women *do* acquiesce to such ideologies, and we must try to understand why.[5] What do institutions, cultures, and religions offer to women in exchange for their submission? For that matter—although it is not quite the same issue—what does the academy offer to feminist scholars, and what sort of submission is the price?

One reason that feminist scholars who study women tend to write about women's hidden power or women's resistance is that most of us are women. That is, we feel loyalty to and solidarity with other women. Furthermore, we are women who have broken gender stereotypes by becoming scholars. Out of an awareness of our own struggles, and whether we realize it or not, we look for similar consciousness in the women we study. Just as we resist oppression, we wish to find women of other cultures or other historical periods who also resisted—women with whom we can identify.[6]

For those of us who study Jewish women, as for others who study their own ethnic, national, or religious group, or their own class, the conflict can be even more complex. We have loyalties to Jewishness and Judaism, as well as to women. For me, the loyalty to Judaism goes deep into my childhood. Judaism is my central identity and source of meaning; I became a scholar of Jewish studies because I am a Jew, and the two aspects of Jewishness, the intellectual and the practical, are not easily separable for me. Even now, as a teacher, I am an advocate for Judaism: I want my students to appreciate its beauty, depth, and power.

Yet clearly, there is a way in which this gorgeous tradition is not addressed to me as a Jewish woman, except very indirectly. And although I have the tools of the scholar—the ability to read classical Jewish texts in their original languages—in some sense I cannot "really" be a Jewish scholar. Analyzing the symbolic use of gender representations can illuminate this dilemma. The feminine gender of the Torah goes far beyond a mere accident of grammar. The Torah is Israel's bride, and the consummation of the marriage is celebrated every time the Torah is undressed, opened, and read with a pointer. This gendered trope of Torah study is repeated over and over throughout centuries of Jewish literature. And while this is not my main point, there is a curious overlap, perhaps peculiar to the world of Jewish studies, between secular and religious scholarship. I find that the ghost of the world of the yeshiva hovers over scholarly meetings and that it is not always clear which norms apply.[7] My dilemma is rendered the more peculiar because I could never have studied at a yeshiva in the first place. And this, of course, accounts in part for the hostility I still sometimes meet, to my surprise, when I present my work at meetings of Jewish scholars.

I turned to the study of the *tkhines* in order to find a place to stand within Judaism. At first, I saw my study as a response to and defense against the early feminist critique of Judaism, a critique that claimed that because Judaism excluded women from *public* religious roles, it effectively excluded them from *all* religious life. I thought this critique blindly applied present-day standards to the past and was poorly informed even about the varieties of Jewish practice in history. Partly because I was trained as a folklorist (a group slow to grapple with issues of power)[8] and partly because of my loyalty to Judaism, I began this study with the (mostly unconscious) assumption that my task was to valorize women's religious lives—that is, to describe their vibrant, rich, independent, and resistant women's culture. I further assumed (or at least fervently hoped) that I would be able to accomplish this without implicating Judaism in women's oppression. In fact, I thought that simply demonstrating that women *had* religious lives was enough to show that they were not seriously oppressed.

Yet the deeper I got into my material and the more I tried to give it a precise social and historical location, the more my hopes and assumptions were frustrated and disappointed. I did find some that women had more access to knowledge of the classics of Jewish tradition—in Yiddish translation and paraphrase—than is usually assumed. There was a large body of popular religious literature in Yiddish: ethical guides that excerpted a whole range of rabbinic literature, collections of tales from the Zohar and other mystical books, homilies on the weekly biblical portion. I also found that there were many more historically traceable women authors of *tkhines* than the skeptical earlier research literature had led me to believe. But I found neither the independant vibrant culture of resistance I was looking for nor significant contributions by women to any aspect of the so-called mainstream religious tradition— at least not in the materials I was studying. Instead, I found a complicated web of resistance and accommodation, valorization and abnegation. After futile attempts to separate women's culture from men's culture, folk culture from elite culture, that is, to isolate single voices in this multivocal mess, I realized that it was more important to attend to the way different layers of the culture related to each other. But once I began to do that, I found I could no longer avoid seeing the power relations embedded and reproduced within my texts. My efforts to define and valorize an Ashkenazic women's culture—and thus at some level to get "Judaism" off the hook—began to seem naive, as I recognized that the gender representations that controlled women's lives were enmeshed in the very fiber of Ashkenazic Judaism.

It is possible to pursue the project of valorization on a more sophisticated level, for example, by calling for an inclusive view of history or culture (we only understand what "Judaism" is when we know about the religious lives of *all* Jews, women and men, scholars and "ordinary folk"), and this was my strategy for some time.[9] However, I now think it is more important to turn to a consideration of the issues raised by a recognition that women *are* often relatively powerless, that they often acquiesce to this condition, and that otherwise valuable institutions, cultures, religions are implicated in women's powerlessness and acquiescence.

My loyalty to Judaism prompts me to insist that the *value* of these institutions and social practices is crucial here. We must avoid oversimplifying "Judaism:" it is not a monolith. Men's and women's culture, elite or folk, all of it is improvised, inconsistent, various. Most important, for our purposes, there is a great deal to Judaism besides an ideology of male domination. Like all great religious traditions, Judaism contains rich and profound texts, traditions, rituals, and customs. This helps us to understand why women—and nonlearned men—would acquiesce to a system of meaning that, in part, disempowers them. It offers them something in return.[10] Further, it is inaccurate to speak of a *single* ideology of male domination or of a single woman's response—whether of resistance or something else.[11] It's all much messier than that.

One further theoretical reflection on the problem of acquiescence: There can be a variety of motivations for acquiescence. The most brutal is physical coercion. At least under certain conditions, slaves acquiesce or die. The most benign, perhaps, is the one I described above: in order to get the good things inherent in an institution or social practice, one agrees, though not always entirely freely or consciously, to accept some of the bad things. Herman Rebell, in an attempt to theorize hegemonized social experience, describes the dominated individual's situation less benignly, as being caught in a double bind, forced, because of internalized, inescapable, mutually conflicting social roles, to engage in culturally necessary betrayal. Rebell calls the paralysis that results "blocked speech."[12] In other words, the speech required by at least one of the individual's roles is blocked—cannot be uttered, perhaps, cannot even be formulated. The concept of blocked speech provides a way to understand the experience of those eighteenth-century Jewish women who aspired to be scholars, as well as that of those who wish to be both good feminists and good Jews today. Not surprisingly, the *tkhine* authors I feel closest to are those who also felt pain at their complex relationship to the male scholarly tradition.

THE EVIDENCE OF THE *TKHINES*

Let me turn to an investigation of women's power and powerlessness, resistance and acquiescence, in early modern Ashkenazic culture. In the course of the discussion, I will revisit some of the texts discussed earlier in the book, although in a different key. My analysis is based primarily on a reading of the Yiddish *tkhines* published in Western and Eastern Europe from 1648 to 1830 and on a comparison of them with their midrashic or kabbalistic Hebrew sources. Of course, the *tkhines* give us only one window onto Ashkenazic Jewish life; different views could be obtained by using a different set of sources, such as the responsa literature, other genres of devotional literature in Yiddish, sermons, and letters. Nonetheless, the *tkhines* show us five different types of relations between women's religion and elite, male religion: (1) a valorization of women's separate sphere; (2) rituals created by women expressing some sort of women's religious culture; (3) a distancing of women from supposedly "desirable" male activities; (4) an appropriation and transformation of motifs from scholarly culture; and (5) a direct challenge to elite, male gender definitions.

The Valorization of Women's Sphere

Some *tkhines* endow women's separate sphere with religious value, thus lending dignity and holiness to women's lives. Yet the act of valorizing the women's sphere also reinforces traditional roles. One important trope that accomplishes both ends in the *tkhine* literature is the exemplification of women's roles by the biblical matriarchs, Sarah, Rebecca, Rachel, and Leah. Just as the standard Hebrew liturgy appeals to the merit of the patriarchs—Abraham, Isaac, and Jacob—so some *tkhines* appeal to the merit of the matriarchs or to the matriarchs themselves. Some texts depict them as the embodiment of traditional women's roles as mothers and daughters—more rarely wives—who draw from these roles the strength and knowledge to aid the petitioner. Here is an excerpt from the *Tkhine of the Matriarchs for the Shofar*, by Serl, daughter of Jacob of Dubno (the famous "Dubno Maggid," who lived from 1741 to 1804), wife of Mordecai Katz Rappoport, the rabbi of Oleksiniec in Volhynia in the late 1760s.

First we ask our mother Sarah to plead for us in the hour of judgment, that we may go out free from before this tribunal. . . . Have mercy, our mother, on your children. And especially, pray for our little children that they may not be separated from us. For you know well that it is very bitter when a child is taken away from the mother, as it happened to you. When your son Isaac was taken away from you, it caused you great anguish. And now you have the chance to plead for us. For he [at the Rosh Hashanah service] is now blowing the *shofar*, the horn of a ram, so that God will remember for us the merit of Isaac, who let himself be bound like a sheep on the altar. Therefore, Satan will be confused, and cannot at this moment accuse us.[13] So you have a chance to plead for us that the attribute of mercy may awaken towards us.

And I also ask our mother Rebecca to plead for our fathers and mothers, that they may not, heaven forbid, be separated from us. For you know well how one can long for father and mother. When Eliezer, the servant [of Abraham] took you away from your father and mother to your husband, Isaac,[14] you also wept bitterly. Therefore, you know how bad it is without a father and without a mother. May they have a year of life, a good year, and a year of livelihood.[15]

Serl weaves together biblical and midrashic motifs to depict the matriarchs as having compassion for the woman who prays for their assistance because of the similarity of their experiences to her own. Further, the matriarchs' experiences as mothers and daughters endow them with the spiritual power to intervene with God on the petitioner's behalf. Note, however, that their power is limited. Just as their power is drawn from traditional female roles, so too it is exercised in traditional female ways: out of their compassion for the petitioner, the matriarchs plead, beg, and cajole God, rather than, for example, compelling the Godhead through theurgic activity.

Even at the outset, my analysis is caught in a tangle. Showing the holiness of the domestic celebrated in the *tkhines* was my first line of defense against the charge that Judaism oppresses women, and the use of the matriarchs as role models sanctifies women's separate sphere. But I suspect that I also chose this text out of a desire to draw attention to its "flaws," perhaps even out of a desire to shock. See how the matriarchs act as intercessors, just like Christian saints! Notice the "superstition" about Satan! Even without condemning the matriarchs for their feminine means to power (and who has the power to coerce God, anyway?), my choice of this text subtly underlines our distance from its author and her readers. It expresses a certain disappointment at this distance, at the failure of the author to be a role model for me.

Women's Culture

Although I originally expected that I would find in the *tkhines* evidence concerning women's culture among Ashkenazic Jews, traces of an independent female culture have been quite scarce. But perhaps I only see this as a problem because of my continuing loyalty to the idea that there *is* something one could call "folk culture," and that therefore there *must* be something else, similar to it in nature, that one could call "women's culture."[16] In any case, there is *some* evidence in the *tkhines* for rituals created by women. And for the folklorist, rituals are one important site at which culture crystallizes.

One brief example is the prayer, discussed in Chapter 4, for biting off the end of the etrog found in several standard collections of *tkhines*, but also in the *Tsenerene*, or "women's Bible," the enormously popular collection of Yiddish homilies on the weekly biblical portion. The *Tsenerene* introduces the prayer with a description of when and how women recited it. This sounds convincingly like a record of a women's practice. It describes women's custom of biting off the end of the etrog (citron) on Hoshana Rabba (the seventh day of Sukkot, when the etrog is no longer needed), and giving money to charity, and then reciting a *tkhine* that asks God for protection during childbirth: "Lord of the World," the woman says, "because Eve ate of the apple, all of us women must suffer such great pangs as to die. Had I been there, I would not have had any enjoyment from [the fruit]." Thus repudiating Eve's sin, the woman claims that she should be exempt from Eve's punishment, painful childbirth. Indeed, she has been careful to obey God's command by waiting until Hoshanah Rabba before biting off the end of the etrog. "Just so, now I have not wanted to render the etrog unfit during the whole seven days when it was used for a *mitsvah*. . . . And just as little enjoyment as I get from the stem of the etrog would I have gotten from the apple that you forbade."[17]

This text richly illustrates the complexities of trying to track down women's culture. First, there seems no reason to doubt that the custom of biting off the end of the etrog originated among women; and perhaps so did the custom of biting it off on Hoshana Rabba after giving charity. Second, the text implicitly repudiates Eve's sin and thus its consequences (the curse of painful childbirth) for the woman who recites it. The reciter points out that, unlike Eve, who disobeyed God, she has kept God's commandment and not rendered the etrog unfit by biting off the end too soon. She strongly implies that if she had been in Eve's place, she would not have eaten of the forbidden fruit. Thus, this *tkhine* rejects one of the foundational texts of Jewish tradition defining who women are. But third, there is evidence from oral tradition that, especially when etrogim were expensive and scarce, many a woman would not wait until the end of the holiday to bite off the end, fearing that some other woman might beat her to it.[18] Thus, the *tkhine* and the custom as we have them could be domestications of a women's practice, alterations of it to bring it into conformity with "normative" practice, which requires that the etrog be kept intact until the end of Sukkot.

Of course, we have no way of knowing *who*—men or women—undertook this alteration. But we can compare it to another *tkhine*, written by a man, for biting off the end of the etrog. This text, included in Mattithias Sobotki's *Seder tkhines*, contains no hint of the rebelliousness implicit in the *tkhine* recorded in the *Tsenerene*.[19] While Sobotki mentions that Eve's sin is the reason for painful childbirth, he eschews all connection between the etrog and the story of Eve. Instead, he has the woman petition God for an easy childbirth in part because she has kept the *mitsvah* of *blessing* the lulav and etrog. And the text adds, "May I have my child as easily as I bite off the stem of the etrog."

Was Sobotki trying to rein a particular women's prayer and custom in with his version? We cannot be sure, although there are other instances of this in the literature.[20] I read Sobotki as censoring women's traditions, especially the denial that the punishment for Eve's sin should apply to all women. And I cheer on the woman who repudiates Eve's disobedience, even though that may implicate her in the rejection of an even more independent and powerful women's custom, that of biting off the *pittam* during Sukkot.[21]

There is another complexity here as well. Sobotki was one of a very small number of men who took women and their religious lives seriously enough to write for them in Yiddish. Yet, like Simeon Frankfurt, author of a guide to dealing with the sick, dying, and dead, or Benjamin Aaron Solnik, author of a guide to the observance of the three "women's commandments," his concern for women is laced with a prescriptive ideal, to guide women toward what he regarded as their proper role and place. And both Sobotki and Solnik insist on Eve's act as a defining moment for later women.

Distanced Participation

A third stance expressed in the *tkhine* literature is one that takes specifically male activities to be of supreme importance and places women at the margins of those activities. The spatial emblem for this is the architecture of the traditional synagogue, which places men at the center, close to the Holy Ark and the Torah scrolls, and keeps women at a distance, behind the *mehitsah* (partition), or in a balcony or separate room.[22] This also finds textual expression in the *tkhines*.

As we saw in Chapter 1, here are two noteworthy phenomena. First, many *tkhines*, especially those published in Western Europe in the seventeenth and early eighteenth centuries, are direct paraphrases or adaptations of Hebrew models. Second, the Hebrew prayers from which the *tkhines* are adapted were written as part of the great wave of religious revival that swept the Jewish people under the influence of Lurianic Kabbalah and Safed pietism.[23]

It seems indisputable that the rise of *tkhines* as a genre is part of Safed pietism.[24] Nonetheless, the Yiddish adaptations of mystical Hebrew devotions alter them systematically, for example, by omitting kabbalistic material such as divine names (and in the process rendering the prayers close to unintelligible). The woman, it would seem, knows that there is such a thing as mystical prayer but does not know any of the details about how actually to engage in it. This is expressed explicitly in the following *tkhine*:

> One should say this *tkhine* evening and morning before each prayer. . . .
> O Lord of all the world, you are an almighty and merciful God, and you know well that we are only flesh and blood, and have not the power to combine your holy Names and [engage in] all the mystical intentions in all of the prayers and all of the blessings, as they are set out in each prayer and in each blessing. And even if we knew the art of combination and the Names in all the prayers and blessings, we would still be unable to adequately recount your praise and your wonders. For we are only human beings, nothing but flesh and blood . . .

Up until this point it sounds like no "mere human" can engage in proper mystical prayer, but the *tkhine* concludes:

> May my prayer ascend before you to make a crown on your holy head with the other prayers of Jews who do know how to engage in mystical intentions and how to combine the letter combinations for the holy Names that belong to each prayer and blessing, and that bring together unity and holiness even unto the seventh heaven, Amen.[25]

Thus, the woman reciting this *tkhine* knows that there *are* Jews who can pray with the requisite mystical techniques, but she also knows that she is not among them. The reader of this *tkhine* and of other, similar texts, is not made privy to the kabbalistic mysteries, the teachings concerning the Godhead that alone really make sense of the intentions and combinations to which the text refers.

Once again, however, we are dealing with a complex situation: This *tkhine* is a Yiddish adaptation of a Hebrew prayer written by a man, R. Leib Pohavitser, for *men* who were not learned in the kabbalistic mysteries. Ashkenazic Jewry was founded on complex hierarchies: learned men were at the top, then came men who knew enough to read this prayer in Hebrew but did not know any Kabbalah, and finally came women (and even more ignorant men), who needed to read it in Yiddish.

At first blush, this seems like a *tkhine* that we can safely love to hate. But to do so accepts a certain hierarchy of values. Why is it so important to know Kabbalah? Who defines mysticism as the center? Clearly, Safed pietism does. But even male hasidim, who clearly honored Lurianic Kabbalah, and strove as mystics to cleave to God, could recite a prayer like this. As men of a lesser generation, they might say, the old mystical techniques are beyond their ken; all they can do is humbly petition God with broken hearts.

Nonetheless, there is a curious kind of double vision here. The modern field of Jewish studies has struggled over the issue of the centrality of Kabbalah (as opposed to either philosophy or law) in Jewish religious history. In a variety of ways, I have been in the camp of those who wish to see spirituality at the heart of Judaism. This makes it seem terribly important to figure out whether or not women were completely excluded from knowledge of Kabbalah.[26] Yet perhaps this question has assumed too much importance, in view of the actual content of women's spiritual lives. Or perhaps this presumes too narrow a definition of spirituality, one that is too centered in elite, male ways of being Jewish. The study of the *tkhines*—seeing them for the deeply spiritual texts they are—can reawaken a respect for simpler forms of piety.

Transformations

While the Yiddish adaptation of R. Leib Pohavitser's prayer places women outside the margins of mystical prayer looking longingly at the true mystical practitioners, some *tkhines* do adapt material from kabbalistic texts and transform it in the service of women's distinctive practice. The examples of transformation are so complex and extensive that I can merely suggest the outlines of one of them.[27] *Tkhine imrei shifre*, "The *Tkhine* of Shifrah's Words," attributed to Shifrah bas Joseph, and discussed in Chapter 6, was probably written in the 1770s. As we have seen, it contains a great deal of material adapted from the Zohar via an intermediate source, a paraphrase of the Zohar in Yiddish. One of the four *tkhines* contained in this work deals with women's Sabbath observance, especially the kindling of the Sabbath lights.

Rejecting the rabbinic view that the *mitsvah* of lighting the Sabbath candles was imposed upon women because Eve extinguished the light of the world by her sin, Shifrah argues that the real reason that women light candles is in honor of the Shekhinah, the tenth *sefirah*, a feminine aspect of the Godhead. Further, by weaving together two passages from a Yiddish paraphrase of the Zohar, she invests the act of candle lighting with cosmic significance, comparing the woman's act to that of the High Priest kindling the lights in the Temple, which the Zohar takes to be symbolic of the arousal to love and union of the seven lower *sefirot*, or emanations of the Godhead. This union is the goal of mystical prayer and ritual. In contrast to the prayer of Leib Pohavitser quoted above, which excludes women from mystical prayer, this text makes the quintessentially female act of candle lighting into a full-fledged mystical practice.

This is a text that I love. Here we have a woman who clearly had a deep interest in the mystical. Much of her *tkhine* consists of quotations and paraphrases of *Nakhalas Tsevi*, Tsevi Hirsh Khotsh's Yiddish paraphrase of portions of the Zohar.[28] Further, she is creative in her use of sources, combining different passages and adding some material of her own to get the meaning that she wants. And she asserts that women act in honor of the Shekhinah, a feminine aspect of the Godhead. Nevertheless, although this *tkhine* turns the woman who recites it into a mystical practitioner, it does so precisely within the domestic sphere. Thus, this can be seen as yet another version of the valorization of women's traditional roles—although, unlike the matriarchs in the first text we quoted, Shifrah does not beg, plead, or cajole, but acts theurgically.

Challenges to Traditional Gender Definitions

Finally, a few *tkhines* push the boundaries and assert that women should have somewhat greater access to highly valued activities traditionally reserved for men. The most explicit discussion of women's religious roles that I have yet found in the *tkhines* is in the introduction to *Tkhine of the Matriarchs* (*Tkhine imohes*), by Leah Horowitz.[29] This remarkable woman, as we have seen, was known for her expertise in Talmud. The *tkhine* itself shows her familiarity with the Zohar and other kabbalistic sources in the original languages. Of all the women authors of *tkhines*, Leah alone wrote in Hebrew and Aramaic, as well as in Yiddish. Her *tkhine* has a Hebrew introduction, an Aramaic liturgical poem, and a Yiddish prose paraphrase of the liturgical poem.

Leah has little patience with those who would deny her the authority to deal with halakhic matters and calls them "fools." Yet her view of family roles seems quite traditional. When, according to Leah, should a woman resist her husband's authority? Only when he neglects the study of Torah, or causes his sons to neglect it; otherwise, she says, "Let him wear the pants in the family." Most interesting for our purposes, however, is her discussion of the nature of women's spiritual power:

> Well-known are the words of Rav Aha that are cited in Yalkut Ruth,[30] that the generations are redeemed only by the merit of women. And this would appear puzzling . . . for men have more commandments. Why are they denigrated when it is in their power to bring the redemption? And one can say that it is written in the verse, "And with weeping they shall come," and that tears are common among women.[31] But "the prayer of a person is not heard except in synagogue."[32] If this is the case, it is proper for the women of our day, "for the day of the Lord is near,"[33] to go to the synagogue morning and evening to pray with "copious tears . . ."[34] for the sake of the Shekhinah . . . and then perhaps by their merit, "a redeemer will come to Zion,"[35] Amen.

Leah argues that women have the power to bring redemption with their tearful prayer for the exiled Shekhinah—if only they would pray regularly in synagogue. Thus, her point is twofold: First, women's prayer is more powerful than is usually supposed. Second, although it is not according to established custom in her day, women *ought* to pray regularly in synagogue, because only in synagogue can their prayers be heard and have their full redemptive effect.

Yet whatever Leah had to say on this topic and on the others she takes up in the introduction, her voice was effectively silenced. Or perhaps it would be more precise to say that there was no audience who could hear her. This may be an example of blocked speech: some things could not be said, even when someone tried to say them. Leah tried to be both woman and scholar, two mutually contradictory roles in Ashkenazic culture. The introduction to her *tkhine* was in Hebrew, as any work that made a claim to being valid scholarship must be. As I discussed in Chapter 7, this cost her her chosen audiences. The women could not read Hebrew and the scholarly men did not read *tkhines*.

Leah Horowitz, unlike most other *tkhine* authors, is clearly angry and in pain. The deck is stacked against her. Despite her learning, she cannot make herself heard. Is the learning itself a trap? Does it imply acceptance of someone else's rules? I wonder about this for myself as well. Because I can read texts and have classical training, I am a "respectable" feminist scholar. Indeed, I have always been very careful to speak and write in such a way as to be credible in the world of academic Jewish studies. Especially early in my career, I deliberately gave my articles long, boring (and thus scholarly sounding and nonthreatening) titles.[36] Have I lost something by acting this way? Compromised my solidarity with my less-well-educated, more radical fellow feminists? Or, perhaps, have I been "writing in Hebrew," as Leah did, because I have been more concerned to make my case to an audience of scholarly men than with anyone else? Why did I pick this particular audience? Does it represent "legitimate authority" for me?

If hegemony includes the silent, unarticulated, and unnoticed ways in which a system maintains its power, and ideology the articulated and thus directly contestable ways in which it justifies that power, this essay has moved from *tkhines* that submit to hegemony, or resist it in a muted way, to those that contest ideology. The *Tkhine of the Matriarchs for the Shofar* acquiesces to (and sanctifies) women's separate sphere. The *tkhine* for biting off the tip of the etrog resists and submits at the same time. It repudiates Eve as the paradigm for later women, yet constrains women's practice within the limitations of *halakhah*. R. Leib Pohavitser's prayer, transposed into Yiddish, definitely shuts women out of mystical prayer and practice. Yet, by making that exclusion articulate, it raises it to the conscious level, and thus opens it to challenge. Shifrah's candle-lighting *tkhine* incorporates and transforms the rabbinic and mystical traditions in the service of enhancing women's own religious performance, yet keeps that performance within the domestic arena. Leah Horowitz offers a direct challenge to the exclusion of women from scholarly and mystical discourse, articulating a mystical theory of the power of women's prayer and of her own power to engage the male world of scholarship. Yet this portion of her work found no audience and disappeared.

In trying to pull all this together, we should note one important feature common to all of these varieties of women's religion in Ashkenaz. Women's Judaism did not exist in a vacuum; its terms are set by "Judaism," to which women must respond. The religious world we can infer from the *tkhine* literature is, essentially, a set of female variants of male

Jewish culture. It does not comprise a Judaism that takes women as its starting point. The *tkhines* do show that women were influenced by the major religious movements that swept Judaism in the seventeenth and eighteenth centuries. But they do not provide any evidence that women created, shaped, or even influenced these religious movements.

Note the asymmetry. Traditional Judaism is structured in such a way as to endow learned men with the power to interpret or define "Judaism" in all its wondrous variety. Women, if they are to be Jews, *must* heed the teachings of scholars, whether they accept, reject, or transform these teachings. But learned men were by and large free to ignore women, or at the least to consider women's religious lives unimportant and uninteresting. To put it slightly differently, Judaism does have a textual tradition and a way of life, however multifaceted, of which learned men are the arbiters. Further, the values of the culture are such that it is the duty of these men to impose, as best they can, their views of religious life on the less learned.

Finally—and here is the real hook—in order to be Jews, women had to (still have to?) accept the basic values of the system, including the central place of Torah study and thus the authority of Torah scholars.[37] While they could respond to this system, with its implied exclusion of virtually all women from positions of authority, in a variety of ways, some responses were still not possible—as long as those women still wanted to be Jews. And it is perfectly clear that all of those whose voices are present in these texts, however they felt about being women within Judaism, *did* want to be Jews—or, more precisely, could not think of stepping outside.

It should be apparent that I am also talking about myself here. If *I* want to be a Jew, if I want to participate in that rich, powerful, and beautiful system of meaning, which I love, what can I and can I not say, as a scholar, as a woman, as a Jew, about the place of women within Judaism? The range of possible responses is different for me than it was for Serl, Leah, and Shifrah, but the dilemma is the same: What does loyalty to Judaism demand? What does loyalty to women demand? What does loyalty to scholarship demand? Some days I reach a point at which the conflicting loyalties block any response but silence.

THE SIXTH RELATION

In the course of completing work on this study, I have come to see ever more clearly the outlines of Ashkenazic women's religious culture. True, women were not among the founders and shapers of the Safed revival or Hasidism. Nonetheless, the *tkhines* reveal a whole world of women's religious lives, concerns, customs, and settings for prayer. These texts are deeply spiritual, no less so than complex and esoteric mystical works. The women who composed these prayers addressed the spiritual issues of their day, whether on the level of domestic piety or national redemption. The *tkhines* themselves are at home in the literature produced for the intellectual middle class at this period; they belong among the guides to the upright life, books of customs, condensations of guides to pious practices, and digests of mystical teachings that were read by householders and artisans. Indeed, the *tkhines* show how much women were also a part of this intellectual and spiritual world.

Yet the *tkhines* also made their own unique contribution to this world, and here we can add a sixth relation to the five enumerated in the previous chapter between women's religion and elite, male religion: the *tkhines* provided a directness of passionately emotional personal prayer, mostly absent from the more collective and formalized male worship experience. Indeed, the struggle for emotional engagement in liturgical prayer was constant throughout Jewish history; for this reason, the hasidic master Nahman of Bratzlav required his disciples to set aside time each day to cry out their own personal prayers to God in their own language—Yiddish. Because they were men, obligated and accustomed to pray the fixed liturgy in Hebrew, they needed to be instructed to speak to God in Yiddish; only through the power of the spoken language could they bind their hearts in intimate relation with the divine.[1] The *tkhines*, supplications in Yiddish, provided precisely this power, enabling women to pour out their hearts to God.

NOTES

Part of this preface is taken from my essay "Traditional Yiddish Literature: A Source for the Study of Women's Religious Lives." The Jacob Pat Memorial Lecture, February 26, 1987, Harvard University Library. Published as a separate pamphlet by Harvard University Library, 1988.

1. *Berkhes* is the Western Yiddish word for the braided Sabbath bread, called *hallah* by some Eastern European Jews.

2. *Tkhines* (Amsterdam: 1648), col. [5c], and in many later editions of the same collection, usually entitled *Seder Tkhines*.

3. The Yiddish word *tkhine* (pl. *tkhines*) derives from the Hebrew *tehinnah* (pl. *tehinnot*), meaning "supplication."

4. Isaac Benjacob, *Otsar ha-sefarim* (Vilna: Romm, 1880), letter *tav*, no. 562. On Benjacob's bibliography, see Shimeo Brisman, *A History and Guide to Judaic Bibliography* (Cincinnati: Hebrew Union College Press; New York: Ktav, 1977), 19–23.

5. With rare exceptions, the only *tkhines* Benjacob lists individually are attributed to male authors. By contrast, Moritz Steinschneider, the greatest nineteenth-century bibliographer of Hebraica, did not ignore works in Yiddish, nor *tkhines* in particular. However, his listings of them, in the *Catalogus Librorum Hebraeorum in Bibliotheca Bodleiana* (Berlin, 1852–1860) and in a series of articles in the bibliographical periodical *Serapeum*, in 1848–1849 and 1864–1866, include only works published before about 1730, thus excluding most of the Eastern European materials, which were published later.

6. Eleazar Shulman, *Sefat yehudit ashkenazit ve-sifrutah* (Riga: E. Levin, 1913), esp. 67–69; Israel Zinberg, *Old Yiddish Literature from its Origins to the Haskalah Period*, vol. 7 of Zinberg, *A History of Jewish Literature* (Cincinnati: Hebrew Union College Press; New York: Ktav, 1975; first published in Yiddish 1929–1937), esp. 249–59; Max Weinreich's most fully developed statement on this literature is found

in his *History of the Yiddish Language* (Chicago: University of Chicago, 1980), first published in Yiddish as *Geshikhte fun der yidisher shprakh* (New York: YIVO, 1973), esp. 259–62; on Shmuel Niger, see n. 7.

7. Niger, "Di yidishe literatur un di lezerin," reprinted in his *Bleter geshikhte fun der yidisher literatur* (New York, Sh. Niger Bukh-Komitet, 1959; first published in 1912), 35–107; now available in an abridged English translation by Sheva Zucker, "Yiddish literature and the female reader," in *Women of the Word*, ed. Judith R. Baskin (Detroit: Wayne State University Press, 1994), 70–90. Niger takes an essentialist view of women's literature; one of the main points of the essay is that "women's nature" determines the character of Yiddish literature for women. See the analysis of this essay in Naomi Seidman, *A Marriage Made in Heaven* (Berkeley: University of California Press, 1997), 3–15. See also Ezra Korman, ed., *Yidishe dikhterins* (Chicago: L. M. Shteyn Farlag, 1928), an anthology of works by Yiddish women poets, including several from the sixteenth and seventeenth centuries.

8. For the exponents of the *shpilman* theory, see Max Erik, *Di geshikhte fun der yidisher literatur* (New York: Alveltlekher ydisher kultur-kongres, 1979; 1st ed. 1927), 27–202; Zinberg, *Old Yiddish Literature*, chap. 3. On the appeal of the *shpilman* in particular, and of the courtly romances and biblical epics more generally, see Khone Shmeruk, "*Medresh Itsik* and the Problem of its Literary Traditions," in Itsik Manger, *Medresh Itsik* (Jerusalem: Magnes Press, 1984). Shmeruk also mentions the lack of interest in *tkhines* and other forms of popular religious literature in Yiddish. For a summary of Shmeruk's arguments against the *shpilman* theory, and references to his earlier works on the subject, see Shmeruk, "Can the Cambridge Manuscript Support the *Spielmann* Theory in Yiddish Literature?" in Chava Turniansky, ed., *Studies in Yiddish Literature and Folklore* (Jerusalem: Institute of Jewish Studies, Hebrew University, 1986), 1–36.

9. See, for example, Erik's discussion of the rise of Yiddish religious literature in Poland, which he contrasts unfavorably with earlier secular literature, in *Geshikhte*, 223–26.

10. Zinberg, *Old Yiddish Literature*, chap. 8.

11. Whether or not Jews ever recited the statutory prayers of the liturgy in Yiddish rather than Hebrew is still a matter of debate; for a recent contribution to the debate, see David Fishman, "Mikoyekh davenen af yidish: a bintl metodologishe bamerkungen un naye mekoyrim," *Yivo Bleter* n.s. 1 (1991): 69–92.

12. Freehof, "Devotional Literature in the Vernacular," *CCAR Yearbook* 33 (1923): 375–474.

13. Ibid., 380.

14. Ibid., 376n.

15. Or perhaps he simply could not imagine that premodern Jewish women could be authors of liturgy. Reform Judaism readily incorporated works by such nineteenth- and twentieth-century poets as Nina Salamon and Emma Lazarus into its liturgy. My thanks to Arthur Green for drawing this to my attention.

16. Tracy Guren Klirs, ed., *The Merit of Our Mothers: A Bilingual Anthology of Jew-

ish Women's Prayers (Cincinnati: Hebrew Union College Press, 1992); Rivka Zakutinsky, ed., *Techinas: A Voice from the Heart* (Brooklyn, NY: Aura Press, 1992); and
Norman Tarnor, ed., *A Book of Jewish Women's Prayers: Translations from the Yiddish* (Northvale, N.J.: Jason Aronson, 1995). All of these volumes contain *tkhines*
from the nineteenth and twentieth centuries, or, as in the case of Klirs, nineteenth-
century editions of eighteenth-century works. My study deals primarily with
tkhines from the seventeenth and eighteenth centuries.

INTRODUCTION

1. Among Scholem's numerous works, his basic introduction to Kabbalah is *Major
Trends in Jewish Mysticism* (New York: Schocken Books, 1954).

2. Moshe Idel, *Kabbalah: New Perspectives* (New Haven: Yale University Press,
1988).

3. See Moshe Idel, *The Mystical Experience in Abraham Abulafia* (Albany: SUNY
Press, 1988).

4. See Gershom Scholem, "Kabbalah and Myth," in his *On the Kabbalah and Its
Symbolism* (New York: Schocken Books, 1965), 87–117, and Louis Jacobs, "The Uplifting of Sparks in Later Jewish Mysticism," in *Jewish Spirituality from the
Sixteenth-Century Revival to the Present,* ed. Arthur Green (New York: Crossroad,
1987), 99–126.

5. The classic work on the Sabbatian movement during Sabbatai Zevi's lifetime is
Gershom Scholem, *Sabbatai Zevi, the Mystical Messiah* (Princeton: Princeton University Press, 1973).

6. See Gershom Scholem, "Redemption through Sin," in *The Messianic Idea in Judaism* (New York: Schocken Books, 1971), 78–141.

7. On these debates, see the recent work of Moshe (Murray) Rosman, especially
The Lord's Jews (Cambridge: Harvard University Press, 1990) and *Founder of Hasidism* (Berkeley: University of California Press, 1996).

8. See Gershom Scholem, "*Devekut,* or Communion with God," *Messianic Idea in
Judaism,* 203–226.

9. For recent discussions of the teachings of early hasidism, see Rivka Schatz Uffenheimer, *Hasidism as Mysticism* (Princeton: Princeton University Press, 1993)
and Moshe Idel, *Hasidism: Between Ecstasy and Magic* (Albany: State University
of New York Press, 1995).

10. Both recent and classic essays on the history and teachings of hasidism are col-
lected in *Essential Papers on Hasidism,* ed. Gershon David Hundert (New York:
New York University Press, 1991). See also the newest scholarship in Ada
Rapoport-Albert, ed., *Hasidism Reappraised* (London: Vallentine Mitchell, 1996).

11. See Ada Rapoport-Albert, "On Women in Hasidism," in *Jewish History: Essays
in Honour of Chimen Abramsky,* ed. Steven J. Zipperstein and Ada Rapoport-Albert
(London: Halban, 1988), 495–525.

12. See Chapters 1 and 6 for further discussion.

CHAPTER I. THE *TKHINES*

This chapter draws upon several previously published essays: "The Traditional Piety of Ashkenazic Women," in *Jewish Spirituality from the Sixteenth-Century Revival to the Present*, ed. Arthur Green (New York: Crossroad, 1987), 245–75; "Traditional Yiddish Literature: A Source for the Study of Women's Religious Lives," The Jacob Pat Memorial Lecture, February 26, 1987, Harvard University Library (published as a separate pamphlet by Harvard University Library, 1988); "Prayers in Yiddish and the Religious World of Ashkenazic Women," in *Jewish Women in Historical Perspective*, ed. Judith Baskin (Detroit: Wayne State University Press, 1991), 159–81.

1. Mendele Mokher Seforim, *Of Bygone Days*, in *A Shtetl and Other Yiddish Novellas*, ed. Ruth Wisse and trans. Raymond Scheindlin (New York: Behrman House, 1973), 300–301.

2. Recent works have begun the task of describing the religious lives of "ordinary Jews." Especially important for Ashkenazic Judaism in the early modern period are the following: Zeev Gries, *Sifrut ha-hanhagot* (Jerusalem: Mosad Bialik, 1989) and *Sefer, sofer, ve-sipur be-reshit ha-hasidut* (Tel-Aviv: Hakibbutz Hameuchad Publishing House, 1992); Sylvie-Anne Goldberg, *Crossing the Jabbok* (Berkeley: University of California Press, 1996); Avriel Bar-Levav, "Rabbi Aharon Berachiah mi-Modena ve-rabbi Naftali ha-Kohen Katz, avot ha-mehabrim sifrei holim u-metim," *Asufot* 9 (1995): 189–274. For the early modern Italian Judaism, see Robert Bonfil, *Jewish Life in Renaissance Italy* (Berkeley: University of California Press, 1994); David Ruderman, *Kabbalah, Magic, and Science* (Cambridge: Harvard University Press, 1988); and the works of Elliot Horowitz: "Speaking of the Dead: The Emergence of the Eulogy among Italian Jewry in the Sixteenth Century," in *Preachers of the Italian Ghetto*, ed. David Ruderman (Berkeley: University of California Press, 1992), 127–62; "Coffee, Coffeehouses, and the Nocturnal Rituals of Early Modern Jewry," *AJS Review* 14 (1989): 17–46; "The Eve of Circumcision: A Chapter in the History of Jewish Nightlife," *Journal of Social History* 23 (1989): 46–69; and "The Rite to be Reckless: On the Perpetration and Interpretation of Purim Violence," *Poetics Today* 15 (1994): 9–54. For Ashkenazic Judaism in the medieval period, see Ivan Marcus, *Rituals of Childhood* (New Haven, Yale University Press, 1996).

3. In many Jewish communities throughout the ages most women were probably not literate. Ashkenazic women seem to have had a higher rate of literacy than Jewish women in many other communities; there are many more books aimed at women in Yiddish than there are in the other Jewish vernaculars. On nineteenth-century Eastern Europe, see Shaul Stampfer, "Gender Differentiation and Education of the Jewish Woman in Nineteenth-Century Eastern Europe," in *From Shtetl to Socialism*, ed. Antony Polonsky (London: Littman Library of Jewish Civilization, 1993), 187–211.

4. Two recent publications acquaint us with the prayers of non-Ashkenazic women. A fifteenth-century manuscript translation of the daily, Sabbath, and holiday

prayers into Ladino, made for a woman, has recently been published in a critical edition; see Moshe Lazar, ed., *Siddur Tefillot: A Woman's Ladino Prayer Book,* limited ed. (Culver City, Ca.: Labyrinthos, 1995). For a translation of the private prayers in Hebrew of an eighteenth-century Italian Jewish women, see Nina Beth Cardin, ed. and trans., *Out of the Depths* (Northvale, N.J.: Jason Aronson, 1991).

5. This literature was the primary reading material of Glikl bas Judah Leib, also known as Glückel of Hameln (1646/7–1724), whose memoirs are the only direct record we have of the life of a woman from this period. As Natalie Zemon Davis has shown, Glikl made wonderful use of the stories and morality tales she found in the ethical literature in Yiddish. See *The Memoirs of Glückel of Hameln,* trans. Marvin Lowenthal (New York: Schocken, 1977); the somewhat fuller translation, *The Life of Glückel of Hameln,* trans. Beth-Zion Abrahams (London: East and West Library, 1962); and the study by Natalie Zemon Davis, *Women on the Margins* (Cambridge: Harvard University Press, 1995), 1–62.

6. There was also a large secular literature in Yiddish, including (at different periods) Arthurian romances, epic poems on biblical and historical themes, plays, chapbooks, travelogues, and historical works. And there is evidence of an extensive oral tradition of prayers, remedies, and rituals.

Much has been published on many of these genres of popular Yiddish writings. The most important works include: Israel Zinberg, *Old Yiddish Literature from Its Origins to the Haskalah Period,* vol. 7 of Zinberg, *A History of Jewish Literature,* trans. and ed. by Bernard Martin (Cincinnati and New York: Hebrew Union College Press and Ktav Publishing House, 1975); S. Niger, "Di yidishe literatur un di lezerin," in his *Bleter Geshikhte fun der yidisher literatur* (New York: Sh. Niger Bukh-komitet baym alveltlekhn yidishn kultur-kongres, 1959); now available in an abridged English translation, "Yiddish Literature and the Female Reader," in *Women of the Word,* ed. Judith Baskin (Detroit: Wayne State University Press, 1994), 70–90. See also the recent analysis of this essay by Naomi Seidman, *A Marriage Made in Heaven* (Berkeley: University of California Press, 1997), 3–5. For a comprehensive annotated bibliography of the tales and other narrative literature in Yiddish, see Sara Zfatman, *ha-Siporet be-yidish me-reshitah ad 'Shivhei ha-Besht' (1504–1814)* (Jerusalem: Institute of Jewish Studies of the Hebrew University, 1985). An excellent introduction to the ethical literature is found in the introduction to the exemplary study by Chava Turniansky, an annotated edition of Alexander ben Isaac Pfaffenhofen, *Sefer Massah u-merivah* (Jerusalem: Magnes Press, 1985), esp. chap. 3. The *Tsenerene,* by Jacob ben Isaac Ashkenazi of Yanov, first published about 1600 (Zinberg, *Old Yiddish Literature,* 130), became known as the "woman's Torah." Not a literal translation of the Pentateuch into Yiddish, the *Tsenerene* instead contains rabbinic legends, ethical maxims, and exemplary tales interwoven with the biblical narrative. It is now available in a sometimes flawed and tendentious three-volume English translation by Miriam Stark Zakon (New York: Artscroll Press, 1983–84). The classic article on this work is Khone Shmeruk, "Di mizrekh-eyropeishe nuskhoos fun der Tsenerene," *For Max Weinreich on his 70th Birthday* (The Hague: Mouton, 1964), 320–33b; also available in Hebrew, "ha-

Nushaot ha-mizrah-eropeiyot shel ha-'tse'enah u-re'enah,'" in Shmeruk, *Sifrut yidish be-polin* (Jerusalem: Magnes Press, 1981), 147–64. See also Khone Shmeruk, *Sifrut yidish: perakim le-toldoteha* (Tel Aviv: Porter Institute for Poetics and Semiotics, Tel Aviv University, 1978), chaps. 1–5, and *Sifrut yidish be-polin*, part 1.

7. All of these are taken from *Seder tkhines u-vakoshes* (Fürth, 1762), which will be discussed below.

8. As with men, so, too, with women: there were men of mystical bent and men of philosophical bent, men of keen halakhic insight and men of simple piety, the learned men and the unschooled; and among the women there were the learned women and the unlettered (although, except in a few cases, women were learned only in the Yiddish devotional literature). There were women of varying spiritual gifts and varying literary powers. Even as women wrote so much less than men, making it that much harder to discern the varieties of their spiritual lives, we nonetheless can find in their *tkhines* evidence of a range of spiritual concerns and religious sensibilities.

9. On *tkhine loshn* and terms for God in early *tkhines*, see Devra Kay, "Words for 'God' in Seventeenth Century Women's Poetry in Yiddish," in *Dialects of the Yiddish Language*, ed. Dovid Katz (Oxford: Pergamon Press, 1988), 57–67.

10. In a recent article, Devra Kay argues that the *tkhines* should be seen as an alternative liturgy for women; that they are meant to replace the prayer book and are modeled on central prayers of the liturgy. Although Kay draws some interesting parallels between the content of some of the *tkhines* and some of the prayers of the Hebrew liturgy, I do not find her argument persuasive. Some of the parallels she draws are quite general and show no specific influence in wording. Further, her argument applies only to *Seder tkhines* and does not account for the many other collections, which were on occasion combined into a larger work such as *Seder tkhines u-vakoshes* (see below). Most important, if I am right about the place of *tkhines* as part of Safed pietism, then, like other genres, they are essentially *paraliturgical* rather than liturgical and may most cogently be compared with the voluntary Hebrew prayers for men that arose at about the same time. See Devra Kay, "An Alternative Prayer Canon for Women: the *Seyder tkhines*," in *Zur Geshichte der jüdischen Frau in Deutschland*, ed. Julius Carlebach (Berlin: Metropol, 1993), 49–96.

11. At least in principle. In fact, once written, many *tkhines* were quite stable over several centuries, changing only linguistically and in minor details. However, new *tkhines* continued to be written and published into the twentieth century.

12. On the *zogerke* see Zinberg, *Old Yiddish Literature*, 23–24; Shmuel Lifshits, "Esther-Khaye the Zogerin ['Sayer']," in *From a Ruined Garden: The Memorial Books of Polish Jewry*, trans. and ed. Jack Kugelmass and Jonathan Boyarin (New York: Schocken, 1983), 76–78; Niger, "Di yidishe literature un di lezerin," 52. Mark Zborowski and Elizabeth Herzog, in *Life Is with People* (New York,: Schocken, 1962), describe the *zogerke* thus: "[The women] repeat the prayers after the *zogerkeh*—a woman who, unlike most of them, is able to read and understand Hebrew.

She reads the prayer and they repeat it after her, following each syllable and intonation. When she says, 'women, now you must weep,' the women weep" (54).

13. In fact, various eighteenth-century editions of *Seder tkhines* were printed as appendices to editions of the prayer book. And in the nineteenth and twentieth centuries, *tkhines* intended to be recited in conjunction with the synagogue service were printed interspersed with the Hebrew prayers at the appropriate point in the liturgy, for example, preceding the prayer announcing the new moon.

14. The folklorist N. Prylucki quotes three "kugel songs" collected in Galicia. [His source was a brief note, "Reime bei der Bereitung des 'kigl'," signed simply A. L., from Brody, that appeared in *Mitteilungen der Gesellschaft für jüdische Volkskunde* 7 (1901): 85–86.] Kugel—a pudding, sweet or savory, of noodles, potatoes, or flour and fat—was a highlight of the Sabbath meal. These songs are in rhymed dialectical Yiddish, though they include some Hebrew phrases. One of them begins thus:

> Leave me alone, I have no time,
> I have to go prepare for Sabbath
> If I had a bigger noodle pot
> You would not have to laugh at me.

Another runs:

> Kugel, kugel, I make you truly
> Truly will I make you
> So that no one will laugh at me.
> Into the oven you go,
> Then into the mouth just so.
> May you be as good as Jacob
> and as red as Esau.

In the third example, by contrast, the lines alternate between Hebrew and Yiddish, as in some printed *tkhines*. Even though one of the Hebrew phrases faintly echoes the theme of regret for the destroyed Temple and altar found frequently in the liturgy and the *tkhines*, they seem to be chosen chiefly for their rhymes rather for their meaning. To give some sense of the play of language, the text is given both in romanization according to the Ashkenazic pronunciation (as it appears in the article in *Mitteilungen*), so as to make the rhymes apparent, and in translation.

Jihi rûtsn milfunâj (H)	May it be My will
Kigl zây mir gitrây; (Y)	Kugel, be true to me;
Eyn lûnu misbeiach (H)	We have no altar
Solst mar sân fet in weiach; (Y)	May you be rich and soft;
Migûdl w'ad kûtn (H)	From the great to the small
Solst mar taki girûtn (Y)	May you come out well.

As Prylucki points out, these are not really prayers. Nonetheless, they show Sabbath preparations—and, by implication, the Sabbath itself—as matters of concern to the woman, who wishes to prepare a memorable Sabbath meal. The continuation of the first song quoted above apostrophizes the kugel, "May we remember you all week!" Further, the third example shows familiarity not only with a certain amount of Hebrew but also with a literary form in which Yiddish and Hebrew are interspersed. This stylistic device had the effect of associating the woman's down-to-earth activities in cooking for the Sabbath, which are described in Yiddish, with the world of holiness and tradition connoted by the Hebrew phrases.

It was suggested to me by Khone Shmeruk that, rather than being actual folk rhymes or prayers about kugel, these verses form part of a tradition of poems in German and Yiddish parodying Friedrich Schiller's poem, "Das Lied von der Glock" (The Song of the Bell). One such parody, by Joseph Ahrons, is entitled "Das Lied vun die Kuggel" (Altona, 1842). However, the kugel poems quoted above resemble Schiller's poem in neither subject matter nor rhyme and meter. Cf. Khone Shmeruk, *Sifrut yiddish: Perakim le-toledoteha* (Tel Aviv: Porter Institute for Poetics and Semiotics of Tel Aviv University, 1978), 169ff.

15. Cf. Susan Sered, *Women as Ritual Experts* (New York: Oxford University Press, 1992).

16. For further discussion of *tkhines* by *maskilim*, see Chapter 9. See also Niger, "Yidishe literatur," 82–94 (which includes a list of known female authors), and Zinberg, *Old Yiddish Literature*, 250–59. Both Niger and Zinberg make the point about the maskilim. Cynthia Ozick gives the erroneous impression that virtually all *tkhines* were forged by indigent male yeshiva students. See Ozick, "Notes toward Finding the Right Question," in *On Being a Jewish Feminist*, ed. Susannah Heschel (New York: Schocken, 1983), 132–33. Ozick relies for this information on an outdated article in the *Jewish Encyclopedia* (New York: Funk and Wagnalls, 1904), 4:551. To avoid using any of these works by the *maskilim* (except in Chapter 9), I have included in this study only *tkhines* that can be documented to have existed before 1840. Solomon Freehof seems to assume that authors of *tkhines* were male: "The books were written by humble men for humble men and women"; see Freehof, "Devotional Literature in the Vernacular," *CCAR Yearbook* 33 (1923), 375–415, quote at 377.

17. On biographical sources for Leah Horowitz, see chapter 7 below. For Leah Dreyzl, see below in this chapter. Part of a *tkhine* by Serl bas Jacob is discussed in Chapter 10. It is usually easiest to trace *tkhine* authors through their male relatives.

18. My discussion of seventeenth- and eighteenth-century Ashkenazic piety and the factors that influenced it is indebted to the pioneering work of Zeev Gries and Avriel Bar-Levav. On contrafraternities, see Bonfil, *Jewish Life*; Elliot S. Horowitz, *Jewish Contrafraternities in Seventeenth Century Verona: A Study in the Social History of Piety* (Ph.D. dissertation, New Haven: Yale University, 1982); and Goldberg, *Crossing the Jabbok*. On new liturgies, see, e.g., Avraham Yaari, "Sifrei tikkunim u-tefillot le-fi Sefer Hemdat yamim," *Kiryat Sefer* 38 (1962): 97–112; and Daniel Goldschmidt, "Tefillot le-erev rosh hodesh," in Goldschmidt, *Mehkerei tefillah u-fiyyut* (Jerusalem: Magnes Press, 1980), 322–335. On liturgies connected to death, see Avriel Bar-Levav, "Rabbi Aharon Berachiah"; and Goldberg, *Crossing the Jabbok*. On books of pious practices, see Zeev Gries, *Sifrut ha-hanhagot*. For the in-

fluence of mysticism on synagogue architecture, see Thomas Hubka, "Bet ha-keneset be-Gwodzdziec - Shaar ha-shamayim: hashpaat Sefer ha-Zohar al ha-omanut veha-adrikhalut," in *ha-Mitos be-yahadut*, ed. Havivah Pedayah (Jerusalem: Hotsa'at ha-sefarim shel Universitat Ben Gurion ba-negev, 1996), 263–316, and Hubka, "Jewish Art and Architecture in the East European Context: The Gwozdziec-Chodorow Group of Wooden Synagogues," *Polin* 10 (1997): 140–82, esp. 168–69.

19. The comparison of the *tkhines* with similar materials in Central and Eastern European popular piety remains a scholarly desideratum. Influences on popular piety may well have crossed ethnic lines, and, in any case, the Zeitgeist may have produced parallels. German pietist women may well have composed prayers similar to *tkhines*. I have been unable to locate any studies of the piety of Polish Catholic women in the eighteenth century, although I have stumbled across a few tantalizing references to groups of village women, known as "Mary circles," who gathered in homes to pray, as well as references to special prayers to be recited while preparing festival breads; on breads, see Danuta Cetera, *Chleba Naszego* (Tarnów: Muzeum Okregowe, 1995). Eighteenth-century Eastern Orthodoxy, like Judaism, produced religious revival movements; certainly the nature of women's piety in these movements would prove a valuable comparison to *tkhines* by Jewish women from Podolia.

20. See, for example, Elhanan Reiner, "The Ashkenazi Elite at the Beginning of the Modern Era: Manuscript versus Printed Book," *Polin* 10 (1997): 85–98.

21. Gries, *Sifrut ha-hanhagot*, xvii.

22. Moshe Idel argues that Cordovero's writings are the crucial underpinnings for the hasidic theory of mystical leadership, and that early Hasidim, while venerating Luria's memory, ignored the mystical system transmitted by his disciples. Arthur Green suggests, by contrast, that the Hasidim made similar use of both Cordovero's and Luria's thought: "Revivalists have no use for *any* systematic theology other than to mine it for inspiring nuggets." See Idel, *Hasidism: Between Ecstasy and Magic* (Albany: State University of New York Press, 1995), esp. chap. 1, and Green's review in the *Journal of Religion* 77 (1977): 190–92.

23. Gries, *Sefer, sofer, ve-sipur*, 22. In this context, Gries is speaking of hasidism, and he attributes the phrase "from mythos to ethos" to Martin Buber. But the insight can be extended to Safed pietism as well; cf. Avriel Bar-Levav, "Rabbi Aharon Berachiah," 190, 197.

24. Ellus bas Mordecai Reb Mikhoels of Slutsk, trans., *Shomrim la-boker* (Frankfurt an der Oder, 1704); Aaron Berachiah of Modena, *Kitsur maavar yabbok*, trans. Ellus bas Mordecai (Frankfurt an der Oder, 1704). *Shomrim la-boker* has three rabbinic approbations (*haskamot*). This is virtually unique in Yiddish books by women and is a testimony of her learning, her determination, her family connections, or all three. The first approbation, by Hillel Levi Mintz, rabbi of Leipnik (Lipnik), refers to Ellus as "the chaste, wise woman of rabbinical family, the *dabranit* [the *zogerke*, women's prayer leader]." Mintz mentions that Ellus and her husband, Aaron, son of Eliakum Goetz, author of *Even ha-shoham* (Dyhernfurt: 1739), for-

mer rabbi of Snipiskes (formerly Shnipeshok; now a neighborhood in Vilnius), were on their way to settle in Palestine. However, because of difficult conditions, they were temporarily staying in Moravia, where her husband had become a preacher. The second approbation, by Rabbi Menahem Mendel of Tsilts, preserves the rabbi's dignity by making it clear that Ellus approached the rabbi by means of his wife, rather than directly. The third approbation is by Judah Leib son of Elhanan, rabbi of Hotzenplotz (Osoblaha).

25. *Tehinnot hadashot she-hiber ish elohim kadosh . . . Yitshak Luria* (Prague: 1709). The lengthy text on the title page explains, in rhyme, that this is a translation of Nathan Nata Hannover's *Shaarei Tsiyyon*; it attributes the prayers therein to Luria.

26. See Chapter 7 below.

27. See *Encyclopaedia Judaica*, s.v. "Horowitz, Isaiah ben Abraham ha-Levi." Part of Horowitz's monumental work, *Shenei Luhot ha-Berit* (The Two Tables of the Covenant) is now available in an English translation by Miles Krassen, *The Generations of Adam* (New York: Paulist Press, 1996).

28. Nathan Nata Hannover, *Shaarei Tsiyyon* (n.p.: Hotsaat benei yisrael, [1960s]). See also *Encyclopaedia Judaica*, s.v. "Hannover, Nathan Nata."

29. Freehof, "Devotional Literature," 405–15. Freehof was unaware that the Yiddish tkhines supposedly based on the prayers for the days of the week found in *Shaarei Tsiyyon* were published in a *tkhine* collection that appeared in 1648, fourteen years before the publication of *Shaarei Tsiyyon*. However, as *Shaarei Tsiyyon* contains a compilation of earlier material, this does not present an insuperable problem.

30. In disagreeing with Freehof, I am also taking issue with Zelda Kahan Newman, "Kabbalistic Ideas in the Women's Yiddish Prayer Book, *Tkheenes*," in *Identity and Ethos: A Festschrift for Solomon Liptzin*, ed. Mark Geller (New York: P. Lang, 1986), 37–48. While Newman is correct in criticizing Freehof's chronology, and in pointing out that some *tkhines* containing kabbalistic ideas were published at an earlier date than the Hebrew works that are supposedly their sources, her notion of Kabbalah is unsophisticated: she takes every mention of Satan or of angels as a reference to kabbalistic doctrine. Yet Satan and various angels appear in the Bible, not to mention pre-kabbalistic rabbinic works. A further difficulty with Newman's essay is her uncritical use of a late (and corrupt) collection of *tkhines*, *Shas tkhine* (New York, n.d. [20th c.]; reprint of a late 19th c. Vilna ed.) as the basis for her analysis.

31. On the mysticism of the chariot, based on the vision in Ezekiel, chap. 1, see Gershom Scholem, *Major Trends in Jewish Mysticism* (New York: Schocken, 1961), chap. 2, and *Jewish Gnosticism, Merkabah Mysticism, and Talmudic Tradition*, 2d ed. (New York: Jewish Theological Seminary of America, 1965).

32. Occasionally the *tkhines* speak of making one's prayers a "crown" for God's holy head. However, this is probably not a reference to the *sefirah keter* (crown) but rather a use of the motif of the coronation of God by prayers, used frequently in pre-kabbalistic *piyyut* (liturgical poetry). For a comprehensive study of the motif of

the crown of God in Jewish mysticism, see Arthur Green, *Keter* (Princeton, N.J.: Princeton University Press, 1997).

33. *Seder tkhines u-vakoshes*, no. 3.

34. Or for non-learned men. This *tkhine* is a translation of a Hebrew prayer for men who were not learned in mystical techniques of prayer; see Judah Leib Pohavitser, S. *Divrei hakhamin* (n.p., 1692 or 1693), pt. 2, *solet belulah, hilkhot tefillah*, 19d, quoted in Isaiah Tishby, *Netivei Emunah u-minut* (Jerusalem: Magnes Press, 1982), 121–22. For further discussion of the implications of this fact, see the concluding chapter.

35. Known as *mesirat modaah*; *Shaarei tsiyyon*, 350–53. However, men sometimes also recited this privately, as part of daily devotions.

36. There are prayers in *Shaarei tsiyyon* and also in *Tkhines* for recovery from illness, for rain in the time of drought, for offspring, and those to be said on the eve of the new moon, on fast days, on Sabbaths, and on holidays.

37. See the discussion of themes in Chapter 2.

38. In the nineteenth century, devotional works for Jewish women in German adapted the *tkhines* to a more modern sensibility. On these works, see the excellent new monograph by Bettina Kratz-Ritter, *Für "fromme Zionstöchter" und "gebildete Frauenzimmer"* (Hildesheim: Georg Olms Verlag, 1995).

39. Published in Amsterdam in 1648. See the bibliography of editions appended to Devra Kay, "An Alternative Prayer Canon for Women," 86–88.

40. The author/translator/compiler nowhere states that he is a man, but it seems fairly clear from the language of the introduction that he is; he speaks about women as if he is not one of them.

41. Judah ben Samuel (d. 1217), *Sefer hasidim*, ed. Reuven Margoliot (Jerusalem: Mosad ha-Rav Kook, 1964), no. 588. The Yiddish clearly echoes the text of *Sefer hasidim*, which suggests that women and men who do not know Hebrew learn the prayers in a language they understand, and also that they pray in a language they understand: "for prayer only occurs with the comprehension of the heart, and if the heart does not know what his mouth speaks, what good is it; better he should pray in the language he understands."

42. Numbers Rabba 3:4; Zohar II:3b–4a.

43. Not all women felt that it was necessary to understand the language in which they prayed, however. As Max Weinreich writes, in the *History of the Yiddish Language* (Chicago: University of Chicago Press, 1980), "A high school principal in Frankfort on the Main, named Schudt, told an instructive anecdote on this point at the beginning of the eighteenth century. He had asked two Jewish women how they could pray in Loshn-koydesh [the holy tongue] without understanding the meaning of the words. One answered: When a physician writes a prescription for me, it is immaterial whether I can read it or not if the apothecary can. The other said even more pointedly: Indeed I don't understand what I am saying, but God does. Intelligibility is an enormously important thing, but in this case, as seen, it

was not decisive. Factors are apparently involved in the matter of prayer that are stronger at times than rational considerations" (261).

44. It was a matter of debate among Jews in the seventeenth and eighteenth century whether women should recite the statutory prayers in Yiddish if they did not understand Hebrew; and it is a matter of debate today among scholars if women ever did so. See Shmeruk, *Sifrut yidish be-polin* (Jerusalem: Magnes Press, 1982), 63–68, and David Fishman, "Mikoyekh davenen af yidish," *YIVO Bleter* n.s. 1 (1991): 69–92.

45. In addition to the edition published in Amsterdam, 1648, I have seen the following editions (all, except as otherwise noted, in the collection *Yiddish Books on Microfiche*, selected by Khone Shmeruk, issued as part of the Jewish Studies Microfiche Project by the Interdocumentation Company AG, Zug, Switzerland): *Seder tkhines* (Amsterdam, 1650); *Seder tkhines*, printed as part of the prayer book *Tefillah ke-fi minhag ha-ashkenazim* . . . (Wilhelmersdof, 1725); *Tkhines* (Dyhernfurth, ca. 1750); *Seder tkhines* (n.p., 1666); Jewish Theological Seminary; *Seder tkhines* (Amsterdam, 1752); Jewish Theological Seminary.

46. Women sometimes recited cemetery prayers in groups. In addition, a woman might engage another, more expert woman to recite graveside prayers on her behalf in her presence. See Gisela Suliteanu, "The Traditional System of Melopeic Prose of the Funeral Songs Recited by the Jewish Women of the Socialist Republic of Rumania," in *Folklore Research Center Studies*, ed. Issachar Ben-Ami (Jerusalem: Magnes, 1972), 3:291–341. The two most important collections of cemetery prayers published during this era are *Maaneh lashon* (Amsterdam, 1723, and many other earlier and later editions) and Simeon Frankfurt, *Sefer ha-hayyim* (Amsterdam, 1703, and many later editions). For more on *Sefer ha-hayyim*, see Chapter 8.

47. Many of these *tkhines* are quite similar to the Hebrew prayers said for the same occasions by Italian Jewish women; cf. Cardin, *Out of the Depths*. However, the extant Italian works, all of them in manuscript, are from the eighteenth century and thus cannot easily be the source of the Yiddish prayers in the 1648 collection. More research is required to clarify their common source.

48. The publisher's motives seem to have been primarily commercial. The title page states: "We have learned that the *tkhines* in Yiddish can no longer be obtained. Thus, I have considered, and translated them into Yiddish, for these [*tkhines*] have never yet been printed. . . . Therefore, come running quickly, and buy these lovely *tkhines* soon. . . . By the hands of Moses the Typesetter from Amsterdam the Capital." Even if no author is named, the printer may simply be a printer; we should not jump to conclusions about Moses's role beyond the technical production of the book.

49. Some *tkhines* written or published in Prague will be discussed in the section on Eastern European *tkhines*, below.

50. This collection also had a long life independent of *Seder tkhines u-vakoshes*. It was reprinted into the twentieth century under the title *Preger tkhine* (*Tkhine* from

Prague). Interestingly, it later became anonymous; subsequent editions were published either with no author statement at all, or with the following Yiddish rhyme:

> Di heylige tkhine iz fun nayen vorn os getrakht
> Es hot zi keyn shlekhter man gemakht
> Ver zi vet leynen un vet zi nemen in akht
> Azo vellin zi far zikhert zeyn far beyze geshekhnish tog un nakht

"This holy *tkhine* has been newly thought up / it was no bad man who made it / whoever reads it and keeps it in mind / will be protected from evil occurrences day and night" (*Preger tkhine*, n.p., n.d. [early 19th c.]). This rhyme does let the reader know that the author was male, and it echoes statements from Sobotki's introduction.

51. Another work by Sobotki, a lament in memory of those who died in the plague that struck Prague in 1713, was published in 1719 and is listed in Otto Muneles, Bibliographical Survey of Jewish Prague (Prague: Orbis, 1952), no. 235.

52. The edition I used was published in Fürth in 1762 and is owned by the Jewish Theological Seminary of America, in New York City. The title page of this edition actually reads *Seder tkhines bakoshes*, omitting the particle for "and" (*u-*); however, most other editions of this work are entitled *Seder tkhines u-vakoshes*. This edition has no page numbers; instead, the individual prayers are numbered. This is the earliest edition I have seen, but I have no reason to believe it is the first edition. The bibliographer H. D. Friedberg refers to a Fürth edition of 1755; perhaps this was the first edition. He also lists the Fürth, 1762 edition, as well as Fürth, 1765 and 1768, Sulzbach, 1794, Dyhernfurth, 1798, Sulzbach, 1798 (the edition used by Freehof), and Fürth, 1811. Friedberg notes that the editions are not identical to each other; Friedberg, *Bet eked sefarim*, 2d rev. ed. (Tel Aviv: M. A. Bar-Judah, 1951), 1098.

   Although I have identified the major sources of *Seder tkhines u-vakoshes*, many thorny bibliographic problems have yet to be resolved, and the sources of many of its individual prayers remain unknown. See also the *tkhines* cited and summarized in Max Grünbaum, *Jüdischdeutsche Chrestomathie* (Leipzing: F. A. Brockhaus, 1882), 328–35.

53. This count includes prayers for the holidays, which will also be enumerated separately below.

54. The holiday of Sukkot, or Tabernacles (Booths), which falls in late September or early October, celebrates the autumn harvest and commemorates the Israelites' wandering in the desert. The holiday observance includes the use of the lulav and etrog: during portions of the morning service on this holiday, each worshiper holds a palm frond, two willow twigs, and three myrtle twigs, together called the lulav, in his right hand, and a citron, the etrog, in his left. This "festival bouquet" is waved to the four points of the compass and up and down (see Lev. 23:33–36, 39–44). After the morning service of the final day of Sukkot, which became a minor holiday in its own right called Hashana Rabba, the lulav and etrog were no longer needed.

55. Under the influence of mystical pietism, men began to observe the eve of the

new moon as a day of penitence and fasting, known among Ashkenazim as Yom Kippur Katan, the minor day of atonement. As a parallel to this, women developed special *tkhines* to be said on the Sabbath before the new moon, for the portion of the liturgy in which the upcoming new moon is announced. Such *tkhines* appear in *Seder tkhines* (Amsterdam, 1752) and in *Seder tkhines u-vakoshes*, as well as in Eastern European *tkhines* such as *Tkhine imohos* by Leah Horowitz, to be discussed in Chapter 7.

Women in sixteenth-century Safed observed the eve of the new moon as a penitential day along with men; see Lawrence Fine, *Safed Spirituality* (New York: Paulist Press, 1984), 42, 51. It is not clear to me whether or not Ashkenazic women also observed Yom Kippur Katan.

56. *Tkhine zu*, usually cited as the earliest collection of *tkhines*, is quite different from later works. It is almost completely bilingual, with two pages of Hebrew text followed by a little over three pages of Yiddish translation. Nothing about it indicates that it was intended for women in particular. It was simply to be recited "every day" and contained prayers for forgiveness, for the ability to repent, for material success, and for the destruction of the reciter's enemies. Because it is so unlike the later collections, I will not include it in my discussion. On the authorship of this work, see Khone Shmeruk, *Sifrut yidish be-polin*, 51, no. 20. Many questions remain about this work.

57. In 1988, Brother Claus Columben Lethen of the Dormition Abbey, Jerusalem, presented this work, along with another early Yiddish book, to the Jewish National and University Library, Jerusalem. A collector of old Yiddish and Hebrew books, Brother Lethen had received these works from a friend in Scotland, *Hebrew University News* (Winter 1988/89), 26. The work is found in the JNUL, shelf mark R8° 894501. Nonetheless, a great many early Eastern European *tkhines* have undoubtedly been lost. See Khone Shmeruk, *Sifrut yidish be-polin*, 65. Isolated *tkhine* texts found within other works have been preserved from the sixteenth century.

58. See Yitshak Yudlov, "'Sheyne tkhine' ve-'Orah hayyim': shenei sifrei yiddish bilti yedu'im," *Kiryat Sefer* 62 (1989): 457–58.

59. Jews were expelled from Vienna (for a second time) in 1669–70.

60. Both of these texts are found in the Bodleian Library, Oxford. The term Beila used to describe herself, *shraybern*, is not a usual term for authorship during this period; it can mean "writer" or "scribe." Rachel, rather than being an author of the *tkhine*, may simply be the "managing editor." The Yiddish phrase used to describe Rachel's role on the title page is a translation of the Hebrew term for this role, *mevi le-vet ha-defus*. On the managing editor at a slightly later period, see Zeev Gries, "The Hasidic Managing Editor as an Agent of Culture," in *Hasidism Reappraised*, ed. Ada Rapoport-Albert (London: Littman Library of Jewish Civilization, 1997), 141–55.

61. This was typical of all genres of popular religious literature in Yiddish published during this period, whether intended for a male or a female audience. See Zeev Gries, *Sifrut ha-hanhagot* (Jerusalem: Mosad Bialik, 1989), xiv.

62. Two linguistic notes: It is possible that *ha-rabbanit*, a word usually translated as "the rabbi's wife," means in this context "of rabbinical family"; the masculine grammatical equivalent, *ha-rabbani*, was sometimes used in this way. (This was first suggested to me by David Fishman.) Second, the word *amtahah* (pouch, satchel) occurs in eighteenth-century Hebrew book titles to denote a collection of remedies and charms for healing, as in Benjamin Beinish ben Judah Leib ha-Kohen of Krotoshin, *Amtahat Binyamin* (Wilhelmsdorf, 1716); see Zeev Gries, *Sifrut ha-hanhagot*, 97.

63. All of the *tkhines* attributed to male authors other than Mattithias Sobotki are Yiddish translations or adaptations of previously existing Hebrew materials. Among the authors whose works were so adapted are Rabbi Eleazar ben Arakh (1st century); Isaiah Horowitz (1570–1626), some of whose prayers were incorporated in *Seder tkhines u-vakoshes*, and later also separately published in Yiddish; his son Shabbetai Sheftel [referred to on *tkhine* title pages as "R. Sheftel of Poznan"(he was appointed rabbi of Poznan in 1645)]; and Rabbi Judah Hasid. I have not yet determined whether this was Judah the Pietist (d. 1217), or, more interestingly, the Sabbatian prophet also known as Judah Hasid (1660?–1700).

64. I have examined two editions of each text, all published without date or place of publication noted. All the editions are in the *tkhine* pamphlet collection of the Jewish National and University Library, call no. R41A460. The editions of *Tkhine es rotsn* are found in vol. 7, nos. 5 and 6; the editions of *Tkhine shaarei tshuve* are found in vol. 9, nos. 3 and 6; the texts in vol. 7, no. 6, and vol. 9, no. 3 were printed at the same press, probably in the second decade of the nineteenth century, which accords well with the biographical information we have; see below.

The titles of the *tkhines* appear to have been bestowed by the publisher. The title pages read: "We have called this *tkhine Es rotsn* because it is founded upon the entire month of Elul, and especially on Rosh Hashanah, and these are days on which everyone's prayer is accepted by God with favor." "We called this *tkhine Shaarey tshuve* because by means of these *tkhines* one can take to heart great *musar* to repent."

65. On the complexities of the question of whether the Baal Shem Tov, a mystic, preacher, and faith healer, can be regarded as the founder of a movement as opposed to the central figure of a loose-knit circle of disciples, see Moshe Rosman, *Founder of Hasidism* (Berkeley: University of California Press, 1996).

66. All of the information on Leah Dreyzl and her family is from Meir Wunder, *Meorei galitsiyah* (Jerusalem: Makhon le-hantsahat yahadut galitsiyah, 1978), vol. 1, cols. 35–38; and see sources cited there. All of the editions of the *tkhines* give her name as Leah Reyzl; I have corrected it to Dreyzl in accordance with Wunder.

67. *Tkhine es rotsn* consists of two leaves, *Tkhine shaarei tshuve* of four.

68. The skill of the author becomes apparent when one compares the description of the process of dying and the sufferings that follow death found in *Tkhine shaarei tshuve* with the more pedestrian treatment of the same material (probably from a

common source) in *Tkhine tshuve tfile utsedoke* by Mamila (or Memael) bas Tsevi Hirsh (Lvov: 1797, and other, undated editions).

69. Zinberg, *Old Yiddish Literature*, 251. See also n. 12.

70. There is a well-known rabbinic trope, originating in Targum Yonatan, Genesis 1:27, that makes a correspondence between human anatomy and God's commandments. According to this traditional physiology, human beings have 248 limbs and 365 organs, corresponding to the numbers of positive and negative commandments, respectively, and adding up to 613, the traditional number of commandments in the Torah. However, this only applies to males; women, with a different anatomy, are traditionally supposed to have 252 limbs. Thus, it is a little odd that Leah Dreyzl uses these numbers in a text clearly intended to be recited by a female speaker. Women's extra limbs were sometimes thought to correspond to the three "women's commandments" plus the obligation to serve one's husband; this may have been in Leah Dreyzl's mind, as the next sentence mentions these commandments. In any case, the overall implication of the sentence is clear: By using the body for material rather than spiritual ends, by following the evil inclination and disobeying the commandments, the speaker has created blemishes and deformities in the spiritual equivalent of the physical body.

71. Ps. 55:23; the verse concludes: "He will never let the righteous man collapse," which may be reflected in the continuation of the Yiddish.

72. A paraphrase from the High Holidays liturgy; note that Leah Dreyzl uses the grammatically correct feminine form in Hebrew: *Ani mele'ah avon.*

73. *Tkhine shaarei tshuve*, 1a-2a. Much of this passage is in rhymed prose.

74. *Tkhine shaarei tshuve*, 2b-3a.

75. See, for example, Immanuel Etkes, "The Zaddik: The Interrelationship between Religious Doctrine and Social Organization," in *Hasidism Reappraised*, ed. Ada Rapoport-Albert (London: Littman Library, 1997), 159–67; Joseph G. Weiss, "Reshit tsemihatah shel ha-derekh ha-hasidit," *Zion* 16 (1951): 46–105; and, for an earlier period, Jacob Elbaum, *Teshuvat ha-lev ve-kabbalat yisurim* (Jerusalem: Magnes Press, 1992).

76. It is, nonetheless, interesting that specific hasidic teachings such as the doctrine of the *tsaddik* as intermediary between earthly and divine spheres and worship through corporeal means are absent from Leah Dreyzl's *tkhines*.

77. For a discussion of *tkhines* for the second of the women's commandments, the observance of menstrual prohibitions and purification, see Chapter 4; for *tkhines* to be recited before or after kindling Sabbath lights, see Chapter 6.

78. Mishnah Shabbat 2:6, phrased negatively: "Women die in childbirth for three transgressions: because they do not take care in observing marital separation, setting aside the portion of dough, and kindling the Sabbath light."

79. These commandments were also incumbent on men. Male bakers separated dough; husbands were, of course, obligated to avoid touching their wives during

menstruation (although obviously they could not perform the inspection and immersion); and if there was no woman in the house the man lit the Sabbath candles.

80. See Rachel Biale, *Women and Jewish Law* (New York: Schocken, 1984), chap. 1.

81. Hannah's prayer for a son (1 Sam. 1:10–18) was taken by the rabbis to be the exemplar of proper prayer. In the course of talmudic discussion of Hannah's prayer, Rabbi Jose, son of Rabbi Hanina, states that Hannah repeated the phrase "your maidservant" three times in her prayer to remind God that she never transgressed the commandments of menstrual separation, separating dough, and lighting Sabbath candles (Berakhot 31b). Here the commandments are not listed in the order that makes an acrostic of Hannah's name.

82. Or for twelve days in all, whichever is longer.

83. Since the Bible forbids lighting a fire on the Sabbath (see Exod. 35:3), it was required that the lights be kindled before the sun set and the Sabbath began.

84. Bettina Kratz-Ritter further compares the *tkhines* for the women's mitzvot to nineteenth-century devotions in German for Jewish women on the same topic; see Kratz-Ritter, *Für "fromme Zionstöchter,"* 144–57.

85. Sarah bas Tovim is the subject of Chapter 8. She seems to have composed this *tkhine* in the mid-eighteenth century.

86. *Seder tkhines u-vakoshes*, no. 45.

87. *Shloyshe sheorim* does not include the Hebrew blessing for ritual immersion or a *tkhine* for this religious act.

88. There is considerable scholarly disagreement as to the exact meaning of this verse. *Shloyshe sheorim*, however, translates the verse according to the rabbinic understanding of the *mitsvah* of *hallah*: "The meaning of the verse is: The first part of your dough you shall separate as *hallah*."

89. The word *hallah* adds up to forty-three in Hebrew numerology.

90. *Tkhines* uses the Western Yiddish term *berkhes*. In some varieties of Eastern Yiddish, however, the Sabbath loaf is also called *hallah* (*khale*), because one must separate *hallah* in order to prepare it. *Seder tkhines* also contains a *tkhine* for taking *hallah* that recalls the sacrifices and the tithes, although it stops short of explicitly identifying the taking of *hallah* with the bringing of a sacrifice.

CHAPTER 2. STUDYING WOMEN'S RELIGION

An earlier version of this chapter was published as "The Religion of Traditional Ashkenazic Women: Some Methodological Issues," *AJS Review*, 12 (Spring 1987): 73–94.

1. Scott's lecture was published as "Women in History II: The Modern Period," *Past and Present* 101 (1983): 141–57. See also Scott's more recent work, *Gender and the Politics of History* (New York: Columbia University Press, 1988). The literature on

women's history is now vast. Among the scholars whose work has most influenced my own are Carroll Smith-Rosenberg, especially *Disorderly Conduct* (New York: Oxford University Press, 1985); Natalie Zemon Davis, numerous conversations and essays, including several of those in *Society and Culture in Early Modern France* (Stanford: Stanford University Press, 1975) and *Women on the Margins* (Cambridge: Harvard University Press, 1995); Caroline Walker Bynum, *Jesus as Mother* (Berkeley: University of California Press, 1982), *Holy Feast and Holy Fast* (Berkeley: University of California Press, 1987), and *Fragmentation and Redemption* (New York: Zone Books, 1991). Together with Stevan Harrell and Paula Richman, Bynum has also edited an excellent collection of essays, *Gender and Religion* (Boston: Beacon, 1986). On studying women's religion in antiquity, see Ross Kraemer, *Her Share of the Blessings* (New York: Oxford University Press, 1992). A recent anthropological study of elderly Middle-Eastern Jewish women is Susan Starr Sered, *Women as Ritual Experts* (New York: Oxford University Press, 1992). There is a brief discussion of *tkhines* in Gerda Lerner, *The Creation of Feminist Consciousness* (New York: Oxford University Press, 1991), 110–14.

2. On the question of women's authorship of *tkhines*, see the discussion in Chapter 1. See Shmuel Niger, "Di yidishe literatur un di lezerin" in Niger, *Bleter geshikhte fun der yidisher literatur* (New York: Sh. Niger Bukh-komitet baym alveltlekh yidishn kultur-kongres, 1959), esp. 82–83; now available in English as Niger, "Yiddish Literature and the Female Read," trans. and abridged by Sheva Zucker, in *Women of the Word*, ed. Judith Baskin (Detroit: Wayne State University Press, 1994), 70–90; and Israel Zinberg, *History of Jewish Literature*, trans. Bernard Martin, vol. 7, *Old Yiddish Literature from Its Origins to the Haskalah Period* (New York: Ktav; Cincinnati: Hebrew Union College Press, 1972–78), 252–53. According to both Niger and Zinberg, *maskilim* began to write *tkhines* to which they attached women's names beginning in the 1860s. Niger gives a list of female authors of *tkhines* and other Yiddish works on pp. 88–94. For a discussion of the identification of Yiddish with femaleness and Hebrew with maleness, see Naomi Seidman, *A Marriage Made in Heaven: The Sexual Politics of Hebrew and Yiddish* (Berkeley: University of California Press, 1997); her analysis of Niger's essay appears on pp. 3–7.

3. On the *Brantshpigl*, see Zinberg, *Old Yiddish Literature*, 157–59; also Max Erik, "Bletlekh tsu der geshikhte fun der elterer yidisher literatur un kultur: I. Der 'Brantshpigl'—Di entsiklopedye fun der yidisher froy in XVII yorhundert," *Tsaytshrift* (Minsk) l (1926): 171–77; and M. N. Rosenfeld, "Der Brant shpigl: mahadurah bilti noda'at shel ha-sefer ve-zihui mehabro," *Kiryat sefer* 55 (1980): 617–21.

4. Another fascinating genre that raises such questions is the guide to the observance of women's commandments, known in several related versions. The earliest extant manuscript dates from 1504, and the first published editions of each version date from 1535, 1552, and 1577. These works deal with the three women's commandments: lighting Sabbath candles (10 chapters in the Basel, 1602, edition); separating dough for *hallah* (15 chapters); and, especially, the observance of menstrual avoidances and purification (105 chapters). For a definitive study of these works, see Agnes Romer Segal, "Sifrei mitsvot ha-nashim be-yidish ba-me'ah ha-16" (Mas-

ter's thesis, Hebrew University, Jerusalem, 1979) and "Yiddish Works on Women's Commandments in the Sixteenth Century," in *Studies in Yiddish Literature and Folklore*, ed. Chava Turniansky, Research Projects of the Institute of Jewish Studies, Monograph Series no. 7 (Jerusalem: Hebrew University, 1986), 37–59.

5. The *Mayse Bukh* has appeared in an annotated English translation: *The Ma'aseh Book: Book of Jewish Tales and Legends*, trans. from the Judeo-German by Moses Gaster (c. 1935; reprint, Philadelphia: Jewish Publication Society, 1981). For the literary history and sources of the *Mayse Bukh*, see Zinberg, *Old Yiddish Literature*, 185–98; Jacob Meitlis, *Das Ma'assebuch, seine Enstehung und Quellengeschichte* (Berlin: Mass, 1933); and Sara Zfatman, "*Mayse Bukh*: Kavim li-demuto shel zhaner be-sifrut yidish ha-yeshanah," *Ha-Sifrut* 28 (1979): 126–52. See also Zfatman's comprehensive bibliography of the tale literature in Yiddish from 1504 to 1814, *ha-Siporet be-yidish me-reshitah ad Shivhei ha-besht* (Jerusalem: Institute of Jewish Studies of the Hebrew University, 1985).

6. Adler, "The Jew Who Wasn't There," *Response* 7, no. 22 (Summer 1973), 77–82; reprinted in *On Being a Jewish Feminist*, ed. Susannah Heschel (New York: Schocken, 1983), 12–18.

7. Conversations with Natalie Davis and Virginia Reinburg about Catholic devotional literature in early modern France were very helpful to me. See Reinburg's doctoral dissertation, "Popular Prayers in Late Medieval and Reformation France" (Ph.D. dissertation, Princeton University, 1985).

8. On the structure of the traditional Ashkenazic community, see Jacob Katz, *Tradition and Crisis*, new ed., trans. and with afterword by Bernard Dov Cooperman (New York: Schocken, 1993; 1st English ed. 1961). For social stratification, see esp. pp. 170–79.

9. On the *Tsenerene*, see Khone Schmeruk, "Di Mizrekh-eyropeishe nuskhoes fun der Tsenerene (1786–1850)," in *For Max Weinreich on His Seventieth Birthday* (The Hague: Mouton, 1964), 320–36.

10. See, for example, Yosef Svirski, in his article on Jewish life in Vilna, "Zikhronot shel yerushalayim de-lita," *Yeda am* 33–34 (1967–68): 108–16. He writes: "The book *Tsenerene*, the Torah in Yiddish for women, played an important role in our culture in past generations. Our mothers used to sit on every Sabbath after their afternoon nap and read it aloud, chanting, with emphasis. And we children would listen sometimes, to hear the beautiful parables and the words of explanation, which the author would quote in the names of the commentators on the Torah" (p. 109; my translation).

11. On these guides, see note 4 above.

12. Translation from Zinberg, *Old Yiddish Literature*, 160.

13. Ibid., 161. "Householders" (*balebatim*), of course, are hardly at the bottom of the social ladder.

14. See the short story by I. L. Peretz, "A Farshterter shabes," in Peretz, *Ale verk*, vol. 2, *Dertseylungen, mayselekh, bilder* (New York: Cyco Bikher-Farlag, 1947), 211–

19. He lists the devotional works read by a traditional Jewish woman: "Seril is an accomplished woman; she reads *ivre-taytsh* [the special variety of Yiddish in which this literature was written] fluently: She knows the *Taytsh-khumesh* [i.e., the *Tsenerene*] and the *Kav ha-yashar* and the *Reyshis hokhme* and other such books" (p. 214; my translation).

15. On Sarah bas Tovim and the making of candles for Yom Kippur, see Chapter 8.

16. *Tsenerene* (Amsterdam, 1702–3), 4b (parashat bereshit); *Seder tkhines u-va-koshes* (Fürth, 1762), no. 89. For a more detailed discussion of this practice, see Chapter 4.

17. *Sefer ha-hayyim*, by Simeon ben Israel Judah Frankfort, was first published in Amsterdam in 1703; the second edition, slightly enlarged, appeared in Amsterdam in 1716. I have used the Kötten, 1717 edition. From its first edition, and in all of its many subsequent editions, *Sefer ha-hayyim* was a bilingual work, its first half in Hebrew, the second in Yiddish. The intended audience for the work was the *hevra kadisha*, the burial society. Men prepared male corpses for burial while women prepared female corpses; thus the first half of the book is intended for the male members of the burial society, and the second half for the women. The Hebrew and Yiddish sections of the work differ substantially. For more on this work and on the custom of measuring graves, see Chapter 8.

18. *Ma'aneh lashon*, by Jacob ben Abraham Solomon, appeared in Prague (in Hebrew) in 1615. Steinschneider regards this as the second edition. It was enlarged, according to Steinschneider, by Eliezer Liebermann Sofer ben Loeb. This enlarged edition was first published in Prague, about 1658. Beginning with the Frankfurt edition of c. 1688, it was frequently published in Yiddish translation. The bilingual edition (Amsterdam, 1723) is the one on which I have chiefly relied.

19. On the sources of the *Mayse bukh*, see Zfatman, "*Mayse bukh*," 131–36, and the notes to Gaster's translation.

20. Zinberg, *Old Yiddish Literature*, 185–86. I have altered the translation slightly, primarily by substituting "Yiddish" for "German" as the translation for "taytsh."

21. Making halakhic materials available in Yiddish could be controversial; see Zinberg, *Old Yiddish Literature*, 216–18, for a discussion of rabbinic reaction to the publication of extracts from the *Shulhan Arukh* as an appendix to Elhanan Kirchhan's Yiddish ethical work, *Simkhas ha-nefesh*. On rabbinic opposition to the publication in Yiddish of laws concerning the women's commandments, see Romer Segal, "Sifrei mitsvot ha-nashim be-yidish," 2–3. And, in fact, despite the claims made on the title page, the *Mayse bukh* contains virtually no halakhic material.

22. Chava Turniansky, personal communication, 1985.

23. Solomon Freehof, "Devotional Literature in the Vernacular," *CCAR Yearbook* 33 (1923): 375–424.

24. On the transformations of one of the passages from the Zohar in *The Three Gates* and other Yiddish popularizations, see Chapters 1 and 5. *Sefer hemdat yamim* originated in heretical Sabbatian messianic circles and contains some hidden ref-

erences to messianic beliefs. The passage in *The Three Gates*, in the prayer for the new moon, that implores the patriarchs, Moses, and the Messiah to beseech God to bring the redemption, originates in *Sefer hemdat yamim*, 4 vols. (Jerusalem: Makor, 1969–70; photo offset of Constantinople, 1734–35 ed.), vol. 2 (*Rosh Hodesh*), 12b–13b (*Enkat Asir*). For more on this connection, see Chapter 8.

25. *Sefer ma'asei Adonai*, pt. 1, 1st ed. (Frankfurt-am-Main, 1691); pt. 2, 1st ed. (Fürth, 1694); edition that combines pts. 1 and 2 (Amsterdam, 1708). *Abir Yankev*, 1st ed. (Sulzbach: 1700). *Kav ha-yashar*, Hebrew text first published 1705; Yiddish translation 1724. Later editions were bilingual.

The Safed revival is discussed in the Introduction. See also Gershom Scholem, *Major Trends in Jewish Mysticism* (New York: Schocken, 1961), 244–86; Solomon Schechter, "Safed in the Sixteenth Century," in Schechter, *Studies in Judaism*, 2d ser. (1908), 203–306; R. J. Zwi Werblowsky, *Joseph Karo: Lawyer and Mystic* (Philadelphia: Jewish Publication Society, 1977), esp. 38–83; Lawrence Fine, *Safed Spirituality* (New York: Paulist Press, 1984). On the popularization of Jewish mysticism in the wake of the Safed revival, see Gershom Scholem, "Ha-tenu'ah ha-shabta'it be-polin," in *Bet Yisrael be-polin* (Jerusalem: ha-Mahlakah le-inyane ha-noar shel ha-histadrut ha-tsiyyonit, 1953–54), 2: 36–76, esp. 36–40; and idem, *Sabbatai Sevi* (Princeton: Princeton University Press, 1973), 66–92. But see also Bernard Weinryb, *The Jews of Poland* (Philadelphia: Jewish Publication Society, 1976), 225–28; Weinryb describes "Polish Jewry's lack of great interest in cabala." My thanks to Ivan Marcus for drawing this to my attention. Moshe Idel also argues against the claim that Lurianic kabbalah was widespread among Ashkenazim; see Idel, "Ehad me-ir u-shenayim me-mishpahah," *Peamim* 44 (1990): 5–30. A different way of approaching this controversy is found in Zeev Gries, *Sifrut ha-hanhagot* (Jerusalem: Mosad Bialik, 1989), and Avriel Bar-Levav, "Rabbi Aharon Berechiah mi-modena ve-rabi Naftali ha-Kohen Katz," *Asufot* 9 (1995): 189–274. Gries and Bar-Levav argue that the spread of Safed pietism had more to do with a spreading of a ritualized ethos than with a detailed conceptual understanding of the esoteric teachings of Luria. See the Introduction and Chapter 1.

26. Works concerning the sick, dying, and dead, such as *Sefer ha-hayyim* and *Ma'aneh lashon* (noted above) are particularly rich sources for investigating these questions. A related work is *Ma'avar yabbok*, by Aaron Berachiah of Modena (Mantua, 1626), a Hebrew book containing prayers for the dying and a very interesting kabbalistic commentary on caring for the dying and the dead, and on mourning practices. On this and related questions, see the excellent new study by Sylvie-Anne Goldberg, *Crossing the Jabbok* (Berkeley: University of California Press, 1996), as well as Bar-Levav, "Rabbi Aharon Berachiah mi-Modena."

27. On Sarah Rebecca Rachel Leah Horowitz, see Chapter 7.

28. The issue of the relationship of oral tradition to the written *tkhines* is taken up in an exchange between the folklorists S. Ansky and N. Prylucki. Ansky reviewed Prylucki's book *Yidishe folkslider*, vol. 1 (Warsaw: Bikher-far-ale, 1910–11) in *Evreskaia Starina* (1911), 591. (Volume 2 was published in Warsaw, Nayer Ferlag, 1912–13.) I translate from Prylucki's Yiddish translation of portions of the review. Pry-

lucki responded in "Polemik: A tshuve eynem a retsenzent," in *Noyekh Prilutskis zamelbikher far yidishen folklor, filologye, un kulturgeshikhte* (Warsaw: Nayer Ferlag, 1912), 1: 154–66. Ansky criticized Prylucki for including as "folk songs" material he regarded as stereotypical printed women's prayers. Prylucki quotes a portion of Ansky's review, which is of interest here: "Some of these [Yiddish women's] prayers are included in the women's prayer books and [books of] *tkhines*, but the majority of them circulate in oral tradition, possessing a multitude of variants." Ansky lists the following topics as particularly common for women's oral prayer: candle lighting, separating dough for *hallah*, ritual immersion, laying the wicks for memorial candles for the dead, pregnancy, and entering the synagogue. For a wide-ranging discussion of the relationship between book-culture and orally transmitted or "mimetic" culture, see Haym Soloveitchik, "Rupture and Reconstruction: The Transformations of Contemporary Orthodoxy," *Tradition* 28:4 (1994): 64–130.

29. Historians have questioned the usefulness of the category "popular religion." See, for example, Peter Brown's critique of the "two-tiered system" (elite versus popular religion) in *The Cult of the Saints* (Chicago: University of Chicago Press, 1981), esp. 12–22. He traces our concept of popular religion to David Hume's essay, "The Natural History of Religion." For a critique of the concept of "popular religion" as used by historians of early modern Europe, see Natalie Zemon Davis, "From 'Popular Religion' to Religious Cultures," in *Reformation Europe: A Guide to Research*, ed. Steven Ozment (St. Louis, Mo.: Center for Reformation Research, 1982). See also Davis, "Some Tasks and Themes in the Study of Popular Religion," in *The Pursuit of Holiness in Late Medieval and Renaissance Europe*, ed. Charles Trinkaus (Leiden: Brill, 1974), 306–336. More recently, postmodern theory has called attention to the ways in which categories such as popular religion, folk culture, and local culture are imbricated in the construction of their opposites, elite religion, high culture, modern culture. See, for example, Amy Shuman, "Dismantling Local Culture," *Western Folklore* 52, nos. 2, 3, 4 (1993): 345–64.

30. One might argue, of course, that the additive *is* ultimately transformative, that adding something to an account inevitably changes that account in some fundamental way.

31. Scott, "Women in History, II," 152.

32. Hannover, *Shaarei Tsiyyon* (Livorno, 1860), *tikkun keriat shema al ha-mitah*, 76a–78a. The first edition was published in Prague in 1662.

33. For a more detailed discussion of this cycle of *tkhines*, see Chapter 4.

34. *Seder tkhines u-vakoshes*, no. 93.

35. The one such problem they do address is the possibility that the woman, as well as the man, may be thinking of someone other than the spouse during intercourse. Proper sexual behavior is discussed in *Seder mitsvas noshim* (Basel, 1602), 21a–22a (chaps. 72–73); and in the *Brantshpigl* (Hanau, 1626), chap. 38. See also *Shenei luhot ha-berit, sha'ar ha-otiyot*, s.v. "*kedushah*."

36. For discussions of the erotic element in kabbalistic symbolism, see, for example, Gershom Scholem, *On the Kabbalah and Its Symbolism* (New York: Schocken,

1965), esp. chaps. 3, 4, and *Major Trends in Jewish Mysticism*, esp. chap. 6; Moshe Idel, "Sexual Metaphors and Praxis in the Kabbalah," in *The Jewish Family*, ed. David Kraemer (New York: Oxford University Press, 1989), 197–224; and Elliot R. Wolfson, *Circle in the Square* (Albany: State University of New York Press, 1995). For a provocative analysis of such symbolism in its historical and cultural context, see David Biale, *Eros and the Jews* (New York: Basic Books, 1992), chaps. 5, 6.

37. An illuminating treatment of these issues primarily from the point of view of their impact on males can be found in David Biale, *Eros and the Jews*, chaps. 3, 5, 6. Biale traces the changes in sexual morality brought about by the introduction and popularization of kabbalistic views on sexuality among Ashkenazic Jews in the sixteenth through the eighteenth centuries. According to Biale, medieval rabbinic and popular sources before this period were affirming of eroticism within marriage, while kabbalistic morality imposed great asceticism.

38. See A. Romer-Segal, "Sifrut yidish u-kehal koreha ba-meah ha-16," *Kiryat Sefer* 5 (1978): 779–90; and, for a later period, the provocative discussion by Seidman, *A Marriage Made in Heaven*, chap. 1, "Engendering Audiences: Hebrew, Yiddish, and the Question of Address."

39. S. *maaneh lashon* (Amsterdam, 1723), 63b–66b (nos. 19–20). There were prayers to be recited at the graves of a whole spectrum of relatives, from maternal or paternal grandparents down to little children. These can help us to understand how all of these different family roles were conceptualized.

40. *Seder tkhines u-vakoshes*, no. 47. On this motif, see Chapter 6.

41. On these texts, see Chapter 5.

42. *Maaseh gadol mi-rabi Shim'on bar Yohai* (Hanau, 1620). See also the later, more garbled version, *Ayn sheyn mayse oyz den Zohar parshes Lekh lekha [sic]* (Fürth, 1692–98).

43. Sarah bas Tovim, *Tkhine shloyshe sheorim* (n.p., n.d., 18th c.) Similar declarations are found in the book that was Sarah's source, Simeon Akiva Ber ben Joseph, *Sefer Maasei Adonai* (Amsterdam, 1708). See Chapter 5.

44. "Derekh ets hayyim ve-inyanei Gan Eden," appended to Jacob ben Abraham Solomon, *Sefer maaneh lashon* (Amsterdam, 1723), 149b–154b; quoted passage is on 152b. In addition to the Zohar, this description may be influenced by Moses de Leon, *Seder gan eden*, a manuscript work published in modern times by Adolph Jellinek, *Bet ha-Midrasch*, 3. Theil, 3 Aufl. (reprint, Jerusalem: Wahrmann, 1967). For another reworking of the description of the women's Paradise that also stresses women's domestic virtues, see Yehiel Mikhl Epstein, S. *Derekh ha-yashar le-olam ha-ba* (Frankfurt-am-Main, 1713), chap. 25.

45. However, nineteenth-century versions of these texts tend to change or omit the assertion that women studied Torah, or otherwise dilute the expressions of women's power found in some of the earlier versions.

46. See Chapter 5.

47. Some of the themes of the present chapter receive further attention in "On Law,

Spirituality, and Society in Judaism: An Exchange between Jacob Katz and Chava Weissler," *Jewish Social Studies* (new series) 2, no. 2 (1996): 87–115.

CHAPTER 3. THE CONSTRUCTION OF GENDER IN YIDDISH DEVOTIONAL LITERATURE

An earlier version of this chapter was published as "'For Women and For Men Who Are Like Women': The Construction of Gender in Yiddish Devotional Literature," *Journal of Feminist Studies in Religion* 5 (Fall 1989): 3–24.

1. For a somewhat different view of the distinction between social and symbolic definitions of gender, see Leslie W. Rabine, "No Lost Paradise: Social Gender and Symbolic Gender in the Writings of Maxine Hong Kingston," *Signs* 12 (1987): 471–92.

2. On the *Brantshpigl*, see Israel Zinberg, *Old Yiddish Literature from its Origins to the Haskalah Period*, trans. Bernard Martin (Cincinnati: Hebrew Union College Press; New York: Ktav, 1975), 157–59; Max Erik, "Bletlekh tsu der geshikhte fun der elterer yidisher literatur un kultur I: Der 'Brantshpigl'—di entsiklopedye fun der yidisher froy in XVII yorhundert," *Tsaytshrift* (Minsk: Institut far vaysruslendishe kultur) 1 (1926): 173–77; Khone Shmeruk, *Sifrut yidish be-polin* (Jerusalem: Magnes, 1981), 44, 96.

3. Reflections on gender are found in all varieties of traditional Hebrew literature, including Midrash, philosophy, and Kabbalah. I have chosen to contrast the Yiddish material with halakhah (Jewish law) because halakhah alone had *normative* force in the Ashkenazic world, as it did in other traditional Jewish societies. By contrast nonhalakhic works, whether in Yiddish or Hebrew, could be more flexible and playful in their gender definitions, because they did not need to concern themselves as directly with regulating actual behavior.

4. A good survey in English of the halakhic status of women can be found in Rachel Biale, *Women and Jewish Law* (New York: Schocken, 1984).

5. In this they differ from nonhalakhic works in Hebrew, which were also not intended to rule on actual practice.

6. The ethical work *Meineket Rivkah* (Prague, 1609) was written by a woman, Rebecca bat Meir Tiktiner. However, it is extremely rare, and I have not yet been able to examine a copy of it. On Rebecca Tiktiner, see Shmeruk, *Sifrut yidish be-polin*, 56–62, and "Ha-Soferet ha-yehudit ha-rishonah be-polin: Rivkah bat Meir Tiktiner ve-hibureha," *Gal-ed* 4–5 (1978): 13–23.

7. According to Jewish law, women are excused from Torah study despite the fact that Torah study does not fall into the category of time-bound commandments, from which women were excused in order to attend to their domestic responsibilities. The halakhic literature contains extensive discussion about whether and what subjects women are *permitted* to study; the usual view is that they could study the

written, as opposed to the oral, Torah, and the commandments that had practical applications in their own lives, such as the dietary laws, Sabbath observance, and menstrual restrictions. For discussions of the halakhic literature concerning women's Torah study, see Biale, *Women and Jewish Law*, 29–41; David Oyerbakh, S. *Halikhot Beitah* (Jerusalem: Makhon Shaarei Ziv, Yeshivat Shaar ha-shamayim, 1982–83), 388–97.

8. On Safed pietism and the related Sabbatian messianic movement, see the Introduction. On the question of legal and mystical materials as competing areas of study, see Jacob Katz, "Halakhah ve-kabbalah ke-nosei limmud mitharim" in Katz, *Halakhah ve-kabbalah* (Jerusalem: Magnes, 1984), 70–101, published in English as "Halakhah and Kabbalah as Competing Disciplines of Study," in Green, *Jewish Spirituality*, 2:34–63.

9. The third reason is that one should begin with little things and that he, describing himself as a "youth," will leave the task of writing in Hebrew for men to those older and wiser than himself. The fourth reason is, as he candidly puts it, "I thought I would have more customers this way."

10. Note that the inability to read was not necessarily a barrier to becoming part of the audience for this book; elsewhere the author directs his audience to read the book frequently or to have it read aloud to them.

11. Exod. 19:3; the verse concludes, "and declare to the children [literally: "sons"] of Israel." The context here is the revelation at Sinai.

12. Tractate Ba-hodesh 2.

13. This builds on the standard rabbinic exegesis of "house" as referring to "woman" or "wife."

14. Exodus Rabba 28 (2).

15. On *Nakhalas Tsevi*, see Zinberg, *Old Yiddish Literature*, 347–50. On its author, see *Encyclopaedia Judaica* (1972), s.v. "Chotsh, Zevi Hirsh ben Jerahmeel."

16. This was especially the case among Ashkenazim; Sefardim were less reluctant to teach it more widely.

17. Niddah 30b.

18. On the Sabbatian messianic movement, see the Introduction.

19. On this question, see Chapter 5.

20. However, *Avir Ya'akov* does not actually contain more technical kabbalistic material than *Nakhalas Tsevi*.

21. See the fuller discussion of the women's commandments in Chapter 1.

22. This motif appears elsewhere and earlier as well. The earliest occurrence known to me is found in *Tkhines* (Amsterdam, 1648), reprinted in other editions of this collection appearing in 1650, 1666, 1725, and c. 1750 (and probably others as well). This same text was also incorporated into a later collection, *Seder Tkhines-u-vakoshes* (Fürth, 1762), which was reprinted a number of times in the eighteenth

and nineteenth centuries. In this text, the comparison of the woman lighting candles to the High Priest appears as one of many motifs and is not given any particular prominence. See also Chapter 6.

23. See the discussion of Sarah bas Tovim in Chap. 8, and Zinberg, *Old Yiddish Literature*, 252–57.

24. "May my *hallah* be accepted as the sacrifice on the altar was accepted." "May this [performance of the] commandment of *hallah* count as if I had given the tithe." The *tkhine* for separating the dough for *hallah* in *Tkhines* (Amsterdam, 1648, and subsequent editions) also connects this act with the ancient system of priestly tithes. It stresses the disjunction between the present era of exile and the era when the Temple was standing: "Now we have been punished because of our sins and the sins of our forebears, so that Jerusalem, the holy city, was destroyed, and the holy House in which your name was sanctified by the priests who brought sacrifices to the altar in great purity. . . . And now we have no priest who can maintain himself in purity according to the commandments of your holy Torah. Nonetheless will I keep your commandment, and separate out a portion of the dough."

This text also expresses hope for the restoration of Temple worship, but it stops far short of comparing the performance of the commandment to separate dough to the actual bringing of a tithe or sacrifice.

25. This *tkhine*, particularly the passage discussed here, is the subject of Chapter 6, in which it is set into historical context and analyzed more fully in relation to its sources and in relation to a somewhat different set of questions.

26. The edition I used, found in the Jewish National and University Library, Jerusalem, contains no date or place of publication. The same is the case for a different edition in the collection of the Jewish Theological Seminary, New York. Ch. B. Friedberg, *Bet eked sefarim* (Jerusalem[?] 1969 or 1970; photo-offset of Tel-Aviv, 1951), 1: 90, no. alef 2258, lists a [Sudylkow, 1837] edition. The title of this *tkhine* appears to be a play on the common book title, *Imrei Shefer*, which, in Genesis 49:21 meant "lovely fawns" but eventually came to mean "beautiful words," i.e., words of Torah. Authors of Hebrew books often incorporated their names into their book titles, for example *Kedushat Levi* (The Holiness of Levi) by Levi Isaac of Berdichev. The only other *tkhine* known to me that incorporates the name of the author is *Tkhine imohes Sore Rivke Rokhl Leye* (The *Tkhine* of the Matriarchs Sarah Rebecca Rachel Leah), by Sarah Rebecca Rachel Leah Horowitz, who is the subject of Chapter 7.

27. Genesis Rabba, end of 17; Tanhuma, beginning of Noah, and near end of Metsora.

28. This is the macrocosm-microcosm correspondence mentioned above.

29. Some portions of this passage are a paraphrase of Zohar I:48b; however, the exegesis of Numbers 8:2 does not appear in this form in the Zohar. (My thanks to Elliot Wolfson for help in identifying zoharic sources.) However, it *does* appear in *Nakhalas Tsevi*. The author of the *tkhine* has combined two passages from *Nakhalas Tsevi*. The discussion of women, Sabbath candles, and the Shekhinah is found in *para-*

shat Bereshit, col. 5b, also numbered col. 130 (in the first edition, Frankfurt-am-Main, 1711), while the discussion of the High Priest is found near the beginning of *parashat Behaalotekha*, col. 8a, also numbered col. 281. The bringing together of these two motifs is the work of the author of the *tkhine*. For a more extended discussion, see Chapter 6.

30. On the remythologization process, see Gershom Scholem, *On the Kabbalah and Its Symbolism* (New York: Schocken, 1960), esp. chaps. 3, 4. On the mystical significance of the Sabbath, including some mention of the lighting of the candles, see Elliot K. Ginsburg, "The Sabbath in the Kabbalah," *Judaism* 31 (1982): 26–36.

31. See also Chapter 7, in which I discuss Leah Horowitz's *Tkhine imohes*, its use and transformation of kabbalistic sources for women.

CHAPTER 4. *MITSVOT* BUILT INTO THE BODY

This chapter was first published as "*Mitzvot* Built into the Body: *Tkhines* for Menstruation, Pregnancy, and Childbirth," in *People of the Body*, ed. Howard Eilberg-Schwartz (Albany: SUNY Press, 1992), 101–15. Used by permission.

1. The definitive study of this work and others of the same genre is Agnes Romer-Segal, "Sifrei mistvot ha-nashim be-yidish ba-meah ha-tet-zayin" (M.A. thesis, Hebrew University, 1979).

2. On the *Brantshpigl*, see Chapter 3.

3. See Chapter 1 for a discussion of the women's commandments.

4. Targum Jonathan, Genesis 1:27. In the Talmud, the correspondence is given differently: 613 commandments were revealed to Moses at Sinai, 365 being prohibitions equal in number to the solar days, and 248 being mandates corresponding in number to the limbs of the human body (B. Makkot 23b). Another talmudic passage states that the disciples of R. Ishmael, by dissecting the corpse of a prostitute who had been executed, determined that women have 252 limbs (B. Bekhorot 45a). The additional "limbs" are various parts of the female genitals.

5. According to B. Hagigah 12a, God, in contemplating future human sin, hid the primordial light that shone during the seven days of creation. With this light one could see from one end of the world to the other, and God saved it as a reward for the righteous in Paradise.

6. *Tkhines* (Amsterdam, 1648), no. 1.

7. One further numerical correspondence suggests that women's and men's bodies must be considered in relation to one another. The number of male and female limbs, 248 and 252, respectively, add up to 500. (In traditional Jewish anatomy at least, women are not *lacking* something but have *more* anatomical features than men.) This figure is used to explain why women light two candles on the eve of the Sabbath. After mentioning other explanations, Sarah bas Tovim, in a section of *The*

Three Gates entitled *Dinim fun lekht tsindn*, states: "'**Ner, ner' adds up numeri-cally to 500.** This means, the numerical equivalent of **candle**, twice, comes out to 500, corresponding to the **organs of man and woman**, the number of organs of the man and of the woman. By the merit of this [commandment], God, blessed be he, will heal the limbs of man and woman. Therefore, one should kindle the lights with great seriousness, and God, blessed be he, will enlighten your children in the Torah."

8. Tanhuma, beginning of parashat Noah; see also variant readings in Midrash Tan-huma, ed. Salomon Buber (Vilna: Romm, 1885), vol. 2, 27–29. Tanhuma is one of the few sources that explicitly state that the women's *mitsvot* function as an atone-ment. Yalkut Shimoni, Genesis 3:31, is dependent on Tanhuma. An earlier source is Avot de-Rabbi Nathan, version B, chap. 9, which, however, was not published until the twentieth century (Solomon Schechter, ed., *Aboth de-Rabbi Nathan* [New York: Feldheim, 1945], 13). For other texts that connect the three women's commandments to Eve's sin, but without the idea of atonement, see Genesis Rabba 17 (end); B. Shabbat 31b–32a, and Rashi, J. Shabbat 2:6.

For a discussion of the passages in Genesis Rabba and the Jerusalem Talmud, see Daniel Boyarin, *Carnal Israel* (Berkeley: University of California Press, 1993), 88–94. Boyarin argues that the misogyny of this midrash is exceptional in rabbinic Judaism but becomes dominant in medieval Judaism. For the development in the laws of *niddah* that transforms them from regulations of temporary ritual impurity in the rabbinic period to a conceptualization of women as dangerously contaminat-ing in the early medieval period, see Shaye D. Cohen, "Menstruants and the Sacred in Judaism and Christianity," in Sarah B. Pomeroy, ed., *Women's History and An-cient History* (Chapel Hill: University of North Carolina Press, 1991), 271–99, and "Purity and Piety: The Separation of Menstruants from the Sancta," in Susan Grossman and Rivka Haut, eds., *Daughters of the King* (Philadelphia: Jewish Publi-cation Society, 1992), 103–15. David Biale reflects on the social changes in Jewish life in the medieval period that might have led to greater anxiety about sexuality and women in *Eros and the Jews* (New York: Basic Books, 1992), chap. 3.

9. B. Erubin 100b; Avot de-Rabbi Nathan, chap. 1.

10. Benjamin Aaron Solnik, *Ayn shoen froen bukhlein (Seder mitsvas ha-noshim)* (Basel, 1602), 3b–4a; all page citations from this work are from this edition. I have been unable to locate a midrashic source for Eve's beating of Adam; this motif does not appear at Genesis 3:12 in Genesis Rabba, Midrash ha-Gadol, Avot de-Rabbi Nathan, Sefer ha-Yashar, Pirkei Rabbi Eliezer, Yalkut Shim'oni, nor does it appear in M.D. Gross, *Otsar ha-aggadah* (Jerusalem: Mosad ha-Rav Kook, 1982). It is not cited by Menahem Kasher, *Torah shelemah* (Jerusalem, 1929); nor by Louis Ginz-berg, *Legends of the Jews* (Philadelphia: Jewish Publication Society, 1913–1938). Nor is it found in the Yiddish sources Moses Henoch Altshuler, *Brantshpigl* (Ha-nau, 1626) and *Odom ve-Khave Lid* (Prague, [1658–1705]). Mordechai A. Friedman suggests that the origin of this interpretation may be that the Aramaic root *yehav* means both "to give" and "to beat or strike"; the Yiddish *gebn* also has both meanings (personal communication, 1991). (This meaning is also found in English, as in, "He really gave it to him.")

11. Solnik, *Seder mitsvas ha-noshim*, 4a.

12. Ibid., 4a.

13. Note, however, that in neither the *musar* literature nor the *tkhines* is Eve's sin described as sexual seduction. Cf. Boyarin, *Carnal Israel*, chap. 3, in which Boyarin points out that Hellenistic Judaism, unlike rabbinical texts, regards sexuality as sinful from the outset, and Eve as the initiator of sexuality.

14. Solnik, *Seder mitsvas ha-noshim*, 4a–4b.

15. Ibid., 4b.

16. Ibid., 39b. Solnik's statement that women can bring about the end of death (the messianic redemption and the resurrection of the dead) by observing the women's commandments with care does appear to give women great mythic power. This may be related to the statement in *Shloyshe sheorim* by Sarah bas Tovim that just as Adam and Eve brought death to the world, so too could they bring the end of death by rectifying their sin; see Chapter 8.

17. Altshuler, *Brantshpigl*, chap. 25, p. 118b, for *niddah*; chap. 36, p. 166a, for *hallah*; chap. 37, p. 166a–b, for *hadlakah*.

18. See the discussion of this in Chapter 1.

19. Cf. Exodus Rabba 30:13.

20. *Seder tkhines* (Amsterdam, 1650), 5b.

21. *Seder tkhines u-vakoshes* (Fürth, 1762), no. 100.

22. Ibid., no. 91.

23. The etrog, or citron, is used, along with the lulav, the palm branch together with myrtle and willow twigs, during the liturgy of the week-long fall harvest festival of Sukkot. The etrog must be intact to be fit for ritual use: in particular, the raised tip at the blossom end of the fruit (the *pittam*) must not have broken off. There were two, probably interrelated, folk beliefs concerning the *pittam* of the etrog. First, attested in twentieth-century ethnographic and literary materials, is the belief that childless women would conceive if they bit off and swallowed the *pittam*; second, and this is what I find in the *tkhines*, the belief that by biting off the *pittam*, pregnant women would ensure a safe and easy childbirth.

24. Jacob ben Isaac of Yanov, *Tsenerene* (Amsterdam, 1703), 4b. In addition, the text of the prayer, but not the introduction, is found in *Seder tkhines u-vakoshes*, no. 89.

25. Interestingly enough, there is another, later *tkhine* for biting off the end of the etrog, written by a man. See Mattithias Sobotki, *Seder tkhines* (Prague, 1718), no. 19. While Sobotki mentions that Eve's sin of disobedience, which brought death to the world, is the reason for painful childbirth, he removes all connection between the etrog and the story of Eve. Instead, he has the woman petition God for an easy childbirth in part because she has kept the *mitsvah* of *blessing* the lulav and etrog. Also, she says, "May I have my child as easily as I bite off the stem of the etrog." While this text distinguishes the woman who recites it and has obeyed God's commandment from disobedient Eve, it blunts the power of the earlier prayer. For more on Sobotki's *Seder tkhines*, see Chapter 1.

26. *Tkhines* (1648), no. 14; *Seder tkhines u-vakoshes*, no. 92.

27. *Seder tkhines u-vakoshes*, no. 93. This *tkhine* also describes how to consummate the act of marital intercourse in a holy manner. The oldest dated *tkhine* extant has rather similar content, although with less explicit discussion of the manner of intercourse. It is found in Solnik, *Seder mitsvas ha-noshim*, no. 49.

28. The use of the term *treyf* for the menstruating woman requires further investigation. While in Yiddish *"treyf"* can mean not only forbidden food but also forbidden in a more general sense, it is not usually applied to people, except in an extremely pejorative sense. Boyarin discusses the use of food metaphors for sexual activity but does not appear to find the use of "kosher" and "treyf" in rabbinic sources. See Boyarin, *Carnal Israel*, 70–76, 116–17.

29. Altshuler, *Brantshpigl*, chap. 34, p. 121. The origin of this idea may be in Tikkunei Zohar, tikkun 40, p. 80a. See also B. Shabbat 146a, B. Yebamot 103b, and B. Avodah Zarah 22b; the Talmud sees the impure venom as the source of human lust and as an explanation of the fact that Adam, Abraham, and Isaac all fathered evil sons as well as righteous ones. See also Boyarin, *Carnal Israel*, 78–83. Zohar I 54a and Tikkunei Zohar, tikkun 70, 128b, continue the Talmud's concern with evil progeny as the offspring of the serpent's impure venom. An early *piyyut* draws a different but related connection between Eve's sin and menstrual blood, stating that the color of menstrual blood is reminiscent of the wine that Eve made Adam drink. (In this reading, the Tree of Knowledge was a grapevine.) Z. M. Rabinovitz, ed., *Mahzor piyyutei Rabbin Yannai la-Torah vela-moadim* (Jerusalem and Tel-Aviv, 1985), 435, cited by Mordechai A. Friedman, "Harhakat ha-niddah veha-minut et-sel ha-geonim, ha-Rambam, u-veno R. Avraham, al pi kitvei genizat Kahir," *Maimonidean Studies* 1 (1990): 1–21.

30. Altshuler, *Brantshpigl*, chap. 34, p. 120b.

31. See, for example, ibid., chap. 3, pp. 11a–12a, in which Altshuler explains why he is writing this book in Yiddish for women.

32. See Nisson E. Shulman, *Authority and Community: Polish Jewry in the Sixteenth Century* (Hoboken, N.J.: Ktav, 1986), 22–25, 148, 187. This is a historical study based on Solnik's halakhic works.

CHAPTER 5. WOMEN IN PARADISE

An earlier version of this chapter was published as "Women in Paradise," *Tikkun* 2 (April–May 1987): 43–46, 117–20.

1. This seems to be a well-known traditional oral motif in Eastern European Ashkenazic culture. However, I have been unable to trace it to any literary source earlier than a short story by Isaac Loeb Peretz (1851–1915), "Sholem bayis," in Peretz, *Ertseylungen* (New York: Farlag "Idish," 1920), vol. 3.

2. B. Berakhot 17a.

3. These works are *Nakhalas Tsevi*, also known as the *Taytsh* Zohar (the Yiddish Zohar), by Tsevi Hirsh Khotsh, first published in 1711; and, more important for our present purpose, in part 2 of *Sefer maasei Adonai*, by Simon Akiva Ber ben Joseph, first published in 1694. The Yiddish translation of this passage in *Nakhalas Tsevi* is quite close to the original Zohar text.

4. These versions appear as separate sections of other books. They include "*Maaseh gadol me-rabi Shim'on bar Yohai*," appended to *S. Olam ha-ba* (Hanau, 1620), a lengthy description of Paradise, 7a–8a; "*Ayn vunder sheyn mayse oyz den* Zohar *parshas Lekh Lekha*[sic]," which is followed by another brief tale (Prague, c. 1665); "*Ayn sheyn mayse oyz den* Zohar *parshas Lekh Lekha*[sic]," printed as an addendum to *Ayn sheyn getlikh lid Orah Hayyim* (Fürth, 1692–98), a poem describing the ethical life, 8a–8b. For further discussion of these tales, see Chapter 2 above.

5. Although a Bithia, daughter of Pharaoh, is mentioned in 2 Chronicles 4:18, it is not clear that she is the same person as the daughter of Pharaoh who rescued Moses (Exod. 2:5–10). The rabbis, however, made this identification and explained her name as meaning "daughter of God" (Lev. Rabba 1:3). This identification was accepted by the author of the Zohar.

6. *Nashim shaananot*; Isa. 32:9.

7. Serah, daughter of Asher, is mentioned in the Bible only in genealogical lists (Gen. 46:17; Num. 26:46; 1 Chron. 7:3). However, later legend portrays her as gently breaking the news to Jacob that Joseph was still alive by playing the harp and singing about it so that Jacob could hear (*Sefer ha-yashar, Va-yiggash*). Other stories are told about her in the Midrash; for a summary, see Yosef Heinemann, *Aggadot ve-toledoteihen* (Aggadah and Its Development) (Jerusalem: Keter, 1974), 56–63.

8. See, for example, Judah ben Samuel, *Sefer Hasidim*, ed. Jehuda Wistinetzki, 2d ed. (1924; Jerusalem: Sifrei Vahrman, 1969) par. 835, which specifies that a man is obligated to teach his daughter the legal rulings that concern her own observance, but that "one does not teach the depth of the Talmud, the reasons for the commandments, or the secrets of the Torah to women or minors." I am indebted to Ivan Marcus for this reference.

9. Part of the reason for the change in terminology may be a simplification for a popular audience. It is possible that women (or nonlearned men) could not be assumed to know what the study of *taamei ha-mitsvot* was.

10. On these tales, see Chapter 3.

11. This section of the passage is important in establishing the chain of literary transmission between the Zohar and the *tkhine*.

12. At least one eighteenth-century Ashkenazic woman, Leah Horowitz, could read the Zohar; see Chapter 7.

13. The fact that the 1708 edition was a combination of parts 1 and 2 was first noted by Sarah Zfatman; see her annotated bibliography, *Yiddish Narrative Prose from Its Beginnings to 'Shivhei ha-Besht' (1514–1814)* (Hebrew) (Jerusalem: Hebrew University, 1985), 92. I am indebted to Dr. Zfatman and to her bibliography for assistance in locating the versions of the "women in Paradise" motif.

14. The evidence, in general, is this: the wording of the *tkhine* is much closer to that of *Sefer maasei Adonai* than it is to any of the other Yiddish sources. Only these two texts, for example, contain the assertions of power and worth by Bithia and Serah. *Nakhalas Tsevi* is more or less a straightforward translation of the Zohar text; the Yiddish tales concerning this motif depart from the original considerably more radically than do either *Sefer maasei Adonai* or *The Three Gates*.

15. See, for example, the 1859 and 1865 editions of *The Three Gates* (Vilna: Romm), which mention Joseph's Torah study in an upper chamber but fail to mention women's Torah study. See also *Tkhine fun rosh khoydesh benshin* (Lemberg [Lvov]: Druck von V. Kübler, 1894), which incorporates many different *tkhines* for the blessing of the new moon, including the one by Sarah bas Tovim (on pp. 11–15). This text removes Bithia and Serah's exclamations of power and worth, but does preserve mention of women's Torah study.

16. See Chapter 9 for a discussion of the *maskilim* and the *tkhines*.

CHAPTER 6. KABBALISTIC CANDLE LIGHTING

An earlier version of this chapter was published as "Woman as High Priest: A Kabbalistic *Tkhine* for Lighting Sabbath Candles," *Jewish History*, 5 (Spring 1991): 9–26, and was also republished in *Essential Papers in Kabbalah*, ed. Lawrence Fine (New York: New York University Press, 1995), 525–46.

1. The lack of female mystics is noted by Gershom Scholem as a distinguishing characteristic of Kabbalah; see Scholem, *Major Trends in Jewish Mysticism* (New York: Schocken, 1946), 37.

2. See I. M. Lewis, *Ecstatic Religion*, 2d ed. (London: Routledge, 1989). In their study of medieval Christian saints, *Saints and Society* (Chicago: University of Chicago Press, 1982), Donald Weinstein and Rudolph Bell speculate that "the social powerlessness of women helps to explain the frequency of supernatural activity in their lives" (228). I believe the matter is more complicated. For a detailed examination of the reasons for and meanings of the related phenomenon of female asceticism in medieval Christianity, see Carolyn Walker Bynum, *Holy Feast and Holy Fast* (Berkeley: University of California Press, 1987). For a fascinating discussion of women's involvement in communing with spirits of a rather different kind, see Alex Owen, *The Darkened Room: Women, Power, and Spiritualism in Late Victorian England* (London: Virago, 1989).

3. As Scholem points out (*Major Trends*, 37), this is not an absolute obstacle to women's mystical activity. Few Christian or Muslim women were learned, yet this did not prevent them from strongly influencing their respective mystical movements.

4. While women seem not to have played a significant role in the leadership of the Sabbatian movement, Eva Frank, Jacob Frank's daughter, was a leader of the

Frankist movement. Frankist theology also accorded a significant place to the feminine aspect of God. See Bernard D. Weinryb, *The Jews of Poland* (Philadelphia, Jewish Publication Society, 1976), 236–61. On women in Hasidism, see Ada Rapoport-Albert, "On Women in Hasidism: S. A. Horodecky and the Maid of Ludmir Tradition," *Jewish History: Essays in Honour of Chimen Abramsky*, ed. Steven J. Zipperstein and Ada Rapoport-Albert (London: Halban, 1988), 495–525. Rapoport-Albert approaches the question of the position of women in Hasidism mainly from the perspective of elite hasidic literature. As I suggest below, it is also important to take popular literature into account.

5. Rapoport-Albert, "On Women in Hasidism." However, see also Nehemiah Polen, "Miriam's Dance: Radical Egalitarianism in Hasidic Thought," *Modern Judaism* 12 (1992): 1–21.

6. I have seen Yiddish *tkhines* attributed to women from Dubno, Krzemieniec, Klewan, and Oleksiniec in Volhynia; Belz, Brody, Bolechów, and Stanislawów in Galicia; and Satanov in Podolia. Other areas are also represented, but more sparsely: Lublin, Mohylev, and Krasnik, for example. This is by no means an exhaustive sample; however, even the *tkhines* published in Vilna in the second half of the nineteenth century, when they contain author attributions, generally note that these authors are from Galicia and Volhynia. Only a small number of *tkhines* contain material of kabbalistic derivation.

7. What is needed is a full analysis of which kabbalistic texts were translated, how they were adapted in translation, and what kinds of Yiddish texts they appeared in. See Israel Zinberg, *A History of Jewish Literature*, vol. 7, *Old Yiddish Literature* (New York: Ktav, 1975), 345–52, for a brief discussion of kabbalistic *musar* literature; Zeev Gries discusses Yiddish kabbalistic *hanhagot* (*regimen vitae*; books of pious customs) in Yiddish in "Itsuv sifrut ha-hanhagot ha-ivrit be-mifneh ha-meah ha-shesh-esreh uva-meah ha-sheva-esreh u-mashmauto ha-historit," *Tarbiz* 56 (1987): 527–81, esp. 531–32, 578–79; see also Gries, *Sifrut ha-hanhagot* (Jerusalem: Mosad Bialik, 1989), esp. 46, 59–63.

8. Simon Akiva Baer ben Joseph, comp. and trans., *Sefer maasei Adonai*, vol. 1 (Frankfurt-am-Main, 1691), vol. 2 (Fürth, 1694), and *Avir Yaakov* (Sulzbach, 1700) (both bilingual in Hebrew and Yiddish); Tsevi Hirsh Khotsh, *Nakhalas Tsevi* (Amsterdam, 1711).

9. For a discussion of a case in which a *tkhine* uses material from *Sefer maasei Adonai* see Chapter 5.

10. Caroline Walker Bynum, "'. . . And Woman His Humanity': Female Imagery in the Religious Writing of the Later Middle Ages," in *Gender and Religion*, ed. C. W. Bynum, S. Harrell, and P. Richman (Boston: Beacon, 1986), 257–88; see also the more general discussion of the different uses women and men make of the symbolism of Christianity in Bynum's *Holy Feast and Holy Fast*, chap. 10.

11. In fact, late twentieth-century Habad (Lubavitch) hasidic women have indeed formulated a mystical view of women's spiritual life that identifies women with the Shekhinah and turns precisely on women's physicality. Specifically, they have made

the menstrual laws (*niddah*) a symbol for God's periodic eclipse, which women on earth embody in their menstrual cycles. This is indeed reminiscent of the strategy of medieval Christian female mystics. See the study by Jody Myers and Jane Rachel Litman, "The Secret of Jewish Femininity: Hiddenness, Power, and Physicality in the Theology of Orthodox Women in the Contemporary World," in *Gender and Judaism*, ed. T. M. Rudavsky (New York: New York University Press, 1995), 51–77. While classical Kabbalah also deals with the menstruation of the Shekhinah, it depicts it in much more negative and demonic terms than do Habad women; see Sharon Koren, "The Shekhinah as *Niddah*," paper presented at the Annual Meeting of the Association for Jewish Studies, December 1996, and included as a chapter in "Mysticism and Menstruation: The Significance of Female Impurity to Jewish Spirituality" (Ph.D. dissertation, Yale University, 1998).

12. *Seder tkhines u-vakoshes* (Fürth, 1762); there was probably at least one earlier edition. On this work, see Chapter 1.

13. For an overview of the *tkhine* literature, see Chapter 1; for discussion of the methodological problems involved in using *tkhines* and other genres of Yiddish popular religious literature for studying the religious lives of women, see Chapter 2. On the connection to mystical private devotions, see Solomon Freehof, "Devotional Literature in the Vernacular," *CCAR Yearbook* 33 (1923): 375–474; and see the discussion in Chapter 2.

14. *Seder tkhines u-vakoshes* (Fürth, 1762), no. 3. This *tkhine* is an adaptation of a Hebrew prayer intended for men who were not learned in Kabbalah. It was composed by Leib Pohavitser and appears in his *Sefer Darkhei Hakhamim* (Frankfort an der Oder, 1683), pt. 2, *Solet belulah, hilkhot tefillah*, 19c. On the motif of the prayers of Israel as a crown for God, see Arthur Green, *Keter* (Princeton: Princeton University Press, 1997), esp. chap. 4.

15. Chapter 8 is devoted to Sarah bas Tovim and her *tkhines*.

16. Part of the *tkhine* for the new moon in *The Three Gates* is a paraphrase of *Sefer hemdat yamim*, 4 vols. (Jerusalem: Makor, 1970; photo-offset of Constantinople, 1735), vol. 2, *Rosh Hodesh*, 12b–13b (*Enkat Asir*). On the history of this anonymous work, see Isaiah Tishby, "Le-heker ha-mekorot shel sefer *Hemdat yamim*," and idem, "Mekorot me-reshit ha-meah ha-shemonah-asar be-sefer *Hemdat yamim*," both reprinted in Tishby, *Netivei emunah u-minut* (Jerusalem: Magnes, 1982), 108–42, 143–68. As Tishby and other scholars have shown, *Hemdat yamim* is a Sabbatian work, although it was not always recognized as such. See further discussion of this in Chapter 8.

17. Leah Horowitz is the subject of Chapter 7.

18. *Tkhine imrei Shifre* (n.p., n.d.; Eastern Europe after 1770?). The edition I used is in the *tkhine* pamphlet collection of the Jewish National and University Library, Jerusalem, call no. R41 A460, vol. 6, no. 8. I compared it with a different edition, also published without date or place of publication, in the uncataloged *tkhine* pamphlet collection of the Jewish Theological Seminary Library, New York. The differences between the two editions are many but small. The title of the *tkhine* is proba-

bly a play on the common book title *Imrei shefer*, from Genesis 49:21 (where it probably means "lovely fawns"); it was later understood to mean "beautiful words," that is, words of Torah.

19. Following its source, this *tkhine* omits references to the *sefirot* in some of its adaptations of zoharic texts.

20. During this period, groups of both hasidim and their opponents, the mitnagdim, immigrated to Palestine. On this migration, see Israel Heilprin, *Aliyot ha-hasidim ha-rishonot le-erets yisrael* (Jerusalem, 1947); Yaacov Barnai [Barniy], *Igrot hasidim me-erets yisrael* (Jerusalem: Yad Yizhak Ben-Zvi, 1980) and *Yehudei erets-yisrael ba-meah ha-yud-het* (Jerusalem, Yad Yizhak Ben-Zvi, 1982); and Rayah Haran, "Mah heni'a et talmidei ha-maggid la-alot le-erets yisrael?" *Cathedra* 76 (1995): 77–95. Unfortunately, none of these works contain references to Shifrah or her husband. Nonetheless, perhaps Shifrah and her husband belonged to one of these groups; or maybe the publisher wished to associate this *tkhine* with the holy lustre of such a move. See below in the text.

21. There is no blank space in the Jewish Theological Seminary edition.

22. This was Ellus bas Mordecai of Slutsk, for her translation of *Shomrim la-boker* (Frankfurt-an-der-Oder, 1704) into Yiddish; it seems clear from the texts of the three *haskamot* in her book that she brought a fair amount of pressure to bear to get them, and that at least one of the rabbis who wrote them was rather embarrassed to be writing a *haskamah* for a woman. See Chapter 1.

23. The first section of the text, a *tkhine* on the bitterness of the exile and the need for repentance, may reflect the difficult conditions of war-torn Poland in 1768–72.

24. In both editions Shifrah's husband's name is followed by an inconsistent string of abbreviations: *n"y '"h p"h*. The first one stands for *nero ya'ir*, implying he is alive; the second for *'alav ha-shalom*, implying he is dead.

I examined the following sources in an unsuccessful search for some reference to Shifrah's husband: Dov Evron, ed., *Pinkas ha-kesherim shel kehillat pozna* (Jerusalem: Mekitsei nirdamim, 1966); Meir Wunder, *Meorei galitsiyah* (Jerusalem: ha-Makhon le-hantsahat yahadut galitsiyah, 1978–86); *Pinkas ha-kehillot, Polin*, vol. 2, *Galitsyah ha-mizrahit* (Jerusalem: Yad va-shem, 1980); Raphael Halprin, *Atlas ets ha-hayyim*, vol. 7 (Tel-Aviv?: Hekdesh ruah Yaakov, 1982); N. M. Gelber, "Aus dem 'Pinax des alten Judenfriedhofes in Brody'(1699–1831)," *Jahrbuch der Jüdisch-Literarischen Gesellschaft* (Frankfurt-am-Main: J. Kauffman, 1920), 119–41. See also the works cited in n. 20 above.

This lack of documentation does not necessarily mean that the author statement on the *tkhine* is fictitious. There were apparently many undocumented rabbis in Brody (Meir Wunder, personal communication conveyed by Shaul Stampfer). In addition, if, as is likely, this *tkhine* was published in the vicinity of Brody, its audience would have known whether there was in fact a *dayyan* named Ephraim Segal, which would have limited the publisher's flights of fancy.

25. On the motivation of the leadership, see especially Haran, "Mah heni'a et talmidei ha-maggid?" whose arguments are more persuasive than those of Barnai, *Yehu-*

dei erets-yisrael, chap. 5. In chapter 4, Barnai notes that the majority of the emigrants in 1777 were from Brody; later he lists the many other locations, including Poznan, from which emigrants came (225).

26. In "Tkhine khadoshe le-khol yom" Shifrah writes: "And I pray you, dear Father, help me [resist] Satan, so that I may have no strange thought. Satan and his accusers hinder my prayer; I cannot overcome him. I pray you, dear God, help me to overcome him." See M. Piekarz, *Bi-yemei tsemihat ha-hasidut* (Jerusalem: Mosad Bialik, 1978), chap. 6, in which discussions of the problem of "strange thoughts" during prayer are quoted from several Yiddish ethical works. These are Tsevi Hirsh Koidanover, *Kav ha-yashar*, chap. 8; Isaac ben Eliakum, *Lev Tov: hilkhot bet ha-keneset*, 8; Yehiel Mikhl Epstein, *Derekh ha-yashar le-'olam ha-ba*. Any (or all) of these could have been Shifrah's source.

Shifrah also uses the term *shefa elyonah* [sic]: "The supernal abundance has removed itself from us; the sages go around without a livelihood." Again, this does not seem to be a specifically hasidic usage of the term *shefa*.

Finally, at one point Shifrah quotes the verse "The 'Dumah' Pronouncement: A call comes to me from Seir, 'Watchman, what of the night? Watchman, what of the night?'" (Isa. 21:11). This verse was a favorite of Frankist exegetes, who understood the Hebrew phrase with which the verse begins, *masa dumah*, to mean "the burden of silence," referring to the secrecy required from Frank's followers. However, Shifrah's interpretation seems impeccably orthodox; if she was a Frankist, she maintained her burden of secrecy.

27. If the author of this *tkhine* were influenced by Hasidic teachings, it would have been by word of mouth or via a manuscript. The earliest published hasidic work, *Toledot Yaakov Yosef*, by Jacob Joseph of Polonnoye, first appeared in 1780. On the significance of the lag between the rise of Hasidism and the publication of hasidic works, see Zeev Gries, *Sefer, sofer, ve-sipur be-reshit ha-hasidut* (Tel Aviv: Hakibbutz Hameuchad Publishing House, 1992).

28. The penultimate paragraph of the *tkhine khadoshe le-khol yom* is similar to part of *Seder tkhines u-vakoshes*, no. 57. A passage in the middle of the third page of the *tkhine khadoshe le-shabes* resembles *Seder tkhines u-vakoshes*, no. 49. Parts of a passage on the third page of the *tokhakhas musar le-shabes* resemble parts of Leah's *Tkhine imohes*. These similarities are not close enough to allow for absolute certainty that Shifrah has indeed used the earlier works; there may be other sources. However, it is clear that she was influenced by the literary tradition of the *tkhines* for lighting Sabbath candles.

29. Num. 8:2. The verse begins: "The Lord spoke to Moses, saying: Speak to Aaron and say to him." The context is the instruction to Aaron (and by implication, the later High Priests) in how to light the candelabrum in the Tabernacle (later, in the Temple). The verse is difficult to understand: it speaks of "raising" when it means "kindling," and it is not clear what is meant by the lamps shining "against the face of" the candelabrum. (The new Jewish Publication Society version translates the rest of the verse: "When you mount the lamps, let the seven lamps throw their light

forward toward the front of the lampstand.") These textual difficulties are used by the *tkhine* (and its sources) in the interpretation of the verse.

30. This is the Yiddish paraphrase of the biblical verse, slightly garbled and out of place; it usually follows the verse but here has become entangled in the interpretation. The text of Shifrah's Yiddish source, below, in which this sentence does not include the verse paraphrase, is much clearer: "By his kindling the candelabrum below, he raised the arousal to the Upper World."

31. See B. Shabbat 23b.

32. *Tkhine imrei Shifre* [6a-6b].

33. The punitive view is found in the Midrash, Genesis Rabba, end of 17; Tanhuma, beginning of Noah and near the end of Metsora. These passages give similar justifications for the other two "women's commandments"—separating a portion of dough for the priestly tithe (*hallah*) and observing menstrual avoidances and post-menstrual purification (*niddah*). See Chapter 4.

34. On the meaning of the Sabbath and its rituals in the Kabbalah, see Elliot K. Ginsburg, *The Sabbath in the Classical Kabbalah* (Albany: State University of New York Press, 1989).

35. There are a number of passages in the Zohar that contain similar themes concerning the High Priest, but none of them correspond to the precise wording of the *tkhine*. Thematic parallels for this motif in the Zohar include correspondence between an earthly priest and tabernacle and a heavenly priest and tabernacle (Zohar I 217a, II 159a, III 134b, 132b [Idra Rabba], 147a); the High Priest kindles the supernal lights (III 34b); and interpretations of the term *be-ha'alotekha* (III 149a: "Come and see, at the time when the priest intended to kindle the lights below, and he would offer incense at that time, then the upper lights would shine"), and see the pages following.

36. The paraphrase was an expansion of a work begun by Khotsh's grandfather, Aviezer Zelig. Khotsh may have been a crypto-Sabbatian. See the (contradictory) statements on this in two articles by Gershom Scholem in the *Encyclopaedia Judaica* (1972), s.v. "Chotsh, Zevi Hirsh ben Jerahmeel"; and s.v. "Shabbetai Zevi," esp. col. 1248.

37. In its intended audience, *Nakhalas Tsevi* is unlike the two other adaptations of kabbalistic material mentioned earlier. The two compendia by Simon Akiva Baer b. Joseph were addressed to both women and men. In fact, *Avir Yaakov* has a rather sweet preface, which recommends that husband and wife read the book together after they arise from their Sabbath nap. Nonetheless, *Nakhalas Tsevi* appears to have been popular reading material for women. For more on attitudes toward women in *Nakhalas Tsevi*, see Chapter 3.

38. Tsevi Hirsh Khotsh, *Nakhalas Tsevi* (Amsterdam, 1711), *Bereshit*, col. 5b, also numbered col. 130.

39. Khotsh, *Nakhalas Tsevi*, *Bemidbar*, col. 8a, also numbered col. 281 (near the beginning of *Be-ha'alotekha*).

40. The Zohar attributes the first view to its own sages (*ve-ukmuha hevraya*). It accepts this as a good explanation (*ve-shafir*) then goes on to discuss, in addition, the secret mystical reason for women to have been assigned this commandment.

41. See Chapter 4 for further discussion of the range of views on the reasons for the women's commandments.

42. *Seder Tkhines u-vakoshes* (Fürth, 1762), no. 47.

43. Sarah bas Tovim, *The Three Gates* (n.p., n.d.; Eastern Europe, late eighteenth c.?) [3b–4a].

44. I am still looking in midrashic literature for the motif in the form it takes in the *tkhines*, namely, an implicit or explicit comparison of the woman lighting candles with the High Priest lighting the candelabrum. *Yalkut Shim'oni* on Num. 8:1 (beginning of *Beha'alotekha*) makes a connection between the candelabrum in the Tabernacle and the Sabbath lights. It further makes the point that while the sacrifices cease after the destruction of the Temple, the kindling of Sabbath lights (taken as symbolic of or related to the priestly blessing) continues throughout the ages.

45. *Nakhalas Tsevi*: "It is proper for the women **below** to act as in the form **above**, to kindle the lights." *Imrei Shifre*: "It is therefore proper for us to do below, in this form, as it is done above, to kindle the lights."

46. *Imrei Shifre*. The wording in *Nakhalas Tsevi* is nearly identical but stops after the word "Shekhinah."

47. For a more theoretical discussion of this issue, see Chapter 3.

48. See Elliot R. Wolfson, "On Becoming Female: Crossing the Gender Boundaries in Kabbalistic Ritual and Myth," in *Gender and Judaism*, 209–228, and *Circle in the Square: Studies in the Use of Gender in Kabbalistic Symbolism* (Albany: State University of New York Press, 1995), esp. chap. 4. Wolfson also argues that the actualized Shekhinah becomes symbolically male.

49. Scholem, *Major Trends*, 37.

CHAPTER 7. TEARS FOR THE SHEKHINAH

1. Some editions, notably that published in Grodno, 1796, give the title of the *tkhine* as *Tkhine imohos Sore Rivke Rokhl Leye* (*Tkhine* of the Matriarchs Sarah Rebecca Rachel Leah). This is one of the few examples of a *tkhine* title that incorporates the name of the author. In addition, Leah worked an acrostic of her full name, Sarah Rivkah Rahel Leah bat ha-Rav Gaon Yaakov Segal (Sarah Rebecca Rachel Leah, daughter of the brilliant Rabbi Jacob the Levite) into both the Aramaic and Yiddish portions of her texts. An acrostic was a common method of claiming authorship.

On this *tkhine*, see Haim Liberman, "'Tehinnah imahot' u-'tehinnat sheloshah shearim'," in Liberman, *Ohel Rahel* (New York: H. Liberman, 1979 or 1980), 432–54, esp. 432–33, 437–38; this was originally published in *Kiryat sefer* 36 (1961): 112–22. Liberman cites a number of the sources that refer to the author.

2. Many other *tkhines* quote biblical verses or passages from the liturgy in Hebrew; some *tkhine* authors composed isolated sentences in Hebrew, which were followed in the text by Yiddish translations or paraphrases. At most, other *tkhines* may contain short paragraphs of a few sentences in Hebrew; Leah's work is the only one I have seen that contains a sustained Hebrew passage running for several pages. However, while Leah was truly exceptional as a *woman* for her scholarship, she was not particularly outstanding as a *scholar*, when compared with her male contemporaries.

3. There are only two editions known to me that contain all three sections of the *tkhine* in their original languages. A copy of one is found in the collection of the Jewish National and University Library, Jerusalem, (shelf mark R41 A460, v. 6, no. 2) and was published in pamphlet format, without mention of place or date of publication. It is printed in small type, is difficult to read, and contains numerous typographical errors. Haim Liberman hypothesized on typographical grounds that this edition was printed in Lvov at the press of Judith Rosanes (active 1788–1805) and that it was the first edition. He was not aware that there is at least one other edition that also contains the complete text. A copy of this other edition, also published without place or date, on bad paper with numerous typographical errors, is found in the uncatalogued *tkhine* pamphlet collection at the Jewish Theological Seminary Library, New York. While the Hebrew and Aramaic portions of this edition differ from the JNUL edition only in small details, the Yiddish portion differs more significantly. I am inclined from my comparison of the two editions to regard the one found at JNUL as the earlier of the two.

A third edition, not noted by Liberman, was published in Horodno (Grodno) in 1796 and is found in the collections of the JNUL (R75 A284). It contains a Yiddish paraphrase of the introduction, the *piyyut* in Aramaic, and the Yiddish *tkhine*. I hope to publish an annotated translation of the *Tkhine of the Matriarchs*, based on these three editions, in the near future.

4. A similarly learned woman of an earlier era was Rebecca Tiktiner, author of *Meineket Rivkah* (Rebecca's nursemaid), a *musar* book for women, and of a Yiddish poem for the holiday of Simhat Torah. See Khone Shmeruk, *Sifrut yidish be-polin* (Jerusalem: Magnes, 1981), 56–63, 65–69, 101–2.

5. *Encyclopaedia Judaica* (1972), s.v. "Horowitz, Jacob Jokel," and see the references there. The article does not mention his daughter Leah. Neither do the genealogies of the Horowitz family: Bernhard Friedberg, *Toldot mishpahat Horovits*, 2d ed. (Antwerp: [s.n.], 1928), lists only the male members of the family; and Hirsch Horowitz, *Toldot mishpahat Horovits* (Cracow: [s.n.], 1934 or 1935), traces the family from its beginnings until the generation of Leah's grandfather. The most extensive information concerning Leah's immediate family is found in Meir Wunder, *Meorei galitsiyah*, v. 2 (Jerusalem: ha-Makhon le-hantsahat yahadut galitsiyah, 1982), col. 123. Wunder lists the (unnamed) author of *Tkhine of the Matriarchs* and Leah as sisters. In my view they are the same person; see note 9 below.

6. According to Wunder, it was his son, R. Isaac, who was involved in the *kloyz*. See Wunder, *Meorei Galitsiyah*, col. 123.

7. Abraham Joshua Heschel, "Rabbi Gershon Kutover: His Life and Immigration to the Land of Israel," in Heschel, *The Circle of the Baal Shem Tov*, ed. Samuel H. Dresner (Chicago: University of Chicago Press, 1985), 51, 55; originally published as Heschel, "R. Gershon Kutover: parashat hayyav ve-aliyyato le-erets yisrael," *Hebrew Union College Annual* 23 (1950–51): pt. 2, 17–71.

8. Heschel states, erroneously, that he settled in Glona (Gliniany) (p. 55n; see also the original Hebrew, p. 26n). According to the *Encyclopaedia Judaica*, Wunder, *Meorei Galitsiyah*, and all other sources, he settled in Glogau, sometimes also called *Glogau-rabbati* or Gross-Glogau.

9. See Wunder, *Meorei Galitsiyah*, cols. 107–8, 123. Wunder lists "the author of *Tkhine of the Matriarchs*, wife of R. Shabbetai ha-Cohen Rappaport, rabbi of Krasny, son of Benjamin" separately from "Leah, wife of Arieh Leib son of the rabbi of Dobromil, renowned as a very learned woman." In my view, it is more likely, as Liberman suggests, that Leah married twice than that there were two separate sisters; Liberman, "'Tehinnah imahot,'" 432n. The best evidence for this is the alphabetical acrostic in *Tkhine of the Matriarchs*, in which the author signs her name: "Sarah Rebecca Rachel Leah, daughter of the brilliant rabbi Jacob of the house of Levi." (The Horowitzes were Levites.) If the author was named Sarah Rebecca Rachel Leah, there was unlikely to be another daughter named simply Leah.

10. A small town in Galicia. The name of Leah's husband given here is not the same as that mentioned in the *Tkhine of the Matriarchs*, in which she is said to be married to Shabbetai, head of the rabbinical court of Krasnik, in Lublin Province. See note 9.

11. Rabbi Solomon ben Isaac (1040–1105), most renowned commentator on the Talmud and the Bible.

12. Ber of Bolechow, *Zikhronot R. Dov mi-Bolihov*, ed. M. Vishnitzer (Berlin: Klal-Verlag, 1922), 44. See also *The Memoirs of Ber of Bolechow*, trans. M. Vishnitzer (New York: Arno, 1973; reprint, London: Oxford University Press, 1922), 78.

13. Ibid., 12.

14. Ber, *Memoirs*, 44–45.

15. Nathanson, *Divre Sha'ul, hidushei agadot* (Lemberg, 1877), 113c, attributes a *kushya* (discussion of a talmudic point) concerning B. Hullin 37b to "the daughter of the eminent Rabbi Yokl." However, this same interpretation is also attributed to Leah's niece, Beila bat Isaac Ha-Levi Horowitz (the mother of Naftali of Ropczyce), by R. Hayyim Eleazar Shapira (the Munkacher Rebbe, 1869–1937), *S. Divrei Torah* (Jerusalem, 1974, reprint of Munkacs, 1929), mahadura tinyana, 65a. Nathanson (1810–1875) could not have had any personal contact with Leah, nor does he even mention her name. Beila, however, was Shapira's ancestor: "I heard in the name of the renowned, scholarly woman, my ancestor [*zekenati*] (the ancestor of our family on the side of my mother Layushta, that righteous woman), i.e., the righteous rabbi's wife, Mistress Beila . . . daughter of . . . R. Isaac ha-Levi Horowitz of Hamburg." It thus seems probable that he had direct knowledge about her, which makes his attribution of this *kushya* to Beila more probable than Nathanson's more

impersonal attribution to Leah. Perhaps the *kushya* became attached to Leah because of her reputation for learning. It is interesting to note that the Horowitz family educated more than one of its daughters along with its eminent sons.

16. Very few editions of this frequently reprinted *tkhine* contain more than the Yiddish portion of the text. As Liberman remarks, "It seems that [this text] was no longer printed in complete form, since men were not interested in *tkhines*, and women did not understand the Aramaic in the *tkhine*, nor the Hebrew in the introduction." Liberman, "'Tehinnah imahot,'" 433.

17. See for example the passage in the daily morning prayers, based on Mishnah Peah 1:1 and B. Shabbat 127a: "These are the things the fruits of which a person enjoys in this world, while the principal remains for him in the hereafter, namely, honoring father and mother, deeds of lovingkindness, early attendance at the house of study morning and evening, hospitality to strangers, visiting the sick, dowering the bride, attending the dead to the grave, devotion in prayer, and making peace between one person and another; but the study of the Torah is greater than all of them."

18. B. Sotah 20a-b.

19. For recent studies of the legend of Beruriah, see Rachel Adler, "The Virgin in the Brothel and Other Anomalies: Character and Context in the Legend of Beruriah," *Tikkun* 3, no. 6 (November-December 1988), 28–32, 102–105; Daniel Boyarin, *Carnal Israel* (Berkeley: University of California Press, 1993), 181–96; and Judith Romney Wegner, "Women in Classical Rabbinic Judaism," in *Jewish Women in Historical Perspective*, ed. Judith Baskin (Detroit: Wayne State University Press, 1991), 76.

20. Mishael Maswari Caspi, *Daughters of Yemen* (Berkeley: University of California Press, 1985), 6. See also Susan Sered, *Women as Ritual Experts* (New York: Oxford University Press, 1992), 16, 66–71.

21. Rachel Biale, *Women and Jewish Law* (New York: Schocken Books, 1984), 29–41; *Sefer Hasidim*, ed. Reuven Margoliot (Jerusalem: Mosad ha-Rav Kook, 1964), para. 313. Two recent guides for Orthodox Jews today take up the question of women's Torah study: David Oyerbakh, *Sefer halikhot beitah* (Jerusalem: Mekhon shaarei ziv, 1983), 388–95, which contains an extensive survey of halakhic sources on women's Torah study; and Isaac Jacob Fuks, *Halikhot bat yisrael* (Jerusalem: Y. Y. Fuks, 1983), 117–26. Fuks is more inclined to permit women to study the Talmud than is Oyerbakh.

22. An interesting example is that of Eva Bacharach (1580–1651), descendant of Rabbi Loew of Prague, grandmother of Yair Hayyim Bacharach, who named his book of responsa *Havvot yair* in her memory. In the introduction to the work, he describes her knowledge of and original commentary on Midrash, liturgical and penitential works, the Bible, and apocrypha.

23. "A woman who studies the Torah has reward for this but it is not as great as the reward of a man who studies, since she is under no legal obligation to study. Even though she has reward for her studies, the rabbis advised against a man teaching

the Torah to his daughter, because the majority of women cannot concentrate properly on their studies, and they interpret the Torah in a stupid way in accordance with the poverty of their minds." Shulhan Arukh, Yoreh Deah, 246, trans. Louis Jacobs, *Jewish Law* (New York: Behrman House, 1968), 154.

24. Tsevi Hirsh ben Aryeh Loeb Levin, also known as Hirschel Lewin, Hirsch Loebel, and Hart Lyon (1721–1800), chief rabbi of Berlin from 1772 to 1800. He was a man of broad intellectual interests and a friend of Moses Mendelssohn, but he was also a vigorous opponent of Naphtali Herz Wessely's proposed reforms. See *Encyclopaedia Judaica* (1972), s.v. "Levin, Zevi Hirsch(-el) ben Aryeh Loeb"; Alexander Altmann, *Moses Mendelssohn, A Biographical Study* (Philadelphia: Jewish Publication Society, 1973), 379–81 and passim.

25. The chief rabbi of the Hague from 1748 to 1785 was Saul Halevi; see *Encyclopaedia Judaica* (1972), s.v. "Hague." The text at this point actually gives the rabbi's name as Tsevi Hirsh; however, this is a typographical error, simply repeating the name of the chief rabbi of Berlin. The next paragraph, which describes some of Dinah's accomplishments as a scholar, refers to her husband, correctly, as "the abovementioned Rabbi Saul."

26. *Hitsoniyut*, or *hitsoniyot*, "external ones," demonic forces.

27. S. *Otsar sihot hakhamim* (Benei-Berak, 1974; photo-offset of Sonik [Sanok], 1914), 42–43. My thanks to Arthur Green for bringing this reference to my attention.

28. Shabbat 30b.

29. For a discussion of "bribing" the powers of evil, see Isaiah Tishby, *Mishnat ha-zohar*, 2d ed. (Jerusalem: Mosad Bialik, 1957), 1:290–92, 352–55; (Jerusalem: Mosad Bialik, 1961), 2:206–10. According to Arthur Green, it was common for hasidic exegetes to understand the telling of a joke at the beginning of study as a bribe to the powers of evil (Green, personal communication).

30. *Al ken amarta hagam de-iteta bi-sevara la shekhihah keter torah munah ve-khu [lei] ule-daati ani mezakah et ha-rabim.* The edition at the Jewish Theological Seminary, New York, reads *amarti* rather than *amarta*, which changes the sense of the sentence to: "Therefore, I said that although a woman rarely participates in reasoned argument, nonetheless, 'The crown of the Torah is left, etc.,' and, in my view, I am bringing merit to the many." This reading makes Leah's struggle for justification internal, while the reading in the edition at the Jewish National and University Library, Jerusalem, depicts a struggle against external critics.

31. Yalkut Shimoni, Ruth, 4.

32. B. Berakhot 6a. Of course, many other sources insist that prayer is heard anywhere, any time. Leah chooses this particular source to make a point about the importance of women's synagogue attendance.

33. In her *Tkhine of Three Gates*, Sarah bas Tovim transforms this critique into autobiography and confesses to the sin of idle talk in the women's section; see Chapter 8. For a sustained treatment of *men's* idle chatter in synagogue, see Isaac ben

Eliakim, *Sefer Lev Tov* (Prague, 1620), *hilkhot bet ha-keneset*. Isaac takes men to task for, among other things, discussing business matters in synagogue (not usually mentioned among the failings of women), but not for discussing their clothing and adornments. There is some gender specificity to these critiques.

34. "It is known that the mother of Rabbi Simeon bar Yohai engaged in idle chatter on the Sabbath, and he said to her, 'My mother, today is the Sabbath, and it is therefore preferable to be silent concerning the things of this world.'" Leah's source for this is probably either J. Shabbat 15:3 or Pesikta Rabbati 23:3.

35. See Rivka Schatz Uffenheimer, *Hasidism as Mysticism* (Princeton: Princeton University Press, 1993), chap. 5. The teaching of the Maggid, from Dov Baer of Mezhirech, *Maggid devarav le-yaakov*, critical ed. by Rivka Schatz Uffenheimer, 2d ed. (Jerusalem, 1990), 25, is quoted in Uffenheimer, *Hasidism*, 148. For the Maggid, prayer for the sake of the Shekhinah was first and foremost *contemplative* rather than theurgical prayer; however, "the Besht and his contemporaries as well as the Maggid and his circle, remained loyal to the concept of prayer on behalf of the Shekhinah, that she be united with her Husband and leave her Exile" (ibid., 164).

A selection of hasidic teachings about prayer for the sake of the Shekhinah is found in *Your Word is Fire*, ed. and trans., with a new introduction, by Arthur Green and Barry Holtz (Woodstock, Vt.: Jewish Lights, 1993), 54, 68–73, 80.

36. For hasidic formulations of this doctrine, see Uffenheimer, *Hasidism*, 163–65.

37. See Louis Jacobs, "The Uplifting of Sparks in Later Jewish Mysticism," in *Jewish Spirituality from the Sixteenth-Century Revival to the Present*, ed. Arthur Green (New York: Crossroad, 1987), 99–126. Discussing the achievement of union between *Ze'ir* and *Nukva* (the Lurianic names for Tiferet and Shekhinah), Jacobs observes, "For *ziwwug* [copulation] to take place, both male and female orgasm are required; the male orgasm is described as 'male waters'; the female orgasm as 'female waters.' The 'male waters' are attained through the flow of grace and power from above, from the higher *sefirot*, but (here is the most startling aspect of the whole doctrine) the 'female waters' are provided by humans who send on high the reclaimed holy sparks. The holy sparks provide the 'female waters' so that the sacred marriage can take place" (107).

38. This makes it unlikely that Leah is actually the author of the other *tkhine* attributed to her, *Tkhine moyde ani* (*Tkhine* of "I acknowledge"). The literary style of this work is quite different from the *Tkhine of the Matriarchs*. It presents a stereotypically "humble" view of women, it contains heartfelt pleas for sustenance and livelihood, and it makes no mention of the exiled Shekhinah.

39. Although in all editions Leah's *tkhine* is clearly associated with the blessing of the month on the Sabbath preceding the new moon, it is possible that she may have intended it to be recited, instead, on the Sabbath that coincides with the new moon. The evidence for this is as follows. The introduction refers to the occasion on which the improper *tkhine* was recited ambiguously as "on every new moon, when the new moon is blessed." Is this the blessing of the month on the Sabbath preceding the new moon, or is it the day of the new moon itself? Further, the Ara-

maic *piyyut* and even more clearly the Yiddish *tkhine* echo themes from the *musaf* prayer for Sabbath that coincides with the new moon. However, this similarity may simply be the result of the fact that the liturgy for the Sabbath that coincides with the new moon was undoubtedly a familiar and easily used literary model.

The *tkhine* to which Leah objects, while unambiguously intended for recitation during the blessing of the month, is derived from a Hebrew prayer from *Shaarei tsiyyon* by Nathan Nata Hannover, first published in 1662, which was recited on Tuesdays (and thus its confessionary formulas were, appropriately, intended for weekday recitation). So far as I know, its first appearance in Yiddish was in *Seder tkhines* (Amsterdam, 1752), 10b-12a, where it was headed "a *tkhine* to be recited when one blesses the new moon." The question of the importance of the blessing of the month for women and the appropriation and adaptation of Hebrew prayers for other occasions, notably the eve of the new moon (which was a penitential day) into Yiddish *tkhines* for this occasion, deserves further study.

40. "Prior to the proclamation of the New Moon, the Ashkenazi ritual contains an introductory prayer, *Yehi Ratson*, which is substantially the private petition recited daily by Rav upon the completion of the *Amidah* (Ber. 16b). . . . This introductory prayer was first recited in the Polish ritual during the first part of the 18th century. It then gradually spread to all Ashkenazi rituals. . . . Many Sephardi and oriental rituals contain introductory prayers for the ingathering of the exiles and the well-being of the rabbis." *Encyclopaedia Judaica* (1971), s.v. "New Moon, Announcement of." The Sephardic prayer, found in David Abudarham, *Sefer Abudarham ha-shalem* (Jerusalem: Even yisrael, 1995), 1:212–13 (Seder Rosh Hodesh), while it does express hopes for the ingathering of the exiles, is unrelated to Leah's text.

41. Translation by David de Sola Pool, *The Traditional Prayer Book* (New York: Behrman, 1960), 262.

42. This is a paraphrase of *Tikkunei Zohar* 6, 22a, part of a long discussion of prayers on the Day of Atonement. The passage contains a play on words. The Aramaic word *hav*, "give!" when repeated, *hav-hav*, means "bow-wow" in Hebrew. The passage from *Tikkunei Zohar* also appears in a popular work of mystical ethics; see Elijah de Vidas, *Reshit hokhmah* (Fürth, 1763), 113b (*shaar ha-teshuvah*, chap. 1). I do not know which of these was Leah's immediate source. Cf. also Dov Baer of Mezhirech: The *Zohar* calls those who pray for themselves and not for the Shekhinah "arrogant dogs who bark, 'Give! Give!'" (quoted in Uffenheimer, *Hasidism*, 148).

43. Leah was not alone in her critique of the new liturgy for blessing the new moon. Her younger contemporary, Rabbi Shneur Zalman of Lyady (1745–1813), the founder of Habad Hasidism, eliminated it from the prayer book used by his followers. He considered these petitions for material benefits unsuitable for Sabbath prayers, and Habad Hasidim, unlike other Ashkenazic Jews, do not recite this prayer to this day (Arthur Green, personal communication).

44. B. Berakhot 17a.

45. A paraphrase of B. Megillah 12b. This proverbial expression means, approximately, that a man is king of his own castle.

46. The Yiddish paraphrase of the introduction omits the entire discussion of when women should prevail over their husbands.

47. For example, the Yiddish paraphrase contains material from Jacob ben Asher's commentary on Exod. 38:8 that Leah did not include in the Hebrew version of the introduction, where she refers to this commentary.

48. Cf. the teaching of one of the disciples of the Maggid: "But the truth is this: that when man prays for his needs this is certainly not called service, but [is referred to] by the language of petition" [Isaac of Radzivilov, *Or Yitshak* (Jerusalem, 1961), 98b–99a, quoted in Uffenheimer, *Hasidism*, 161].

49. Moshe Idel, *Kabbalah: New Perspectives* (New Haven: Yale University Press, 1988), 75–88. In many of the texts Idel cites, weeping is rewarded with a vision of the Shekhinah.

50. Ibid., 197–99.

51. Hayyim Vital, *Ets ha-Daat Tov*, pt. 2 (Jerusalem, 1982), fol. 5b, cited in Idel, *Kabbalah*, 198 (Idel's translation). Note, however, that the occasion and purpose of the theurgical weeping in this passage is not the redemption of the Shekhinah from exile, but rather is mourning (and causing God to mourn by weeping) the death of a righteous man. Yet the need for human initiative to bring about divine action is the same: "God therefore waits for human activity to activate him." See also Zohar II, 12a-b, on the discovery of the baby Moses by Pharaoh's daughter; the passage says that the tears of Israel cause their Mother, the Shekhinah, to weep, and thus bring about redemption.

52. Idel, *Kabbalah*, 198.

53. She also seems to be working within a larger kabbalistic tradition that connects tears and the Shekhinah. There is a well-known legend that one of Luria's contemporaries in Safed, Abraham ben Eliezer ha-Levi Berukhim (c. 1515–c. 1593), had a vision of the Shekhinah after praying, weeping, and tearing his hair in mourning for the exile at the Western Wall in Jerusalem: "He proceeded to the Western Wall where he began to pray and weep bitterly. While doing so he lifted up his eyes and saw upon the Wall the likeness of a woman with her back turned towards him. . . . As soon as he saw her he fell upon his face, crying out and weeping: 'Mother, mother, mother of Zion, woe is me that I have seen you thus!' And he continued to weep bitterly, afflicting himself, tearing hair out of his beard and head until he fainted and fell deeply asleep. Then in a dream he saw the *Shekhinah* coming toward him and, placing her hand upon his face, wipe away the tears from his eyes. She said to him: 'Console yourself, Abraham my son, for "there is hope for thy future," saith the Lord, and "your children shall return to their own border" [Jer. 31:17] "for I will cause their captivity to return, and will have compassion upon them"'" [Jer. 33:26] [Letter by Solomon Shlomiel of Dresnitz, published in Avraham Yaari] *Iggrot Erets Yisrael* (Ramat Gan, 1971), 205–206, as quoted in and translated by Lawrence Fine, *Safed spirituality* (New York: Paulist Press, 1984), 49]. This account, as well as reports by other kabbalists of visions of the Shekhinah brought on by weep-

ing, echoes the midrashim on which Leah also draws in the composition of her *tkhine*.

54. Cf. J. Shabbat 15:3: "R. Abbahu said, as the Holy One, be blessed, rested from saying, so you, too, rest from saying."

55. During the time of the Sanhedrin, the beginning of each month would be declared according to reports of eyewitnesses who had seen the new moon. This procedure is described in the Mishnah, Rosh Hashanah 2:5–7.

56. The hope for scholarly male offspring was natural for a woman of Leah's background, despite her belief that women have the power to bring redemption. I have been unable to discover whether or not Leah had any children. The information concerning her husband(s) found in Wunder, *Meorei galitsiyah*, is inconsistent, and I could find neither of them listed in his own right, which is the only way to track descendants. Under the listing for Benjamin ben Simhah Rappoport (rabbi of Brzezany, and author of *Gevulot Binyamin*), who was supposedly the father of her husband Shabbetai, only two sons are listed, Simhah and Gershon, and an unnamed daughter. There are other inconsistencies; the sources are not altogether reliable.

57. These two goals of mystical prayer are those of the theosophical-theurgical aspect of Kabbalah. Another, more esoteric stream of Jewish mysticism, ecstatic Kabbalah, was directed toward mystical experience. The goal of mystical prayer for these kabbalists was *unio mystica*, or *devekut*. For the distinction, see Idel, *Kabbalah*. I have as yet found no evidence for the influence of ecstatic Kabbalah on the *tkhine* literature.

58. The Yiddish version differs somewhat: "You have also given us new moons, which the Sanhedrin used to consecrate. Today, when we consecrate the new moon, when we say the blessing on the Sabbath which is [before] the new moon, then it is a time to petition God. Therefore, we spread out our hands before God, and say our prayers that you bring us back to Jerusalem, and renew our days as of old. For we have no strength; we can no longer endure the hard, bitter exile, for we are also like the feeble lambs. Our Sabbaths and festivals and our new moons have been ruined. We are like orphans, like sheep who have gone astray without a shepherd. For the nations have too much power over us. **You are a God of Vengeance**; but you, God, are yet always an avenger, and you reckon up accounts with the wicked. Therefore, we pray you, Lord of the world, take revenge on those who cause us suffering, for the sake of the merit of the patriarchs and matriarchs." The entire passage, in both Hebrew and Yiddish, is full of echoes, paraphrases, and quotations of fragments of biblical verses, especially from Lamentations and from Isaiah and other prophets.

59. On Lurianic mystical contemplation, which has as part of its goal the reunification of Tiferet and Shekhinah (in their Lurianic forms as Ze'ir Anpin and Nukva de-Ze'ir), see Lawrence Fine, "The Contemplative Practice of Yihudim in Lurianic Kabbalah," in Green, ed., *Jewish Spirituality*, 64–98.

60. Tishby, *Mishnat ha-zohar*, 1:224–25.

61. Genesis never mentions a daughter of Abraham, only sons. However, some talmudic sages and the kabbalists interpreted "and the Lord had blessed Abraham in all things" (Gen. 24:1) to mean that Abraham must have had a daughter. See below in the text.

62. B. Sukkah 49b. This interpretation of the image in Leah's text is suggested by Liberman, "'Tehinnah imahot,'" 432–54, esp. 437–38.

63. Abraham's daughter is mentioned in B. Baba Batra 16b. The kabbalistic interpretation of this daughter as the Shekhinah first appears in *Sefer ha-bahir*, no. 78 (Margoliot edition). See also Nahmanides on Gen. 24:1; Zohar I 219a, 223a; II 85b; III 276b (Ra'aya Meheimna). My thanks to Elliot Wolfson for drawing my attention to the kabbalistic significance of this phrase and to its sources.

64. Gershom Scholem discusses the terms "Male World" and "Female World" in his article, "Le-heker kabbalat R. Yitshak ben Ya'akov ha-Kohen," pt. 3, *Tarbiz* 3 (1932): 33–67, esp. 40–42 (66–68 of the internal pagination of the article). The sentence quoted is on p. 41.

65. Zohar III 82a (Ra'aya Meheimna).

66. It is possible that someone else made the Yiddish paraphrase of the *piyyut*. However, I think this unlikely. If Leah's whole purpose was to correct the religious practice of women, then she must have planned to include a Yiddish portion of the text from the start and would have wanted it to express her meaning as precisely as possible. It thus seems most plausible that she composed the Yiddish version herself.

67. On the equation of "ignorant men" with women, specifically with reference to study of Kabbalah, see Chapter 3.

68. Many *tkhines* omit Leah from discussions of the merits of the matriarchs or treat her only very briefly. Perhaps since the author was usually called Leah, she was more interested in the matriarch Leah than were other *tkhine* writers.

69. Petihta 24:23–25.

70. On the erotic nature of the sequence of the pleas to God, see Galit Hasan-Rokem, "Ha-kol kol ahoti: demuyot nashim u-semalim nashiyim be-Midrash Eikhah Rabba," in *Eshnav le-hayyehen shel nashim be-havarot yehudiyot*, ed. Yael Azmon (Jerusalem: Merkaz Zalman Shazar le-toldot Yisrael, 1995), 95–111.

The *tkhine* also omits, at least in the Lvov edition, God's explicit capitulation to Rachel's plea. However, the Grodno, 1796, edition contains it in condensed fashion. In that edition, the end of this passage reads: "Thus, even more so, it is undoubtedly fitting for you, God, who are entirely **compassionate and gracious**, to have mercy. God answered her, I acknowledge that you are right, and I will bring your children out of exile."

71. Cf. the transformation, mentioned above, of the Aramaic's address to God as "my beloved" to the Yiddish "our dear father."

There is precedent in kabbalistic literature for the equation of tears with "female fluids"; see Elliot R. Wolfson, "Weeping, Death, and Spiritual Ascent in Sixteenth Century Jewish Mysticism," in *Death, Ecstasy, and Other Worldly Journeys*, ed. John J. Collins and Michael Fishbane (Albany: State University of New York Press, 1995), 209–47. Wolfson, like Idel, discusses weeping primarily in the context of theosophical and ecstatic techniques, as a way to gain access to heavenly secrets or visions of the Shekhinah; he only deals with theurgic weeping as it is relevant to that context. Further, Wolfson argues that although tears are in one sense to be understood as the "female waters," the eye and its fountain of tears are in a more profound sense a phallic symbol in kabbalah. This argument is part of Wolfson's larger project of exploring gender transformation in kabbalistic symbolism; in fact, he argues that the weeping male kabbalist is later transformed into a symbolic female by his identification with the "female waters" of the Shekhinah.

If Wolfson is right, and if Leah knew the literature which supports this point, she may in fact be making a more radical claim for women, that by weeping they become symbolically male—at least until their integration into the Shekhinah.

72. Leah had many sources on which to rely in this portrayal of Rachel. For example, Rashi's commentary to Genesis 48:7 implies that Rachel alone will arise from her grave to plead for Israel; in any case, he does not mention other figures preceding her. See also the *Tsenerene* on this verse.

CHAPTER 8. CANDLES FOR THE DEAD

An earlier version of this chapter was published as "'For the Human Soul is the Lamp of the Lord': The *Tkhine* for 'Laying Wicks'" by Sarah bas Tovim, *Polin: Studies in Polish Jewry* 10 (1997): 40–65.

1. See the epigraph and note 1 to Chapter 1.

2. Sarah's epithet, *bas tovim*, means "daughter of notable [or good] people." The "tovim" were communal officials, but this seems not to be the direct origin of her epithet. "Tuwim" is known as a surname among twentieth-century Polish Jews; some say that the poet Julian Tuwim (1894–1953) was Sarah's descendant (Prof. Dov Noy, personal communication, spring 1985). Different editions of her *tkhines* give somewhat different genealogies: daughter of Mordecai, or sometimes daughter of Isaac or Jacob, of Satanov. All, however, agree that she was the great-granddaughter of "Rabbi Mordecai of Brisk." Some editions of *The Three Gates* append the formula "may she live" after the author's name, indicating she was still alive at the time of its publication.

In the second half of the nineteenth century, *maskilim*, who wrote *tkhines* for small sums, exploited her popularity by using her name on their productions. Because they wrote under her name, some of these *maskilim* thought Sarah had never existed. The literary historian Israel Zinberg asserts that Sarah bas Tovim was indeed a historical figure; using the statements in her *tkhines* that identify the names and places of residence of some of her male ancestors, he hypothesizes that she was probably the great-granddaughter of either Mordecai Zusskind (d. 1684) or

Mordecai Gunzberg (d. 1688), both rabbis in Brisk (Brest-Litovsk). See Zinberg, *History of Jewish Literature*, vol. 7, *Old Yiddish Literature from Its Origins to the Haskalah Period*, trans. Bernard Martin (New York: Ktav and Cincinnati: Hebrew Union College Press, 1975), 252–54.

3. "Der ziveg; oder, Sore bas Tovim," in Peretz, *Ale verk*, vol. 5, *Folkstimlekhe geshikhtn* (New York: Cyco, 1947), 372–79. An English translation of this story appears in I. L. Peretz, *The Case Against the Wind and Other Stories*, trans. and adapted by Esther Hautzig (New York: Macmillan, 1975), 45–53.

4. This is almost unique. I have only seen one or two other *tkhines* in which no husband was mentioned for the author.

5. Some, mostly early but undated editions of *The Three Gates* include the customary formula *she-tihyeh* [may she live] after Sarah's name, indicating she was still alive at the time of publication. Of course, editions containing the formula may be reprinted long after a person's death, but this suggests that at least one edition of the work was published during the author's lifetime. Raphael Mahler lists books mentioned by the censor in Lvov, Galicia, in 1818. See Mahler, *Der kampf tsvishn haskole un khasides in galitsye* (New York: YIVO, 1942), 148–50. The list includes a work entitled *Shloyshe sheorim* which is probably the *tkhine* by Sarah bas Tovim. (There was another *tkhine* by this title published in the eighteenth century, as an addendum to a work entitled *Naye lange rosh khoydesh bentshn tkhine*, but in the nineteenth-century editions, the title of this addendum seems to change to *Shaarei dmoes tkhine*.) Other works listed by the censor include *Tsenerene*, *Korbm minkhe*, *Shivhei ha-Besht*, *Tkhines u-vakoshes*, *Kav ha-yashar*, *Preger gebete*, *Maaneh lashon*, and *Simkhas ha-nefesh*.

6. She introduces the first section, or gate, of *The Three Gates* with the Hebrew rhyme: *Shaar zeh nisyased al sheloshoh mitsvos she-nitstavu ha-noshim, u-shemi Sore be-roshei ha-haruzim* (This gate is founded on the three women's commandments, and my name, Sarah, is found at the beginning of the verses). However, most editions print the following section in such a way as to highlight the *sin* and *resh*, the first two letters, skipping the *heh*, the final letter, and highlighting instead a *het* that begins a later paragraph. The *het* is actually in a more logical place for emphasis. It *is* possible that her name was in fact *Serah*, although that biblical name was very rarely used by Eastern European Jews.

7. This is typical of eighteenth- and early-nineteenth-century Eastern European *tkhines*. Most are printed on bad paper with poor type and numerous typographical errors and give no indication of date or place of publication. I have located only two editions of *The Gate of Unification*, neither of them dated. On typographical grounds I would place these two editions in Eastern Europe between 1780 and 1820. The library of the Jewish Theological Seminary, New York, owns a complete copy of one edition; a defective copy of another edition is found in the library of Agudas Chassidei Chabad, Brooklyn, N.Y. Two or three pages of the latter edition are missing at the end, including over half of the expanded confession and all of the *tkhine* for memorial candles. Unfortunately, the extant portions show this to be the better of the two editions. Interestingly, the author describes herself on the title

page as, "I, the renowned woman Sarah bas Tovim, of distinguished ancestry" (*ikh, ishoh Sarah bas tovim, ha-meyuheses veha-mefursemes*). *The Three Gates* does not contain quite such bold assertions of its author's fame. Of course, such adjectives can always be added by the printer. Other *tkhines*, by contrast, may state that "because of her great piety, the modest woman who composed this *tkhine* concealed her name."

As is the case for many *tkhines*, I am unable to identify *any* edition of *The Three Gates* that I regard as especially good or early, although I *can* identify some editions as late and bad. Unfortunately, these late, garbled, or rearranged editions include all those with dates of publication. The earliest *dated* edition I have seen was published in Vilna, by Romm, in 1838, but I am convinced, on the basis of typography, that earlier editions were published in the eighteenth century. (The 1838 edition is in the collection of the Jewish National and University Library, Jerusalem, *tkhine* pamphlet collection, R41 A460, vol. 1, no. 5. A facsimile of its opening page is printed in the *Encyclopaedia Judaica* (1971), s.v. "Bas-Tovim, Sarah." For a listing of an edition published in Sudylkow in 1824, see M. Pines, *Histoire de la littérature judéo-allemande* (Paris: Jouve, 1911), 564.)

The texts used as the basis for my translations and analysis of *The Three Gates* are primarily two undated Eastern European editions, one found in the Jewish National and University Library, Jerusalem, *tkhine* pamphlet collection, R41 A460, vol. 8, no. 26, and the other in the Jewish Theological Seminary, New York, uncataloged *tkhine* collection, bound in a volume with eight other *tkhines*, the first of them entitled *Tkhine koydem tfile*. Both of these editions are problematic, as are all others I have seen. I have also consulted other editions, most of them similarly undated. The dated editions are all too late to be of much bibliographic value.

8. The textual difficulties of even the early editions led me to wonder whether the entire work known as *The Tkhine of Three Gates* was in fact the work of one author. I have concluded that most of it was. Sarah has a number of distinctive stylistic characteristics, most especially a way of referring to God as "the dear God, blessed be he and blessed be his name," the latter phrase appearing as the abbreviation *b"h u-v"sh*. One finds this locution throughout the text, except in certain passages that have external sources. (All of these occur in the third section of the text.) Even these are woven together with material written in Sarah's characteristic style; this suggests that Sarah herself incorporated them into her text. The only portions about which I am uncertain are two or three paragraphs at the end.

9. I have not yet identified all of her sources. As far as I have been able to determine, however, all of the material that she incorporated into her texts from Hebrew sources came to her through Yiddish paraphrases. She seems to have been quite well read in Yiddish ethical (*musar*) literature.

10. By contrast, late editions were often radically altered by the publisher. For example, an edition published in Vilna by Romm in 1859 (included in an anthology entitled *Seder tkhines u-vakoshes* [Vilna: Romm, 1860]), translated by Norman Tarnor, omits the entire *tkhine* for the making of Yom Kippur candles and substitutes an altogether different text consisting mainly of paraphrases of selections

from the Hebrew liturgy for Yom Kippur. Further, it rearranges the order of the gates, putting the one for Yom Kippur third, thus making it correspond to the order announced on the title page. See Norman Tarnor, "Three Gates Tehinno: A Seventeenth-Century Yiddish Prayer," *Judaism* 40 (1991): 354–67. See, by contrast, the 1865 Vilna edition, included in *The Merit of Our Mothers: A Bilingual Anthology of Jewish Women's Prayers*, comp. Tracy Guren Klirs (Cincinnati: Hebrew Union College Press, 1992), 12–45. It contains all of the original text, in the correct order, but with numerous small editorial changes, some of which substantially alter the meaning.

11. 1st ed., Izmir, 1731–32.

12. In fact, the passage in question contains an internal date; in the Hebrew original, 1669, and in a *tkhine* that contains a Yiddish paraphrase of the entire passage from *Hemdat yamim*, 1735. Sarah probably drew upon the same Yiddish source as this other *tkhine*. However, she incorporated only a portion of the passage, one that did not include the section with the internal date. See further discussion later in the chapter.

13. Prov. 31:30. The verse is part of the praise of a virtuous wife, customarily read by Jewish husbands every Sabbath Eve at table as part of the ceremony beginning the Sabbath meal (Prov. 30:10–31).

14. Prov. 14:1.

15. Esther 3:8; in the *tkhine*, it refers to Sarah's life of wandering. See below.

16. Cf. Avot 3:1.

17. Ps. 80:6.

18. This passage is in the rhymed prose so typical of Sarah's style: *Ikh, oreme froy, ikh bin gevezn mefuzar u-meforad; hob ikh nit gekont shlumin. Hot mayn harts geton in mir brumen. Hob ikh mikh der mont fun vanen ikh bin gekumen. Un vi ikh vel kumen un vi ikh vel vern genumen. Iz of mir a groyse forkht gekumen. Hob ikh gebetn dem lebndign got borukh hu bi-dmoes shalish az di tkhine zol fun mir aros kumen.*

19. This sentence is taken by Zinberg to mean that Sarah was childless and therefore needed to write the *tkhine* because she had no child to say the memorial prayers after her death (*History of Jewish Literature* 7:255, n. 62). I am not sure this inference is justified; many other passages refer to the reciter's husband and children.

20. Note the parallel to the weeping of Rabbi Nahman of Bratzlav (1770?–1810) before he "said Torah" to his disciples (Arthur Green, personal communication). For a description of the intensity of the act of "saying Torah," see Green, *Tormented Master* (New York: Schocken Books, 1981), 150–52.

21. The most popular topic by far is that of the penitential season and the Days of Awe. Most other *tkhines* on these themes differ from Sarah's in their overriding concern with confession, penitence, and obtaining God's forgiveness for sin. (As we shall see below, Sarah's *tkhine* for Yom Kippur candles is primarily concerned with obtaining the intercession of the dead in bringing about the messianic re-

demption.) Other topics that occur frequently in other *tkhines* but that Sarah does not address are the Sabbath (aspects other than kindling Sabbath lights) and prayers for adequate sustenance and livelihood.

22. A word seems to be missing here in all early editions.

23. Much of this *tkhine* is in rhymed prose; this sentence is the first example of rhyme (. . . *mit gantsn grunt fun maynem hartsn, zolstu unz hitn fun payn un shmertsn*).

24. The text refers here to the tradition that the angel Sandalfon fashions a crown for the Holy One out of the prayers of Israel (B. Hagiga 13b and the tosafot there). On this motif, see Arthur Green, *Keter: The Crown of God in Early Jewish Mysticism* (Princeton: Princeton University Press, 1997), esp. chaps. 3 and 4. Sarah thus claims equality for her *tkhines* with other prayers in Hebrew and Yiddish.

25. Alternatively, Sarah may have undertaken a life of wandering as a voluntary penance, a common pietistic act at the time. If so, it would be important evidence that women also engaged in this practice. However, Sarah does not use the usual term for such penitential wandering, *golus*, derived from the Hebrew word for "exile," but instead uses *na ve-nad*, a Hebrew phrase used in Yiddish to express wandering or homelessness. In addition, the language used elsewhere in the text seems to imply that she regarded her homelessness as an involuntary punishment: "Therefore, I warn you, so that you may not, God forbid, be punished as I was punished, with wandering." However, to the extent that she was some sort of public religious figure, perhaps a wandering *zogerke* who led women in prayer and rebuked them for their moral shortcomings such as talking in synagogue, she resembles the wandering petty religious intelligentsia described by Joseph Weiss in "Reshit tsemihatah shel ha-derekh ha-hasidit," *Tsiyyon* 16 (1950–51): 46–105.

26. Rabbi Eleazar (this is the correct form of the name) b. Simeon lived at the end of the second century C. E. I have not found any source for the following incident that mentions Rabbi Eleazar. A version of this motif is found in Isaac Ben Eliakim's *Sefer lev tov* (Book of the Good Heart) (Prague, 1620), a popular ethical work in Yiddish that Sarah is quite likely to have read. "We find in a midrash: Rabbi Yose said, Once I was walking along the way in a field and I saw Elijah the prophet, peace be upon him, and he had four thousand camels with him, all laden. I asked him, With what do you have these camels laden? He spoke thus: I have these camels laden only with destroying angels, who are called wrath and anger. I asked him, For whom have you loaded these camels, or where are you taking them? He spoke thus, I am taking them to hell to repay the people who talk in synagogue **during the prayers**, that is, from *barukh she-amar* until after the *shemoneh esreh*, and after Kaddish that the cantor says after *rahum ve-hanun*. All of that is termed **during the prayers** (*hilkhot tefillah*)."

Another parallel is the following, taken from *Amud ha-avodah* (The Pillar of Worship), which was appended to an edition of *Sefer ha-gan* and *Derekh Mosheh* (Lemberg, 1864). This supplement, extracts from various ethical works, was compiled in 1802 by one Abraham ben Judah Leib. It is divided into days; on Day 26 (p. 33b) we read: "In the name of Midrash Shoher Tov: R. Yose ben Kisma said, Once I was walking on the way, and I met three hundred camels loaded with wrath and anger. And Elijah the prophet met me and said to me, This is for those who engage in idle chatter in the synagogue." I have not yet been able to locate this passage in the midrash named.

27. *Barukh she-amar* ("Blessed is the one who spoke and the world came into being") begins the core of the morning service, and this core ends with the *shemoneh esreh*, the Eighteen Benedictions, which is recited silently and standing. According to Jewish law, one may not speak during this portion of the service but should give one's wholehearted attention to prayer.

28. The preceding two sentences were translated from the edition in the Jewish National and University Library, not from the one at the Jewish Theological Seminary, because the former text is clearer.

29. This rhymes in Yiddish: *Mit dem vos mir tuen oyf unzere zind gedenken, zol Hashem yisborakh dos lebin shenkin.*

30. This Hebrew phrase is from the liturgical poem *Ve-khol maaminim* (And All Believe) said right after *Kedushah* in the *musaf* (additional) service of Rosh Hashanah (my thanks to Tracy Guren Klirs for this reference). I have translated it according to the Yiddish interpretation that Sarah gives for it, which corresponds to one literal sense of the words. However, a more idiomatic translation means almost precisely the opposite: He who is wrathful for a short time, and slow to anger.

31. See the discussion of this motif in Leah Horowitz's *Tkhine imohes* (n.p.: n.d., 18th century), Chapter 7 above.

32. This contrasts with, for example, *Tfilas Kheyn* (n.p., n.d.), in which hunger is clearly a palpable issue for the petitioner.

33. The earliest reference that suggests the existence of this custom is a poem by Eleazar of Worms, written in 1197 as an elegy to his wife, Dulcia, murdered by Crusaders. The poem mentions that Dulcia "makes wicks" and prepares candles for Yom Kippur. See Ivan Marcus, "Mothers, Martyrs, and Moneymakers: Some Jewish Women in Medieval Europe," *Conservative Judaism* 38 (Spring 1986): 34–45. Various other medieval sources, both halakhic and minhagic, refer to aspects of this custom (burning candles for the living and the dead on Yom Kippur, circumambulating the cemetery, and preparing candles from wicks used to measure graves or the cemetery, sometimes for Yom Kippur and sometimes for someone who is ill). My investigation of this material demonstrated to me how difficult it is to track women's customs in male sources, a point also noted by Israel Ta-Shma in a chapter on the custom of women covering their eyes while lighting Sabbath candles, "Kisui ha-einayim be-et hadlakat ner shabat," in *Minhag Ashkenaz ha-kadmon* (Jerusalem: Magnes, 1992), 136–41. I hope to publish a separate study of the evidence concerning the historical evolution of the custom of measuring graves with candlewicking that was then used to make Yom Kippur candles.

34. Frankfurt, *Sefer ha-hayyim*, 1st ed. (Amsterdam, 1703).

35. As I discuss later in this chapter, there is also the possibility that Sarah transcribed or adapted the text *from* oral tradition rather than composing it herself.

36. S. Weissenberg, "Das Feld- und das Kejwermessen," *Mitteilungen zur jüdischen Volkskunde* 6 (1906): 39–42. Weissenberg gives the locale for his account as "southern Russia."

37. Weissenberg does summarize a text for the measuring of a single grave; it is similar to texts collected by Gisela Suliteanu in Romania in the 1960s. See Suliteanu, "The Traditional System of Melopeic Prose of the Funeral Songs Recited by the Jewish Women of the Socialist Republic of Rumania," in *Folklore Research Center Studies*, ed. Issachar Ben-Ami (Jerusalem: Magnes, 1972), 3:291–349. Suliteanu's texts were simply for the visiting, not the measuring, of parents' graves. The bulk of her article is devoted to the musical notation of the performance of the texts; it is important to remember that *tkhines* were often chanted, rather than simply read.

38. Additional ethnographic sources: Yehudah Elzet [Y. L. Zlotnik], "Mi-minhagei Yisrael," *Reshumot* (Tel Aviv) 1 (2d ed.) (1925): 335–77, cf. 352; H. Chajes, "Gleybungen un minhogim in farbindung mitn toyt," *Filologishe shriftn* (Vilna) 2 (1926): cols. 281–328, cf. cols. 292, 295; Yosef Zelikovitsh, "Der toyt un zayne bagleyt-momentn in der yidisher etnografye un folklor," *Lodzher visnshaftlekhe shriftn* 1 (1938): 149–90, cf. 180–81. Brief mentions are also found in "Aus Hausapotheke und Hexenkuch," *Mitteilungen zur jüdischen Volkskunde*, h. 1 (1900): 1–87, cf. 60 n. 201; Dr. Lazarus, "Das Messen," *Mitteilungen zur jüdischen Volkskunde*, h. 6 (1900): 137; S. Ansky [Shloyme Zanvil Rappoport], *Dos yudishe etnografishe program*, vol. 1, *Der Mentsh* (Petrograd: Yosef Luria, 1915), no. 1641; and Joshua Trachtenberg, *Jewish Magic and Superstition* (1939; Cleveland: Meridian Books, 1961), 285 n. 6. Interestingly, twentieth-century Persian Jewish women now living in the United States report that in Iran they were responsible for making candles for Yom Kippur, although they say nothing about measuring graves with candlewick. See Susan Grossman and Rivka Haut, "From Persia to New York: An Interview with Three Generations of Iranian Women," in *Daughters of the King*, ed. Susan Grossman and Rivka Haut (Philadelphia: Jewish Publication Society, 1992), 215–25, cf. 221.

Literary sources (including memoirs): Pauline Wengeroff, *Memoiren einer Grossmutter*, 2d ed. (Berlin: Verlag von M. Poppelauer, 1913), 1:103–4; Bella Chagall, *Brenendike likht* (New York: Folks-farlag, 1945), 77–79. Shemuel Yosef Agnon, *Yamim noraim* (Jerusalem: Schocken, 1956), 202–203, paraphrases several sources that deal with this custom, most notably *Mateh Efrayim* by Ephraim Zalman Margoliot (to be discussed below). Agnon's paraphrase differs substantially from the original and includes the detail that the women recall the names of their departed relatives over each wick, especially of those who had been righteous and who could therefore be good advocates for them in heaven. Agnon may have taken this information from his own observations, or possibly he found it in other written sources.

Particularly valuable for the sense it gives of the emotional tone of the candle-making ritual is the description found in *Of Bygone Days*, the autobiographical novel by Shalom Jacob Abramovitsh (Mendele Mokher Seforim), set in the town of Kapulie (Province of Minsk), in the 1840s. While Mendele never attributes the *tkhine* he quotes to any author, he does describe a group of women making the candles, led by Sarah (the character who represents his mother), a learned and pious woman. See *Ba-yamim ha-hem* [Hebrew version], in *Kol kitvei Mendele Mokher Sefarim* (Tel Aviv: Dvir, 1958), 271; idem, *Shloyme Reb Khayyims* [Yiddish version], in *Ale verk fun Mendele Moykher Seforim* (Cracow: Ferlag Mendele, 1910–11), 2:35–37; idem, *Of Bygone Days* [English translation by Raymond Scheindlin], in Ruth Wisse, ed., *A Shtetl and other Yiddish Novellas* (New York: Behrman House, 1973), 249–358; cf. 300–302. Abramovitsh goes on to quote a text that, while apparently based on *The Three Gates*, differs from it in significant details. He also describes how the women weep as they recite the *tkhine*.

Because of the nature of the differences between Abramovitsh's text and the *tkhine*, I think it more likely that he consciously altered the text, rather than using a different version extant in oral tradition. Briefly, as compared with Sarah's *tkhine*, Abramovitsh's text, in both Hebrew and Yiddish, emphasizes love of all humankind, including non-Jews. It also minimizes the intercessory role of the biblical figures called upon and emphasizes instead the more theologically acceptable reliance upon their *zekhut*, or merit. (Both intercession and *zekhut* are found in Sarah's text, about equally balanced.) These changes were likely to make the *tkhine* more acceptable to Abramovitsh's enlightened audience. It is possible, nonetheless, that he based his version on a text that was already somewhat removed from Sarah's text, whether because of transmission through oral tradition or the alterations of a late publisher. And see now the discussion of this passage in Naomi Seidman, *A Marriage Made in Heaven* (Berkeley: University of California Press, 1997), 61–66. Seidman analyzes the differences between the Hebrew and Yiddish versions of the text and sets them into the larger context of the gendered roles these languages played in nineteenth-century Eastern European Jewish writing.

Recent contemporary evidence of the longevity of this *tkhine* is found in *Tkhine imohos* (*Tkhine* of the Matriarchs), published in Brooklyn, New York, in 1992, and "written and adapted" by Jacob Meshullam Grinfeld. This anthology of *tkhines* shows clear traces of the hasidic origin of its editor. Interestingly, it includes a version of Sarah's *tkhine*, as well as a description of the making of candles for Yom Kippur among the women of the Belzer hasidic community in Europe before the Holocaust. Grinfeld's description, found in a footnote on p. 259 of *Tkhine imohes*, reads as follows (my translation): "It was formerly the custom that righteous women would themselves make the candles for Yom Kippur. They made the wicks, dipping them in melted wax several times until the candle was ready. During the making of the candles, they would pray fervently, with great weeping. It was a custom among the *tsaddikim* of the Belz dynasty to preach a fiery sermon to the women during the making of the candles. The spiritual arousal among the listeners was so great that their weeping rose to the heart of heaven." It is interesting that Grinfeld includes this three-page *tkhine*, since the practice is no longer followed.

See also Ben-Zion Alfes, ed., *Shas tkhine khadoshe* (1911; Brooklyn: Moshe Hoffman, n.d. [1980s?]), 238–39. Alfes provides a *tkhine* for making candles on the eve of Yom Kippur but notes that, in his day, most women bought factory-made candles. He specifies that the *tkhine* should be said as one brings the candles home after purchase. Although the text of the prayer is new, it echoes many of the themes found in *The Three Gates*.

39. Zechariah Mendel ben Arieh Loeb of Cracow, Baer heitev on Shulhan Arukh, Yoreh Deah 376 (4), s.v. 'afar.

40. However, Wengeroff, Memoiren, 1:104, states that the cemeteries or graves were measured in times of illness, while the actual making of the candles from the wicks used for measuring took place on the Eve of Yom Kippur.

41. Margoliot, Mateh Efrayim, 1st ed. (Zolkiew, 1835).

42. He refers to these women, perhaps with a touch of sarcasm, as nashim shaana-not (tranquil women, see Isa. 31:9). This term has a long history in Midrash and Kabbalah.

43. Margoliot, Mateh Efrayim (Warsaw: Bomberg, 1865), 22a-b.

44. While the term mitsvah can mean a simple good deed as well as a divine commandment, it is clear that Sarah is using it here in the latter, more technical sense of a religious obligation. Evidence for this is found in the close linguistic parallel between her tkhine for kindling Sabbath lights (clearly a divine commandment) and the present text. In the first of these, she writes: "Ribono shel olom, mayn mitsve fun di lekht on tsindn zol azo on genumen zayn vi di mitsve fun kohen godol ven er hot lekht in libn beys-hamikdosh getsinden." In the latter she writes: "Ribono shel olom, ikh bet dikh, zeyer der barmiger got, zolst on nemen mayn mitsve fun de lekht vos mir veln makhn fun dayn heylign libn nomen vegn." Sarah is concerned in each instance that the performance of the commandment be acceptable to God. Interestingly, Margoliot refers to these candles as "nerot shel mitsvah" (Mateh Ephraim), 22b.

45. There was a belief that Satan would stand in the heavenly court on Rosh Hasha-nah and Yom Kippur to remind God of the sins of the Israelites, thus making God disinclined to accept their prayers.

46. Ps. 69:2.

47. This is a standard kabbalistic trope for the final redemption.

48. Cf. Ezek. 37:1–14.

49. Many of the martyrs did not receive proper Jewish burial.

50. Those without children, which includes those who died as children, presumably have no descendants to make memorial candles for them.

51. See Genesis 23, in which Abraham purchases the Cave of Machpelah in Hebron as a burial place for his wife Sarah. According to later Jewish tradition, Adam and Eve, as well as Abraham and Sarah, Isaac and Rebecca, and Jacob and Leah, are also buried there.

52. Mishnah Yoma 6:8, building on Isaiah 1:18. Since this sign that the goat for Aza-zel had reached the wilderness occurred during the Temple ceremony on Yom Kippur, the wish to be worthy to see it is as much a wish for the restoration of Temple worship in the messianic era as it is a wish that God may forgive Israel's sins.

53. Zohar III, 70b-71a. Interestingly, the Zohar, as well as later transformations of this passage, repeatedly uses the phrase *modi'i leho,* "inform them," or its Hebrew equivalent. *The Three Gates* uses *modi'a zayn.*

This passage in the Zohar is also one of the sources of the Safed pietistic practice of grave prostration. It is not clear to me whether or not *kneytlakh legn* can be considered a women's "equivalent" of grave prostration. See Lawrence Fine, "The Contemplative Practive of Yihudim in Lurianic Kabbalah," in *Jewish Spirituality from the Sixteenth-Century Revival to the Present,* ed. Arthur Green (New York: Crossroad, 1987), 64–98, esp. 79–83.

54. *Nakhalas Tsevi* (Amsterdam, 1711), *aharei mot*; S. *Mayse Adonai u-mayse nisim* (Amsterdam, 1723), second excerpt from *aharei mot.*

55. Aaron Berachiah of Modena stresses both the satisfaction the dead receive from the visits of their kin and the fact that they can be awakened to pray for the living, in particular through the ritual of bringing a Torah scroll into the cemetery; *Maavar yabok* (n.p., 1732), sec. 3, chap. 24, p. 40b. Explaining and paraphrasing the Zohar (III, 70b-71a), he states: "When people [*benei ha-olam*] are in trouble, and go to the cemetery, the soul [*nefesh,* the lowest of the three parts of the soul, which lingers at the grave site] awakens and flies [*meshotetet*] and rouses the spirit [*ruah*], and the spirit rouses the aspect of the patriarchs in paradise, and it ascends and rouses the higher soul [*neshamah*], and then the Holy One, blessed be he, has mercy on the world" (sec. 3, chap. 25, p. 41a).

56. Some editions say "he," i.e., Isaac.

57. B. Rosh Hashanah 16a.

58. This phrase is the congregational response in the Kaddish, a prayer that marks the major divisions of the service. The Talmud attaches great importance to this response: "Whoever answers 'May his great name be blessed' is assured of life in the world to come" (Berakhot 57a). The kabbalists discovered mystical significance in the fact that the response contains "seven words composed of twenty-eight letters. This corresponds to the number of words and letters in the first verse of the Bible. . . . One who responds to the Kaddish with these words becomes, as it were, God's partner in the creation of the world, which is the theme of the first verse in the Scriptures." Abraham Millgram, *Jewish Worship* (Philadelphia: Jewish Publication Society, 1971), 483.

59. Jer. 31:17.

60. Perhaps this parallels the Christian practice of lighting candles for saints. Herman Pollack, however, interprets the ritual differently: "The act of 'measuring the field' would symbolize the 'transfer' of ownership of the cemetery grounds to living relatives who thereupon acquired the authority to instruct or direct the dead to aid them." Pollack, *Jewish Folkways in Germanic Lands* (Cambridge: MIT Press, 1971), 48.

61. For an example of the discomfort (although also of valuable descriptive mate-

rial), see Pollack's discussion of the custom of visiting graves in *Jewish Folkways*, 47–49, which concludes: "In the main we shall observe that scholars and rabbis did not always challenge popular views and customs." This is in fact an understatement: many rabbis actually supported and believed in the efficacy of imploring the dead for their intercession. The following talmudic texts support (although not always unequivocally) a belief in the intercession of the dead: B. Sotah 34b, B. Taanit 16a, 23b. Later sources are S. Hasidim (Wistinetzki), p. 377, no. 1537; Shulhan Arukh, Orah Hayyim, no. 599 (10) with Baer Heitev and Magen Avraham (primarily opposed to intercession); no. 579 (3) (Shulhan Arukh opposed; Magen Avraham brings positive view); no. 581 (4) with Baer Heitev (opposed); Isaiah Horowitz, *Shaar ha-shamayim* (Amsterdam, 1742), 325a (summarizes various customs and positions).

62. In general, the matriarchs are depicted as somewhat more active than the patriarchs (though not more so than Moses) in their efforts on behalf of Israel. See Weissler, "Traditional piety," in *Jewish Spirituality*, ed. Green, 266–67, where I slightly overstated the case.

63. For a study of the burial society of Prague, as well as other aspects of illness and death in Ashkenazi Judaism, see Sylvie-Anne Goldberg, *Crossing the Jabbok* (Berkeley: University of California Press, 1996).

64. The history of the genre of cemetery prayers requires further study. Some of these prayers may be quite old: *Tsidduk ha-din* (Venice, 1737) attributes a prayer to be said in the cemetery between Rosh Hashanah and Yom Kippur to R. Israel Isserlein (1390–1460); and it attributes a prayer to be said at any time of year when visiting the graves of martyrs, and another such prayer for the Ninth of Av (a fast day commemorating the destruction of the Temple in Jerusalem) to R. Samuel Archivolti (1515–1611). The most significant new research on this topic is that by Avriel Bar-Levav. See Bar-Levav, "Rabi Aharon Berachiah mi-Modenah ve-rabi Naftali ha-Kohen Katz: Avot ha-mehabrim sifrei holim u-metim," *Asufot* 9 (1995): 189–234. This article is based on a portion of Bar-Levav's dissertation, which I have unfortunately not yet had the opportunity to read in full; see Bar-Levav, "ha-Mavet be-olamo shel ha-mekubbal rabi Naftali ha-Kohen Katz" (Ph.D. dissertation, Hebrew University of Jerusalem, 1990).

65. I have examined the following editions: Johann Kellner, Frankfurt, 1724, and Itsik ben Leib, Fürth, 1766, both of which are all Yiddish, and Proops, Amsterdam, 1723, a bilingual edition.

66. Many rabbinic sources say that the reason women are required to kindle Sabbath lights is to atone for Eve's sin; Eve darkened Adam's light (she made him mortal) by persuading him to eat the forbidden fruit. This view is also found in Yiddish ethical literature, although not in *tkhines* for candle lighting. See Chapter 4.

67. Frankfurt, *Sefer ha-hayyim* (Amsterdam, 1716), Yiddish section, pp. 128b–129a; (Koetten, 1717), Yiddish section, pp. 55b-56a.

68. The *tkhine* immediately preceding this one specifies that "the women should say this prayer on the eve of Rosh Hashanah and the eve of Yom Kippur."

69. There are two other possible, if unlikely, relationships between these texts. First, perhaps Sarah was familiar with *Sefer ha-hayyim* and rewrote the *tkhine* she found there. However, it is far more usual for someone to rationalize a text and make it more theologically acceptable by removing certain elements than for someone to take a rationalized text and "remythologize" it. Further, we know that Frankfurter rewrote other texts. Nonetheless, we cannot utterly dismiss the possibility that Sarah got the idea for her *tkhine* from *Sefer ha-hayyim*.

Second, perhaps *The Three Gates*, or at least this portion of it, was written before 1731. Perhaps the entire third gate, containing the material from *Hemdat yamim*, was added later. But although two key passages of the third gate are taken from other books (and other portions of this gate probably also have similar origins), a careful analysis shows that they were woven together by the same author who composed the rest of the *tkhine*. And even leaving aside the dating of the passage from *Hemdat yamim*, the other passage for which I have identified a source, a description of the women's Paradise, is taken from a work published in 1708. This still puts the third gate, and probably the entire work, later than the publication of *Sefer ha-hayyim*.

70. The question of when the sin is described as Eve's and when it is described as Adam's would repay further analysis. In general, it seems to me, if a text is concerned with the nature and fate of humanity, Adam gets "credit" for the sin, but if the text is concerned with the nature and fate of women in particular or the relationship between women and men, Eve is blamed for it.

71. While it is impossible to develop this point fully here, the contrast between Sarah's and Frankfurt's views of the relationship between the living and the dead resembles the contrast between Catholic and Protestant views in early modern France, as described by Natalie Zemon Davis in "Ghosts, Kin, and Progeny: Some Features of Family Life in Early Modern France," in *The Family*, ed. Alice S. Rossi, Jerome Kagan, and Tamara Hareven (New York: W. W. Norton, 1978), 92ff. Catholics can appeal to the saints for help; they are also expected to aid their deceased kin in Purgatory. Further, for Catholics, the dead are simply another "age group" of the extended family. Protestants, however, must relate in a more unmediated way to the divine and also tend to develop more individualistic family strategies. Thus, Frankfurt's thinking may have been influenced by the Protestant Reformation, as well as by political and social changes in Western Europe, whereas Sarah reflected her milieu, where Catholic (and Eastern Orthodox) views continued to prevail.

72. Serl bas Jacob, *Tkhine imohes fun rosh hodesh elul* (Lvov, n.d.); the *tkhine* for the shofar is part of this larger text. My translation of excerpts from this text appears in Ellen M. Umansky and Dianne Ashton, eds., *Four Centuries of Jewish Women's Spirituality* (Boston: Beacon, 1992), 53–54.

73. See Chapter 7.

74. Serl bas Jacob, *Tkhine imohes fun rosh hodesh elul*. The source of this motif is *Sefer ha-yashar*.

CHAPTER 9. AMERICAN TRANSFORMATIONS
OF THE *TKHINES*

This chapter combines portions of two conference papers: "American Transformations of the *Tkhines*," invited lecture at a conference entitled Across Boundaries: A History of Jewish Women in America, University of Maryland, College Park, October 31–November 1, 1993, and "Yiddish *Tkhines* as a Model for Feminist Creativity," invited lecture at a conference entitled, Can There Be Yiddishkeit Without Yiddish? Joseph and Rebecca Meyerhoff Center for Jewish Studies, University of Maryland, College Park, November 3, 1996.

1. Susan Starr Sered, *Women as Ritual Experts* (New York and Oxford: Oxford University Press, 1992), 32–33. For a somewhat different definition of domestic religion, see Barbara Myerhoff, *Number Our Days* (New York: Dutton, 1978), 234–35, 256–58. See also the distinction made by Haym Sloveitchik between mimetic Judaism, characteristic of traditional Eastern European Jewish life, and text-based Judaism, characteristic of American and Israeli Orthodox Judaism in the second half of the twentieth century, in "Rupture and Reconstruction: The Transformation of Contemporary Orthodoxy," *Tradition* 28: 4 (1994): 64–130.

2. Because they are a written genre, the *tkhines* are more closely interwoven with the texts and ideas of the great tradition of Judaism than are the prayers and religious practices that Sered describes. Nonetheless, like the examples she explores, *tkhines* usually do concern themselves with the lives of "particular, usually well-loved individuals" or with occasions rooted in the private lives of individuals rather than with the liturgical calendar. (As will be noted below, this changes somewhat in the nineteenth and twentieth centuries.)

3. On these changes, see David Biale, "Childhood, Marriage and the Family in the Eastern European Jewish Enlightenment," in *The Jewish Family: Myth and Reality*, ed. Steven M. Cohen and Paula E. Hyman (New York: Holmes and Meier, 1986), 45–61, and *Eros and the Jews* (New York: Basic Books, 1992), chap. 7. Jacob Goldberg argues that Jewish marriage patterns, especially arranged marriages and the young age of the couples being wed, began to be criticized— and to change—in the second half of the eighteenth century. See Goldberg, "Jewish Marriage in Eighteenth-Century Poland," *Polin* 10 (1997): 3–39. Economic conditions were such that, in most families, both parents had to work to sustain the family, whatever the ideals.

4. Ben-Zion Alfes, *Shas tkhine khadoshe*, 1st ed. (Vilna: Rosenkrants and Shriftzetser, 1911), cited in Shulamit Z. Berger, "Tehines: A Brief Survey of Women's Prayers," in *Daughters of the King*, ed. Susan Grossman and Rivka Haut (Philadelphia: Jewish Publication Society, 1992), 73–83, 81, n. 14.

5. On Alfes, see Berger, "*Tehines*," and the references there.

6. There were additional routes to modernization for the *tkhines*. In Central and Western Europe in the nineteenth century, *tkhines* were published with more

modern sensibilities first in a germanized Yiddish, and then in German and other Western European languages. On the German books of devotion for Jewish women, see the study by Bettina Kratz-Ritter, *Für "fromme Zionstöchter" und "gebildete Frauenzimmer"* (Hildesheim: Georg Olms Verlag, 1995). Similar works were published in the United States in English, for example *Ruhamah: Devotional Exercises for the Use of the Daughters of Israel,* comp. and trans. from the German of Letteris, Miro, and Stern, and ed. by Morris Jacob Raphall (New York: L. Joachimssen, 1852).

7. For a discussion of Dik's life and fiction, see David Roskies, *A Bridge of Longing* (Cambridge, Mass.: Harvard University Press, 1985), chap. 3.

8. Isaac Meyer Dik, Preface to *Shivim moltsayt* (Vilna, 1877), quoted in Shmuel Niger, "Yiddish Literature and the Female Reader," trans. Sheva Zucker, in *Women of the Word,* ed. Judith Baskin (Detroit: Wayne State University Press, 1994), 70–90, quote at 82.

9. On the maskilic authors of *tkhines,* see Israel Zinberg, *Old Yiddish Literature from its Origins to the Haskalah Period* (Cincinnati: Hebrew Union College Press, 1975), 252–53, and Shmuel Niger, "Di yidishe literatur un di lezerin," in Niger, *Bleter geshikhte fun der yidisher literatur* (New York: Sh. Niger bukh-komitet, 1959), 35–107, esp. 83–85, now available in Sheva Zucker's abridged translation, "Yiddish Literature and the Female Reader."

10. Yitskhok Shloyme Mayer, "Amerikaner [*sic*] tkhines," *YIVO bleter* 39 (1955): 271–75.

11. *Shas Tkhine Rav Peninim* (New York: Hebrew Publishing Company, n.d.) Mayer notes that this edition is "a little later" than 1916, the date of an earlier edition he also mentions. On Aguz, see Mayer, "Amerikaner tkhines," 272, n. 1, and *Leksikon fun der nayer yidisher literatur* (New York: Congress for Jewish Culture, 1956), 1:18–19. The original *Tkhine tsu far hitin di gezund* by Alfes is found in Ben-Zion Alfes, *Shas tkhine khadoshe* (Brooklyn, N.Y.: Moshe Hoffmann: 1980s?), 46–47. It lacks the references to tasty meals, improved hygiene, and women's hypochondria.

12. This proverb is found in the Talmud (B. Pesahim 64b), not the Torah.

13. Ethics of the Fathers 3:17. The full proverb states: If there is no flour there is no Torah, and if there is no Torah there is no flour. The meaning is that body and spirit are interdependent.

14. Moses Maimonides (1135–1204), medieval Jewish philosopher and physician.

15. This is also a saying from the Ethics of the Fathers (4:1): Who is rich? One who rejoices in his own portion.

16. B. Kiddushin 80b.

17. "A New *Tkhine* upon Arising in the Morning," in *Shas tkhine rav peninim* (The Six Orders *Tkhine* Full of Pearls) (New York: Hebrew Publishing Company, c. 1916), 6–7, quoted in Yitskhok Shloyme Mayer, "Amerikaner tkhines," 272. Another, very similar text with the same title is found in *Tkhinas benos Yerushalayim*

(*Tkhine* of the Daughters of Jerusalem) (New York: Star Hebrew Book Co., 1929), 7–8.

18. See Jenna Weissman Joselit, "A Set Table: Jewish Domestic Culture in the New World, 1880–1950," in *Getting Comfortable in New York: The American Jewish Home, 1880–1950*, ed. Susan L. Braunstein and Jenna Weissman Joselit (New York: The Jewish Museum, 1990), 19–73, and *The Wonders of America* (New York: Hill and Wang, 1994), 135–41, 178–83. The Henry Street Settlement House was a social agency on the Lower East Side of Manhattan, founded by Lilian Wald and other German Jews to help and educate the Eastern European Jewish immigrants.

19. *Shas tkhine rav peninim*, quoted in Mayer, "Amerikaner tkhines," 272–73. Mayer does not cite the pages on which this is found in the original.

20. Or was it simply that the author of this *tkhine* thought immigrant women *should* feel discomfort at the desecration of the Sabbath? As my grandmother said to me when I asked her about the traditional ways of the Old Country she had long since abandoned, "You know, I've come a long way since then. And you know what? I'm glad!" A surprisingly large number of immigrants worked on the Sabbath, including those who owned their own businesses; see Joselit, *The Wonders of America*, 252–53.

21. Mayer, "Amerikaner tkhines," passim.

22. The various hasidic groups maintain networks of private, sex-segregated schools. However, in Europe, some of these groups had opposed any form of formal education for girls.

There is a large literature on Hasidim in America. Two recent works are Jerome Mintz, *Hasidic People* (Cambridge: Harvard University Press, 1992); and Janet S. Belcove-Shalin, ed., *New World Hasidism* (Albany: State University of New York Press, 1995). Both address aspects of the lives of women who are part of hasidic communities.

23. Examples of recent Israeli editions are *Tkhinos Rokhl imenu le-khol ha-shanah* (Jerusalem: Levin-Epstein, n.d.) and *Tkhine rav peninim* (Tel Aviv: Sinai, n.d., c. 1980?). These two editions have broadly overlapping content and appear to be photo-offsets of early twentieth-century European editions. Recent American editions include a reprint of Ben-Zion Alfes, *Shas Tkhine khadoshe* (Brooklyn, N.Y.: Moshe Hoffmann, 1980s?). When I purchased this book from Mr. Hoffmann in his bookstore in the Williamsburg section of Brooklyn, he told me very proudly that this was not a reprint of the usual standard collection of *tkhines* and that he had searched out an unusual edition that had been out of print. *Tkhine imohes*, ed. Jacob Meshullam Grinfeld (Brooklyn, N.Y.: Ateres, 1992), will be discussed below.

24. These changes provide further evidence for the shift from a domestically based mimetic Judaism to a religion based increasingly on the sole authority of sacred texts, noted for the non-hasidic Orthodox by Haym Soloveitchik in "Rupture and Reconstruction."

25. See, for example, *tkhines* to be recited by the mother of the bride before her daughter's wedding; the mother tearfully begs God to promote love and harmony

between the young couple (*Tkhinos Rokhl imenu*, 235–36; *Tkhine imohes*, 303–304).

26. This collection contains the same *tkhine* upon arising in the morning as that quoted by Mayer from the early twentieth-century collection, as well as rewritten excerpts from such eighteenth-century works as Sarah bas Tovim's *Shloyshe sheorim* (The Three Gates) and Seril bas Jacob's *Tkhine imohes fun Rosh Hodesh Elul* (*Tkhine* of the Matriarchs for the New Moon of Elul). Evidence of hasidic affiliation of the author includes a prayer by Rabbi Elimelekh of Lizensk, as well as a description of the making of candles for Yom Kippur by the women of the Belzer hasidic community in Europe before the Holocaust.

27. While this view was expressed by some early *tkhine* authors, notably Leah Horowitz in her *Tkhine of the Matriarchs*, many early *tkhines* either insisted or assumed that men had greater spiritual power and religious significance than women. On Leah Horowitz, see Chapter 7.

28. On this tendency toward stringency, see Egon Mayer, *From Suburb to Shtetl: The Jews of Boro Park* (Philadelphia: Temple University Press, 1979), Samuel C. Heilman, *Portrait of American Jews* (Seattle: University of Washington Press, 1995), 144–59, Jack Wertheimer, *A People Divided* (New York: Basic Books, 1993), 114–36, and, most recently, Haym Soloveitchik, "Rupture and Reconstruction."

29. Rivka Zakutinsky, ed., *Techinas: A Voice from the Heart* (Brooklyn, N.Y.: Aura Press, 1992). Ephraim Kanarfogel (personal communication) has mentioned to me that this book is popular among his students at Stern College of Yeshiva University, a women's institution attended primarily by young modern Orthodox students, albeit the more traditional among them.

30. Zakutinsky, *Techinas*, 13–14.

31. In this, Zakutinsky is closer to Myerhoff's conception of domestic religion than Sered's: "'Domestic Religion' . . . [is] acquired in early childhood, completely associated with family and household, blending nurturance and ethnic specificities, and it was this blend that gave hearth-based religion such endurance and depth" (Myerhoff, *Number Our Days*, 256, also 235). Zakutinsky's memories also hark back to a mimetic Judaism, learned at one's parents' side (Soloveitchik, "Rupture and Reconstruction").

32. The Havurah movement arose in the late 1960s as a kind of Jewish counterculture; see Riv-Ellen Prell, *Prayer and Community: The Havurah in American Judaism* (Detroit: Wayne State University Press, 1989), and Chava Weissler, *Making Judaism Meaningful: Ambivalence and Tradition in a Havurah Community* (New York: AMS Press, 1989).

33. On changes in the Conservative movement during this period, see Wertheimer, *A People Divided*, chaps. 4 and 7.

34. *Sabbath and Festival Prayer Book*, ed. and trans. Morris Silverman (New York: Rabbinical Assembly of America, c. 1946, 1973) was intended to be used in synagogue on Sabbaths and holidays. (There was also a prayerbook for weekday ser-

vices.) *Siddur Sim Shalom: A Prayer Book for Shabbat, Festivals, and Weekdays*, ed. and trans. Jules Harlow (New York: Rabbinical Assembly of America and United Synagogue of America, 1985), includes far more of the material found in a full traditional prayer book, including blessings and ceremonies for the home. It also includes English readings for private devotion and reflection and alternative versions of a number of the central prayers of the synagogue liturgy. While the Silverman prayer book included a section entitled "Supplementary Readings," the Hebrew title of the section, *"Likutim le-keriah be-kahal"* (Selections for Congregational Reading) makes it clear that these were intended for inclusion in public worship rather than for use in private devotion.

35. *Siddur Sim Shalom*, 702. Harlow does give source notations for most material derived from external sources.

36. For two dozen variant versions of this prayer, see Noah Prylucki, *Yidishe folkslider*, vol. 1 (Warsaw: Bikher-far-ale, 1911), 15–43. Unlike the more literary *tkhines*, *Got fun Avrohom* was passed down through oral tradition and rarely appeared in print. Many women regarded this prayer as the female equivalent of Havdalah; just as all the restrictions of the Sabbath ended for men as they recited Havdalah as night fell on Saturday evening, so women could return to weekday work after reciting *Got fun Avrohom*. Indeed, the European-born mother of a friend of mine expressed astonishment that her daughter, educated in the great tradition, ended the Sabbath by reciting Havdalah instead of *Got fun Avrohom* (Dina Rosenfeld, personal communication, 1974).

37. *Siddur sim shalom*, 717.

38. Ibid., 720.

39. Jewish continuity is a topic of concern for most modern Jewish movements. There is a real fear that increased secularization and intermarriage, along with the loss of six million Jews in the Holocaust, will lead to the gradual disappearance of the Jewish people. Thus, the concern for Jewish continuity expressed in this prayer is in line with the shift in Jewish education from teaching students knowledge of Judaism to convincing them that it is valuable to remain active Jews.

40. *Siddur sim shalom*, 720–21. The other prayer by Navah Harlow focuses more on the experience of the individual offering the prayer: finding inner peace, hope, and compassion.

41. The introduction to *Siddur sim shalom* contains a section entitled "On Personal Involvement" (in prayer). The section concludes: "It is difficult for many individuals to appreciate the fact that their own words of prayer or reflection are as authentic at certain times as those of an ancient or medieval sage. Individuals should be encouraged to overcome the initial difficulties of expressing their own prayers, just as they should be encouraged to participate actively in the service. . . . The results will be well worth the effort, for their own life of prayer and for that of the congregation" (p. xxx).

42. I have chosen to focus this section on *Siddur Sim Shalom* because it includes prayers that resemble *tkhines* for an occasion on which *tkhines* were actually re-

cited: candle lighting in the home. Here let me briefly review recent prayer books by the other liberal movements of Judaism. As of this writing, the Reconstructionist movement has published a new prayer book for Sabbaths and holidays, *Kol Haneshamah* (Wyncote, Pa.: Reconstructionist Press, 1994), which is focused on public worship. Nonetheless, it does include a translation or adaptation of part of one *tkhine* for candle lighting in its Friday night liturgy: "Almighty God, grant me and all my loved ones a chance truly to rest on this Shabbat. May the light of the candles drive out from among us the spirit of anger, the spirit of harm. Send your blessings to my children, that they may walk in the ways of your Torah, your light" (*Shas Tkhines*, p. 4).

The Reform movement has issued a comprehensive set of new prayer books over the last few decades. Included among them is *Gates of the House: Prayers and Readings for Home and Synagogue*, ed. Chaim Stern (New York: Central Conference of American Rabbis, 1977). This book contains some personal prayers that resemble *tkhines*, in that they are intended for individual devotion on private occasions. They are interspersed with other sorts of materials, primarily in the section entitled "The Path of Life." However, they are not singled out in any way, nor are they aimed in particular at a female audience. Most of them were written by the editor of the volume.

43. New collections of *tkhine* translations include Tracy Guren-Klirs, comp., *The Merit of Our Mothers* (Cincinnati, Ohio: Hebrew Union College Press, 1992); Norman Tarnor, comp. and trans., *A Book of Jewish Women's Prayers* (Northvale, N.J.: Jason Aronson, 1995), and Zakutinsky, *Techinas*.

44. Examples from a variety of points on the religious spectrum include the following: "*Tkhine* 100" and "*Tkhine* 103 from *Seder Tkhines Uvakoshes*," trans. Chava Weissler, in *Lifecycles: Jewish Women on Life Passages and Personal Milestones*, ed. Debra Orenstein, (Woodstock, Vt.: Jewish Lights, 1994), 1:19–20, 22; "Tkhines for Rosh Chodesh," by Tracy Guren Klirs, in *Celebrating the New Moon*, ed. Susan Berrin (Northvale, N.J.: Jason Aronson, 1996), 49–65; "*Tkhines* and *Techinot*: Ancient Prayers," introd. Chava Weissler, trans. Chava Weissler and Shaindy Jacobson, in *Total Immersion: A Mikveh Anthology*, ed. Rivkah Slonim (Northvale, N.J.: Jason Aronson, 1996), 95–99.

45. Elizabeth Resnick Levine, ed., *A Ceremonies Sampler: New Rites, Celebrations, and Observances of Jewish Women* (San Diego, Calif.: Women's Institute for Continuing Jewish Education, 1991); Penina V. Adelman, *Miriam's Well: Rituals for Jewish Women around the Year* (Fresh Meadows, N.Y.: Biblio Press, 1986); Ellen M. Umansky and Dianne Ashton, ed., *Four Centuries of Jewish Women's Spirituality* (Boston: Beacon, 1992). The term "sampler" in the title of the first work listed above bespeaks the eclectic approach to spirituality found in these works.

46. Jennifer Breger, "The Prayers of Jewish Women: Some Historical Perspectives," *Judaism* 42 (1993): 504–15, esp. 509–12, the section of the article entitled "Do These Prayers Provide a Usable Past?"

47. I have also dealt with this question in Weissler, "The *Tkhines* and Women's Prayer," *CCAR Journal* (Fall, 1993): 75–78. See Starhawk, "Ritual as Bonding, in

Weaving the Visions, ed. Judith Plaskow and Carol P. Christ (San Francisco: Harper and Row, 1989), 326–35. Of related interest is the study by Jody Elizabeth Myers, "The Myth of Matriarchy in Recent Writings on Jewish Women's Spirituality," *Jewish Social Studies* (new series) 4 (Fall 1996): 1–27; as Myers shows, the popularity of matriarchal myths is related to the penchant for embodiedness in women's spirituality. However, she would be reluctant to label these forms of women's spirituality as "feminist."

48. Exceptions include ritual gatherings of women for the making of Yom Kippur candles (see Chapter 8) and recitations of *tkhines* during synagogue services by groups of women led by the *zogerke*.

49. Breger, "Prayers of Jewish Women," 511. The isolated nature of *tkhine* performance was also noted as a drawback by Geela Rayzel Raphael, whose *tkhines* will be analyzed below. Raphael suggests that "today's rewrites would include communal voices." Raphael, "Techinot," manuscript, Reconstructionist Rabbinical College, 1993, 13.

50. Jane Litman, "M'ugelet, A Pregnancy Ritual," in *A Ceremonies Sampler*, 5–7.

51. The matriarch Rachel is depicted in Midrash and legend as a caring mother of her children, the people of Israel. Paradoxically, and perhaps because of her own difficulty in conceiving, her tomb has been a pilgrimage site for childless women for centuries. See Susan Starr Sered, "Rachel's Tomb and the Milk Grotto of the Virgin Mary: Two Women's Shrines in Bethlehem," *Journal of Feminist Studies in Religion* 2 (Fall 1986): 7–22.

52. The translation of the original *tkhine*, entitled "*Tkhine* for a woman who is about to have a child," from the collection entitled *Rokhl mevakoh al boneho* (Rachel Weeps for Her Children) (Vilna, 1910) is found in Guren Klirs, comp., *The Merit of Our Mothers*, 128. Guren Klirs has romanized the names of biblical figures and certain other important terms according to their Yiddish pronunciation. The following are their translations, in order: So-and-so, daughter of so-and-so; Sarah, Rebecca, Rachel, and Leah; Miriam, Deborah, Hannah, and Huldah; Yael; Torah; commandments; amen.

53. For example, the prayer to give birth with room to spare appears in *Tkhine* 100 of *Seder tkhines u-vakoshes* (Fürth, 1762). This collection also contains a *tkhine* (no. 93; see also no. 96) in which the pregnant woman asks that her womb not be bewitched, and that she not develop cravings for any unkosher foods—perhaps the inspiration for Litman's prayer to avoid ingesting unhealthy food, drink, or smoke.

54. Breger, "Prayers of Jewish Women," esp. 511. See also her article, "Women's Devotional Literature: An Essay in Jewish Bibliography," *Jewish Book Annual* 52 (1994–95): 73–98.

55. Jewish feminist rituals are similar in this and other characteristics to rituals created by non-Jewish feminists. For a discussion of the fluid quality of Jewish feminist ritual, see Judith Plaskow, *Standing Again at Sinai* (San Francisco: Harper and Row, 1990), 67ff.

56. For the connections between psychotherapy and spirituality, see Lucy Breg-man, "Psychotherapies," in *Spirituality and the Secular Quest*, ed. Peter H. Van Ness (New York: Crossroad, 1996), 251–76.

57. I first noted this drive for individual meaning in my earlier research on the ha-vurah movement. See Chava Weissler, *Making Judaism Meaningful* (New York: AMS Press, 1989). For a discussion of these themes in American society as a whole, see *Habits of the Heart*, ed. Robert Bellah (Berkeley: University of California Press, 1996).

58. Raphael, "Techinot." Raphael has since been ordained as a rabbi.

59. Raphael, "Techinot," 19. Note that in this case, no gathering for ritual purposes is suggested.

60. Clearly, one source of this imagery is Clarissa Pinkola Estés, *Women Who Run with the Wolves* (New York: Ballantine Books, 1992; 1995), a popular book among certain New Age and other feminists.

61. One additional *tkhine* that asks for inspiration and patience to compose the pa-per appears as an epigraph before the portion of her text that reviews the history of the *tkhine* genre, and at the head of the present chapter. The ten *tkhines* Raphael composed are found at the end of the essay.

62. This introduction imitates the author statements found in classical *tkhines*.

63. Heather Altman, "The Dream *Tkhine*" (Honors project in Religion, Emory Uni-versity, 1994). Beyond the purview of the present study, because its author is an Is-raeli of British origin rather than an American, is the beautifully written *tkhine* by Alice Shalvi, "A Techine for Yom Kippur," in Gail Twersky Reimer and Judith A. Kates, eds., *Beginning Anew* (New York: Simon and Schuster, 1997), 274–75.

64. Altman, "Dream *Tkhine*," 2.

CHAPTER 10. THE FEMINIST SCHOLAR
AND THE *TKHINES*

An earlier version of this chapter was published as "Women's Studies and Women's Prayers: Reconstructing the Religious History of Ashkenazic Women." *Jewish So-cial Studies* (New Series), 1 (Winter 1995): 28–47.

1. For a powerful meditation on what it means to be a woman, a feminist, and a classicist, see Amy Richlin, "Hijacking the Palladion: Feminists in Classics," *Gen-der and History* 4:1 (1992): 70–83.

2. See Renato Rosaldo, "Grief and a Headhunter's Rage," in Rosaldo, *Culture and Truth* (Boston: Beacon, 1989). For discussions of anger by feminist philosophers, see Marilyn Frye, "A Note on Anger," in Frye, *The Politics of Reality* (Trumansburg, N.Y.: Crossing Press, 1983); Naomi Scheman, "Anger and the Politics of Naming," in *Women and Language in Literature and Society*, ed. Sally McConnell-Ginet,

Ruth Borker, and Nelly Furman (New York: Praeger, 1980); and Elizabeth V. Spelman, "Anger and Insubordination," in *Women, Knowledge, and Reality*, ed. Ann Garry and Marilyn Pearsall (Boston: Unwin Hyman, 1989).

3. Rosan A. Jordan and Susan J. Kalcik, eds., *Women's Folklore, Women's Culture* (Philadelphia: University of Pennsylvania Press, 1985), and Susan Tower Hollis, Linda Pershing, and M. Jane Young, eds., *Feminist Theory and the Study of Folklore* (Urbana: University of Illinois Press, 1993).

4. An important exception is the work of scholars studying women in conservative, fundamentalist religious groups. See the studies of Elaine J. Lawless on Pentecostal women, notably her essay, "Access to the Pulpit," in Hollis, Pershing, and Young, *Feminist Theory*, 258–276, and *Handmaidens of the Lord* (Philadelphia: University of Pennsylvania Press, 1988). Also interesting in this regard is Helen Hardacre's study of women in the Reiyukai Kodan movement in Japan, *Lay Buddhism in Contemporary Japan* (Princeton: Princeton University Press, 1984). In essence, Lawless and Hardacre argue that women are able to gain power and influence through their engagement with and manipulation of the roles available to women. For studies of the attractiveness of traditional gender roles to modern Jewish women, see Lynn Davidman, *Tradition in a Rootless World* (Berkeley: University of California Press, 1991), and Debra Kaufman, *Rachel's Daughters* (New Brunswick, N.J.: Rutgers University Press, 1991).

5. For a fascinating psychoanalytic study of dominance and submission, see Jessica Benjamin, *The Bonds of Love* (New York: Pantheon, 1988).

6. As Lila Abu-Lughod remarks, "Despite the considerable theoretical sophistication of many studies of resistance and their contribution to the widening of our definition of the political, it seems to me that because they are ultimately more concerned with finding resistors and explaining resistance than with examining power, they do not explore as fully as they might the implications of the forms of resistance they locate. . . . [T]here is perhaps a tendency to romanticize resistance, to read all forms of resistance as signs of the ineffectiveness of systems of power and of the resilience and creativity of the human spirit in its refusal to be dominated. By reading resistance in this way, we collapse distinctions between forms of resistance and foreclose certain questions about the workings of power." See Abu-Lughod, "The Romance of Resistance: Tracing Transformations of Power through Bedouin Women," *American Ethnologist*: 17 (February 1990): 41–55.

7. For example, should I obey the norms of "Torah scholarship" and rise when my teacher comes into the room? Or, by contrast, should I obey the norms of secular scholarship and address a university colleague who has profound and recognized talmudic scholarship—a *gadol be-Torah*—by his first name?

8. On this issue, see Amy Shuman, "Dismantling Local Culture," *Western Folklore* 52 (1993): 345–64.

9. See, for example, Chava Weissler, "The Traditional Piety of Ashkenazic Women," in *Jewish Spirituality from the Sixteenth Century Revival to the Present*, ed. Arthur Green (New York: Crossroad, 1987), 245–75, and *Traditional Yiddish Literature: A*

Source for the Study of Women's Lives, The Jacob Pat Memorial Lecture, February 26, 1987 (Cambridge: Harvard University Library, 1988).

10. On women and nonlearned men, see Chapter 3.

11. See Herman Rebell, "Cultural Hegemony and Class Experience: A Critical Reading of Recent Ethnological-Historical Approaches (Part One)," *American Ethnologist* 16 (1989): 117–36. See also Judith Plaskow, *Standing Again at Sinai* (San Francisco: Harper and Row, 1990), esp. the introduction and chap. 1.

12. Rebell, "Cultural Hegemony," 128–29.

13. There was a folk belief that the blowing of the shofar would confuse Satan and prevent him from reciting the sins of Israel before God on Rosh Hashanah, when they are being judged.

14. Gen. 24.

15. This translation is based on an undated edition published in Lvov, probably between 1780 and 1820. My translation of a longer excerpt from this text appears in Ellen Umansky and Dianne Ashton, eds., *Four Centuries of Jewish Women's Spirituality,* (Boston: Beacon, 1992), 53–54.

16. For a critique of the notion of "folk culture" that shows how it is simply a place-holder that defines its "opposite," "modern culture," see Shuman, "Dismantling Local Culture."

17. Jacob ben Isaac of Yanov, *Tsenerene* (Amsterdam, 1702 or 3), 4b.

18. Prof. Dov Noy, personal communication.

19. Sobotki, *Seder tkhines* (Prague, 1718), no. 19.

20. See, for example, the comparison in Chapter 8 between Sarah bas Tovim's *tkhine* for measuring graves and that composed by Simeon Frankfurt.

21. And the traditional Jew in me is horrified at the idea of rendering the etrog unfit before the end of the holiday.

22. The point of this was for the men to be unaware of, and thus undistracted by, the women's presence, so that they could get on with their required prayer. While women probably usually did make their presence heard, there is an interesting iconographic tradition that shows how women could "disappear" from the margins. The Yiddish custumals (books of *minhagim*) were usually illustrated. The picture for the new moon of Elul and for Rosh Hashanah in the edition published in Venice in 1601, shows a man blowing the shofar before a congregation of men and boys, while women cup their ears to hear from the windows of the women's balcony. In all other editions that I have seen (Venice, 1593 and the editions that follow its tradition of illustration, such as Amsterdam, 1645, Amsterdam, 1662) the windows are blank—the women have disappeared.

23. See the Introduction for background on these religious movements.

24. See the discussion of the relationship of the *tkhines* to the kabbalistic private devotions in Hebrew in Chapters 1 and 2. Solomon Freehof, in a classic article, was the first to notice the relationship between Lurianic devotional literature in He-

brew and the *tkhines*. See Freehof, "Devotional Literature in the Vernacular," *CCAR Yearbook* 33 (1923): 375–424.

25. *Naye tkhines u-vakoshes* (Homburg-vor-der-Hohe, 1729), no. 3. A slightly different text is found in *Seder tkhines u-vakoshes* (Fürth, 1762), no. 3.

26. On the question of the absence of Jewish women mystics, see Chapter 6 above.

27. See Chapter 6 for a fuller discussion of this text.

28. Khotsh, *Nakhalas Tsevi* (Frankfurt-am-Main, 1711; Zolkiew, 1740).

29. For a full discussion of Leah Horowitz and *The Tkhine of the Matriarchs*, see Chapter 7 above.

30. Yalqut Shim'oni, Ruth, 4.

31. Jer. 31:8[9]: "With weeping they shall come, and with supplications I will lead them back, I will make them walk by brooks of water, in a straight path in which they shall not stumble; for I am a father to Israel, and Ephraim is my first born." Cf. also B. Berakhot 32b and B. Baba Metsia 59a: "R. Eleazar said, from the day on which the Temple was destroyed, the gates of prayer were locked . . . , but even though the gates of prayer were locked, the gates of tears were not locked." The text in Baba Metsia also mentions that tears are common among women.

32. B. Berakhot 6a.

33. Joel 1:15; 3:14; Obad. 1:15; Zeph. 1:7.

34. Ps. 80:6.

35. Isa. 59:20.

36. Members of the Feminist Research Group of the Lehigh Valley suggested that instead of "Woman as High Priest: A Kabbalistic Prayer in Yiddish for Lighting Sabbath Candles," I title my article about *Tkhine imrei shifre* "Come on, Baby, Light My Fire!"

37. On the paradoxes of this position for modern Jewish women who have adopted Orthodoxy, see Kaufman, *Rachel's Daughters*, 155–67.

EPILOGUE

1. See Arthur Green's discussion of *hitbodedut* (private prayer) in the teachings of Nahman of Bratzlav, in *Tormented Master* (New York: Schocken, 1981), 144–48.

ACKNOWLEDGMENTS

With a heart full of gratitude, I acknowledge the One whose daily miracles sustain us all, and whose Presence fills creation.

Over the dozen or so years of research, thought, and writing that have gone into the making of this book, I have received the gracious help of institutions, colleagues, and friends. A Fellowship from the National Endowment for the Humanities in 1985 allowed me to spend a semester at the Hebrew University of Jerusalem; there, with the resources of the library and the assistance of colleagues, I was able to begin serious scholarly work on the *tkhines* and their sources. As a Research Associate in Women's Studies in Religion at Harvard Divinity School in 1986–87, I broadened my grasp of feminist theory and its relevance for my research. The wonderful facilities and gracious hospitality of the Annenberg Research Institute (now the Center for Judaic Studies of the University of Pennsylvania) in 1990–1991 were essential to the completion of several important chapters. Research leaves from Princeton University and Lehigh University enabled me to take advantage of the fellowships mentioned above; a sabbatical from teaching at Lehigh University for the fall semester of 1997 enabled me to complete the book. The Gipson Foundation for Eighteenth Century Studies of Lehigh University provided financial assistance towards the purchase of research materials in microform and towards manuscript preparation costs, and the Office of Research and Sponsored Programs of Lehigh University also provided a grant for the technical aspects of manuscript preparation. Finally, the Philip and Muriel Berman Center for Jewish Studies at Lehigh University has provided assistance towards research expenses. I appreciate the generosity of all of these agencies, their founders, and staff. As I was working on the final draft of the manuscript, Philip Berman passed away. His enthusiasm, vision, and generosity have left a lasting legacy in the Berman Center, as well as in his many other charitable endeavours.

Libraries and their staffs are essential for the pursuit of any scholarly project. I have been fortunate in receiving the assistance of many wonderful libraries. I undertook the very beginnings of my research on the *tkhine* literature at the Library of the Jewish Theological Seminary of America in New York, and its staff have been unfailingly helpful ever since. I am especially grateful for the ongoing encouragement of Menahem Schmelzer, for many years the director of the library, and the assistance of Jerry Schwarzbard, of the Rare Book Collection. The Library of the YIVO Institute for Jewish Research, New York, was also helpful in the early stages of my project, and Zachary Baker came to my assistance again at the end. The Jewish National and University Library in Jerusalem had especially rich resources; its *tkhine* pamphlet collection was invaluable for my research, and the treasures of its Judaica reading room are a blessing to all scholars in the field. During my year at Harvard Divinity School, the Judaica collection of Harvard University Library and its director, Charles Berlin, provided much valuable assistance. I have also used the resources of the Library of Hebrew Union College in Cincinnati and the Bodleian Library at Oxford University. Staff at the Bodleian graciously assisted me in obtaining microfilms of early Yiddish materials. Over the past seven and a half years I have spent a great deal of time, and received much help, from the library at the Center for Judaic Studies at the University of Pennsylvania, and am especially grateful for the assistance of Sol Cohen and Judith Leifer. And I have received remarkable help and service from the Inter-Library Loan staff at Lehigh University Library, who wonder what has happened to me if they haven't gotten a request in awhile.

Among the colleagues and friends who helped me in this lengthy enterprise, let me express special appreciation to Arthur Green, who read the entire manuscript, provided detailed comments, and raised many valuable questions.

Conversations with Natalie Zemon Davis helped me to get started on this project. Laurence Silberstein, the director of the Berman Center at Lehigh, has generously read drafts of many chapters and helped me to refine my thinking. Ross Kraemer, colleague and friend, has, over the years in which I have been engaged in this project, read and commented on drafts of numerous articles and chapters and has been an important conversation partner as we have both thought through the difficult issues in studying women's religion.

The past and present members of the Lehigh Valley Feminist Research Group have been a sounding board over the years, and have provided encouragement, "tough love," and detailed feedback on many of the chapters included in this book.

It was my great privilege to have been able to discuss *The Tkhine of the Matriarchs*, by Leah Horowitz, and my translation of it with my teacher Prof. Alexander Altmann a few months before his death. Characteristically, he insisted that there was no need to acknowledge his assistance. If I have gone against his wishes in doing so, it is to acknowledge his profound influence on my work from my undergraduate years until the present. He vigorously encouraged me to pursue a vocation in Jewish scholarship at a time when this was quite an unusual career for women. He had some difficulty in understanding why I would wish to study folk and popular Judaism when all the intellectual and spiritual riches of Kabbalah and philosophy lay before me, but he eventually understood even this, and at our last meeting gave his blessing to my life's work.

Conversations with many friends and colleagues have been invaluable. Many people have read portions of the manuscript (sometimes in article form), encouraged my perseverance in the project, suggested relevant materials, or assisted in locating obscure references. I appreciate the help I have received from Rebecca T. Alpert, Shaye Cohen, Ilana Coven, David Fishman, Talya Fishman, Ezra Fleischer, Mordechai A. Friedman, John Gager, Norman Girardot, Sylvie-Anne Goldberg, Galit Hasan-Rokem, Kathryn Hellerstein, Martha Himmelfarb, Gershon Hundert, Barbara Kirshenblatt-Gimblett, Molly Layton, Ivan Marcus, Ann Matter, Dov Noy, Alexandra Owen, Judith Plaskow, Ada Rapoport-Albert, Michael Raposa, Gail Twersky Reimer, Joseph Reimer, Amy Richlin, Agnes Romer-Segal, David Satran, Khone Shmeruk, of blessed memory, Amy Shuman, Michael Silber, Shaul Stampfer, Hava Tirosh-Samuelson, Chava Turniansky, Elliot Wolfson, Benjamin G. Wright, and Sarah Zfatman. Of course, the responsibility for any errors remains with me.

I want to single out Paula Hyman, not only for the help and encouragement she gave me, but also for her crucial role in creating and maintaining a community of feminist scholars of Judaism and of Jewish history. Without her efforts, none of us would have a context in which to work.

Acknowledgments

Without the assistance of Ilene Cohen, able editor, and more importantly, dear friend, this book would not have been completed. She read and edited the entire manuscript, encouraged me, and kept me focused on the task at hand over many months.

Beacon Press waited patiently for this book for what must have seemed an inordinately long time. I want to thank my first editor, Deborah Chasman, for continuing to encourage me; my second editor, Susan Worst, for helping me find a way to finish the book when I had despaired of completing the project; and my third editor, Amy Caldwell, for seeing the book through publication.

Marian Gaumer, the administrative coordinator of the Department of Religion Studies at Lehigh University, has cheerfully pitched in and helped when it came to the crunch, handling photocopying, mailing, e-mail correspondence, and more. I couldn't have done it without her.

The most personal debts are the hardest to express. My parents, both of them scientists, early instilled in me a love for the life of the mind and a profound respect for intellectual inquiry. My mother, Pearl G. Weissler, has pushed me for years to finish this project; her suggestion (seconded by Gail Reimer) that I engage an editor enabled me to complete the book. She has always been my biggest fan. Sadly, my father, Alfred Weissler, of blessed memory, died just as I began comprehensive revisions of the manuscript. I wish he had lived to see its publication. My brothers, Frederic and Robert, my sister-in-law, Carol Miaskoff, my nephews Samuel, Nathan, and Eli, and my niece Hannah have all been a source of support, love, and joy. Jonathan, Samuel, and Elizabeth Fredland have also cheered me on.

Words cannot express my love and gratitude for the constancy, support, and love of Nancy Fredland.

INDEX